Affect in Social Thinking and Behavior

FRONTIERS OF SOCIAL PSYCHOLOGY

Series Editors:
Arie W. Kruglanski, *University of Maryland at College Park*
Joseph P. Forgas, *University of New South Wales*

Frontiers of Social Psychology is a new series of domain-specific handbooks. The purpose of each volume is to provide readers with a cutting-edge overview of the most recent theoretical, methodological, and practical developments in a substantive area of social psychology, in greater depth than is possible in general social psychology handbooks. The Editors and contributors are all internationally renowned scholars, whose work is at the cutting edge of research.

Scholarly, yet accessible, the volumes in the *Frontiers* series are an essential resource for senior undergraduates, postgraduates, researchers, and practitioners, and are suitable as texts in advanced courses in specific sub-areas of social psychology.

Published titles

Negotiation Theory and Research, Thompson
Close Relationships, Noller & Feeney
Evolution and Social Psychology, Schaller, Simpson, & Kenrick

Forthcoming titles

Automatic Processes in Social Thinking and Behavior, Bargh
Culture, Chiu & Mallorie
Personality and Social Behavior, Rhodewalt
Political Psychology, Krosnick
Science of Social Influence, Pratkanis
Social Cognition, Strack & Förster
Social Communication, Fiedler
The Self, Sedikides & Spencer

For continually updated information about published and forthcoming titles in the *Frontiers of Social Psychology* series, please visit: **www.psypress.com/frontiers**

THE SYDNEY SYMPOSIUM OF SOCIAL PSYCHOLOGY series

This book is Volume 8 in the Sydney Symposium of Social Psychology series. The aim of the *Sydney Symposia of Social Psychology* is to provide new, integrative insights into key areas of contemporary research. Held every year at the University of New South Wales, Sydney, each symposium deals with an important integrative theme in social psychology, and the invited participants are leading researchers in the field from around the world. Each contribution is extensively discussed during the symposium and is subsequently thoroughly revised into book chapters that are published in the volumes in this series. For further details see the website at www.sydneysymposium.unsw.edu.au

Previous Sydney Symposium of Social Psychology volumes:

SSSP 1. FEELING AND THINKING: THE ROLE OF AFFECT IN SOCIAL COGNITION** ISBN 0-521-64223-X (Edited by J. P. Forgas). *Contributors*: Robert Zajonc, Jim Blascovich, Wendy Berry Mendes, Craig Smith, Leslie Kirby, Eric Eich, Dawn Macaulay, Len Berkowitz, Sara Jaffee, EunKyung Jo, Bartholomeu Troccoli, Leonard Martin, Daniel Gilbert, Timothy Wilson, Herbert Bless, Klaus Fiedler, Joseph Forgas, Carolin Showers, Anthony Greenwald, Mahzarin Banaji, Laurie Rudman, Shelly Farnham, Brian Nosek, Marshall Rosier, Mark Leary, Paula Niedenthal, Jamin Halberstadt.

SSSP 2. THE SOCIAL MIND: COGNITIVE AND MOTIVATIONAL ASPECTS OF INTERPERSONAL BEHAVIOR** ISBN 0-521-77092-0 (Edited by J. P. Forgas, K. D. Williams, & L. Wheeler). *Contributors*: William & Claire McGuire, Susan Andersen, Roy Baumeister, Joel Cooper, Bill Crano, Garth Fletcher, Joseph Forgas, Pascal Huguet, Mike Hogg, Martin Kaplan, Norb Kerr, John Nezlek, Fred Rhodewalt, Astrid Schuetz, Constantine Sedikides, Jeffry Simpson, Richard Sorrentino, Dianne Tice, Kip Williams, Ladd Wheeler.

SSSP 3. SOCIAL INFLUENCE: DIRECT AND INDIRECT PROCESSES* ISBN 1-84169-038-4 (Edited by J. P. Forgas & K. D. Williams). *Contributors*: Robert Cialdini, Eric Knowles, Shannon Butler, Jay Linn, Bibb Latané, Martin Bourgeois, Mark Schaller, Ap Dijksterhuis, James Tedeschi, Richard Petty, Joseph Forgas, Herbert Bless, Fritz Strack, Eva Walther, Sik Hung Ng, Thomas Mussweiler, Kipling Williams, Lara Dolnik, Charles Stangor, Gretchen Sechrist, John Jost, Deborah Terry, Michael Hogg, Stephen Harkins, Barbara David, John Turner, Robin Martin, Miles Hewstone, Russell Spears, Tom Postmes, Martin Lea, Susan Watt.

* Published by Psychology Press
** Published by Cambridge University Press

Affect in Social Thinking and Behavior

Edited by
Joseph P. Forgas

Ψ Psychology Press
Taylor & Francis Group

NEW YORK AND HOVE

Published in 2006
by Psychology Press
Taylor & Francis Group
270 Madison Avenue
New York, NY 10016
www.psypress.com

Published in Great Britain
by Psychology Press
Taylor & Francis Group
27 Church Road
Hove, East Sussex BN3 2FA
www.psypress.co.uk

Psychology Press is an imprint of the Taylor & Francis Group, an informa business

Typeset by Macmillan India Ltd, Bangalore, India
Printed and bound in the USA by Sheridan Books, Inc., Ann Arbor, MI, on acid-free paper
Cover design by Lisa Dynan

10 9 8 7 6 5 4 3 2 1

Library of Congress Cataloging in Publication Data

Affect in social thinking and behavior / edited by Joseph P. Forgas.

  p. cm. – (Frontiers of social psychology)

 Includes bibliographical references and index.

 ISBN-13: 978-1-84169-454-2 (hardback : alk. paper)

 ISBN-10: 1-84169-454-1 (hardback : alk. paper) 1. Interpersonal relations. 2. Social interaction. 3.
Affect (Psychology) 4. Emotions. 5. Social perception. I. Forgas, Joseph P. II. Series.

 HM1106.A34 2006

  302'.1–dc22

                        2006005426

ISBN13: 978-1-84169-454-2 (hbk)

ISBN10: 1-84169-454-1 (hbk)

Contents

About the Editor

Joseph P. Forgas is a Scientia Professor of Psychology at the University of New South Wales, Sydney. He received his DPhil degree from the University of Oxford and subsequently was awarded a DSc degree from the same university. He has written or edited 14 books and is the author of more than 120 scholarly articles and papers. He is a fellow at the Academy of Social Sciences, Australia; the American Psychological Society; and the Society of Personality and Social Psychology. His current research focuses on the role of affect in social thinking and interpersonal behavior. This work has received international recognition, including the Research Prize from the Alexander von Humboldt foundation (Germany) and a Special Investigator Award from the Australian Research Council.

Contributors

Danu B. Anthony
University of Waterloo
Ontario, Canada

Jamie Arndt
University of Missouri
Columbia, MO, USA

Roy F. Baumeister
Florida State University
Tallahassee, FL, USA

John T. Blackledge
University of Wollongong
Wollongong, Australia

Herbert Bless
University of Mannheim
Germany

Christopher T. Burke
New York University
New York, NY, USA

John T. Cacioppo
University of Chicago,
Chicago, IL, USA

Joseph Ciarrochi
University of Wollongong
Wollongong, Australia

Gerald L. Clore
University of Virginia
Charlottesville, VA, USA

Bieke David
Vanderbilt University
Nashville, TN, USA

Elizabeth W. Dunn
University of British Columbia
Vancouver, Canada

Eric Eich
University of British Columbia
Vancouver, Canada

Ralph Erber
DePaul University
Chicago, IL, USA

Klaus Fiedler
University of Heidelberg
Germany

Joseph P. Forgas
University of New South Wales
Sydney, Australia

Martie G. Haselton
University of California, Los Angeles
Los Angeles, CA, USA

John G. Holmes
University of Waterloo
Ontario, Canada

E. J. Horberg
University of California, Berkeley
Berkeley, CA, USA

Felicia A. Huppert
University of Cambridge
Cambridge, UK

Eric R. Igou
Tilburg University
Tilburg, The Netherlands

Janice R. Kelly
Purdue University
West Lafayette, IN, USA

Dacher Keltner
University of California, Berkeley
Berkeley, CA, USA

Timothy Ketelaar
New Mexico State University
Las Cruces, NM, USA

Leslie D. Kirby
Vanderbilt University
Nashville, TN, USA

Simon M. Laham
University of New South Wales
Sydney, Australia

Dawn Macaulay
University of British Columbia
Vancouver, Canada

Susan Markunas
DePaul University
Chicago, IL, USA

Christopher Oveis
University of California, Berkeley
Berkeley, CA, USA

Clay Routledge
University of Southampton
Southampton, UK

Constantine Sedikides
University of Southampton
Southampton, UK

Craig A. Smith
Vanderbilt University
Nashville, TN, USA

Jennifer R. Spoor
Purdue University
West Lafayette, IN, USA

Justin Storbeck
University of Virginia
Charlottesville, VA, USA

Dianne M. Tice
Florida State University
Tallahassee, FL, USA

Yaacov Trope
New York University
New York, NY, USA

Kathleen D. Vohs
University of Minnesota
Minneapolis, MN, USA

Tim Wildschut
University of Southampton
Southampton, UK

Piotr Winkielman
University of California
San Diego, CA, USA

Carrie L. Wyland
University of New South Wales
Sydney, Australia

Introduction

1

Hearts and Minds: An Introduction to the Role of Affect in Social Cognition and Behavior

JOSEPH P. FORGAS, CARRIE L. WYLAND,
and SIMON M. LAHAM

INTRODUCTION

*H*istorically, most writers and philosophers have assumed that it is the unique human capacity for reason and rational thought that makes us truly human. Affect and emotion were traditionally relegated to a subsidiary role, as inferior, more primitive, and invasive response systems. Yet affect lies at the heart of most of the things that really concern us in our daily lives. How much do I love my partner and how much does he or she love me? Why do I feel envious of my high-flying colleague? How can I be less anxious in social situations? How can I control my anger? Why do I think so ineffectively when I am upset? How could I become a happier person? Questions such as these are of enduring concern to most of us, yet reason alone rarely leads to satisfactory answers. A better understanding of the role of affect in social thinking and behavior is arguably one of the most important tasks for psychology. This book aims to review the most important empirical and theoretical developments in recent social psychological research on affect and social life.

This introductory chapter aims to set the context for much of what follows. We will begin with a brief overview of some of the key issues and historical approaches to affect and social behavior. Next, some contemporary affect-cognition models will be considered. Finally, we will conclude with a brief overview of the structure and main themes of the book.

BACKGROUND, BASIC ISSUES, AND DEFINITIONS

Affect: Noise or Information?

The traditional assumption that emotions have a dangerous, invasive influence on higher mental processes can be traced throughout 2000 years of Western philosophy. Plato thought that affect represented a primitive, animalistic response system, an idea that found its most potent recent expression in Freud's psychoanalytic concept of the irrational id. Freud's hydraulic model suggests that one of the main functions of the conscious, rational ego is to control, manage, and repress unacceptable emotional impulses. Psychoanalysis also provided an influential vocabulary that entrenched the view of affect as primitive, uncontrollable, and incompatible with reason. The "bad press" that emotions have received is also illustrated in Arthur Koestler's otherwise impressive works. For Koestler, the human inability to properly understand and control emotions suggests a fatal evolutionary flaw, a lack of integration between affect and reason that may ultimately lead to the extinction of our species (Koestler, 1978).

The last two decades of research in evolutionary psychology, neuropsychology, and cognition suggest a contrary view, however. According to convergent lines of evidence (see Haselton & Ketelaar, this volume; Winkielman & Cacioppo, this volume), affective reactions are often a highly useful and even necessary adjunct to rationality and effective social decisions (Damasio, 1994; De Sousa, 1987; Lieberman, 2003; Oatley & Jenkins, 1992, 1996). Thus, affect may be thought of as a fundamental response system in its own right, one that feeds into higher mental processes and provides essential input for social action. It seems that Blaise Pascal's speculations over 350 years ago that "the heart has its reasons which reason does not understand" (1643/1966, p. 113) are finally receiving empirical support. Although it is now increasingly recognized that affect represents a useful and adaptive response system, there still remains much confusion about just how affect and other psychological processes such as cognition, motivation, and behavior are related. We shall turn to this question next.

The Relationship between Affect, Thinking, and Behavior

Psychology's subject matter is often classified into three basic categories: thinking (cognition), feeling (affect), and motivation and behavior (conation; Hilgard, 1980). This subdivision of the human psyche into three distinct faculties has its origins in 18th century philosophy. In his historical discussion of the origins of this idea, Hilgard (1980) identified Christian Wolff (1714–1762) as among the first to distinguish between a *facultas cognoscivita* and a *facultas appetiva*—knowing and desire. This view was expanded further a few decades later by Moses Mendelssohn (1729–1789), who introduced a threefold classification of the fundamental faculties of the soul— understanding, feeling, and will. This tripartite classification was also used by Kant, probably the most influential philosopher of his period. For Kant, "pure reason corresponds to intellect or cognition, practical reason to will, action, or conation, and judgment to feeling pleasure or pain, hence affection" (Hilgard, 1980, p. 109).

It is interesting, and somewhat surprising, that the philosophical subdivision of psychology into cognition, affect, and motivation/behavior continued to influence the empirical discipline of psychology as it emerged in the 20th century. Early experimentalists, such as Wundt and Titchener, believed that these three faculties could only be understood jointly, as different but complementary dimensions of unitary psychological experiences. Subsequent paradigms however increasingly saw affect, cognition, and conation as independent, isolated faculties and indeed isolated research fields, largely ignoring the close interdependence between them. Much of psychology in the first half of the 20th century was dominated by a fundamentalist paradigm, behaviorism, which explicitly excluded the study of cognition and affectivity from its subject matter. For a radical behaviorist, all unobservable mental events—such as feelings and affect—were by definition outside the scope of scientific psychology. All that remained were some early behaviorist experiments that explored some of the environmental conditioning processes that might impact on emotional responses, as in Watson's well-known "little Albert" studies. Other lines of investigation within the behaviorist paradigm focused on the environmental manipulation of basic drive states such as hunger and thirst as a substitute for studying affectivity. It is not surprising then that behaviorist research contributed very little to our understanding of the functions and consequences of affect in everyday social life.

Behaviorism's stifling domination of psychology was overturned by the "cognitive revolution" of the 1950s and 1960s. Unfortunately, the ascendancy of cognitivism was also characterized by a persistent lack of interest in affect (Neisser, 1982). Traditional cognitive theories saw affect, if considered at all, as a source of disruptive influence on "proper," that is, cold, affectless, thinking. By the 1980s, this assumption came to be challenged from several directions. Within social psychology, Zajonc (1980) argued for the primacy of affective phenomena and their independence from the dominance of cognitive approaches. Within cognitive psychology proper, Neisser (1982) asserted that the fiction of "cold" cognition as a universal paradigm for studying thinking is flawed, as almost all everyday thinking also involves feelings, desires, and affect. Of course, this view was also anticipated in the influential "new look" research by Bruner (1957) and his colleagues.

By the early 1980s, the Zeitgeist was ripe for attempts to reintegrate affect into the study of mental phenomena in general and cognitive psychology in particular. Such influential publications as Bower's (1981) paper on mood and memory did much to place affect on the agenda for cognitive psychologists, just as Zajonc (1980) had done for social psychologists. Several of the chapters in this volume testify to the ultimate success of this endeavor, reporting the impressive achievements of mature research domains that have benefited greatly from the reintegration of affect into cognition (see, for example, Bless and Fiedler, this volume; Baumeister, Vohs, & Tice, this volume; Eich & Macaulay, this volume; Forgas, this volume; Sedikides, Wildschut, Arndt, & Routledge, this volume; Trope, Igou, & Burke, this volume). But what exactly is the nature of the relationship between affect, cognition, and behavior?

The Contemporary Status and Definitions of Affect

Perhaps as a result of the historical neglect of affective phenomena, there continues to be a fundamental theoretical controversy in the field about whether affect should be seen as a separate and in some ways independent and primary response system as Zajonc (1980, 2000) argued, or as an integral part of the cognitive-representational system (see, for example, Bless & Fiedler, this volume; Clore & Storbeck, this volume; Eich & Macaulay, this volume; Forgas, this volume; Winkielman & Cacioppo, this volume). Those who argue for a "separate-systems" view (e.g., Zajonc, 2000) propose that affective reactions often precede, and are psychologically and neuroanatomically distinct from cognitive processes. Most existing research however, including recent fMRI studies (Lieberman, 2003), seems to support a more integrative, interactionist conceptualization of the links between affect and cognition. One's position in this debate does of course partly depend upon the breadth of the definition of "cognition." Arguments for a primary, separate system of affective reactions are only sustainable if cognition is narrowly defined as consisting only of high-level, systematic, and elaborative processes, but excluding early attentional and interpretational mechanisms that are inevitably involved in stimulus identification before any response (affective or otherwise) is possible (Lazarus, 1984).

The interactionist position is also supported by the long philosophical tradition in psychological theorizing that recognizes the interdependence of feeling, thinking, and behavior, going back to the work of Wundt, Titchener, and James. Most contemporary affect-cognition approaches in social psychology also assume, explicitly or implicitly, that affect is part of a single, integrated cognitive representational system, at least in the sense that "the experience of an emotion *is* a cognition" (Laird & Bresler, 1991, p. 24). Most of the chapters here also review substantive research areas that are consistent with such an interactionist view. Further, according to all available evidence there is clearly a bidirectional link between affect and cognition. Not only does affect influence various social-cognitive functions and behaviors in predictable and systematic ways (Forgas, 2002; see also Baumeister et al., this volume; Clore & Storbeck, this volume; Eich & Macaulay, this volume; Holmes & Anthony, this volume; Keltner, Horberg, & Oveis, this volume; Kelly & Spoor, this volume; Trope et al., this volume), but cognitive processes also play a crucial role in the elicitation and management of affective states (Bless & Fiedler, this volume; Erber & Markunas, this volume; Smith, David, & Kirby, this volume).

Affect, Mood, and Emotion: Toward a Definition

Despite the dramatic growth of research on affect, mood, and emotions during the past two decades, the precise definition of these terms remains somewhat elusive. However, one accepted approach might be to define *affect* as a broad, generic, and inclusive term that refers to a variety of specific affective states, including both *moods* and *emotions* (Forgas, 1995, 2002). *Moods* in turn may be defined as relatively low-intensity, diffuse, subconscious, and enduring affective states that have no salient antecedent cause and therefore little cognitive content (such as feeling generally good or bad). In contrast, distinct *emotions* are more short-lived, conscious, and intense; usually have a highly accessible and salient cause, and clear, prototypical cognitive content (e.g., disgust, anger, or fear). Both emotions and moods do have an influence on social thinking and behavior, but the nature of that influence may be quite different and mediated by different cognitive mechanisms (see, for example, Keltner et al., this volume).

It is interesting to observe that research on *moods* and research on *emotions* have evolved as distinct and relatively independent fields. *Mood* researchers are typically interested in the cognitive and behavioral *consequences* of these affective states (see, for example, chapters by Clore & Storbeck, this volume; Eich & Macaulay, this volume; Forgas, this volume; Trope et al., this volume), while *emotion* researchers' primary focus has been the cognitive and contextual *antecedents* of various emotional reactions (see especially the chapter by Smith et al., this volume). This dichotomy in research orientation between mood researchers and emotion researchers has, however, been breached in recent years as a growing number of researchers have began exploring the judgmental and behavioral consequences of distinct emotions such as anger, fear, anxiety, and the like (Keltner et al., this volume).

BASIC PERSPECTIVES ON AFFECT AND COGNITION

Although psychologists have only recently begun to empirically explore the relationship between affect, thinking, and behavior, there are a number of theoretical perspectives that have broadly informed this enterprise. We shall briefly discuss some of the more important of these as they relate to affect research.

The Learning-Conditioning Perspective

We have seen above that radical learning theorists were not interested in studying internal mental processes such as affectivity. However, conditioning theories nevertheless had, and continue to have, an important influence on contemporary research on affectivity. The basic idea of classical conditioning research that spatial and temporal contiguity alone can produce powerful associations between pre-existing, unconditioned affective reactions and new, previously neutral stimuli was first demonstrated by Watson in his well-known "little Albert" studies. The same fundamental principle was re-visited in experimental studies by Byrne and Clore (1970), Clore and Byrne (1974), Griffitt (1970), Gouaux (1971), and Gouaux and Summers (1973). These experiments showed that conditioning mechanisms may go some way towards explaining how affective states can be "attached" to otherwise unrelated experiences and judgments. In the Byrne and Clore studies, for example, participants were exposed to environments that elicited an unconditioned positive or negative affective reaction (such as noisy, unpleasant rooms, or pleasant rooms). When participants then met a new person in an aversive or rewarding environment, their evaluations and judgments were influenced by the incidental affective state they experienced. In other words, mere spatial and temporal contiguity between the unconditioned stimulus (the environment) and the conditioned stimulus (the new person) was sufficient to elicit a conditioned response, influencing the affective tone of judgments.

With the emergence of a more cognitive orientation in psychology, such "blind" conditioning principles fell from favor. However, the idea that affective states can spontaneously "attach" themselves to otherwise neutral stimuli, and thus influence responses, continues to exert considerable influence on recent social cognition theorizing (Berkowitz, 1993; Clore, Schwarz, & Conway, 1994; Wyer & Srull, 1989; see also Clore and Storbeck, this volume). Instead of using a conditioning explanation, contemporary models emphasize a more mentalistic account, suggesting that misattribution processes can account for such incidental associations. For example, the affect-as-information model proposed by Schwarz and Clore (1983) suggests a direct link between affect and subsequent evaluative judgments, a model that makes very similar predictions to Clore and Byrne's (1974) earlier findings couched in conditioning terminology.

The Psychodynamic Perspective

During the first half of the 20th century, the psychoanalytic perspective represented one of the major alternatives to the stifling dominance of conditioning theories. Freud's speculative psychodynamic theory had a great deal to say about the interplay between affect and cognition, and arguably played an important role in focusing attention on affective phenomena well before it became fashionable to do so in empirical psychology. Within the psychoanalytic framework, consistent with the historical disdain for affectivity within Western philosophy, affective states were located within the id, and were conceptualized as seeking expression and exerting "pressure" against the countervailing force of rational, controlled ego mechanisms. In psychodynamic terms, affect has an invasive, dynamic quality that can potentially subvert a wide variety of cognitive processes and behaviors unless adequate psychological effort is employed to control it.

Psychodynamic theories also stimulated a number of empirical attempts to demonstrate affect infusion. For example, Feshbach and Singer (1957) induced fear and anxiety using electric shocks, and then instructed subjects to repress their fear or not, before making social judgments about a target person. As predicted, anxious and fearful people were indeed more likely to "perceive another person as fearful and anxious" (p. 286), and this effect was enhanced precisely when they were trying to suppress their fear. This pattern was interpreted by Feshbach and Singer (1957) as consistent with the psychodynamic process of projection, as "suppression of fear facilitates the tendency to project fear onto another social object" (p. 286). Indeed, Feshbach and Singer (1957) in a prescient passage describe this process as indicating the "infusion of affect into cognition", a concept that continues to be important in contemporary research. It is interesting that it took several more decades of research before the precise cognitive mechanisms responsible for such affect infusion or its absence could be systematically explored (Forgas, 1995, 2002).

Although studies such as Feshbach and Singer's and Byrne and Clore's represent impressive early attempts to explore the interface between affect and thinking, ultimately, neither conditioning nor psychoanalytic theories could offer a plausible explanation for such affect infusion processes. Following Popper's devastating criticisms of psychoanalysis, and the difficulty of obtaining coherent empirical support for Freud's speculative theories, psychodynamic explanations declined in popularity. By excluding the possibility of constructing mentalistic (i.e., cognitive) explanations, conditioning theories also fell far short of accounting for affect infusion phenomena. Although conditioning may well play a role in mediating some affective reactions (Berkowitz, 1993), it cannot provide a complete theory of affect influences on social thinking and behavior because of the absence of a well-articulated cognitive dimension mediating these effects (Forgas, 1992a, 1992b). In keeping with the changing Zeitgeist in psychology during the last few decades, cognitive, information processing approaches became dominant in offering explanations for the role of affect in social thinking and behavior, as we shall see below.

The Cognitive, Information Processing Perspective

The impressive growth of research on affectivity in the last two decades owes much to the influence of cognitive, information processing theories on this field. Since the early 1980s, most research on affectivity focused on three major research issues: (1) How can we explain the apparent affect congruence of many social judgments and behaviors? (*the affect-congruence problem*), (2) How does affect influence information processing? (*the processing problem*), and (3) How do people appraise situations in producing an affective response? (*the appraisal problem*). In all of these three fields, information processing theories often adapted from cognitive research played a major role in producing novel hypotheses, and guiding the research effort.

The Affect Congruence Problem   Much of the early research on affect and cognition focused on the question of how mood and emotion can influence the content of cognition. There have been two main cognitive theories developed to explain this effect, *affect-priming* (Bower, 1981; Bower & Forgas, 2001; see also Eich & Macaulay, this volume) and the *affect-as-information* model (Schwarz & Clore, 1983, 1988; see also Clore and Storbeck, this volume). We will briefly explore the theoretical background and implications of these models and recent developments in this field.

The *affect-priming* account is derived from associative network models of memory as first outlined by Bower (1981). Affect priming occurs when an affective state selectively primes and makes more accessible past memories and knowledge structures associated with that affective state in memory. Such affective associations can occur because (a) the affective state at retrieval matches the affective state experienced when the memory was first encoded (*mood-state-dependent retrieval*), and (b) the mood state matches the affective valence of material stored in memory (*mood-congruent retrieval*). The better availability of affect-congruent information from memory should, in turn, have a widespread influence on a variety of constructive cognitive processes leading to affect-congruent judgments and behaviors. Indeed, there has been considerable cumulative evidence supporting such a view, showing significant congruence effects linked to the selective retrieval of mood-congruent information from memory (e.g., Fiedler, 1990, 1991; Forgas, 1991, 1992a, 1993; Forgas & Bower, 1987; see also Eich & Macaulay, this volume; Forgas, this volume).

Affect priming is not the only cognitive mechanism that can produce affect congruence in social judgments and behaviors. An alternative *affect-as-information* model was proposed by Schwarz and Clore (1983), who suggested a more simple, conscious, inferential mechanism for affect infusion, when people in effect ask themselves "How do I feel about that?" and use their existing affective state as information in constructing a response. This heuristic of responding by misattributing a pre-existing feeling state in fact describes the same kind of process that Clore and Byrne (1974) identified in their conditioning experiments, but the explanation now emphasizes inferential (cognitive) rather than conditioning (behavioral) principles.

However, there are several important qualifications that apply to this model. Most obviously, this is not so much a model of social judgment, but of misjudgment, to the extent that the real features of the judgmental target as well as relevant memory-based information is simply bypassed and only the irrelevant affective state is used to infer a response. It is for this reason that the affect-as-information heuristic is most likely to produce mood-congruence in social judgments when the judge has little interest, involvement, motivation, or resources to compute a more thorough response (Forgas & Moylan, 1987).

On the other hand, if the misattributed affective state is just one of several sources of information used, then we need an additional model to explain how various information categories (affect, target features, memories, and associations, etc.) combined to produce a response. Several attempts have been made to propose an explanation for such context-specificity in reactions (Abele & Petzold, 1994), suggesting that affective states have no invariable informational value, but their meaning depends on the context in which they are experienced (Martin, 2000).

Can we empirically distinguish between these two mechanisms of affect congruence? It is sometimes claimed that the affect-as-information model is supported by findings that correctly attributed moods are no longer informative (misattributable) (Schwarz & Clore, 1983). However, this is by no means a robust finding. There are many experiments where participants must have been highly aware of the correct source of their moods, yet strong affect congruence is obtained (for example, using highly salient and undisguised mood induction methods such as the Velten method, autobiographical recall, etc.).

Further, the claim that the misattribution manipulation can selectively support the affect-as-information model seems both logically and empirically flawed. Logically, just because an effect can be eliminated by an additional manipulation (i.e., by emphasizing the source of the affective state), this is not informative about how a mood-congruent effect is actually produced when this additional manipulation is absent. And empirically, a procedure that calls attention to the person's affective state can easily eliminate any affect-congruent pattern, howsoever caused, simply because it may motivate a person to control and reverse an affective bias that he/she has just now been made aware of. Indeed, calling attention to the affective state can eliminate affect congruence due to affect priming by producing a contrast effect (Berkowitz, Jaffee, Jo, & Troccoli, 2000). Ultimately, the misattribution manipulation cannot provide selective support for the affect-as-information model, despite claims to that effect.

One recent integrative theory, the affect infusion model (AIM; Forgas, 1995, 2002), specifically predicts that affect congruence should be more likely to occur when some form of constructive processing is used. The AIM further distinguishes between heuristic processing and substantive processing as the two strategies implicated when affect-as-information and affect-priming mechanisms operate, respectively. This model suggests that the way in which affect infuses judgments is highly dependent on what kind of cognitive strategies are involved.

If constructive processing is indeed essential for affect priming to be effective, an interesting counterintuitive hypothesis could also be derived from the AIM: more difficult and demanding tasks that should recruit more constructive and elaborate processing and increase the likelihood that affectively primed information will influence the response. Numerous experiments now support this prediction, showing for example that more complex and unusual people, couples, and situations call for longer processing and produce greater affect congruence in judgments (Forgas, 1993, 2002; Sedikides, 1995).

Numerous studies also looked at processing latencies as a suitable technique for determining how a task is performed. These experiments typically show that with realistic tasks more extensive processing increases affect congruence, as predicted by the affect-priming model (Forgas, 1993, 1995; Forgas & Bower, 1987).

In conclusion, we may consider the affect-priming and the affect-as-information models as complementary mechanisms, producing affect congruence when simple, heuristic processing is called for in superficial, irrelevant situations (affect-as-information), and when more elaborate, substantive processing is required (affect-priming). More generally, the development of integrative theories such as the AIM seem central to gaining an understanding of the way in which affect and cognition interact.

The Processing Problem   In addition to influencing *what* people think, affect may also influence *how* people think, that is, the processing strategies they use. Initially, it was thought that people in a positive mood tend to use more heuristic, superficial, and rapid and flexible thinking to make decisions and judgments (Isen, 1987). On the other hand, negative mood seems to trigger a more effortful, systematic, analytic, and vigilant processing style (Bless & Fiedler, this volume; Fiedler, 1991; Forgas, 2002; Schwarz, 1990; Schwarz & Bless, 1991). It appears then that both positive and negative moods can benefit or hinder mental processes, depending on the task and the situation.

Why should positive and negative affective states trigger different processing strategies? At least three early explanations were advanced to explain this processing dichotomy. According to functionalist, evolutionary theories, positive and negative affect have adaptive significance as they signal benevolent or dangerous situations, and accordingly call for more or less vigilant processing (Schwarz, 1990). An alternative, motivational account suggests that negative affect motivates more systematic and effortful thinking in order to ameliorate an aversive state, while positive affect reduces processing effort in order to preserve a favorable affective state (Clark & Isen, 1982). Finally, capacity explanations suggest that positive affect can consume cognitive capacity and therefore limit attentional resources—however, it is not clear whether positive or negative affect is more likely to impose such capacity constraints (Ellis & Ashbrook, 1988; Mackie & Worth, 1991).

A recent integration of the evidence by Bless and Fiedler (this volume) suggests that positive and negative affect do not simply influence processing effort, but rather trigger fundamentally and qualitatively different processing styles: accommodative thinking, focusing on the external stimulus situations (in negative affect), and assimilative thinking, relying on pre-existing schemata and knowledge structures (Bless, 2000; Fiedler, 1991). There is strong support for the view that affective states do perform such a cognitive regulatory function.

The Appraisal Problem   Thus far we have focused primarily on the *consequences* of affective states, including their informational and processing effects. However, another thriving research tradition has focused on the cognitive and situational *antecedents* of affect, and in particular the appraisal processes people use when producing an emotional reaction (see Smith et al., this volume). Appraisal theorists want to find answers to questions such as: what is the social character of emotions?, how do emotional responses reflect social rules and customs?, and how can we explain the large individual differences in emotional response to highly similar situations? *Structural models* seek to systematize and explain the appraisal conditions that produce particular affective reactions. Overall, they suggest highly similar appraisal dimensions (e.g., desirability, coping ability, responsibility, etc.) that determine the strength or intensity of the resulting emotional reaction.

Alternatively, *procedural models* explore the cognitive operations and processes involved in emotion appraisal, and distinguish between slower, conscious, and verbal appraisals (conceptual processing), and automatic, spontaneous appraisals (schematic processing), a dichotomy that closely matches the heuristic-substantive processing distinction in other theories such as the AIM (Forgas, 2002). Finally, as Smith et al. (this volume) suggest, a third kind of *relational model* is also being developed, seeking to explain emotion appraisals in terms of the relationship between situational affordances and personal needs, goals, and capacities. Relational models and the research they stimulate in particular pave the way towards the development of a truly social conceptualization of emotional reactions.

There is also an emerging convergence between these two research traditions, those who are mainly interested in the antecedents of emotions (appraisal research), and those who are focusing on the cognitive and behavioral consequences of moods (affect congruence and affective influences on information processing). It turns out that the kinds of processing theories developed to explain affect congruence, for example, also have their applications in understanding how emotions are appraised. And in turn, distinct emotional states can produce strong and reliable cognitive consequences, influencing judgments, decisions, and behaviors (Lerner & Keltner, 2000, 2001; see also Keltner et al., this volume). This book and the research reviewed here should play an important role in promoting this convergence.

The Functionalist, Evolutionary Perspective

While cognitive theories are typically invoked to explain the proximal mechanisms involved in the influence of affect on social cognition, recent work has also begun to focus on more distal causes. The dominant view in Western thought has been that emotions are at best irrelevant, and at worst a danger to rational human functioning. This view has recently been challenged by the emerging evolutionary paradigm in our field (Buss, 1999). In general, the application of evolutionary ideas has produced a renewed emphasis on the biological basis of many of our affective reactions and a focus on the fundamentally functional, adaptive character of our affective experiences (see Haselton & Ketelaar, this volume; Winkielman & Cacioppo, this volume).

It is clear that some emotions can facilitate reproductive fitness. Fear of predators, for example, often triggers a "fight or flight" response that aids survival. Not all emotions, however, so clearly improve reproductive fitness. More often, as we shall see in many of the chapters in the book (see Bless & Fiedler, this volume; Erber & Markunas, this volume; Forgas, this volume; Haselton & Ketelaar, this volume, for example), the functional consequences of affective states are subtle, indirect, and elusive. Haselton and Ketelaar (this volume), for example, argue that it is likely that emotions evolved in order to assist complex social decision-making when detailed rational analysis would be neither feasible nor helpful in producing a suitable response. Emotions such as guilt and love, for example, can serve as decision inputs that counter the general tendency to underweight long-term gains. Fear and anger can influence the way we perceive others and disgust may play a central role in the development of morality.

In addition, affective reactions typically interact with other mental processes that can direct and influence behavior at the level of perception, attention, inference, memory, motivation, and more. For example, Bless and Fiedler (this volume) suggest that mild positive and negative moods spontaneously promote two distinct styles of information processing. Positive affect seems to produce assimilative thinking, facilitating reliance on existing knowledge, schematic ideas, and the use of top-down processing. In contrast, negative affect calls for more accommodative thinking, and greater focus on novel, external information and bottom-up processing. Although subtle, such an affectively triggered processing dichotomy has obvious adaptive significance, influencing the way people respond to a given situation. Consistent with this view, several experiments found that, somewhat counterintuitively, negative affect can produce better cognitive and social outcomes through directing attention to new, external information. For example, those in a negative mood were found to be more resistant to common judgmental biases such as the fundamental attribution error (Forgas, 1998), were less likely to suffer from distortions in their eyewitness memories (Forgas, Vargas, & Laham, 2005), and were better able to detect deception (East & Forgas, 2005) than were people experiencing positive affect.

Although many of their effects may be subtle, indirect, and unconscious, affective states are nevertheless part and parcel of our evolutionary make-up. This is not to deny that more intense emotional states, such as anger, fear, anxiety, or euphoria, can and do sometimes interfere with rational thinking and may have a negative impact on cognitions But there is now strong support for the view that emotions and affect also have important adaptive functions which have arisen from natural selection in order to solve the adaptive problems faced by our ancestors (Tooby & Cosmides, 1990).

The Affective Neuroscience Perspective

Another rapidly developing recent approach for understanding the influence of affect on cognition and behavior focuses on the neuropsychological underpinnings of these processes. It seems self-evident that in order to fully understand the role of emotions in human social behavior, it is necessary to consider their underlying neural substrates and circuitry. This endeavor has received a huge boost recently with the increasing availability of neuroimaging techniques. Consequently, social psychologists have been in the vanguard of exploring the fundamental physiological mechanisms underlying social thinking and behavior. As argued by Panksepp (1998), it is clear that different neural systems have developed in order to specialize in solving different adaptive problems. Further, these systems have a complex pattern of interaction in which lower-level processes (i.e., emotions) both influence and are influenced by higher-level processes (i.e., cognitions). The development of higher-level cognitions in turn allows us to regulate our emotions (albeit rather imperfectly; see Erber & Markunas, this volume).

Extensive research in recent years examined the systems and brain areas that are at the core of the processing of emotions. The integration of techniques from cognitive neuroscience, including neuroimaging (namely, fMRI and PET), has allowed us to get a much clearer understanding of how the brain processes affect and affective stimuli. For example, the amygdala, which is known to process evaluative and emotional stimuli, especially related to threat (e.g., fearful expressions), has reciprocal connecting pathways with the prefrontal cortex, which is the home of higher cognitive functioning in humans (e.g., LeDoux, 1989; see also Winkielman & Cacioppo, this volume). The frontal cortex serves a key role in regulating our emotional reactions when making decisions. As shown by Damasio (1994), the influence of emotion on our cognitions is vital to successful decision-making. Without emotions to inform our cognitions, as is the case with patients who have suffered orbitofrontal lesions, social behaviors tend to be dysfunctional and irrational, even if no other intellectual impairment is present, leading to serious social and relationship problems (Damasio, 1994).

It is particularly relevant to the theme of this book that according to newly emerging evidence, emotion and cognition are neurally interdependent and have a strong influence on one another (Lieberman, 2003; Winkielman & Cacioppo, this volume). When informed by well-formulated and testable psychological theories, the neuropsychological approach has the potential to provide dramatic new insights into the interplay of emotion and cognition, and the specific mechanisms by which affect can influence thinking and social behavior.

OVERVIEW OF THE BOOK

The book is organized into four main sections. Following this introductory chapter, Part I reviews some *basic ideas and paradigms* that have informed recent social psychological research on affect. These chapters discuss the role of functional, evolutionary processes in affectivity (Haselton & Ketelaar, Chapter 2), the role of neuropsychological mechanisms in affective reactions (Winkielman & Cacioppo, Chapter 3), the interplay between affect and information processing strategies (Bless & Fiedler, Chapter 4), and recent developments in the appraisal perspective on affect research (Smith et al., Chapter 5). Part II discusses recent research on the role of *affect in cognitive processes*, reviewing evidence for the role of affect in social memory (Eich & Macaulay, Chapter 6), inferential processes (Clore & Storbeck, Chapter 7), decision-making processes (Baumeister, Vohs, & Tice, Chapter 8), moral judgments (Keltner et al., Chapter 9), and affective forecasting phenomena (Dunn & Laham, Chapter 10). Part III addresses recent work exploring the links between *affect and the "social self"*, including the construction of self-representations and self-related emotions such as nostalgia (Sedikides et al., Chapter 11), the role of affect in goal setting and goal pursuit (Trope et al., Chapter 12), the role of positive emotions in well-being and life satisfaction (Huppert, Chapter 13), and affect regulation (Erber & Markunas, Chapter 14). The final, fourth section examines recent work on the way *affective states influence social behaviors*. Topics covered in this section include mood and interpersonal behavior (Forgas, Chapter 15), the role of emotional intelligence in social behavior (Ciarrochi & Blackledge, Chapter 16), affect and group behavior (Kelly and Spoor, Chapter 17), and the role of affect in personal relationships (Holmes et al., Chapter 18). Consistent with the objectives of the Frontiers series to provide up-to-date overviews of a substantive field, each of the chapters will present a comprehensive theoretical and empirical review, the main lines of research in these areas, and a conceptual integration of the current status of the field.

REFERENCES

Abele, A., & Petzold, P. (1994). How does mood operate in an impression formation task? An information integration approach. *European Journal of Social Psychology, 24*, 173–188.

Berkowitz, L. (1993). Towards a general theory of anger and emotional aggression. In T. K. Srull & R. S. Wyer (Eds.), *Advances in social cognition* (Vol. 6, pp. 1–46). Hillsdale, NJ: Lawrence Erlbaum Associates, Inc.

Berkowitz, L., Jaffee, S., Jo, E., & Troccoli, B. T. (2000). On the correction of feeling-induced judgmental biases. In J. P. Forgas (Ed.), *Feeling and thinking: The role of affect in social cognition*. New York: Cambridge University Press.

Bless, H. (2000). The interplay of affect and cognition: The mediating role of general knowledge structures. In J. P. Forgas (Ed.), *Feeling and thinking: The role of affect in social cognition*. New York: Cambridge University Press.

Bower, G. H. (1981). Mood and memory. *American Psychologist*, 36, 129–148.

Bower, G. H., & Forgas, J. P. (2001). Mood and social memory. In J. P. Forgas (Ed.), *The handbook of affect and social cognition* (pp. 95–120). Mahwah, NJ: Lawrence Erlbaum Associates, Inc.

Bruner, J. S. (1957). On perceptual readiness. *Psychological Review*, 64, 123–152.

Buss, D. M. (1999). *Evolutionary psychology: The new science of the mind*. Needham Heights, MA, US: Allyn & Bacon.

Byrne, D., & Clore, G. L. (1970). A reinforcement model of evaluation responses. *Personality: An International Journal*, 1, 103–128.

Clark, M. S., & Isen, A. M. (1982). Towards understanding the relationship between feeling states and social behavior. In A. H. Hastorf & A. M. Isen (Eds.), *Cognitive social psychology* (pp. 73–108). New York: Elsevier-North Holland.

Clore, G. L., & Byrne, D. (1974). The reinforcement affect model of attraction. In T. L. Huston (Ed.), *Foundations of interpersonal attraction* (pp. 143–170). New York, NY: Academic Press.

Clore, G. L., Schwarz, N., & Conway, M. (1994). Affective causes and consequences of social information processing. In R. S. Wyer & T. K. Srull (Eds.), *Handbook of social cognition* (2nd ed.). Hillsdale, NJ: Lawrence Erlbaum Associates, Inc.

Damasio, A. R. (1994). *Descartes' error*. New York: Grosste/Putnam.

De Sousa, R. J. (1987). *The rationality of emotion*. Cambridge, MA: The MIT Press.

East, R., & Forgas, J. P. (2005). On being happy and gullible. Unpublished manuscript.

Ellis, H. C., & Ashbrook, T. W. (1988). Resource allocation model of the effects of depressed mood state on memory. In: K. Fiedler & J. P. Forgas (Eds.), *Affect, cognition and social behaviour* (pp. 25–43). Toronto: Hogrefe.

Feshbach, S., & Singer, R. D. (1957). The effects of fear arousal and suppression of fear upon social perception. *Journal of Abnormal and Social Psychology*, 55, 283–288.

Fiedler, K. (1990). Mood-dependent selectivity in social cognition. In W. Stroebe & M. Hewstone (Eds.), *European review of social psychology* (Vol. 1, pp. 1–32). New York: Wiley.

Fiedler, K. (1991). On the task, the measures and the mood in research on affect and social cognition. In J. P. Forgas (Ed.), *Emotion and social judgments* (pp. 83–104). Oxford: Pergamon.

Forgas, J. P. (1991). Mood effects on partner choice: Role of affect in social decisions. *Journal of Personality and Social Psychology*, 61, 708–720.

Forgas, J. P. (1992a). Affect in social judgments and decisions: A multi-process model. In M. Zanna (Ed.), *Advances in experimental social psychology* (Vol. 25, pp. 227–275). New York: Academic Press.

Forgas, J. P. (1992b). Affect and social perceptions: Research evidence and an integrative model. In W. Stroebe & M. Hewstone (Eds.), *European review of social psychology* (Vol. 3, pp. 183–224). Chichester: Wiley.

Forgas, J. P. (1993). On making sense of odd couples: Mood effects on the perception of mismatched relationships. *Personality and Social Psychology Bulletin*, 19, 59–71.

Forgas, J. P. (1995). Mood and judgment: The affect infusion model (AIM). *Psychological Bulletin*, 117(1), 39–66.

Forgas, J. P. (1998). On being happy and mistaken? Mood effects on the fundamental attribution error. *Journal of Personality and Social Psychology*, 75, 318–331.

Forgas, J. P. (2002). Feeling and doing: Affective influences on interpersonal behavior. *Psychological Inquiry, 13*, 1–28.

Forgas, J. P., & Bower, G. H. (1987). Mood effects on person perception judgments. *Journal of Personality and Social Psychology, 53*, 53–60.

Forgas, J. P., & Moylan, S. J. (1987). After the movies: The effects of transient mood states on social judgments. *Personality and Social Psychology Bulletin, 13*, 478–489.

Forgas, J. P., Laham, S. M., & Vargas, P. (2005). Mood effects on eyewitness memory: Affective influences on susceptibility to misinformation. *Journal of Experimental Social Psychology, 41*, 574–588.

Gouaux, C. (1971). Induced affective states and interpersonal attraction. *Journal of Personality and Social Psychology, 20*, 37–43.

Gouaux, C., & Summers, K. (1973). Interpersonal attraction as a function of affective states and affective change. *Journal of Research in Personality, 7*, 254–260.

Griffitt, W. (1970). Environmental effects on interpersonal behavior: Ambient effective temperature and attraction. *Journal of Personality and Social Psychology, 15*, 240–244.

Hilgard, E. R. (1980). The trilogy of mind: Cognition, affection, and conation. *Journal of the History of the Behavioral Sciences, 16*, 107–117.

Isen, A. M. (1987). Positive affect, cognitive processes and social behaviour. In L. Berkowitz (Ed.), *Advances in experimental social psychology* (Vol. 20, pp. 203–253). New York: Academic Press.

Koestler, A. (1978). *Janus: A summing up*. London: Hutchinson.

Laird, J. D., & Bresler, C. (1991). The process of emotional experience: A self-perception theory. In M. Clark (Ed.), *Review of personality and social psychology* (Vol. 14, pp. 213–234). Beverly Hills: Sage.

Lazarus, R. S. (1984). On the primacy of cognition. *American Psychologist, 39*, 124–129.

LeDoux, J. E. (1989). Cognitive–emotional interactions in the brain. *Cognition and Emotion, 3(4)*, 267–289.

Lerner, J. S., & Keltner, D. (2000). Beyond valence: Toward a model of emotion-specific influences on judgment and choice. *Cognition and Emotion, 14*, 473–493.

Lerner, J. S., & Keltner, D. (2001). Fear, anger and risk. *Journal of Personality and Social Psychology, 81*, 146–159.

Lieberman, M. D. (2003). Reflexive and reflective judgment processes: A social cognitive neuroscience approach. In J. P. Forgas, K. D. Williams, & W. von Hippel (Eds.), *Social judgments: Implicit and explicit processes* (pp. 44–67). New York: Cambridge University Press.

Mackie, D., & Worth, L. (1991). Feeling good, but not thinking straight: The impact of positive mood on persuasion. In J. P. Forgas (Ed.), *Emotion and social judgments* (pp. 201–220). Oxford: Pergamon.

Martin, L. (2000). Moods don't convey information: Moods in context do. In J. P. Forgas (Ed.), *Feeling and thinking: The role of affect in social cognition*. New York: Cambridge University Press.

Neisser, U. (1982). Memory: What are the important questions? In U. Neisser (Ed.), *Memory observed*. San Francisco: Freeman.

Oatley, K., & Jenkins, J. M. (1992). Human emotions: Function and dysfunction. *Annual Review of Psychology, 43*, 55–85.

Oatley, K., & Jenkins, J. M. (1996). *Understanding emotions*. Oxford: Blackwell.

Panksepp, J. (1998). *Affective neuroscience: The foundations of human and animal emotions*. New York: Oxford University Press.

Pascal, B. (1966/1643). *Pensees*. Baltimore: Penguin books.

Schwarz, N. (1990). Feelings as information: Informational and motivational functions of affective states. In E. T. Higgins & R. Sorrentino (Eds.), *Handbook of motivation and cognition: Foundations of social behaviour* (Vol. 2, pp. 527–561). New York: Guilford Press.

Schwarz, N., & Bless, H. (1991). Happy and mindless, but sad and smart? The impact of affective states on analytic reasoning. In J. P. Forgas (Ed.), *Emotion and social judgments* (pp. 55–71). Oxford: Pergamon Press.

Schwarz, N., & Clore, G. L. (1983). Mood, misattribution and judgments of well-being: Informative and directive functions of affective states. *Journal of Personality and Social Psychology, 45,* 513–523.

Schwarz, N., & Clore, G. L. (1988). How do I feel about it? The informative function of affective states. In K. Fiedler & J. P. Forgas (Eds.), *Affect, cognition, and social behavior* (pp. 44–62). Toronto: Hogrefe.

Sedikides, C. (1995). Central and peripheral self-conceptions are differentially influenced by mood: Tests of the differential sensitivity hypothesis. *Journal of Personality and Social Psychology, 69(4),* 759–777.

Tooby, J., & Cosmides, L. (1990). The past explains the present: Emotional adaptations and the structure of ancestral environments. *Ethology and Sociobiology, 11(4–5),* 375–424.

Wyer, R. S., & Srull, T. K. (1989). *Memory and cognition in its social context.* Hillsdale, NJ: Lawrence Erlbaum Associates, Inc.

Zajonc, R. B. (1980). Feeling and thinking: Preferences need no inferences. *American Psychologist, 35,* 151–175.

Zajonc, R. B. (2000). Feeling and thinking: Closing the debate over the independence of affect. In J. P. Forgas (Ed.), *Feeling and thinking: The role of affect in social cognition.* New York: Cambridge University Press.

Part I

Basic Approaches to Affect and Social Behavior

2

Irrational Emotions or Emotional Wisdom? The Evolutionary Psychology of Affect and Social Behavior

MARTIE G. HASELTON and TIMOTHY KETELAAR

Irrational Emotions	**Emotional Wisdom**
"A human being is a bundle of useless passions." John-Paul Sartre, Philosopher	"The heart has its reasons which reason knows nothing of." Blaise Pascal, Philosopher
"Show me a guy who has feelings, and I'll show you a sucker." Frank Sinatra, Singer and Movie Star	"Your intellect may be confused, but your emotions will never lie to you." Roger Ebert, Film Critic

INTRODUCTION

Get a grip...control your emotions...don't let your feelings get in the way! Listen to your heart...get in touch with your emotions...express yourself! These messages from the academic community, as well as popular treatments of emotion, are contradictory. The rationalist history of Western thought portrays emotions as fundamentally flawed, and something we must therefore control (Haidt, 2001). Yet, there has been another voice in history—and one echoed in recent evolutionary treatments of emotion—that suggests that emotions are wise and not to be ignored (Buss, 2001; Clore, 2005; Keltner & Haidt, 1999; Ketelaar, 2004, 2005; Ketelaar & Clore, 1997).

Emotions do indeed pose a paradox. There is little doubt that emotions are a ubiquitous and a universal feature of our human nature (e.g., Ekman, 1992; Ekman & Friesen, 1971; Fessler, 1999), and thus it is hard to believe that emotions emerged through evolution only to disrupt judgment and decision-making.

On the other hand, the phenomenology of emotion certainly suggests otherwise: The effects of emotion often seem objectively irrational and we feel the need to get them under control (Baumeister, Vohs, & Tice, this volume; Forgas & Ciarrochi, 2002; Kahneman, 1999; Varey & Kahneman, 1992).

In this paper we argue that an evolutionary perspective on emotions and behavior may help to resolve this paradox. To do so, we review two promising evolutionary approaches to emotion, discuss research linking particular emotions to specific adaptive problems, and argue that these theoretical arguments and empirical findings are consistent with the claim that the emotions often display evidence of being designed to aid, rather than hinder, social decision-making. Finally, we conclude by suggesting that mismatches between our evolved emotional responses and the novel modern environments in which they currently operate often lead to outcomes we can legitimately view as suboptimal.

EVOLUTIONARY THEORIES OF EMOTION

Although numerous adaptive-evolutionary treatments of emotion have emerged over the years (e.g., Ekman & Davidson, 1994; Plutchik, 1994), an *evolutionary-psychological* approach distinguishes itself from other evolutionary approaches by adopting an explicitly adaptationist perspective (Barkow, Cosmides, & Tooby, 1992). An adaptationist perspective is guided by the simple assumption that the mind comprises many mental adaptations, each of which is the product of natural and sexual selection operating over many generations during the course of human evolution (Buss, Haselton, Shackelford, Bleske, & Wakefield, 1998).

Our ancestors faced a multitude of adaptive problems—evading predators, gathering food, finding shelter, attracting mates, caring for kin, and communicating with conspecifics, to name just a few (Barkow, Cosmides, & Tooby, 1992; Buss, 2006). Because each of these adaptive problems required a unique solution (escaping a predator involves different skills than acquiring a mate), evolutionary psychologists argue that we should expect that our minds consist of a great variety of distinct psychological mechanisms, each shaped to address a specific adaptive challenge (Barrett, 2005; Symons, 1979). Similarly, we argue that it is reasonable to expect that humans have evolved a multitude of distinct emotions, each designed to deal with a specific set of adaptive problems.

Emotions affect the way we think and behave in a variety of personal and social contexts (Clore, Schwarz, & Conway, 1994; Holmes & Anthony, this volume; Morris & Keltner, 2000; Zeelenberg & Pieters, 2005). Evolutionary approaches to emotion and social decision-making have ranged from broad theoretical models of emotion (Buck, 1999; Cosmides & Tooby, 2000; Tooby & Cosmides, 1990) to empirical investigations of specific emotions (Ketelaar & Au, 2003). One of the broadest theoretical approaches to emotion and decision-making (emotions-as-commitment devices) uses the tools of experimental economics to explore game-theoretic aspects of emotions. A second theoretical approach proposes that emotions are superordinate cognitive programs that coordinate thoughts and behaviors in response to specific adaptive challenges. We describe each of these approaches before turning to a brief review of recent empirical research linking specific emotions to specific adaptive problems.

Emotions as Commitment Devices

Humans can be coldly calculating and selfish and, like many animals, humans have preferences for immediate gains due to heavy discounting of the future (Ainslie, 1975; Ainslie & Herrnstein, 1981; Frederick, Loewenstein, & O'Donoghue, 2003). Theorists from Adam Smith (1759/2000) to Robert Trivers (1971) and more recently economists Jack Hirshleifer (1987) and Robert Frank (1988) have argued that emotions operate as mechanisms for sustaining subjective commitments to strategies that run counter to speciously attractive immediate rewards. Frank summarized the logic of the theory as follows (Frank, 1988, p. 82):

> The idea is that if the psychological reward mechanism is constrained to emphasize rewards in the present moment, the simplest counter to a specious reward from cheating is to have a current feeling that tugs in precisely the opposite direction. ...because [the emotion] coincides with the moment of choice...it can negate the spurious attraction of the imminent material reward.

Frank illustrated this view with examples of how emotions such as love and guilt can influence social decision-making. When one experiences feelings of love for a romantic partner, for example, the immediate positive reward the emotion produces counteracts the pull of desire for an attractive other. Likewise, feelings of guilt immediately punish thoughts of selfishly cheating an ally and thus prevent the individual from compromising a cooperative relationship. In doing so, these emotions help us to stick with strategies that lead to rewards in the long run despite the fact that they often necessitate forgoing smaller immediate gains. For example, if one were drawn away from every possible romantic commitment by the prospect of finding a still more attractive mate, one could never reap the fitness benefits of long-term mateship, including cooperative child rearing (Hurtado & Hill, 1992; Marlowe, 2003; Pillsworth & Haselton, 2005) and assurance of mutual care in times of dire need (e.g., Nesse, 2001).

The bulk of the work on the commitment-device theory has been purely analytical (e.g., testing theoretical assumptions with mathematical models; see Hirshleifer, 1987; Nesse, 2001, for reviews). Recently, however, this theory has also been subject to empirical tests. For example, in one study of the effects of guilt on cooperation, participants played an Ultimatum Game and emotions recorded after the first transaction were used to predict behavior 1 week later (Ketelaar & Au, 2003). In an Ultimatum Game, participants are assigned the role of the proposer or respondent. The proposer is allotted a sum of money and allowed to give some percentage of it to the responder, who then decides whether to accept or refuse the offer. If the offer is accepted, the proposer and respondent split the money as proposed; if the offer is rejected neither party receives any money. In this study, the researchers found that over 90% of subjects who felt guilty after proposing an unfair offer (less than 50–50 split) reversed their behavior a week later and made a generous monetary offer (Ketelaar & Au, 2003). By contrast, less than 25% of the individuals who experienced no feelings of guilt made a similarly generous offer; in fact, the vast majority of them (>75%) continued making selfish offers a week later. The effects of guilt on social decision-making observed in this study are consistent with the claim that individuals under the influence of certain emotions often make decisions that forego immediate benefits in favor of more profitable long-term outcomes (e.g., a cooperative alliance; Frank, 1988).

In sum, the immediate rewards or punishments that we feel when we experience certain emotions can serve as a potent counterweight to our tendency to overweight short-term gains. These emotions may appear irrational in the short run because they lead us to forgo sure gains, but ultimately they lead us to acquire still greater long-term benefits.

Superordinate Coordination Theory

Perhaps the broadest and most inclusive evolutionary theory of emotions is one that views these states as superordinate cognitive programs (e.g., Cosmides & Tooby, 2000; Levenson, 1999; Tooby & Cosmides, 1990). If evolution has created a multitude of "microprograms," serving many different functions with outputs that sometimes conflict, there must be some way for the brain to selectively activate only the subset of programs needed when an organism faces a particular adaptive problem. Otherwise, the action of these mechanisms would be chaotic and self-defeating—does one flee or court, collect food or seek shelter, sleep or eat?

Cosmides and Tooby (2000; Tooby & Cosmides, 1990) propose that the emotions serve precisely this sort of governing function by orchestrating systems of perception, attention, goal pursuit, and energy and effectiveness, as well as by activating specialized inferences, recalibrating decision weightings, and regulating behavior. They illustrate using the emotion of fear: You can imagine walking alone at night and hearing some rustling in the brush. Your energies are aroused to ready you for action, you become acutely aware of sounds that could indicate that you are being stalked, the threshold for detecting movement is lowered, you no longer feel pangs of hunger, attracting a mate is the farthest thing from your mind, you recall where there are good places to hide, and you act—by running, hiding, fighting, or ceasing all movement, depending on the circumstances.

Cues associated with ancestrally recurrent threats and opportunities such as being cloaked in darkness, viewing naked, nubile mates, or smelling delicious food can automatically turn on particular emotions, thereby activating specialized strategies that in ancestral environments would have led to targeted adaptive responses. Our everyday experiences provide evidence that this general hypothesis holds some merit. Fear, for example, results in protective responses including flight, whereas sexual desire results in the pursuit of a desired mate. In the next section, we also describe several lines of research demonstrating that (1) ancestrally recurrent cues readily elicit specific emotions and (2) specific emotions lead to targeted, functional outcomes. The relevant literature has grown substantially over the last several decades (see Haidt, 2003; Ketelaar, 2005; Keltner & Haidt, 1999 for reviews). In our brief review, we have selected examples that (1) demonstrate the function-specificity of emotions, (2) would be difficult to understand without evolutionary theorizing, and (3) represent the latest updates on important theoretical questions in the study of emotion.

ANCESTRAL CUES ELICIT SPECIFIC EMOTIONS

Fear and Ancestral Sources of Danger

As we have already hinted, perhaps nowhere does there exist better evidence for the domain-specificity of emotion than in the domain of fear. Modern environments possess an abundance of lethal threats that hardly evoke a moment's notice. Humans routinely operate speeding automobiles, work around sources of electrical hazard, and expose themselves to carcinogenic agents without breaking a sweat. Yet, a single harmless stinging insect can bring about behavioral changes that are detectable for several city blocks. Why do humans appear to lack fear of objects that can kill (automobiles and electrical outlets) and yet display an almost debilitating fear of objects that present only a small threat (spiders and snakes)? In this section, we illustrate how an adaptationist view on the functional-specificity of emotions allows us to make sense of this otherwise puzzling array of fear responses.

Evolutionary psychologists argue that the nonrandom distribution of fear stimuli is a legacy of the evolutionary past. The absence of fear responses to evolutionarily novel sources of danger (automobiles, electrical outlets, etc.), for example, suggests that emotional responses are not simply the product of rational deliberation. Instead, human fears are the result of domain-specific mechanisms that correspond to ancient sources of harm such as dangerous animals, bodily insults, heights, social evaluation, and the risk of social exclusion (Costello, 1982; Marks & Nesse, 1994; Nesse, 1990; Öhman & Mineka, 2001; Seligman, 1971). Snake fear is perhaps the best-researched example. Although snakes do not pose much of a risk in modern environments, snakes and humans have coexisted for millennia and snakebites can be lethal. In the laboratory, researchers can condition people to fear snakes and snake-like stimuli using mild electrical shocks. By contrast, it is difficult to condition fear to other stimuli, even those with strong semantic associations with shock (e.g., damaged electrical outlets; see Öhman & Mineka, 2001 for a review). Unlike responses to evolutionarily novel sources of harm, biologically prepared fear responses (snakes, spiders, etc.) are notoriously difficult to extinguish (see Cook & Mineka, 1990; Marks & Nesse, 1994; Mineka, 1992; Nesse, 1990; Seligman, 1971, for reviews).

One of the curiosities of evolved fear responses is that they often appear overresponsive (Nesse, 1990, 2005). For example, prey animals express startle and flight responses at rates that suggest that they overestimate risk (Bouskila & Blumstein, 1992), and the human tendency to acquire and retain snake fears on the basis of slim evidence can also be conceived of as a bias (Haselton & Nettle, 2006). Rather than indicating irrationality, this hypersensitivity to particular environmental cues may be due to error management (Haselton & Buss, 2000; Haselton & Nettle, 2006). For example, when the costs of expressing a defensive reaction are small (e.g., a few calories spent on fleeing), whereas the consequences of failing to do so can be deadly (failing to evade a predator), it pays to err on the side of making false positive errors rather than false negative errors, even if this increases overall error rates (Bouskila & Blumstein, 1992; Haselton & Nettle, 2006; Nesse, 1990). In sum, adaptive over-responsiveness in our emotional reactions may sometimes lead to the mistaken impression that defensive emotions (fear, anxiety, and aggression) are not well-designed.

Specific Emotions and Sex-Linked Adaptive Problems

Function specificity is evident not only in cross-species conflicts (humans vs. dangerous animals), but also appears in a variety of within-species conflicts for which humans appear to have evolved special-purpose emotional machinery. For example, men and women have historically faced different adaptive problems in the domain of mating, and evolutionary psychologists have therefore proposed that the sexes have evolved different solutions to a number of sex-linked adaptive problems.

Differences in parental investment can produce some of the largest conflicts between the sexes. Because men's reproductive investments can be very small, the upper limit on reproductive success for males is predicted, quite simply, by the number of fertile partners to whom they gain access (Symons, 1979; Trivers, 1972). Women's investments, on the other hand, are always large—at minimum 9 months of pregnancy, typically followed by years of breastfeeding in traditional societies. Thus, the optimal strategy for a man and a woman will often be in conflict. For women, mate quality looms larger than mate quantity, whereas for some men who are able to successfully pursue a short-term mating strategy, the reverse can certainly be true (see Gangestad & Simpson, 2000), and a variety of robust sex differences support this proposal. Women, for example, tend to desire longer delays before sex in order to assess a mate's quality and disposition to invest. Men, on average, desire sex earlier in relationships and maintain a desire for sexual variety even after finding a long-term mate (Schmitt et al., 2003; also see Buss, 2003, for a review).

Differences in the evolved desires that underpin these sex-differentiated adaptive problems can result in sexual strategies that produce conflict. Buss (1989) proposed that negative emotions such as anger and fear may aid an individual in dealing with the attempts of others to interfere with one's strategic goals: When a source of interference is detected, negative emotions (e.g., anger) can draw attention to the source of interference, mark important events for storage in memory, and activate behavioral routines that serve to minimize current and future interference. To the degree that the sources of strategic interference differ between the sexes, one expects to observe sex differences in the emotional responses that they elicit.

An extensively researched example is sexual jealousy. Due to internal female fertilization, men are uncertain of paternity, whereas women are always certain of maternity and hence they do not face this problem. Thus, evolutionary psychologists proposed that men should experience greater jealousy in response to cues to sexual infidelity than women do (Buss, Larsen, Westen, & Semmelroth, 1992; Daly, Wilson,

& Weghorst, 1982). Although research on this hypothesis is fraught with controversy (Buller, 2005; Buss & Haselton, 2005; Harris, 2003; Sagarin, 2005), the bulk of the evidence, including many cross-cultural studies, has found that men report greater jealousy in response to imagined infidelity than do women, though clearly both men and women find all forms of infidelity extremely upsetting (e.g., Buss et al., 1992; Buss & Haselton, 2005; Haselton, Buss, Oubaid, & Angleitner, 2005; Sagarin, 2005). Also consistent with the jealousy hypothesis, men express more jealousy if their partners are higher in reproductive value (younger and or more attractive; Buss & Shackelford, 1997) and when their partners are nearing ovulation and the likelihood of extra-pair conception as a result of an affair is greatest (Gangestad, Thornhill, & Garver, 2002; Haselton & Gangestad, 2005).

In the realm of mating deception, women respond with far greater upset in response to a partner exaggerating his feelings in order to have sex or failing to maintain commitments after sex, whereas men respond with greater upset in response to being sexually led on (Haselton et al., 2005). Deceptive exploitations of sex-linked mate preferences also produce sex differences in degree of emotional upset. Women are more upset if a partner exaggerates his income or status, whereas men's upset is piqued by a long-term partner exaggerating her faithfulness or under-reporting her level of sexual experience (Haselton et al., 2005).

Emotions also track experience-contingent shifts in costs and benefits for the sexes. First-time intercourse signals the possibility of pregnancy for a woman and therefore the importance of securing commitment from her partner. For men who pursue a short-term mating strategy, first-time sex signals both that a goal has been achieved and that there is a possibility of becoming entangled in an unwanted long-term relationship. After first-time sex, the feelings men and women experience do indeed differ. Women more than men experience a positive affective shift toward increased feelings of commitment for their partners (Haselton & Buss, 2001), whereas men who have had many sex partners (and therefore successfully pursue a short-term strategy) experience a negative affective shift marked by a drop-off in physical attraction to their partners (Haselton & Buss, 2001). These effects are hypothesized to prompt behaviors to secure investment (for women) or to extricate oneself from a potential romantic entanglement (for short-term oriented men).

The sexes may also differ in their feelings of regret surrounding sex. The affective experience of regret is hypothesized to function to improve future decision-making by enabling people to avoid mistakes that have important consequences (Haselton, Poore, von Hippel, Gonzaga, & Buss, 2005; Roese, 2005; Zeelenberg, 1999). If this hypothesis is correct, feelings of regret should track sex-differentiated adaptive problems including problems of careful partner choice for women (more than men) and problems of attracting multiple mates for men (more than women). Haselton and colleagues proposed that missed sexual opportunities (sexual omission) would have been more reproductively costly for ancestral men than for women, whereas sexual encounters with an undesirable or noninvesting partner (sexual commission) would have been more reproductively costly for women than for men (Haselton et al., 2005). As predicted, in response to hypothetical regret scenarios, women more than men reported that they would regret having sex in a relationship that turned out to be only short-term, whereas men more than women reported they would regret missing an attractive sexual opportunity (Haselton et al., 2005). These effects were corroborated by participants' spontaneous reports of past experiences: Although women and men both listed more sexual commission regrets than sexual omission regrets, women reported that they regretted acts of sexual commission more intensely than did men.

In sum, there is growing evidence that the emotions men and women experience are differentially sensitive to cues linked with the specific adaptive problems each sex faced during evolutionary history. Men react more strongly to sexual infidelity, being sexually led on, and being deceived about a partner's tendency to be faithful. Men experience predictable affective shifts after first-time sex, and they report that they would strongly regret missed sexual opportunities. Women, on the other hand, react more strongly to being deceived about a man's level of commitment in order to get sex and about his level of status. Women experience a predictable increase in feelings of commitment to a partner after first-time sex, and they experience stronger regrets after having sex with a partner who turned out not to be desirable as first believed.

The Function-Specificity of Moral Disgust

Emotions should be sensitive not only to the on-average differences in fitness costs and benefits between the sexes but also to individuating circumstances that confront members of the same sex. We now turn to two such examples in the domain of disgust.

Many theorists have proposed that disgust is designed to reject toxic or pathogenic substances (e.g., Rozin, Lowery, & Ebert, 1994) and to prevent costly sexual behaviors—for example, engaging in sex with biological relatives (Fessler & Navarrete, 2003; Lieberman, 2003). Many sources of evidence indicate that feelings of disgust are indeed opposed to feelings of sexual desire (see Fessler & Navarrete, 2003, for a review).

Lieberman (2003; Lieberman, Tooby, & Cosmides, 2003) proposed that a reliably occurring cue to siblingship is coresidence during childhood, and therefore length of coresidence should be associated with greater disgust in response to imagined sexual activities with a sibling and to greater moral disapproval of third party incest. Not surprisingly, Lieberman found that length of coresidence strongly predicted degree of relatedness, but length of coresidence also positively predicted the degree of disgust men and women reported in response to imagining sexual activities with siblings, ranging from tongue-kissing to having sexual intercourse (Lieberman, 2003; Lieberman et al., 2003). Siblings who coresided for longer periods of time also expressed greater moral sentiments prohibiting sex between relatives (Lieberman et al., 2003; also see Fessler & Navarrete, 2004, for converging results). Coresidence time predicted incest aversions after controlling for actual degree of relatedness, suggesting that time spent living together is possibly the cue to which the evolved psychology of incest avoidance is most strongly attuned (Lieberman et al., 2003). These results are striking given that the subjects in these studies (Western undergraduates) have access to explicit information about true sibship, and yet the effects of relatedness are trumped by the hypothesized ancestral cue (coresidence).

The onset of ovulation signals greater risk of conception for women and hence greater costs of suboptimal matings. Thus, Fessler and Navarrete (2003) proposed that near ovulation women should experience greater disgust sensitivity in the sexual domain but not in other domains (e.g., food, body envelope violations, or hygiene). As predicted, they found that women's probability of conception based on self-reported cycle day significantly predicted disgust sensitivity in the sexual domain, and only in the sexual domain, of the Disgust Scale (Haidt, McCauley, & Rozin, 1994). In sum, these results demonstrate that two cues which were likely to predict ancestral costs of sex—length of coresidence and female cycle position—elicit sexual disgust.

EMOTIONS AND BEHAVIORAL OUTCOMES

We have already shown that emotions show an adaptive fit with the circumstances that elicit them, presumably because emotions tended to lead to adaptive outcomes in those circumstances ancestrally. However, emotions do not simply evolve because they are activated by highly specific stimuli; rather, they evolve because they yielded functional responses with real fitness effects—for example, by adaptively shifting perceptions, behaviors, and decisions. Examples of emotional influences on perception, behavior, and decision-making are well-known (Clore, Schwarz, & Conway, 1994; Clore & Storbeck, this volume; Ketelaar & Clore, 1997), yet much of this research has focused on detailed accounts of the proximate mechanisms through which emotions influence these phenomena. In the next section, we focus an evolutionary lens on these domains to illustrate how an adaptationist perspective can shed light on the ultimate cognitive and behavioral functions of emotions.

Emotions and Perceptual Shifts: Fear versus Romantic Arousal

One prediction of Cosmides and Tooby's superordinate coordination theory (2000) is that emotions should change our perceptions of others in evolutionarily predictable ways. There are several recent empirical examples that are consistent with this expectation.

In ancestral environments, between-group differences in appearance and behavior (e.g., tribal markers, signaled differences in coalition membership, etc.) would have activated the psychology of intergroup conflict. To the degree that this intergroup psychology has been shaped by evolutionary selection pressures, we might expect that features of modern environments that resemble these intergroup cues and markers will activate this ancient psychology (Kurzban, Tooby, & Cosmides, 2001; Sidanius & Veniegas, 2000). Moreover, as previously noted, emotions might play an important role in determining how we process these cues. Specifically, certain emotions might make us more responsive, and in some cases over-responsive to particular cues that would have been predictive of specific threats and opportunities in ancestral environments. Ambient darkness, for example a danger/fear cue, increases racial and ethnic stereotypes connoting violence, but has little effect on other negative stereotypes such as laziness or ignorance (Schaller, Park, & Mueller, 2003).

Maner and colleagues (Maner et al., 2005) hypothesized that fear would increase biases toward inferring aggressiveness in others (particularly members of coalitional outgroups), whereas sexual arousal would increase men's bias toward overinferring sexual interest in women (Haselton & Buss, 2000). They showed men and women clips of scary or romantically arousing films, and then asked them to interpret "microexpressions" in photographs of people who had relived an emotionally arousing experience but were attempting to conceal any facial expressions that would reveal it (the faces were actually neutral in expression). In the fear condition, the study participants, who were mostly White, "saw" more anger on male faces, especially the faces of outgroup males (Blacks and Arabs). The fear manipulation had no effect on perceptions of sexual arousal in the faces. In the romantically arousing film condition, men perceived greater sexual arousal in female faces, particularly when the faces were attractive. The arousal manipulation did not increase men's perceptions of sexual arousal in other men's faces nor did it increase women's perceptions of sexual arousal in any of the faces. Thus, the effects were emotion and target specific, and for sexual arousal, sex specific. When fearful, men and women perceived greater threat from ethnic outgroup members; when sexually aroused, men but not women perceived greater arousal in attractive opposite-sex faces.

Love and Commitment

Humans pursue a mix of mating strategies. Some highly desirable men can and do engage in a multiple-female mating strategy, either through maintaining simultaneous affairs with several women (Gangestad & Simpson, 2000), or through serial remating of progressively younger women—effectively dominating the reproductive careers of many females (Buss, 2003). Men who are less able to pursue such strategies can still gain fitness advantages by committing to an exclusive long-term partnership and investing heavily in each child, thus ensuring greater offspring survival, health, and success in adulthood (Hurtado & Hill, 1992; Marlowe, 2003; also see Gangestad & Simpson, 2000). Women also engage in mixed mating strategies (Gangestad & Simpson, 2000), though most evidence suggests that they have a stronger preference for long-term partnerships than short-term affairs (Buss, 2003).

Although the optimal mating strategy for every ancestral human was not the same, many (perhaps the majority) would have benefited from exclusive coupling, at least at some point in their lives (Pillsworth & Haselton, 2005). Given the temptation of romantic alternatives, and humans' proclivity to overweight short-term temptations, Frank (1988; also see above) hypothesized that the emotion of love serves as a commitment device. Just as feelings of guilt evoked while considering cheating can deter romantic defection, feelings of love while contemplating one's mate can compel the individual to stay committed (Ketelaar & Goodie, 1998).

Indeed, people in love seem to believe that there is no one more desirable than their own partner and they recurrently experience pleasant feelings toward their partner that may counteract the temptation to pursue alternative mating opportunities.

If love is a commitment device, as Frank proposed, it should suspend or suppress mate search. Along these lines, Gonzaga and colleagues (Gonzaga, Haselton, Davies, & Smurda, 2005) predicted that inductions of feelings of love should cause attractive alternatives to be less tempting. They further hypothesized that a closely related emotion, sexual desire, which is theoretically not a commitment device (e.g., Fisher, Aron, Mashek, Li, & Brown, 2002), would not yield the same effect. To test the hypothesis they made use of a subtle psychological phenomenon, thought suppression. Numerous studies have shown that when people attempt to suppress exciting thoughts they experience a paradoxical surge of the thoughts (the rebound effect) as compared to individuals who do not attempt to suppress those thoughts (e.g., Wegner, Schneider, Carter, & White, 1987; also see Wegner, Shortt, Blake, & Page, 1990). It follows that if love acts as a commitment device, this emotion may facilitate the suppression of thoughts of romantic alternatives, and thereby reduce or eliminate the rebound effect. To test this hypothesis, Gonzaga and colleagues asked participants to either suppress or express the thought of an attractive other while writing essays about experiences of intense love or sexual desire for their current romantic partner. Consistent with their evolutionary hypothesis, after attempting to suppress the thought of the attractive other and relative to the sexual desire condition, participants in the love condition had fewer thoughts of the attractive other, indicating successful suppression of thoughts of the attractive other (Wegner & Gold, 1995).

These results provide support for the commitment theory of emotion and suggest that discrete emotions have discrete effects—although love and desire were both elicited in reference to participants' romantic partner, only love facilitated suppression of thoughts of attractive others.

Specific Emotions and Decision-Making: Fear, Anger, and Disgust

Social cognition research on emotion and decision-making has traditionally focused on the proximate mechanisms through which valenced mood states (positive and negative affects) influence decision-making. Recently, a number of researchers have highlighted the benefits of moving beyond the study of valence to look at the influence of specific emotional states on decision-making (Lerner & Keltner, 2000, 2001; Van Kleef, de Dreu, & Manstead, 2004). Some of this research has focused on the *intrapersonal functions* of emotions, such as when post-decision regret motivates one to subsequently pursue an opportunity he or she had previously rejected (Zeelenberg & Pieters, 2005). An equally promising line of research has focused on the *interpersonal functions* of emotions such as when anger motivates one to punish a selfish contributor in a public goods game (Fehr & Gaechter, 2002).

Studies that emphasize domain-specific influences of emotion quickly lead to the realization that not all negative emotions have the same effects on decision-making.

For example, Fessler, Pillsworth, and Flamson (2004) proposed that although anger and disgust are similar in valance (both negative) they would have distinct effects on behavior. Anger is a response to experiencing a transgression and attempting to deter it through action against the source. Disgust, in contrast, is a response to a potential contaminant and it motivates distancing from the source. It follows that these two negative emotions should have very different effects on risk-taking—anger should increase it and disgust should decrease it (see Lerner & Keltner, 2000, 2001; Lerner, Small, & Loewenstein, 2004 for nonevolutionary routes to this same conclusion). In addition, Fessler, Pillsworth, and Flamson hypothesized that there will be sex differences in the impact of these emotions on risk-taking, with men responding more to risks associated with intrasexual (male–male) competition and women responding more on risks in the domain of reproduction and child-rearing. These predictions are based on the notion that, historically, the risk of being bested by a rival is likely to have exacted a larger fitness cost on men than on women, and thus men are expected to be particularly prone to take risks when primed to feel anger. Similarly, the risk of contamination is likely to have exacted a larger fitness cost on women than on men (e.g., through risks associated with pregnancy), and thus women are expected to be particularly averse to risks when primed to feel disgust. Consistent with these hypotheses, relative to controls, anger primes significantly increased male risk-taking in an economic game with real monetary stakes; disgust primes had no such effect. Women's risk-taking in the game was not affected by anger, but was substantially decreased by disgust. For women, one might expect even more dramatic effects if the task involved risks directly linked with contamination.

DISCUSSION

Functional approaches to emotion are not new in psychology. A variety of clinical, personality, and social-cognitive approaches to emotion have emphasized the role of emotion in social adjustment, mental health, subjective happiness, and well-being (e.g., see reviews in Baumeister, Vohs, & Tice, this volume; Clore & Storbeck, this volume; Erber & Markunas, this volume; Holmes & Anthony, this volume; Huppert, this volume; Trope, Igou, & Burke, this volume). What is unique about an evolutionary approach to function, however, is its focus on *why* emotions operate in the manner that they do (questions about ultimate function) rather than questions about *what* emotions do (descriptions of proximate functions). We argue that this focus on ultimate functions yields novel insights (Ketelaar & Ellis, 2000) and in some cases can illustrate how seemingly irrational emotions aid rather than hinder reasoning. When viewed through a Darwinian lens, many of the proximate effects of emotion that appear to illustrate defects in reason can be viewed, instead, as evidence for well-designed influences on perception, decision-making, and behavior.

A focal point of any evolutionary psychological treatment of emotion is the concept of adaptation. Adaptations are specialized problem-solving machinery produced through natural and sexual selection operating over many generations during the course of human evolution (Buss et al., 1998). In this chapter we have attempted to support the utility of this adaptationist approach by illustrating empirical and theoretical contributions to our understanding of evolutionary fears and modern dangers, sex-linked adaptive problems, and the corresponding emotions that arose to address these problems, as well as a variety of emotion-outcome linkages (fear and perception, love and commitment, disgust and decision-making) that, as a collective, make sense only when viewed in light of evolution.

There are several implications of an adaptationist approach to emotion that future emotion research might consider. First, because emotions themselves are treated as cognitive programs (Cosmides & Tooby, 2000; Tooby & Cosmides, 1990), there is no dividing line between "emotion" and "cognition" that would make it sensible to contrast emotion with reason. Second, because we expect that emotions are tailored to a variety of distinct ancestral problems, we also expect to observe a great variety of emotions (rather than only a few), each with their own specialized functions. Moreover, when a single emotion operates in a variety of different domains in modern environments, we expect to observe that their effects will be moderated by contextual cues that harken back to ancestral adaptive problems. Finally, the perceptual behavior and decision-making outcomes produced by emotions in these circumstances may sometimes make sense only when viewed from an adaptationist perspective.

Importantly, we wish to note that a focus on evolutionary insights does not entail that traditional approaches to emotion and cognition are somehow flawed. Instead, an evolutionary approach adds novel insights to current and previous emotion research, contributing to, rather than taking away from, our understanding of emotion and human nature. For example, empirical findings regarding the emotions-as-commitment devices approach are quite consistent with the familiar affect-as-information model in social cognition research (Schwarz & Clore, 1983, 1988). A central assumption of an affective-information view revolves around the idea that emotions can influence decision-making by virtue of providing information about outcomes. Research from this perspective shows us that individuals routinely consult their emotions (How do I feel about this choice?) before acting. Although this approach suggests that affective feelings provide valuable information for decisions, it does not tell us what this "information" actually refers to. Researchers using an evolutionary approach to affect-as-information have argued that "affective information" should be designed to provide information about the fitness relevant payoffs/utilities associated with particular strategy choices (Ketelaar, 2005; Ketelaar & Au, 2003; Ketelaar & Todd, 2001). Positive emotions and feeling states (happiness, lust) portend fitness benefits, whereas negative emotions (guilt, jealousy) portend fitness costs. When the influence of emotion on judgment is viewed in this light—as providing valuable information about likely future consequences—we believe that the traditional affect-as-information perspective is enriched and elaborated rather than critiqued and constrained. In this same spirit, we conclude that an adaptationist approach to emotion actually complements existing research by shedding light on the ultimate functions that may lie beneath the proximate effects that we observe in the lab.

Throughout this chapter we have argued that emotions show evidence of adaptive design, and therefore are not fundamentally irrational. Indeed, our emotions are wisely adapted to potent ancestral threats—dangerous animals, hostile humans, strategic conflict arising in mating—and to ancestral opportunities—pursuing attractive mates, cementing cooperative alliances. It is the case, however, that because emotions have evolved to operate in ancestral worlds different from our own, we will often observe a mismatch between our evolved emotional responses and the novel modern environments in which they currently operate (Fessler & Haley, 2003; Sripada & Stich, 2004). This can lead to outcomes that appear to be suboptimal or irrational in the modern world. Moreover, evolution operates to maximize reproduction, whereas our personal aspirations might instead be to maximize other outcomes, such as subjective happiness (Fessler & Haley, 2003). In pursuing our personal goals, we may therefore wisely choose not to always follow the mandates of our emotions. This tension between the strong pull of our evolved adaptations and our differing current goals is a potential solution to the paradox of emotions.

REFERENCES

Ainslie, G. (1975). Specious reward: A behavioral theory of impulsiveness and impulse control. *Psychological Bulletin*, *82*, 463–496.

Ainslie, G., & Herrnstein, R. J. (1981). Preference reversal and delayed reinforcement. *Animal Learning and Behavior*, *9*, 476–482.

Barkow, J. H., Cosmides, L., & Tooby, J. (Eds.). (1992). *The adapted mind: Evolutionary psychology and the generation of culture*. New York: Oxford University Press.

Barrett, H. C. (2005). Enzymatic computation and cognitive modularity. *Mind and Language*, *20*, 259–287.

Baumeister, R. F., Vohs, K. D., & Tice, D. M. (2006). Emotional influences on decision making. In J. Forgas (Ed.), *Affect in social thinking and behavior*. New York: Psychology Press.

Bouskila, A., & Blumstein, D. T. (1992). Rules of thumb for predation hazard assessment: Predictions from a dynamic model. *The American Naturalist*, *139*, 161–176.

Buck, R. (1999). The biological affects: A typology. *Psychological Review*, *106*, 301–336.

Buller, D. J. (2005). Evolutionary psychology: The emperor's new paradigm. *Trends in Cognitive Sciences*, *9*, 277–283.

Buss, D. M. (1989). Conflict between the sexes: Strategic interference and the evocation of anger and upset. *Journal of Personality and Social Psychology*, *56*, 735–747.

Buss, D. M. (2001). Cognitive biases and emotional wisdom in the evolution of conflict between the sexes. *Current Directions in Psychological Science*, *10*, 219–223.

Buss, D. M. (2003). *The evolution of desire: Strategies of human mating*. New York: Basic Books.

Buss, D. M. (2006). *The handbook of evolutionary psychology*. Hoboken, NJ: Wiley.

Buss, D. M., & Haselton, M. G. (2005). The evolution of jealousy: A response to Buller. *Trends in Cognitive Science*, *9*, 506–507.

Buss, D. M., Haselton, M. G., Shackelford, T. K., Bleske, A. L., & Wakefield, J. (1998). Adaptations, exaptations, and spandrels. *American Psychologist*, *53*, 533–548.

Buss, D. M., Larsen, R. J., Westen, D., & Semmelroth, J. (1992). Sex differences in jealousy: Evolution, physiology, and psychology. *Psychological Science*, *3*, 251–255.

Buss, D. M., & Shackelford, T. K. (1997). From vigilance to violence: Mate retention tactics in married couples. *Journal of Personality and Social Psychology, 72*, 346–361.

Clore, G. L. (2005). For love or money: Some emotional foundations of rationality. *The Chicago-Kent Law Review, 80*, 1151–1166.

Clore, G. L., Schwarz, N., & Conway, M. (1994). Affective causes and consequences of social information processing. In R. S. J. Wyer & T. K. Srull (Eds.), *Handbook of social cognition* (pp. 323–417). Hillsdale, NJ: Lawrence Erlbaum Associates, Inc.

Clore, G. L., & Storbeck, J. (2006). Affect as information about liking, efficacy, and importance. In J. Forgas (Ed.), *Affect in social thinking and behavior.* New York: Psychology Press.

Cook, M., & Mineka, S. (1990). Selective associations in the observational conditioning of fear in rhesus monkeys. *Journal of Experimental Psychology: Animal Behavior Processes, 16*, 372–389.

Cosmides, L., & Tooby, J. (2000). Evolutionary psychology and the emotions. In M. Lewis & J. M. Haviland-Jones (Eds.), *Handbook of emotions* (2nd ed., pp. 91–115). New York: Guilford.

Costello, C. G. (1982). Fears and phobias in women: A community study. *Journal of Abnormal Psychology, 91*, 280–286.

Daly, M., Wilson, M. I., & Weghorst, S. J. (1982). Male sexual jealousy. *Ethology and Sociobiology, 3*, 11–27.

Ekman, P. (1992). An argument for basic emotions. *Cognition and Emotion, 6*, 169–200.

Ekman, P., & Davidson, R. J. (1994). *The nature of emotion: Fundamental questions.* New York: Oxford University Press.

Ekman, P., & Friesen, W. (1971). Constants across cultures in the face and emotion. *Journal of Personality and Social Psychology, 17*, 124–129.

Erber, R., & Markunas, S. (2006). Managing affective states. In J. Forgas (Ed.), *Affect in social thinking and behavior.* New York: Psychology Press.

Fehr, E., & Gaechter, S. (2002). Altruistic punishment in humans. *Nature, 10*, 137–140.

Fessler, D. M. T. (1999). Toward an understanding of the universality of second order emotions. In A. L. Hinton (Ed.), *Biocultural approaches to the emotions.* (pp. 75–116). New York: Cambridge University Press.

Fessler, D. M. T., & Haley, K. (2003). The strategy of affect: Emotions in human cooperation. In P. Hammerstein (Ed.), *The genetic and cultural evolution of cooperation* (pp. 7–36). Cambridge, MA: MIT Press.

Fessler, D. M. T., & Navarrete, C. D. (2003). Domain-specific variation in disgust sensitivity across the menstrual cycle. *Evolution and Human Behavior, 24*, 406–417.

Fessler, D. M. T., & Navarrete, C. D. (2004). Third-party attitudes toward sibling incest: Evidence for westermarck's hypotheses. *Evolution and Human Behavior, 25*, 277–294.

Fessler, D. M. T., Pillsworth, E. G., & Flamson, T. J. (2004). Angry men and disgusted women: An evolutionary approach to the influence of emotions on risk taking. *Organizational Behavior and Human Decision Processes, 95*, 107–123.

Fisher, H. E., Aron, A., Mashek, D., Li, H., & Brown, L. L. (2002). Defining the brain systems of lust, romantic attraction, and attachment. *Archives of Sexual Behavior, 31*, 413–419.

Forgas, J. P., & Ciarrochi, J. (2002). On managing moods: Evidence for the role of homeostatic cognitive strategies in affect regulation. *Personality and Social Psychology Bulletin, 28*, 336–345.

Frank, R. H. (1988). *Passions within reason: The strategic role of the emotions.* New York: Norton.

Frederick, S., Loewenstein, G., & O'Donoghue, T. (2003). Time discounting and time preference: A critical review. In G. Loewenstein & D. Read (Eds.), *Time and decision: Economic and psychological perspectives on intertemporal choice* (pp. 13–86). New York: Russell Sage Foundation Press.

Gangestad, S. W., & Simpson, J. A. (2000). The evolution of human mating: Trade-offs and strategic pluralism. *Behavioral and Brain Sciences, 23,* 573–644.

Gangestad, S. W., Thornhill, R., & Garver, C. E. (2002). Changes in women's sexual interests and their partners' mate retention tactics across the menstrual cycle: Evidence for shifting conflicts of interest. *Proceedings of the Royal Society of London: B Biological Sciences, 269,* 975–982.

Gonzaga, G., Haselton, M. G., Davies, M. S., & Smurda, J. (2005). *Love, desire, and the suppression of thoughts of attractive others.* Manuscript under review.

Haidt, J. (2001). The emotional dog and its rational tail: A social intuitionist approach to moral judgment. *Psychological Review, 108,* 814–834.

Haidt, J. (2003). The moral emotions. In R. J. Davidson, K. R. Scherer, & H. H. Goldsmith (Eds.), *Handbook of affective sciences* (pp. 852–870). New York: Oxford University Press.

Haidt, J., McCauley, C., & Rozin, P. (1994). Individual differences in sensitivity to disgust: A scale sampling seven domains of disgust elicitors. *Personality and Individual Differences, 16,* 701–713.

Harris, C. R. (2003). A review of sex differences in sexual jealousy, including self-report data, psychophysiological responses, interpersonal violence, and morbid jealousy. *Personality and Social Psychology Review, 7,* 102–128.

Haselton, M. G., & Buss, D. M. (2000). Error management theory: A new perspective on biases in cross-sex mind reading. *Journal of Personality and Social Psychology, 78,* 81–91.

Haselton, M. G., & Buss, D. M. (2001). Emotional reactions following first-time sexual intercourse: The affective shift hypothesis. *Personal Relationships, 8,* 357–369.

Haselton, M. G., Buss, D. M, Oubaid, V., & Angleitner, A. (2005). Sex, lies, and strategic interference: The psychology of deception between the sexes. *Personality and Social Psychology Bulletin, 31,* 3–23.

Haselton, M. G., & Gangestad, S. W. (2005). *Conditional expression of female desires and male mate retention efforts across the human ovulatory cycle.* Manuscript under review.

Haselton, M. G., & Nettle, D. (2006). The paranoid optimist: An integrative evolutionary model of cognitive biases. *Personality and Social Psychology Review, 10,* 47–66.

Haselton, M. G., Poore, J., von Hippel, B., Gonzaga, G., & Buss, D. M. (2005, June). *Sexual Regret.* Paper presented at the Human Behavior and Evolution Society Conference, Austin, TX.

Hirshleifer, J. (1987.) On the emotions as guarantors of threats and promises. In J. Dupré (Ed.), *The latest on the best: Essays on evolution and optimality* (pp. 307–326). Boston: MIT Press.

Holmes, J. G., & Anthony, D. B. (2006). Affect and the regulation of interdependence in personal relationships. In J. Forgas (Ed.), *Affect in social thinking and behavior.* New York: Psychology Press.

Huppert, F. A. (2006). Positive emotions and cognition. In J. Forgas (Ed.), *Affect in social thinking and behavior.* New York: Psychology Press.

Hurtado, A. M., & Hill, K. R. (1992). Paternal effect on offspring survivorship among Ache and Hiwi hunter-gatherers: Implications for modeling pair-bond stability. In *Father–child relations: Cultural and biosocial contexts* (pp. 31–55). Hawthorne, NY: Aldine de Gruyter.

Kahneman, D. (1999). Objective happiness. In D. Kahneman, E. Diener, & N. Schwarz (Eds.), *Well-being: Foundations of hedonic psychology* (pp. 3–27). New York: Russell Sage Foundation Press.

Keltner, D., & Haidt, J. (1999). Social functions of emotion at four levels of analysis. *Cognition and Emotion, 13,* 505–521.

Ketelaar, T. (2004). Ancestral emotions, current decisions: Using evolutionary game theory to explore the role of emotions in decision-making. In C. Crawford & C. Salmon (Eds.), *Evolutionary psychology, public policy and personal decisions* (pp. 145–168). Mahwah, NJ: Lawrence Erlbaum Associates, Inc.

Ketelaar, T (2005). The role of moral sentiments in experimental economics. In D. DeCremer, K. Murnighan, &. M. Zeelenberg (Eds.), *Social psychology and economics.* Mahwah, NJ: Lawrence Erlbaum Associates, Inc.

Ketelaar, T., & Au, W. T. (2003). The effects of guilty feelings on the behavior of uncooperative individuals in repeated social bargaining games: An affect-as-information interpretation of the role of emotion in social interaction. *Cognition and Emotion, 17,* 429–453.

Ketelaar, T., & Clore, G. L. (1997). Emotions and reason: The proximate effects and ultimate functions of emotions. In G. Matthews (Ed.), *Personality, emotion, and cognitive science* (pp. 355–396). Amsterdam: Elsevier.

Ketelaar, T., & Ellis, B. J. (2000). Are evolutionary explanations unfalsifiable?: Evolutionary psychology and the Lakatosian philosophy of science. *Psychological Inquiry, 11,* 1–21.

Ketelaar, T., & Goodie, A. S. (1998). The satisficing role of emotions in decision making. *Psykhe: Revista de la Escuela de Psicología, 7,* 63–77.

Ketelaar, T., & Todd, P. (2001). Framing our thoughts: Ecological rationality as evolutionary psychology's answer to the frame problem. In H. R. Holcomb III (Ed.), *Conceptual challenges in evolutionary psychology.* Dordrecht: Kluwer.

Kurzban, R., Tooby, J., & Cosmides, L. (2001). Can race be erased? Coalitional computation and social categorization. *Proceedings of the National Academy of Sciences, 98,* 15387–15392.

Lerner, J. S., & Keltner, D. (2000). Beyond valence: Toward a model of emotion-specific influences on judgment and choice. *Cognition and Emotion, 14,* 473–493.

Lerner, J. S., & Keltner, D. (2001). Fear, anger, and risk. *Journal of Personality and Social Psychology, 81,* 146–159.

Lerner, J. S., Small, D. A., & Loewenstein, G. (2004). Heart strings and purse strings: Carry-over effects of emotions on economic transactions. *Psychological Science, 15,* 337–341.

Levenson, R. W. (1999). The intrapersonal functions of emotion. *Cognition and Emotion, 13,* 481–504.

Lieberman, D. (2003). *Mapping the cognitive architecture of systems for kin detection and inbreeding avoidance: The Westermarck Hypothesis and the development of sexual aversions between siblings.* Ph.D. Thesis, University of California, Santa Barbara, CA.

Lieberman, D., Tooby, J., & Cosmides, L. (2003). Does morality have a biological basis? An empirical test of the factors governing moral sentiments regarding incest. *Proceedings of the Royal Society of London: B Biological Sciences, 270,* 819–826.

Maner, J. K., Kenrick, D. T., Becker, D. V., Robertson, T. E., Hofer, B., & Neuberg, S. L., Delton, A. W., Butner, J., & Schaller, M. (2005). Functional projection: How fundamental social motives can bias interpersonal perception. *Journal of Personality and Social Psychology, 88,* 63–78.

Marks, I. M., & Nesse, R. M. (1994). Fear and fitness: An evolutionary analysis of anxiety disorders. *Ethology and Sociobiology, 15,* 247–261.

Marlowe, F. (2003). A critical period for provisioning by Hadza men: Implications for pair bonding. *Evolution and Human Behavior, 24,* 217–229.

Mineka, S. (1992). Evolutionary memories, emotional processing, and the emotional disorders. *Psychology of Learning and Motivation, 28,* 161–206.

Morris, M. W., & Keltner, D. (2000). How emotions work: An analysis of the social functions of emotional expressions in negotiations. *Research in Organizational Behavior, 22,* 1–50.

Nesse, R. (1990). Evolutionary explanations of emotions. *Human Nature, 1,* 261–289.

Nesse, R. M. (2001). *Evolution and the capacity for commitment.* New York: Russell Sage Foundation Press.

Nesse, R. M. (2005). Natural selection and the regulation of defenses: A signal detection analysis of the smoke detector problem. *Evolution and Human Behavior, 26,* 88–105.

Öhman, A., & Mineka, S. (2001). Fears, phobias, and preparedness: Toward an evolved module of fear and fear learning. *Psychological Review, 108,* 483–522.

Pillsworth, E. G., & Haselton, M. G. (2005). The evolution of coupling. *Psychological Inquiry, 16,* 98–104.

Plutchik, R. (1994). *The psychology and biology of emotion.* New York: Harper Collins.

Roese, N. J. (2005). *If only.* New York: Broadway Books.

Rozin, P., Lowery, L., & Ebert, R. (1994). Varieties of disgust faces and the structure of disgust. *Journal of Personality and Social Psychology, 66,* 870–881.

Sagarin, B. J. (2005). Reconsidering evolved sex differences in jealousy: Comment on Harris (2003). *Personality and Social Psychology Review, 9,* 62–75.

Schaller, M., Park, J. H., & Mueller, A. (2003). Fear of the dark: Interactive effects of beliefs about danger and ambient darkness on ethnic stereotypes. *Personality and Social Psychology Bulletin, 29,* 637–649.

Schmitt, D. P., & the 118 member of the International Sexuality Description Project (2003). Universal sex differences in the desire for sexual variety: Tests from 52 nations, 6 continents, and 13 islands. *Journal of Personality and Social Psychology, 85,* 85–104.

Schwarz, N., & Clore, G. L. (1983). Mood, misattribution, and judgments of well-being: Informative and directive functions of affective states. *Journal of Personality and Social Psychology, 45,* 513–523.

Schwarz, N., & Clore, G. L. (1988). How do I feel about it? Informative functions of affective states. In K. Fiedler & J. Forgas (Eds.), *Affect, cognition, and social behavior* (pp. 44–62). Toronto: Hogrefe International.

Seligman, M. E. P. (1971). Phobias and preparedness. *Behavior Therapy, 2,* 307–320.

Sidanius, J., & Veniegas, R. C. (2000). Gender and race discrimination: The interactive nature of disadvantage. In S. Oskamp (Ed.), *Reducing prejudice and discrimination* (pp. 47–69). Mahwah, NJ: Lawrence Erlbaum Associates, Inc..

Smith, A. (2000). *The theory of moral sentiments.* New York: Prometheus Books. (Original work published 1759)

Sripada C., & Stich, C. (2004). Evolution, culture and the irrationality of the emotions. In D. Evans & P. Cruse (Eds.), *Emotion, evolution and rationality.* New York: Oxford University Press.

Symons, D. (1979). *The evolution of human sexuality.* New York: Oxford University Press.

Tooby, J., & Cosmides, L. (1990). The past explains the present: Emotional adaptations and the structure of ancestral environments, *Ethology and Sociobiology, 11,* 375–424.

Trivers, R. L. (1971). The evolution of reciprocal altruism. *Quarterly Review of Biology, 46,* 35–57.

Trivers, R. L. (1972). Parental investment and sexual selection. In B. Campbell (Ed.), *Sexual selection and the descent of man, 1871–1971* (pp 136–179). Chicago, IL: Aldine Publishing Company.

Trope, Y., Igou E. R., & Burke, C. T. (2006). Mood as a resource in structuring goal pursuit. In J. Forgas (Ed.), *Affect in social thinking and behavior.* New York: Psychology Press.

Van Kleef, G. A., de Dreu, C. W. W., & Manstead, A. S. R. (2004). The interpersonal effects of emotion in negotiations: A motivated information processing approach. *Journal of Personality and Social Psychology, 87,* 510–528.

Varey, C., & Kahneman, D. (1992). Experiences extended across time: Evaluation of moments and episodes. *Journal of Behavioral Decision Making, 5,* 169–186.

Wegner, D. M., & Gold, D. B. (1995). Fanning old flames: Emotional and cognitive effects of suppressing thoughts of a past relationship. *Journal of Personality and Social Psychology, 68,* 782–792.

Wegner, D. M., Schneider, D. J., Carter, S. R. I., & White, T. L. (1987). Paradoxical effects of thought suppression. *Journal of Personality and Social Psychology, 53,* 5–13.

Wegner, D. M., Shortt, J. W., Blake, A. W., & Page, M. S. (1990). The suppression of exciting thoughts. *Journal of Personality and Social Psychology, 58,* 409–418.

Zeelenberg. M. (1999). Anticipated regret, expected feedback and behavioral decision-making. *Journal of Behavioral Decision Making, 12,* 93–106.

Zeelenberg, M., & Pieters, R. (2005). *Feeling is for doing: A pragmatic approach to the study of emotions in decision-making.* Manuscript under review.

3

A Social Neuroscience Perspective on Affective Influences on Social Cognition and Behavior

PIOTR WINKIELMAN and JOHN T. CACIOPPO

OVERVIEW

*P*sychological research on the mechanisms underlying affective influences on social cognition goes back several decades and has generated an exciting empirical literature, as illustrated by other chapters in this book. More recently, our understanding of these mechanisms has been enriched by advances in social neuroscience (e.g., Cacioppo et al., 2002; Harmon-Jones & Winkielman, in press; Winkielman, Berntson, & Cacioppo, 2001). A premise underlying work in social and affective neuroscience, as well as cognitive neuroscience, is that our understanding of information processing mechanisms can be informed by studying the operation of the central nervous system (brain) and the peripheral nervous system (body). Consequently, social and affective neuroscientists study how stimulation or lesion of a circumscribed nervous circuit influences a specific mental function and how performing a specific mental function influences activity of a circumscribed nervous circuit.

In neuroscience, just like in psychology, there are often theoretical disputes regarding what precisely constitutes a system responsible for a function. However, there is general agreement regarding several broad domains of processing that can be distinguished from one another. The traditional and richly investigated domain of cognitive neuroscience is object knowledge (Gazzaniga, 2004). This chapter is devoted to the two other highly investigated domains: (1) affect, with processes ranging from basic affective reactions to complex social emotions such as guilt, shame, embarrassment, or pride; and (2) social cognition, with processes ranging from face perception to complex inferences about social norms.

In our chapter, we aim to provide a brief and accessible review of what is known about neural circuits underlying affect and social cognition. More importantly, however, we aim to illustrate how social and affective neuroscience can offer a new perspective on some classic phenomena from the psychological affect and social cognition literature, contribute to the discovery of new phenomena, and lead towards more comprehensive explanations.

Our chapter is structured as follows. In the first section, we consider the organization of the brain in the evolutionary context. Our main point in this section is that affective processes are represented and interact across multiple levels of neural organization. This message is reinforced in the second section, where we review the particular roles of major subcortical and cortical structures in elicitation, experience, and regulation of affect. In the third section, we explore the implications of findings from affective neuroscience for the debate about conscious and unconscious affective influence. In the fourth section, we explore the interactions between neural circuits involved in affective and social processing. Our main point in this section is that social cognitive and affective processes piggyback on each other in terms of both neural representation and psychological function.

EVOLUTION AND MULTILEVEL ORGANIZATION OF AFFECT THROUGHOUT THE BRAIN

To appreciate the biological underpinnings of affective influences on social cognition, it is worth highlighting a few facts about the evolution of the nervous system (for an accessible overview, see Allman, 1999). Millions of years of evolution have resulted in a heterarchical structure of the nervous system, with networks that process affect in a distributed fashion at multiple levels of organization (Berntson & Cacioppo, in press; Konorski, 1967). The most primitive protective responses to immediate nociceptive and aversive stimuli are organized at the level of the spinal cord. This is demonstrated by the fact that withdrawal reflexes to noxious (e.g., pain) stimuli can be seen even after spinal trans-sections. Those spinal mechanisms could possibly be as old as simple vertebrates, which emerged over 500 million years ago. The primitive protective reactions are expanded at higher levels of the nervous system. Thus, as discussed shortly, the networks of the brainstem and limbic system endow organisms with an expanded behavioral repertoire, including basic pleasure/displeasure reactions, escape reactions, aggressive responses, and even a rudimentary ability to anticipate and avoid aversive encounters. In fact, reptiles, which emerged over 300 million years ago, already possess networks responsible for specific affective behaviors, such as aggression, fear, play, and mating (Panksepp, 1998). Although these networks have been expanded upon and modified in mammals, there are remarkable similarities between fish, reptiles, birds, and mammals in both affective neurochemistry and neuroanatomy (Berridge, 2000; Goodson & Bass, 2001; Martinez-Garcia, Martinez-Marcos, & Lanuza, 2002). The emergence of primates (about 60 million years ago) and particularly hominids (10 million years ago, or the last 0.2% of the evolutionary history of vertebrates) is, of course, associated with rapid encephalization, or the growth of the neocortical mantle. Our own species, which emerged only about 100,000 million years ago, has a particularly large neocortex (particularly prefrontal white matter) even when compared to other advanced mammals (Dorus et al., 2004; Schoenemann, Sheehan, & Glotzer, 2005). Presumably, this neural hardware endows us with the ability for symbolic representation, transformations and computations, rapid learning, language, complex social interaction, as well as a rich sense of self-awareness and theory of mind (Dunbar, 2003).

No doubt, much of the emotional and social life of humans depends on cortical contributions. A rat can lose its entire neocortex and continue to live a remarkably normal life (Berridge, 2003), whereas even seemingly mild damage to the human neocortex can result in significant affective, cognitive, and behavioral changes (National Institutes of Health, 1998). Nevertheless, the biological underpinnings of affective influences on human social behavior are best understood as reflecting a multiplicity of older and newer mechanisms, which are not localized to a single neural level, but are instead represented across the nervous system. At progressively higher levels of organization, there is a general expansion in the range and complexity of contextual controls and in the breadth and flexibility of behavioral responses. But, though the higher mechanisms certainly confer greater flexibility, they do not eliminate lower level mechanisms (e.g., Berntson & Cacioppo, in press). Furthermore, even though evolutionary forces have rigidly canalized some aspects of behavior, these forces also forged many *interacting* neural systems. For these reasons, one should be cautious of any account of human affect that primarily focuses on one level (e.g., the "low route" or "old mechanism" explanations) or posits some limited number of qualitatively different systems (e.g., the currently fashionable "two systems" explanations). In short, there is a great amount of anatomical and functional interactivity in neural processing (we will return to this point later).

In the forthcoming sections, we will focus more specifically on the contribution of various neural systems to affective processing. In our discussion, we will refer to several subcortical and cortical brain structures (Figure 3.1 shows their approximate locations). We wish to note that our brief presentation cannot fully capture the complexity of neuroanatomy and neurochemistry of these structures, or their additional roles in affect and cognition. The interested reader is encouraged to consult recent reviews (e.g., Berridge, 2003).

SUBCORTICAL AND CORTICAL NETWORKS UNDERLYING AFFECTIVE REACTIONS AND AFFECTIVE EXPERIENCE

Affective influences reflect a wide spectrum of mechanisms (Cacioppo & Gardner, 1999; Cacioppo, Larsen, Smith, & Berntson, 2004). At the bottom end of the spectrum, affective influence may involve simple physiological priming of defense reflexes (Davis, 1997; Lang, 1995), preparation of simple motor responses (Cacioppo, Priester, & Berntson, 1993), automatic modulation of perception and

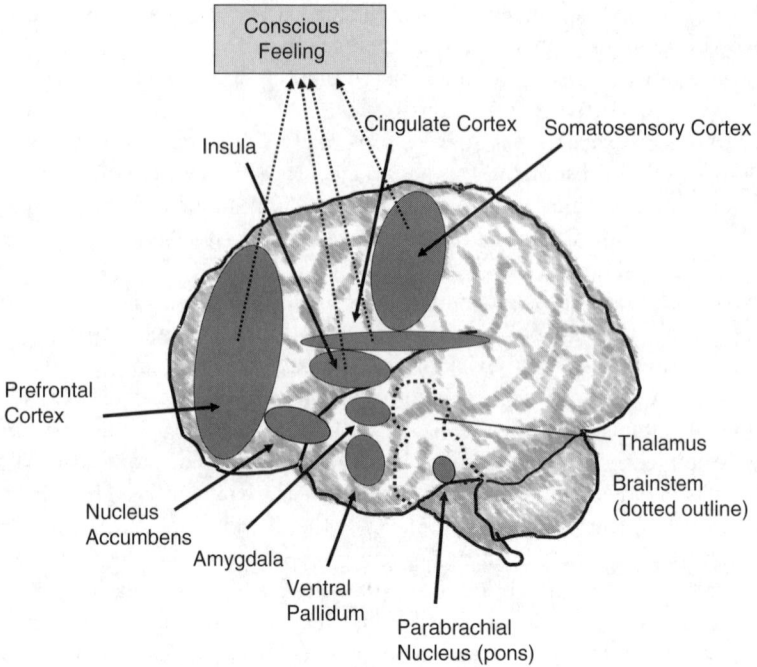

FIGURE 3.1 Some neural regions involved in affect and social cognition. Regions indicated with dashed lines are believed to be critical for the conscious affective experience.

attention (Niedenthal & Kitayama, 1994; Öhman, Flykt, & Lundqvist, 2000), or semantic priming within the associative memory system (Bless & Fiedler, this volume; Forgas, this volume). At the top end of the spectrum, affective influence may involve complex inferences from conscious feelings (Clore, this volume), anticipation of feeling changes as a result of certain actions (Baumeister, Vohs, & Tice, this volume), and strategic attempts at mood regulation (Erber & Markunas, this volume). Recent work in affective neuroscience has identified some critical structures and pathways underlying these various types of affective influence. Below, we review some illustrative findings. For clarity, we organize our presentation by the critical brain structures, though as mentioned earlier the underlying mechanisms typically involve complex networks instantiated across multiple structures.

Brainstem

We have already mentioned that the most basic responses are organized at the level of the spinal cord. On the top end of the spinal cord, near the base of the skull, sits the brainstem. Many psychologists think of the brainstem as a merely reflexive structure, perhaps only slightly more complex than the spinal cord. However, the brainstem is critically involved in multiple affective phenomena, including elicitation of basic facial expressions, reactions to pleasurable and painful stimuli, and affective modulation of memory.

A particularly poignant demonstration of the brainstem's role in basic affective reactions is offered by a cruel experiment of nature. As a result of a birth defect, some infants have a congenitally malformed brain, possessing only a brainstem, but no cortex and little else of the forebrain (i.e., no amygdala, nucleus accumbens, etc.). Yet, in these anencephalic infants the sweet taste of sugar still elicits facial expressions indicative of "liking" reactions, such as lip smacking and elevation of mouth corners, whereas bitter tastes elicit facial expressions indicative of "disliking" reactions, such as mouth gapes or nose wrinkling (Steiner, 1973). This finding is consistent with observations that positive facial expressions to sweetness are emitted by chimpanzees, orangutans, and gorillas, various monkeys, and even rats (Berridge, 2000; Steiner, Glaser, Hawilo, & Berridge, 2001). Of course, the pattern of positive facial expression becomes less and less similar to humans as taxonomic distance increases. But, all of these species share some reaction components that are homologous to ours, suggesting common evolutionary ancestry and a similar neural mechanism that might be anchored in the brainstem.

The brainstem is also critically involved in processing hedonic value of basic sensory stimuli. For example, the brainstem's parabrachial nucleus (PBN) receives ascending signals from many sensory modalities, including taste sensations from the tongue.[1] Not surprisingly, the PBN plays a role in generating positive responses to tasty foods. Thus, when a rat's PBN is tweaked by microinjections that activate its benzodiazepine/GABA receptors, the rat produces greater "liking" reactions to sugar, such as tongue protrusions and lip licking (Berridge & Pecina, 1995). In the domain of negative affect, the brainstem's periaqueductal gray modulates human and animal responses to pain (Willis & Westlund, 1997).

Our final example of the brainstem's role in more complex aspects of affect–cognition interface comes from research on the well-known phenomenon of enhanced memory for emotional events (McGaugh, 2003). Affective neuroscience research suggests that this phenomenon involves the brainstem's nucleus of the solitary tract (NTS) and the feedback it receives from the viscera, i.e., heart, lungs, stomach, etc. (Berntson, Sarter, & Cacioppo, 2003). Specifically, during emotional activation, the adrenal medulla releases the hormone epinephrine into the bloodstream, causing the well-known "fight-or-flight" response in the viscera. This visceral response activates the ascending fibers of the vagus nerve, which stimulate the NTS. In turn, the NTS neurons, via their ascending projections, cause the release of the neurotransmitter norepinephrine into the amygdala and hippocampus, leading to the enhanced encoding of memory (Hassert, Miyashita, & Williams, 2004).

Amygdala

One of the most "famous" affective structures is the amygdala. The amygdala consists of a pair of almond-shaped structures located in the medial temporal lobe, just anterior to the hippocampus. The amygdala is richly and reciprocally connected to several cortical areas involved in cognitive and affective processing, as well as subcortical areas involved in physiological regulation (sympathetic and parasympathetic control of cardiovascular activity, respiration, hormone levels, muscular responses, etc.). Unsurprisingly, the amygdala is involved in several interesting affective phenomena, including the generation of responses to rudimentary features of significant stimuli, affective modulation of attention and memory, and affect regulation. We will briefly discuss these affective phenomena now, but will later return to amygdala's involvement in more general aspects of social cognition.

Significance Detector   Animal and human studies suggest that the amygdala responds to significant sensory stimuli, such as emotional facial expressions, or sounds and sights associated with punishments (Atkinson & Adolphs, 2005; Phelps, 2005). In fact, the amygdala can be activated even without the conscious recognition of the stimulus, such as when fearful or angry facial expressions are presented subliminally (Whalen, Rauch, Etcoff, McInerney, Lee, & Jenike, 1998) or under condition of binocular rivalry (Williams, Morris, McGlone, Abbott, & Mattingley, 2004).

Some earlier reports have suggested that the amygdala is particularly important for processing fear, as indicated by the impairments of the amygdala patients in recognition of facial expressions of fear (Adolphs, Tranel, Damasio, & Damasio, 1994). More recent work suggests that this specificity is explained by the role that the information from the eye region plays in fear recognition (Adolphs, Gosselin, Buchanan, Schyns, Tranel, & Damasio, 2005). In fact, the amygdala seems particularly important in processes of gaze information (Adams, Gordon, Baird, Ambady, & Kleck, 2003) and can be activated even by rudimentary eye features, such as the sclera (Whalen et al., 2004).

High Versus Low Route   The amygdala receives sensory input via several pathways, including a slow, ventral pathway from the sensory cortex, and a fast, direct pathway from the sensory thalamus (LeDoux, 1996). This connectivity led several researchers to propose that the amygdala responses primarily reflect the "low" road. Unfortunately, in most studies, it is unclear to what extent the "low road" is responsible for amygdala activation, or, more importantly, for the contribution of the amygdala to judgment and behavior (see Clore & Storbeck, this volume). Fortunately, a few studies suggest that, at least under some conditions, the "low" route mediates the amygdala responses to basic emotional stimuli, such as facial expressions. Thus, patients with damage to the primary visual cortex rely on the "low route" and show amygdala activation to anger expressions presented in their "blind field" (Morris, DeGelder, Weiskrantz, & Dolan, 2001; Morris, Öhman, & Dolan, 1999). Further, in healthy individuals, the amygdala responds to significant stimuli presented with low-spatial frequency (e.g., highly blurred fear faces), which are processed by the "low" visual route (Vuilleumier, Armony, Driver, & Dolan, 2003).

Attention   The amygdala not only receives input from the sensory areas but is also reciprocally connected to them, allowing for early affective modification of sensory processing. One example is the amygdala's role in attentional modification, as demonstrated by research on the phenomenon of attentional blink. This phenomenon refers to the observation that after identifying the first target, participants are impaired in the identification accuracy of the rapidly following second target. Interestingly, normal participants show a substantial reduction in attentional blink to emotionally charged stimuli (e.g., when the second target word is "murder"). However, this normal reduction of attentional blink is eliminated in patients with amygdala damage, suggesting an important modulatory role of amygdala in early sensory processing (Anderson & Phelps, 2001).

Memory   The amygdala is also involved in the most basic form of affective learning—the acquisition of conditioned fear responses. The now classic studies demonstrated that patients with congenital and acquired amygdala damage, yet intact hippocampus, show impairments in acquisition of conditioned fear responses, as measured by skin conductance, while showing relatively unimpaired declarative memory (Bechara, Tranel, Damasio, Adolphs, Rockland, & Damasio, 1995).

But the role of the amygdala is not limited to simple conditioning. Earlier, we mentioned that the well-known phenomenon of the emotional enhancement of memory involves interactions between the amygdala and the brainstem (McGaugh, 2003). Consistently, patients with bilateral damage to the amygdala do not show the typical memorial advantage for emotionally arousing stimuli, such as taboo words (Anderson & Phelps, 2002).

Cortical Influences   The amygdala is also connected to the higher cortical areas, including the prefrontal cortex, involved in symbolic processes and executive functions. This connectivity plays a role in top–down influences on affective responses. Thus, a verbal induction of fear (e.g., "you will receive an electric shock upon seeing a blue slide") leads to amygdala activation and physiological arousal, an effect that is reduced in amygdala-damaged patients (Phelps, O'Connor, Gatenby, Gore, Grillon, & Davis, 2001). In normal participants, the amygdala response to affectively charged pictures is modulated by cognitive efforts of affect regulation (Ochsner, Bunge, Gross, & Gabrieli, 2002). In short, the reviewed research suggests that the amygdala, through its cortical connections, may participate in social psychological phenomena that rely on strategic management of affective responses (Baumeister et al., this volume; Erber & Markunas, this volume).

Subjective Experience   Finally, and perhaps surprisingly, amygdala does not seem to be critical for the subjective experience of emotion. This finding is suggested by the fact that patients with damage to the amygdala show little, if any, impairment in their subjective experience of emotion, at least as measured by the magnitude and frequency of self-reported positive or negative affect (Anderson & Phelps, 2002). The finding may be initially surprising to readers familiar with the proposal that amygdala is the critical structure of the "emotional brain" (LeDoux, 1996). However, as we discuss shortly, the mechanisms underlying conscious feelings appear to be primarily supported by cortical circuitry.

Nucleus Accumbens and Related Structures

Near the bottom of the front of the brain, in the area called the basal forebrain, lie several nuclei rich in dopamine and opioid neurotransmitters. One of those nuclei, the nucleus accumbens, sometimes referred to as the *ventral striatum*, is famous for its association with reward. In fact, many affective neuroscientists view activation of dopamine projections to the accumbens and related targets as a neural "common currency" for reward. Presumably, this common coding of qualitatively different rewards allows the brain to represent a variety of different pleasures on a similar hedonic metric (Cabanac, 1992). There is actually evidence that accumbens reflects not "pleasure", or "liking" of the stimulus, but rather an incentive salience, or "wanting" of the stimulus (Berridge & Robinson, 1998). However, for our purposes here, it is only important to highlight the role of the accumbens in the modulation of positive affective reactions to a variety of simple and complex social and nonsocial stimuli. For example, brain microinjections of drug droplets that activate opioid receptors in the accumbens cause increased "liking" for sweetness in rats (Pecina & Berridge, 2000). In fMRI studies on humans, accumbens and related areas activate not only to drug cues, but also to other rewarding stimuli, including foods, drinks, sexual partners, attractive faces, and money (Knutson, Adams, Fong, & Hommer, 2001; O'Doherty, Deichmann, Critchley, & Dolan, 2002). Recent research has even suggested the involvement of these areas in coding the rewarding aspects of complex social behavior. Thus, the accumbens and related structures activate to signals of cooperation in prisoner's dilemma games (Rilling, Gutman, Zeh, Pagnoni, Berns, & Kilts, 2002), and during "altruistic punishment", as when a person punishes a transgressor against her group by sacrificing her own benefit (de Quervain et al., 2004). Finally, there is evidence that projections from the accumbens to the prefrontal cortex may contribute to conscious affective experience. For example, the intense feeling of pleasure experienced by heroin users appears to involve accumbens-to-cortex signals (Wise, 1996). In another example, self-reports of "excitement" in typical participants are related to the degree of activation in the nucleus accumbens and prefrontal cortex (Knutson, Bjork, Fong, Hommer, Mattay, & Weinberger, 2004).

Cortical Networks

Of course, one cannot talk about affect and emotions in humans without discussing the cortex. Below we focus on two areas, the somatosensory cortices and the prefrontal cortex (see Figure 3.1). We highlight the roles of these areas in the perception of emotion, generation and regulation of affective experience, and in the integration of emotion and cognition.

Somatosensory Cortices and Insula

The primary somatosensory cortex (S1) runs top–down behind the central sulcus and is responsible for body sensation (e.g., touch) and proprioception (i.e., state of muscles and joints). S1 is organized in a roughly topographic fashion, containing a receptive field for every body part, with larger receptive fields devoted to more highly innervated parts (e.g., lips). The secondary somatosensory cortex (S2) lies inferior to S1 and is mostly buried in the lateral sulcus. Functionally, S2 serves as a higher order association area for body sensations and may be involved in the creation of "body image" (Ramachandran & Blakeslee, 1998). Near the base of the somatosensory cortex, almost at the intersection of the frontal, parietal, and temporal lobes, lies the insula (Adolphs, Damasio, Tranel, Cooper, & Damasio, 2000). The insula receives inputs from limbic structures, such as the amygdala, and cortical structures, such as the prefrontal cortex and the anterior cingulate. Functionally, the insula appears particularly important for introception, or monitoring the state of internal organs (Craig, 2003; Critchley, Wiens, Rotshtein, Oehman, & Dolan, 2004), and for sensations, including pain (Peyron, Laurent, & Garcia-Larrea, 2000) and pleasure (O'Doherty et al., 2002).

There is reason to believe that somatosensory cortices may be involved in the "embodiment" phenomena, many of which have been initially reported by social psychologists (for review see Hatfield, Cacioppo, & Rapson, 1994; Niedenthal, Barsalou, Winkielman, Krauth-Gruber, & Ric, 2005). One class of such phenomena involves facilitation of affect perception by congruent bodily responses and impairment of affective perception by incongruent bodily responses (Cacioppo et al., 1993; Neumann, Förster, & Strack, 2003). For example, participants are more efficient in detecting changes in a person's emotional facial expression when they are free to mimic the expression, as opposed to being prevented from mimicking (Niedenthal, Brauer, Halberstadt, & Innes-Ker, 2001). Interestingly, neuroimaging studies found activation in somatosensory cortices during perception of emotional stimuli (Carr, Iacoboni, Dubeau, Mazziotta, & Lenzi, 2003). A more causal evidence comes from studies showing that patients with somatosensory lesions are worse than controls in classifying emotional expressions from the face (Adolphs et al., 2000) and from the body (Heberlein, Adolphs, Tranel, & Damasio, 2004). According to the "embodiment" account of such finding, recognition of emotional expressions (facial or bodily) involves simulation of the expression using the perceiver's own somatosensory resources, and experiencing the resulting somatosensory feedback (Niedenthal et al., 2005). Interestingly, the insula tends to activate during both experiences, as well as observation of affective situations with a large "visceral" component. For example, human studies show involvement of the insula in the experience and observation of pain (Singer, Seymour, O'Doherty, Kaube, Dolan, & Frith, 2004), and the experience and observation of disgust (Wicker, Keysers, Plailly, Royet, Gallese, & Rizzolatti, 2003). These data are again consistent with the embodiment account.

Finally, there is also evidence that somatosensory cortices and the insula might be critically involved in generating conscious emotional experiences. One mechanism for this presumably involves building a model of the current body state, including its current hormonal, muscular, and visceral conditions (Damasio, 1999). For example, neuroimaging studies show that recall of emotional memories is associated with extensive activation of the somatosensory cortex and the insula (Damasio et al., 2000), whereas damage to these regions is associated with reduction in intensity of conscious affective experiences (Craig, 2003; Critchley et al., 2005).

Prefrontal Cortex

The prefrontal cortex, which, unsurprisingly, lies at the very front of the brain, is involved in many aspects of affect and social cognition. In fact, the famous case of Phineas Gage, who showed radical changes in affect, personality, and social behavior after a metal rod went through his brain, was later determined to involve damage to the prefrontal cortex (Damasio, 1999). In this section, we review how different parts of the prefrontal cortex may be preferentially involved in the assignment of stimulus value, the use of affective feedback in decision making, affect regulation, and conscious affective experience. Later, we will return to the prefrontal cortex to discuss its involvement in other aspects of social cognition.

Orbitofrontal Cortex   The ventral, or bottom one third of prefrontal cortex, sitting right above the eyes, is most elaborately developed in humans and other primates. This region plays a role in one of the most fundamental aspects of affect–cognition interaction—linking cognitive representation of the stimulus with the representation of its corresponding reinforcement value. The orbitofrontal cortex (OFC) plays a critical role in this process, as demonstrated by selective firing of OFC neurons to stimuli associated with rewards or punishments (Rolls, 1999). Importantly, these neurons are highly flexible in their coding properties, and will not fire when the reward properties of a stimulus change (e.g., when a stimulus that was previously associated with food delivery is no longer associated with food). Further, the OFC neurons will only fire to a stimulus when it is motivationally relevant. For example, neurons that fire to a particular food (e.g., a banana) when the animal is hungry will not fire to this food when the animal is satiated (Rolls, 1999).

Recent work has also highlighted the role of the OFC in more complex affective processes, such as appraisals involved in generating self-conscious emotions, such as embarrassment and shame. For example, compared to neurological controls, patients with OFC damage are less likely to feel embarrassed by their inappropriate social behavior (Beer, Heerey, Keltner, Scabini, & Knight, 2003).

Medial and Ventramedial Prefrontal Cortex   A meta-analysis of functional neuroimaging literature on emotion found that the medial prefrontal cortex (mPFC) was commonly activated and that this activation was not specific to a particular emotion or induction method (Phan, Wagner, Taylor, & Liberzon, 2002). A more circumscribed, ventral section of the medial prefrontal cortex (vmPFC) appears to be especially important for the ability to incorporate somatic feedback into judgment and decisions (Damasio, 1999). This process is fundamental to social cognition and may contribute to the phenomena such as the use of affect-as-information (Clore & Storbeck, this volume) and strategic use of affect in decision making (Baumeister et al., this volume).

Several studies in affective neuroscience explored the role of somatic feedback in decision making using the "Iowa Gambling Task" developed by Bechara, Damasio, Tranel, and Damasio (1997). In a standard version of the task, participants select cards from four different decks. Two decks have cards associated with moderate payments and moderate losses, and two decks have cards associated with large payments and occasional large losses. The rules of the game are complex enough to prevent the players from easily figuring out payoffs associated with each deck, thus maximizing participants' reliance on somatic feedback. Bechara et al. (1997) used the Iowa Gambling Task to compare decision making of vmPFC-lesioned patients and controls while monitoring skin conductance responses (SCR). The results showed that after playing the game for a while, controls started to show anticipatory SCRs to decks associated with a huge loss and began to avoid taking cards from these decks. The vmPFC patients, however, showed no anticipatory SCRs to these decks and continued to take cards from them. Interestingly, these autonomic and behavioral differences emerged even though controls and prefrontal patients did not differ in their explicit understanding of the payoff rules at this point of the game. Bechara et al. (1997) interpreted these results to mean that the ability to make good decisions is at least partly dependent on intact mechanisms of somatic feedback, which involve interconnections between the vmPFC, amygdala, and insula. This interpretation is consistent with a more recent finding that patients with lesions of the vmPFC, or with right unilateral lesions of the amygdala or the right insular cortices, perform poorly on the general measures of emotional intelligence and social functioning (Bar-on, Tranel, Denburg, & Bechara, 2003). Furthermore, this finding holds even when the patients are matched to controls on cognitive intelligence, executive functioning, perception, memory, personality, and psychopathology.

Importantly, more recent work on decision making has emphasized that depending on the structure of the task, the presence of the somatic feedback might be advantageous or disadvantageous to decision making. Specifically, in the original version of the Iowa Gambling Task, the expected value of "risky" option (high wins, high losses) was lower than the "safe" option (medium wins and losses). Shiv, Loewenstein, Bechara, Damasio, and Damasio (2005) set up a card game in an alternative way such that the "risky" option, while still associated with occasional losses, had an overall higher expected value. In such a scenario, the vmPFC patients made economically more advantageous decisions and frequently chose the risky option. In contrast, the controls tended to choose in an overly conservative fashion, presumably reflecting the typical phenomenon of loss aversion.

Lateral Prefrontal Cortex   Cognitive neuroscience research has documented that the lateral prefrontal cortex is important for "executive control" skills, such as the selection, maintenance, and application of goal-directed strategies (Ochsner & Gross, 2004). This raises the possibility for involvement of lateral prefrontal cortex in the strategic up and down regulation of affective processes, especially given descending projections from the prefrontal cortex to the amygdala and the accumbens (Damasio, 1999; Davidson, Jackson, & Kalin, 2000; Phan et al., 2002). Consistent with this idea, recent research found lateral prefrontal cortex activation during tasks involving up-regulation and down-regulation of affect (Ochsner & Gross, 2004). As mentioned earlier, these findings suggest a potential biological substrate for processes that may underlie strategic use and regulation of affect (Erber & Markunas, this volume).

CONTRIBUTION OF SUBCORTICAL AND CORTICAL NETWORKS TO CONSCIOUS AND UNCONSCIOUS AFFECTIVE INFLUENCES

As our brief review indicates, both subcortical systems and cortical systems participate in emotion as a complex set of interconnected loops. Accordingly, any isolated focus on subcortex or cortex cannot do justice to the wide spectrum of human emotion. However, within these loops, subcortical systems seem essential for orchestrating basic affective reactions and for mobilizing physiological support of a behavioral response. In contrast, cortical systems seem essential for supporting symbolic appraisal processes, integrating affective reactions with cognitive representations of stimuli, regulating one's affect, and generating conscious affective experience. Specifically, the conscious experience, the phenomenal aspect of emotion, appears to involve an interaction between cortical and subcortical structures, as the cortex hierarchically re-represents and feeds back on subcortical processes.[2]

Doing without Feeling

The just described organization of the brain raises the possibility for functional decoupling, where an emotional stimulus has an impact on behavior but does not trigger any conscious feelings. This possibility is consistent with our research on "unconscious affect" (Berridge & Winkielman, 2003; Winkielman & Berridge, 2004). Specifically, we have recently conducted two studies assessing participants' behavior towards a novel beverage after exposing them to several subliminal emotional facial expressions, such as happiness and anger (Winkielman, Berridge, & Wilbarger, 2005). Immediately after the subliminal exposure, participants rated their current feelings (mood and arousal) and consumed and evaluated the beverage. The order of feeling ratings and consumption behavior was counterbalanced. In both studies, there was no evidence of any change in mood or arousal. Yet subliminal expressions influenced participants' consumption behavior and evaluation, particularly when participants were thirsty. Specifically, after happy faces thirsty participants poured more drink from the pitcher, and drank more from their cup than after angry faces (Study 1). Thirsty participants were also willing to pay more for a drink after happy, rather than angry expressions (Study 2). These results suggest that under some conditions an affective process strong enough to influence behavior can occur without producing a conscious experience.

Here is a possible neuroscientific account of this effect. The subliminal facial expressions might initially activate the amygdala (Whalen et al., 1998). The amygdala might then project to the adjacent structures, such as the nucleus accumbens, involved in the processing of natural incentives (Berridge, 2003). Altered responsiveness of the nucleus accumbens, constituting unconscious "liking", could then bias the affective reaction when participants are exposed to the sight and taste of the beverage (Rolls, 1999). Such differential reaction would in the end translate to different behavior towards the beverage as well as different ratings of its value. In other words, we propose a process that at the level of core neural mechanisms is not unlike what happens when a morphine microinjection into a rat's shell of accumbens enhances the rat's affective reaction to sweetness, and leads to behavioral reaction of greater "liking". Again, all of this can happen without generating conscious affective experience. Such experience presumably requires mapping one's current body state, which, as mentioned earlier, is supported by the insula and somatosensory cortices, and integrating this body map with the representation of the self, which is supported by the prefrontal cortex (Damasio, 1999; Decety & Sommerville, 2003).

Our findings on "unconscious affect" and its putative neural mechanisms have interesting implications for social psychological theorizing on affect influence. One implication is that the impact of basic affective reactions can fall outside the domain of models that postulate a critical role for conscious feelings in affective influence (e.g., the "feeling-as-information" model, Schwarz & Clore, 2003). Instead, we propose that basic affective stimuli can act via unconscious processes to directly alter the target's incentive value. Consistent with this assumption, attributional manipulations, which typically modulate the impact of conscious feelings on judgments, do not modulate the impact of unconscious affective stimuli on judgment and behavior (Winkielman, Zajonc, & Schwarz, 1997).

Finally, it is worth emphasizing that affective stimuli are not unique in their ability to drive behavior independent of conscious experience (for broad disscussion see Feldman Barrett, Niedenthal, & Winkielman, 2005). As documented in research on "vision for action" (Goodale & Milner, 2004) and "blindsight" (Weiskrantz, 1996), under certain conditions, visual information can drive the action system without ever reaching brain areas responsible for conscious visual experience. For example, a patient with a visual form of agnosia, caused by damage to the ventral stream regions of the temporal lobe, is unable to provide a correct perceptual report of the orientation of a letter slot. However, the patient shows no difficulty when asked to insert an actual letter into the slot (Goodale & Milner, 2004).

INTERACTION OF SOCIAL AND EMOTIONAL PROCESSING ACROSS SUBCORTICAL AND CORTICAL NETWORKS

In the last part of our chapter, let us turn to the interactions between the neural circuits underlying affect and social cognition. Before we start, it is worth highlighting that there is little in a typical human life that does not involve some interplay between affect and social cognition. Without a doubt, for most people the greatest pleasures of life are social (e.g., successful relationship, professional recognition), as most of life's pains (e.g., loss of loved one, social rejection). But, affect and social cognition are closely intertwined even at the level of most basic mental processes. For example, in going about our daily business, we need to recognize people's faces. Most of the time, these faces carry an emotional expression that communicates something important about the social situation. Similarly, every day we make inferences regarding people's reasons for their actions. These inferences are often either triggered by or led to an emotional response. In yet another example, we often figure out how to behave in the social world through observation of others' behavior. This observation, and imitation, is often of emotional actions.

Because of the inherent connections between social and emotional processes, we have argued that these processes may share some basic neural mechanisms (Norris, Chen, Zhu, Small, & Cacioppo, 2004). Specifically, the adaptive advantage of discerning social signals and organizing flexible responses to social stimuli may have been achieved in part by co-opting and building on selected neural systems that originally evolved for dealing with hedonic events (threats, appetitive stimuli). Although the neural substrates of emotion and social cognition are best thought of as organized by circuits, rather than individual structures, the available literature has focused so far on associating structures with specific behavioral functions. Accordingly, in this section, we again organize our brief overview by structure.

Amygdala

Earlier we described the involvement of the amygdala in affective processes. This structure is also highly important for social cognition (Brothers, 1990). One of the first hints comes from research that reported massive disturbances in the social behavior of primates with extensive damage to the temporal lobe, including the amygdala (Kluver & Bucy, 1939/1997). Recent research, with more selective and complete lesions of the amygdala, has re-evaluated some of the early claims and reported more restricted changes, such as less caution in novel social interaction among the amygdala-lesioned animals (Amaral et al., 2003). However, it appears clear that the amygdala is significantly involved in many subtle aspects of social cognition. For example, Heberlein and Adolphs (2004) report that SM, a patient with bilateral amygdala damage, does not spontaneously provide a social inter-pretation of the famous Heider and Simmel movie. Interestingly, SM performed normally on direct questions regarding the film that rely on social attributions (e.g., "What was the large triangle like?"), suggesting that her impairment lies in automatically inferring social meaning from a nonsocial stimulus. Other research suggests amygdala involvement in evaluating trustworthiness of unknown individ-uals (Adolphs, Tranel, & Damasio, 1998; Winston, Strange, O'Doherty, & Dolan, 2002) and in attributing internal states, beliefs, and desires to other people (Baron-Cohen, Ring, Bullmore, Wheelwright, Ashwin, & Williams, 2000).

It is interesting to note, however, that many of the studies on the amygdala conflate social and emotional processes. For example, in order to determine the social meaning of the stimulus, the observer must typically process the emotional context. And in order to determine the emotional meaning, the observer must dis-till the social context. Accordingly, impairment in one process necessarily impacts the other. As a consequence, in many lesion studies and in many functional imag-ing studies, it is often not clear whether the contribution of the amygdala is due to the social or the emotional nature of the stimulus, or both.

To address this concern, Norris et al. (2004) recently conducted an fMRI study to investigate the interactive and independent effects of social and emotional processes on activation of the amygdala and other neural regions involved in affect and social cognition. In this study, participants viewed a set of IAPS pictures that varied in two dimensions. First, each picture was either neutral or emotional (collapsed across positive and negative valence). Second, each picture was either social (i.e., contained one or more faces or bodies of conspecifics) or nonsocial (i.e., scenes, objects). Animals were excluded from the design, and all four groups of pictures were matched on complexity and arousal. Results for the amygdala indicated two main effects. First, the amygdala activation was greater for emotional than for neutral stimuli. Second, the amygdala activation was greater for social than for nonsocial stimuli. One interpretation of these findings is that the amygdala is involved in directing sensory and attentional processes to stimuli that, upon rudimentary analysis, appear to have potential motivational significance. Because emotional and social stimuli have motivational significance, they can have additive effects on amygdala activation.

Cortical Regions

The findings on cortical regions further support the notion that social cognition and emotion are subserved by common neural systems. As we describe next, the "emotion" regions tend to be involved in processing of social stimuli, and the "social cognitive" regions tend to be involved in processing of emotional stimuli. Interestingly, this notion can be traced all the way back to the case of the Phineas Gage, in whom damage to the prefrontal cortex resulted in joint social and emotional impairments (Damasio, 1999).

Orbitofrontal Cortex   Earlier we discussed the role of OFC in the representation of stimulus value and self-conscious emotion. Interestingly, OFC seems to support both emotional and social cognitive processes (Stone, in press). For example, compared to matched controls, patients with OFC damage from frontotemporal dementia were impaired on both emotion and mental state items from various theory-of-mind tasks, including the "Reading the Mind in the Eyes" task (Gregory et al., 2002).

Medial Prefrontal Cortex   As mentioned earlier, another region commonly associated with emotion processing is the mPFC (Phan et al., 2002). Interestingly, the just described fMRI studies by Norris et al. (2004) found greater mPFC activation in participants who viewed pictures that depicted conspecifics than those that did not. This finding again suggests that both emotional and social stimuli recruit similar regions for dealing with significant events.

Fusiform Gyrus   An enormous amount of research effort in cognitive neuroscience has focused on neural regions involved in processing of faces, especially the fusiform gyrus located on the ventromedial surface of the temporal and occipital lobes. Again, this region appears sensitive to the emotional value of stimuli. One of the first demonstrations of this sensitivity comes from a PET study by Geday, Gjedde, Boldsen, and Kupers (2003). In this study, participants viewed a set of pictures that varied both in social complexity, from low (e.g., faces) to high (e.g., social situations), and in emotional valence (positive, negative, neutral). The results demonstrated that regional cerebral blood flow in the fusiform gyrus was not only greater when participants viewed more complex, versus less complex, social stimuli, but was also greater when participants viewed emotional (i.e., positive and negative), as compared to neutral, stimuli (see also Dolan, Fletcher, Morris, Kapur, Deakin, & Frith, 1996; Vuilleumier, Armony, Driver, & Dolan, 2001). Norris et al. (2004) replicated the finding that the fusiform gyrus is more active to emotional than to neutral stimuli. Furthermore, they found that this pattern was driven by activation to social stimuli, a result that is consistent with the proposed role of the fusiform in social cognition. In sum, it appears that a neural region classically involved in face perception is also sensitive to emotional significance.

Inferior Frontal Gyrus   Much attention in recent years also has been devoted to the inferior frontal gyrus (IFG), or the region in the lower portion of the frontal lobe, near the Broca's area. This region has been suggested as a location of the "mirror neurons" that discharge both when an action is performed and merely observed (cf. Rizzolatti, Fogassi, & Gallese, 2001). Such findings have led to suggestions that "mirror neurons" support the process of imitation, and might be critical for social cognition in general (Gallese, Keysers, & Rizzolatti, 2004).

Consistent with the idea of the intermingling between social and emotional processes, findings suggest that the IFG might be particularly important for empathy, an emotion that derives its meaning from social context, and may function through imitative mechanisms (Decety & Sommerville, 2003). The findings on mirror neurons are also consistent with the previously described "embodiment" literature, which reports similar effects for the perception and observation of emotions such as disgust or pain (Niedenthal et al., 2005). Finally, the earlier described study by Norris et al. (2004) found the IFG region to be sensitive to both emotion and social stimuli.

In summary, the evidence reviewed in this section of our chapter converges on the notion that many neural structures traditionally associated in emotional processing, such as the amygdala and mPFC, also participate in social information processing. And, conversely, many neural structures involved in social cognition, such as the OFC and mPFC, fusiform gyrus, and IFG, are also involved in emotional processing. These findings make sense in light of evolutionary considerations that common pressures for dealing with significant stimuli resulted in the co-mingling of structure and function in the social and emotional brain (Brothers, 1990).

CONCLUSION

In this chapter, we have offered a social neuroscience perspective on the affective influences on social cognition. We reviewed neural circuits underlying elicitation, experience, and regulation of affect and emotion. We also have highlighted neural pathways by which affect interacts with social cognition. In the course of this chapter we have emphasized the following four points: (1) the neural systems supporting affect and social cognition reflect multiple levels of organization;

(2) subcortical and cortical circuits are involved in affective influences on perception, memory, judgment, and decision making; (3) under certain conditions, affective stimuli can have independent effects on affective behavior and conscious affective experience; and (4) social and affective processing shares many neural structures, which have probably coevolved to deal with stimuli of high significance.

As our review makes clear, we are still far from a complete understanding of the neural mechanisms of affective and social processing. However, these two domains, and their interactions, are the "hot" topics in neuroscience, and exciting contributions appear weekly in the best journals. We hope that social and affective neuroscientists will continue to collaborate with researchers trained in psychological theories and methods. Together we can reach a more complete understanding of the multilevel processes that shape the social and emotional brain and mind.

ACKNOWLEDGMENTS

We thank Joe Forgas, Mark Starr, and Jenny Trujillo for their helpful comments. Preparation of this chapter was supported by the National Science Foundation Grant BCS-0350687 to PW and the National Institute on Mental Health Grant P50 MH72850 to JTC.

NOTES

1. Some have suggested that in humans the PBN also participates in generating the "protoself", an unconscious but coherent representation of the momentary state of the body (Damasio, 1999).

2. Importantly, our point here is not about anatomical separation—a neat division of labor whereby subcortical networks instantiate unconscious processes and cortical networks instantiate conscious processes. Our point is that mechanisms of consciousness, including affective consciousness, require circuitry able to support demanding computations. Such computations presumably involve an ability to represent different modal, autonomous inputs in a common representational workspace; coordinate the functioning of these inputs; enable verbal access to these inputs; and create a rudimentary representation of self (Baars, 1997; Crick & Koch, 2003; Dennett, 1991). These computational mechanisms could be intermixed within the same brain divisions, or the same brain divisions could have both conscious and unconscious modes.

REFERENCES

Adams, R. B., Gordon, H. L., Baird, A. A., Ambady, N., & Kleck, R. E. (2003). Effects of gaze on amygdala sensitivity to anger and fear faces. *Science, 300*, 1536.

Adolphs, R., Damasio, H., Tranel, D., Cooper, G., & Damasio, A. R. (2000). A role for somatosensory cortices in the visual recognition of emotion as revealed by 3-D lesion mapping. *Journal of Neuroscience, 20*, 2683–2690.

Adolphs, R., Gosselin, F., Buchanan, T. W., Schyns, P., Tranel, D., & Damasio, A. R. (2005). A mechanism explaining impaired fear recognition in amygdala damage. *Nature, 433*, 68–72.

Adolphs, R., Tranel, D., & Damasio, A. R. (1998). The human amygdala in social judgment. *Nature, 393,* 470–474.

Adolphs, R., Tranel, D., Damasio, H., & Damasio, A. (1994). Impaired recognition of emotion in facial expressions following bilateral damage to the human amygdala. *Nature, 372,* 669–672.

Allman, J. M. (1999). *Evolving brains.* New York: Scientific American Library.

Amaral, D. G., Bauman, M. D., Capitanio, J. P., Lavenex, P., Mason, W. A., Mauldin-Jourdain, M. L., Mendoza, S. P. (2003). The amygdala: Is it an essential component of the neural network for social cognition? *Neuropsychologia, 41,* 517–522.

Anderson, A. K., & Phelps, E. A. (2001). Lesions of the human amygdala impair enhanced perception of emotionally salient events. *Nature, 411,* 305–309.

Anderson, A. K., & Phelps, E. A. (2002). Is the human amygdala critical for the subjective experience of emotion? Evidence of intact dispositional affect in patients with lesions of the amygdala. *Journal of Cognitive Neuroscience, 14,* 709–720.

Atkinson, A. P., & Adolphs, R. (2005). Visual emotion perception: Mechanisms and processes. In L. Feldman-Barrett, P. Niedenthal, & P. Winkielman (Eds.), *Emotion and consciousness.* New York: Guilford Press.

Baars, B. (1997). *In the theater of consciousness: The workspace of the mind.* New York: Oxford University Press.

Bar-On, R., Tranel, D., Denburg, N. L., & Bechara, A. (2003). Exploring the neurological substrate of emotional and social intelligence. *Brain, 126,* 1790–1800.

Baron-Cohen, S., Ring, H. A., Bullmore, E. T., Wheelwright, S., Ashwin, C., & Williams, S. C. R. (2000). The amygdala theory of autism. *Neuroscience and Biobehavioral Reviews, 24,* 355–364.

Bechara, A., Damasio, H., Tranel, D., & Damasio, A. R. (1997). Deciding advantageously before knowing the advantageous strategy. *Science, 275,* 1293–1295.

Bechara, A., Tranel, D., Damasio, H., Adolphs, R., Rockland, C., & Damasio, A. (1995). Double dissociation of conditioning and declarative knowledge relative to the amygdala and hippocampus in humans. *Science, 267,* 1115–1118.

Beer, J. S., Heerey, E. H., Keltner, D., Scabini, D., & Knight, R. T. (2003). The regulatory function of self-conscious emotion: Insights from patients with orbitofrontal damage. *Journal of Personality and Social Psychology, 85,* 594–604.

Berntson, G. G., & Cacioppo, J. T. (in press). The neuroevolution of motivation. In J. Shah & W. Gardner (Eds.), *Handbook of motivation science.* New York: Guilford Press.

Berntson, G. G., Sarter, M., & Cacioppo, J. T. (2003). Ascending visceral regulation of cortical affective information processing. *European Journal of Neuroscience, 18,* 2103–2109.

Berridge, K. C. (2000). Measuring hedonic impact in animals and infants: Microstructure of affective taste reactivity patterns. *Neuroscience and Biobehavioral Reviews, 24,* 173–198.

Berridge, K. C. (2003). Comparing the emotional brain of humans and other animals. In R. J. Davidson, H. H. Goldsmith, & K. Scherer (Eds.), *Handbook of affective sciences* (pp. 25–51). New York: Oxford University Press.

Berridge, K. C., & Pecina, S. (1995). Benzodiazepines, appetite, and taste palatability. *Neuroscience and Biobehavioral Reviews, 19,* 121–131.

Berridge, K. C., & Robinson, T. E. (1998). What is the role of dopamine in reward: Hedonic impact, reward learning, or incentive salience? *Brain Research—Brain Research Reviews, 28,* 309–369.

Berridge, K. C., & Winkielman, P. (2003). What is an unconscious emotion: The case for unconscious 'liking'. *Cognition and Emotion, 17,* 181–211.

Brothers, L. (1990). The social brain: A project for integrating primate behaviour and neuropsychology in a new domain. *Concepts in Neuroscience, 1*, 27–51.

Cabanac, M. (1992). Pleasure: The common currency. *Journal of Theoretical Biology, 155*, 173–200.

Cacioppo, J. T., Berntson, G. G., Adolphs, R., Carter, C. S., Davidson, R. J., McClintock, M. K., McEwen, B. S., Meaney, M. J., Schacter, D. L., Sternberg, E. M., Suomi, S. S. & Taylor, S. E. (Eds.). (2002). *Foundations in social neuroscience*. Cambridge, MA: MIT Press.

Cacioppo, J. T., & Gardner, W. L. (1999). Emotion. *Annual Review of Psychology, 50*, 191–214.

Cacioppo, J. T., Larsen, J. T., Smith, N. K., & Berntson, G. G. (2004). The affect system: What lurks below the surface of feelings? In A. S. R. Manstead, N. H. Frijda, & A. H. Fischer (Eds.), *Feelings and emotions: The Amsterdam conference*. New York: Cambridge University Press.

Cacioppo, J. T., Priester, J. R., & Berntson, G. G. (1993). Rudimentary determinants of attitudes. II: Arm flexion and extension have differential effects on attitudes. *Journal of Personality and Social Psychology, 65*, 5–17.

Carr, L., Iacoboni, M., Dubeau, M.-C., Mazziotta, J. C., and Lenzi, G. L., (2003). Neural mechanisms of empathy in humans: A relay from neural systems for imitation to limbic areas. *Proceedings of the National Academy of Sciences, 100*, 5497–5502.

Craig, A. D. (2003). Interoception: The sense of the physiological condition of the body. *Current Opinion in Neurobiology, 13*, 500–505.

Crick, F., & Koch, C. (2003). A framework for consciousness. *Nature Neuroscience, 6*, 119–126.

Critchley, H.D. (2005). Neural mechanisms of autonomic, affective and cognitive integration. *Journal of Comparative Anatomy, 493*, 154–166.

Critchley, H. D., Wiens, S., Rotshtein, P., Oehman, A., & Dolan, R. J. (2004). Neural systems supporting interoceptive awareness. *Nature Neuroscience, 2*, 189–195.

Damasio, A. R. (1999). *The feeling of what happens: Body and emotion in the making of consciousness*. New York: Harcourt Brace.

Damasio, A. R., Grabowski, T. J., Bechara, A., Damasio, H., Ponto, L. L., Parvizi, J., & Hichwa, R. D. (2000). Subcortical and cortical brain activity during the feeling of self-generated emotions. *Nature Neuroscience, 3*, 1049–1056.

Davidson, R. J., Jackson, D. C., & Kalin, N. H. (2000). Emotion, plasticity context, and regulation: Perspectives from affective neuroscience. *Psychological Bulletin, 126*, 890–909.

Davis, M. (1997). The neurophysiological basis of acoustic startle modulation: Research on fear motivation and sensory gating. In P. Lang, R. Simons, & M. Balaban (Eds.), *Attention and orienting: Sensory and motivational processes* (pp. 69–98). Mahwah, NJ: Lawrence Erlbaum Associates, Inc.

Decety, J., & Sommerville, J. A. (2003). Shared representations between self and others: A social cognitive neuroscience view. *Trends in Cognitive Science, 7*, 527–533.

de Quervain, D. J.-F., Fischbacher, U., Treyer, V., Schellhammer, M., Schnyder, U., Buck, A., & Fehr, E. (2004). The neural basis of altruistic punishment. *Science, 305*, 1254–1258.

Dennett, D. (1991). *Consciousness explained*. Boston: Little Brown.

Dolan, R. J., Fletcher, P., Morris, J., Kapur, N., Deakin, J. F., & Frith, C. D. (1996). Neural activation during covert processing of positive emotional facial expressions. *NeuroImage, 4*, 194–200.

Dorus, S., Vallender, E. J., Evans, P. D., Anderson, J. R., Gilbert, S. L., Mahowald, M., Wyckoff, G. J., Malcom, C. M., & Lahn, B. T. (2004). Accelerated evolution of nervous system genes in the origin of *Homo sapiens*. *Cell, 119*, 1027–1040.

Dunbar, R. I. M. (2003). The social brain: Mind, language and society in evolutionary perspective. *Annual Review of Anthropology, 32,* 163–181.

Feldman-Barrett, L., Niedenthal, P., & Winkielman, P. (2005). *Emotion and Consciousness.* New York: Guilford Press.

Gallese, V., Keysers, C., and Rizzolatti, G. (2004). A unifying view of the basis of social cognition. *Trends in Cognitive Sciences, 8,* 396–403.

Gazzaniga, M.S. (2004). *The cognitive neurosciences.* Cambridge, MA: MIT Press.

Geday, J., Gjedde, A., Boldsen, A.-S., & Kupers, R. (2003). Emotional valence modulates activity in the posterior fusiform gyrus and inferior medial prefrontal cortex in social perception. *NeuroImage, 18,* 675–684.

Goodale, M. A., & Milner, M. A. (2004). *Sight unseen: An exploration of conscious and unconscious vision.* Oxford: Oxford University Press.

Goodson, J. L., & Bass, A. H. (2001). Social behavior functions and related anatomical characteristics of vasotocin/vasopressin systems in vertebrates. *Brain Research Reviews, 35,* 246–265.

Gregory, C., Lough, S., Stone, V. E., Erzinclioglu, S., Martin, L., Baron-Cohen, S., et al. (2002). Theory of mind in frontotemporal dementia and Alzheimer's disease: Theoretical and practical implications. *Brain, 125,* 752–764.

Harmon-Jones, E., & Winkielman, P. (in press). *Fundamentals of social neuroscience.* New York: Guilford Press.

Hassert, D. L., Miyashita, T., & Williams, C. L. (2004). The effects of peripheral vagal nerve stimulation at a memory modulating intensity on norepinephrine output in the basolateral amygdala. *Behavioral Neuroscience, 118,* 79–88.

Hatfield, E., Cacioppo, J., & Rapson, R. L. (1994). *Emotional contagion.* New York: Cambridge University Press.

Heberlein, A. S., & Adolphs, R. (2004). Impaired spontaneous anthropomorphizing despite intact perception and social knowledge. *Proceedings of the National Academy of Sciences of the United States of America, 101,* 7487–7491.

Heberlein, A. S., Adolphs, R., Tranel, D., and Damasio, H. (2004). Cortical regions for judgments of emotions and personality traits from point-light walkers. *Journal of Cognitive Neuroscience, 16,* 1143–1158.

Kluver, H., & Bucy, P. C. (1939/1997). Preliminary analysis of functions of the temporal lobes in monkeys. *Journal of Neuropsychiatry & Clinical Neurosciences, 9,* 606–620.

Knutson, B., Adams, C. M., Fong, G. W., & Hommer, D. (2001). Anticipation of increasing monetary reward selectively recruits nucleus accumbens. *Journal of Neuroscience, 21,* 1–5.

Knutson, B., Bjork, J. M., Fong, G. W., Hommer, D. W., Mattay, V. S., & Weinberger, D. R. (2004). Amphetamine modulates human incentive processing. *Neuron, 43,* 261–269.

Konorski, J. (1967). *Integrative activity of the brain: An interdisciplinary approach.* Chicago: University of Chicago Press.

Lang, P. J. (1995). The emotion probe: Studies of motivation and attention. *American Psychologist, 50,* 372–385.

LeDoux, J. (1996). *The emotional brain: The mysterious underpinnings of emotional life.* New York: Simon & Schuster.

Martinez-Garcia, F., Martinez-Marcos, A., & Lanuza, E. (2002). The pallial amygdala of amniote vertebrates: Evolution of the concept, evolution of the structure. *Brain Research Bulletin, 57,* 463–469.

McGaugh, J. (2003). *Memory and emotion: The making of lasting memories.* New York: Columbia University Press.

Morris, J. S., DeGelder, B., Weiskrantz, L., & Dolan, R. J. (2001). Differential extra-geniculostriate and amygdala responses to presentation of emotional faces in a cortically blind field. *Brain, 124*, 1241–1252.

Morris, J. S., Öhman, A., & Dolan, R. J. (1999). A subcortical pathway to the right amygdala mediating "unseen" fear. *Proceedings of the National Academy of Sciences, 96*, 1680–1685.

National Institutes of Health. (1998). *Rehabilitation of ersons with traumatic brain injury.* Paper presented at the NIH consensus statement, Washington, DC.

Neumann, R., Förster, J., & Strack, F. (2003). Motor compatibility: The bidirectional link between behavior and evaluation. In J. Musch & K. C. Klauer (Eds.), *The psychology of evaluation* (pp. 371–391). Mahwah, NJ: Lawrence Erlbaum Associates, Inc.

Niedenthal, P. M., Barsalou, L., Winkielman, P., Krauth-Gruber, S, & Ric, F. (2005). Embodiment in attitudes, social perception, and emotion. *Personality and Social Psychology Review, 9*, 184–211.

Niedenthal, P. M., Brauer, M., Halberstadt, J. B., & Innes-Ker, A. H. (2001). When did her smile drop? Contrast effects in the influence of emotional state on the detection of change in emotional expression. *Cognition and Emotion, 15*, 853–864.

Niedenthal, P. M., & Kitayama, S. (Eds.) (1994). *The heart's eye: Emotional influences in perception and attention.* New York: Academic Press.

Norris, C. J., Chen, E. E., Zhu, D. C., Small, S. L., & Cacioppo, J. T. (2004). The interaction of social and emotional processes in the brain. *Journal of Cognitive Neuroscience, 16*, 1818–1829.

Ochsner, K. N., Bunge, S. A., Gross, J. J., & Gabrieli, J. D. E. (2002). Rethinking feelings: An fMRI study of the cognitive regulation of emotion. *Journal of Cognitive Neuroscience, 14*, 1215–1299.

Ochsner, K. N., & Gross, J. J. (2004). Thinking makes it so: A social cognitive neuroscience approach to emotion regulation. In R. F. Baumeister & K. D. Vohs (Eds.), *Handbook of self-regulation: Research, theory, and applications* (pp. 229–255). New York: Guilford Press.

O'Doherty, J., Deichmann, R., Critchley, H. D., & Dolan, R. J. (2002). Neural responses during anticipation of a primary taste reward. *Neuron, 33*, 815–826.

Öhman, A., Flykt, A., & Lundqvist, D. (2000). Unconscious emotion: Evolutionary perspectives, psychophysiological data and neuropsychological mechanisms. In R. D. Lane, L. Nadel, & G. Ahern (Eds.), *Cognitive neuroscience of emotion* (pp. 296–327). New York: Oxford University Press.

Panksepp, J. (1998). *Affective neuroscience: The foundations of human and animal emotions.* Oxford, UK: Oxford University Press.

Pecina, S., & Berridge, K. C. (2000). Opioid eating site in accumbens shell mediates food intake and hedonic 'liking': Map based on microinjection Fos plumes. *Brain Research, 863*, 71–86.

Peyron, R., Laurent, B., & Garcia-Larrea, L. (2000). Functional imaging of brain responses to pain. A review and meta-analysis. *Clinical Neurophysiology, 30*, 263–288.

Phan, K. L., Wagner, T., Taylor, S. F., & Liberzon, I. (2002). Functional neuroanatomy of emotion: A meta-analysis of emotion activation studies in PET and fMRI. *Neuroimage, 16*, 331–348.

Phelps, E. A. (2005). The interaction of emotion and cognition: Insights from studies of the human amygdala. In L. Feldman-Barrett, P. Niedenthal, & P. Winkielman, *Emotion and consciousness.* New York: Guilford Press.

Phelps, E. A., O'Connor, K. J., Gatenby, J. C., Gore, J. C., Grillon, C., & Davis, M. (2001). Activation of the left amygdala to a cognitive representation of fear. *Nature Neuroscience, 4,* 437–441.

Ramachandran, V. S., & Blakeslee, S. (1998). *Phantoms in the brain.* New York: William Morrow.

Rilling, J. K., Gutman, D. A., Zeh, T. R., Pagnoni, G., Berns, G. S., & Kilts, C. D. (2002). A neural basis for social cooperation. *Neuron, 35,* 395–405.

Rizzolatti, G., Fogassi, L., & Gallese, V. (2001). Neurophysiological mechanisms underlying the understanding and imitation of action. *Nature Reviews Neuroscience, 2,* 661–670.

Rolls, E. T. (1999). *The brain and emotion.* Oxford: Oxford University Press.

Schoenemann, P. T., Sheehan, M. J., & Glotzer, L. D. (2005). Prefrontal white matter volume is disproportionately larger in humans than in other primates. *Nature Neuroscience, 8,* 242–252.

Schwarz, N., & Clore, G. L. (2003). Mood as information: 20 years later. *Psychological Inquiry, 14,* 296–303.

Shiv, B., Loewenstein, G., Bechara, A., Damasio, H., & Damasio, A. (2005). Investment behavior and the negative side of emotion. *Psychological Science, 16,* 435–439.

Singer, T., Seymour, B., O'Doherty, J., Kaube, H., Dolan, R. J., & Frith, C. D. (2004). Empathy for pain involves the affective but not sensory components of pain. *Science, 303,* 1157–1162.

Steiner, J. E. (1973). The gustofacial response: Observation on normal and anencephalic newborn infants. *Symposium on Oral Sensation and Perception, 4,* 254–278.

Steiner, J. E., Glaser, D., Hawilo, M. E., & Berridge, K. C. (2001). Comparative expression of hedonic impact: Affective reactions to taste by human infants and other primates. *Neuroscience and Biobehavioral Reviews, 25,* 53–74.

Stone, V. E. (in press). An evolutionary perspective on domain-specificity in social intelligence. In Harmon-Jones, E., & Winkielman, P. (Eds.). *Fundamentals of social neuroscience.* New York: Guilford Press.

Vuilleumier, P., Armony, J. L., Driver, J., & Dolan, R. J. (2001). Effects of attention and emotion on face processing in the human brain: An event-related fMRI study. *Neuron, 30,* 829–841.

Vuilleumier, P., Armony, J. L., Driver, J., & Dolan, R. J. (2003). Distinct spatial frequency sensitivities for processing faces and emotional expressions. *Nature Neuroscience, 6,* 624–631.

Weiskrantz, L. (1996). Blindsight revisited. *Current Opinion in Neurobiology, 6,* 215–220.

Whalen, P. J., Kagan, J., Cook, R. G., Davis, F. C., Kim, H., Polis, S., McLaren DG, Somerville LH, McLean AA, Maxwell JS, Johnstone T. (2004). Human amygdala responsivity to masked fearful eye whites. *Science, 306,* 2061.

Whalen, P. J., Rauch, S. L., Etcoff, N. L., McInerney, S. C., Lee, M. B., & Jenike, M. A. (1998). Masked presentations of emotional facial expressions modulate amygdala activity without explicit knowledge. *Journal of Neuroscience, 18,* 411–418.

Wicker, B., Keysers, C., Plailly, J., Royet, J.-P., Gallese, V., & Rizzolatti, G. (2003). Both of us disgusted in my insula: The common neural basis of seeing and feeling disgust. *Neuron, 40,* 655–664.

Williams, M. A., Morris, A. P., McGlone, F., Abbott, D. F., & Mattingley, J. B. (2004). Amygdala responses to fearful and happy facial expressions under conditions of binocular suppression. *Journal of Neuroscience, 24,* 2898–2904.

Willis, W. D., & Westlund, K. N. (1997). Neuroanatomy of the pain system and of the pathways that modulate pain. *Journal of Clinical Neurophysiology, 14,* 2–31.

Winkielman, P., Berntson, G. G., & Cacioppo, J. T. (2001). The psychophysiological perspective on the social mind. In A. Tesser & N. Schwarz (Eds.), *Blackwell Handbook of Social Psychology: Intraindividual Processes* (pp. 89–108). Oxford: Blackwell.

Winkielman, P., & Berridge, K. C. (2004). Unconscious emotion. *Current Directions in Psychological Science, 13,* 120–123.

Winkielman, P., Berridge, K. C., & Wilbarger, J. (2005). Unconscious affective reactions to masked happy versus angry faces influence consumption behavior and judgments of value. *Personality and Social Psychology Bulletin, 1,* 121–135.

Winkielman, P., Zajonc, R. B., & Schwarz, N. (1997). Subliminal affective priming resists attributional interventions. *Cognition and Emotion, 11,* 433–465.

Winston, J. S., Strange, B. A., O'Doherty, J., & Dolan, R. J. (2002). Automatic and intentional brain responses during evaluation of trustworthiness of faces. *Nature Neuroscience, 5,* 277–283.

Wise, R. A. (1996). Addictive drugs and brain stimulation reward. *Annual Review of Neuroscience, 19,* 319–340.

4

Mood and the Regulation of Information Processing and Behavior

HERBERT BLESS and KLAUS FIEDLER

INTRODUCTION

*C*onsider the two most famous characters from the TV series Star Trek, Captain Kirk and Mr. Spock. Mr. Spock, a "Vulcan" allegedly unable to experience emotions, bases his judgments and his behavior on a thoughtful consideration of the situation and on a rational integration of the relevant information. In contrast, Captain Kirk's thinking, judgment, and behavior seem often to be influenced by his affective states. Quite in line with Mr. Spock's view, the early approaches in psychology proposed that affect serves to reduce individuals' ability to think rationally, thus impairing their judgments and decisions (for an overview see Forgas, 2000). Research conducted within the last three decades, though, conveys a fundamentally different picture. Affective states need not create irrational behavior but may rather provide a very useful source of information, signals, and motives that are essential for adaptive regulation of cognitive processes and behavior. By "regulation"—the core concept of this chapter—we refer to all kinds of adjustment processes that serve to keep stimuli and reactions within an appropriate range, and to prevent them from exceeding critical boundaries. Regulatory processes occur in various dimensions, such as the intensity and density of stimuli, adjusting social and physical distance, optimal time or effort expenditure, or establishing an acceptable range of behaviors on the conformity versus deviance dimension, or on the novelty versus familiarity dimension.

In the present chapter we discuss how individuals' mood states influence the regulation of a wide spectrum of cognitive processes and behaviors, such as regulation of exposure to pleasant or unpleasant information, temporal regulation, regulation of the motivational system, regulation of abstractness of thinking, regulation of transgression versus conformity, regulation of elaboration versus truncation of thinking and problem solving, and regulation of top-down versus bottom-up processing. We will argue that—contrary to Mr. Spock's perspective—moods are far from being dysfunctional, but may rather play an important role for the adaptive regulation of cognition and behavior. Given the limited scope of the present chapter, we will not be able to elaborate on all aspects of regulation at the same level of detail. We shall rather address some issues in greater depth than others.

A TAXONOMY OF REGULATORY DIMENSIONS

Table 4.1 provides a taxonomy of different dimensions of cognitive and behavioral regulation, as they map onto various paradigms of affect-and-cognition research. The purpose of the table is twofold. First, it affords an advanced organizer, or preview of the entire chapter's contents, intended to facilitate reading and understanding. The second purpose is to sensitize the reader to the distinct modes of cognitive and behavioral regulation that exist, theoretically, and to point out a common theoretical denominator that connects all aspects of regulation listed in Table 4.1, namely, the two complementary adaptive functions, assimilation and accommodation (cf. Piaget, 1954). Assimilation means to impose internalized structures onto the external world, whereas accommodation means to modify internal structures in accordance with external constraints. This distinction between internally driven and externally driven adaptation can be sensibly applied to all aspects of regulation. Moreover, with respect to affective influences on regulatory processes, it will turn out that—as a unifying theme—the role of positive mood is to facilitate assimilation whereas the role of negative mood is to strengthen accommodation functions.

MOOD INFLUENCES ON DIFFERENT REGULATORY DIMENSIONS: AN EMPIRICAL REVIEW

Mood and Hedonic Regulation: Exposure to Pleasant and Unpleasant Information

It is almost a truism that individuals strive for positive affective states and try to avoid negative affective states (e.g., Bentham, 1789). This general assumption is entailed in many approaches that conceptualize the regulation of human behavior and cognitive processes on a hedonistic dimension (see Erber & Erber, 2000; Erber & Markunas, this volume, for an overview). Accordingly, individuals are motivated to maintain positive and avoid negative affective states, and in order to do so they have developed a behavioral and cognitive repertoire that serves this function. In this section, we start by outlining some approaches that build on this general hedonistic notion and relate them to other approaches assuming that—at least under certain boundary conditions—individuals may also expose themselves to situations and stimuli, seek for information, and engage in behaviors that make them feel less positive.

It seems straightforward to assume that individuals' affective states are mainly determined by what is on their minds. In other words, it is assumed that there is a (bi-directional) link between individuals' affective states and the accessibility of pos-

TABLE 4.1   Dimensions of cognitive-affective behavior regulation

Aspect of Regulation	Comments
Hedonism. Avoiding unpleasant stimuli	Although this dimension must not be equated with regulation per se, it is clearly one of the most important regulation dimensions. Research on repression, mood repair, negative-state relief, deliberate information search, etc.
Temporal regulation	Temporal regulation of action plans, as in a typical delay of gratification paradigm. Tradeoff between smaller short-term payoff and larger long-term payoff. Mood and delay of gratification. Temporal construal.
Regulatory focus	Regulation through promotion vs. prevention focus. Little direct evidence available on mood and regulatory focus. One feature of the taxonomy is that it renders missing research, or gaps, visible, as in a periodic system.
Abstraction vs. detail	Regulation through choice of abstractness level, or inclusiveness of categories and concepts, segment width, grain size, etc. Mood and clustering; abstractness of language use; inclusiveness of mental representations.
Transgression vs. conformism	Regulation through testing the limits. The extent to which people confirm to or transgress against rules (idiosyncracy credit). Research on mood and politeness; negotiation; quick and dirty heuristics.
Closure	Regulation on continue vs. truncate dimension. Exhaustiveness of information and stopping rules (mood as input). Mood and correspondence bias.
Knowledge-driven vs. stimulus-driven	Top-down vs. bottom-up processing. Generate new information (based on prior knowledge) vs. conserve stimulus information. Memory for expected vs. unexpected info. Relying on stimulus facts vs. inferences in stereotyping and persuasion.

itive and negative information in working memory (Bower, 1981; Forgas & Bower, 1987; see Eich & Macaulay, this volume). Given that an increased accessibility of negative information may induce unpleasant affective states, the desire to maintain and consume pleasant states should result in strategies that counteract the automatic activation of negative mood-congruent information. Support for this conclusion comes from many findings suggesting that mood-congruent memory is asymmetrical (Fiedler, Nickel, Asbeck, & Pagel, 2003)—a pattern that already emerged in Bower's (1981) seminal paper. On the one hand, happy moods facilitate the recall of happy memories and inhibit the recall of sad memories. On the other hand, however, sad moods may slightly inhibit the recall of happy memories, but rarely increase the recall of sad memories (Isen, Shalker, Clark, & Karp, 1978; see Isen, 1984). Isen (1984, 1987) accounted for this asymmetry by postulating more controlled motivational processes in addition to the automatically spreading associations suggested by Bower (1981). According to this perspective, individuals in negative affective states may be motivated to "repair" their moods by attempting "to stop the process of thinking about negative material that might be cued by sadness" (Isen, 1987, p. 217). These controlled processes may in turn override the automatic impact of sad moods on the accessibility of (sad) mood-congruent material (see Morris, 1989, for a critical review).

The assumption that individuals engage in behavioral and cognitive strategies that either maintain positive affective states or "repair" negative affective states can be found in several approaches. While numerous strategies have been discussed in this respect (see Erber & Markunas, this volume; Morris, 1989; Morris & Reilly, 1987), perhaps the most explicit approach refers to prosocial behavior. It has been suggested that a leading motive for individuals' willingness to engage in helping others is to improve one's own mood (mood repair, "if you feel bad, do good things"). This contention received empirical support from several experiments showing that inducing negative affective states increased individuals' helping behavior (e.g., Cialdini & Kenrick, 1976; Schaller & Cialdini, 1988; see also Baumeister, Vohs, & Tice, this volume). In line with the regulation argument, helping was restricted to those conditions in which individuals subjectively believed in the improvement of their mood (Manucia, Baumann, & Cialdini, 1984). In a related but different vein, it has been suggested that engaging in effortful cognitive processes might interfere with the consumption of positive mood states (Isen, 1987; Wegener & Petty, 1994; Wegener, Petty, & Smith, 1995). Accordingly, individuals might enhance and expand their emotional states by regulating the amount of cognitive work. We will return to this issue and related evidence below.

Empirical evidence that individuals strive for positive affective states and try to avoid negative affective states is widespread (for a critical overview see Erber, 2001). Note, however, that a *regulation* perspective always emphasizes the adaptive value of *variation*, rather than just an invariant striving for positive affect. Various approaches have addressed such a genuine regulation aspect and contrasted it to the notion that individuals inevitably seek positive affect. In this respect Erber and colleagues (e.g., Erber & Erber, 2000; Erber & Markunas, this volume; Erber, Wegner, & Therriault, 1996) proposed that individuals may attenuate their affective states when they expect to interact with others, but they engage in little mood regulation attempts when they are not expecting social interaction or demanding tasks. Thus, contrary to a pure mood-maintenance/mood-repair perspective, individuals are not expected to optimize their affective experience, but they attenuate their hedonic consumption to a less intense level if necessary for the current task demands or interaction goals (see Erber & Erber, 2000, for a more extensive discussion).

The ability to face unpleasant information, and not to negate the existence of threatening aspects of reality, is at the heart of many important adaptation problems that call for tolerance, mastery, and delay of gratification (e.g., medical examination as a key to successful therapy; honest confession to save one's partnership). In this regard, Trope and colleagues (Raghunathan & Trope, 2002; Trope, Igou, & Burke, this volume; Trope, Ferguson, & Raghunathan, 2001) suggest that positive affect may serve as a resource that gives one the backing-up for tackling unpleasant but necessary tasks. Individuals are more likely to expose themselves to potentially negative information when they are in a happy rather than a sad mood. Positive affect functions as a resource that counteracts the threat and burden of negative information. Trope and colleagues suggest that this benevolent effect is most pronounced when the information in question implies negative self-relevant feedback of high informational value.

Consistent with this buffer function of happy mood, depressive patients have been shown to be unable to deliberately expose themselves to negative stimuli (Fiedler, 1991), or to accept a short-term disadvantage in order to gain a stronger long-term advantage (Trope et al., 2001). Their ability to sacrifice part of their payoffs for the sake of curiosity, exploration, or higher social goals is reduced (Forgas & Fiedler, 1996). Even mildly depressed states resulting from watching sad films have been shown to support profit maximization and to restrict strategic flexibility in experimental dilemma games (Hertel & Fiedler, 1994).

Altogether, the reviewed research on hedonic regulation suggests that individuals do not invariably strive for positive information leading to desired states and avoid negative information inducing undesired affective states. Instead, individuals seem to *regulate* their affective states in accordance with the task environment and the adaptive function of different mood states. The available evidence is consistent with the generic assumption that positive mood supports assimilative functions whereas the function of negative mood is accommodative—following the hedonic constraints of the stimulus world. Nevertheless, given the seemingly divergent perspective of mood repair, more research and theorizing is needed on how emotional states trigger various mechanisms of hedonic regulation and what boundary conditions moderate these mechanisms (such as temporal delay in the finding that mood-congruent reactions prevail immediately after a mood-inducing event, whereas the likelihood of mood-incongruent reactions increases with delay, cf. Forgas & Ciarrochi, 2002).

Mood and Regulation of Norm-Conformity Versus Transgression

Variation on the dimension of norm-conforming versus norm-deviant behavior can be considered a special case of social hedonism; the former is desirable whereas the latter is undesirable. The general pattern of mood dependence is indeed the same: Research in several paradigms suggests that good mood gives people the backing-up required for unusual, idiosyncratic, norm-deviant, or even transgressive behavior, whereas bad mood induces norm-conforming, conventional behavior. Relevant evidence includes Forgas' (1998, 1999, this volume) repeated demonstration that happy people engage in more impolite and less restrictive and controlled social behaviors than dysphoric people, as well as the complementary finding that recipients perceive the same communications as less impolite when they are in a good- than in a sad-mood state. In association experiments, good-mood participants would produce more unusual associations, according to common association norms, than do sad-mood participants (Isen, Johnson, Mertz, & Robinson, 1985). Or, in a related vein, in negotiation situations, good mood encourages people to be more risk-seeking than negative affective states, which induce more conservative strategies (Williams & Voon, 1999).

Again, the two opposite adaptation modes, assimilation versus accommodation, afford a sensible interpretation of the behavioral repertoire supported by different mood states. Good mood provides the resources and self-confidence needed to engage in spontaneous, internally determined, daring behavior—all features of assimilative regulation. In contrast, bad mood induces common, norm-conforming behaviors determined by external rules and social conventions—thus fulfilling an accommodative function.

Mood and The Regulation of Processing Depth and Processing Style

When confronted with a problem situation, individuals are not restricted to a single set of cognitive processes to interpret the situation. Rather, there is a whole variety of cognitive tools that may be applied to deal with the same social reality (see Bless, Fiedler, & Strack, 2004). Given this starting point, individuals need to select an "appropriate" mechanism. For example, they have to determine whether to encode a particular stimulus on a more abstract or a more concrete level, how much effort they should invest in the processing of the task situation, and how much they should rely on prior knowledge versus how much emphasis they should give to the incoming information. Several theoretical positions hold that affective states regulate the use of these different mechanisms. In the next sections, we will discuss these theoretical approaches and present empirical evidence that is related to the question of how affective states regulate cognitive processes.

Level of Abstractness

When communicating or thinking about social information, individuals are often free to represent the same behavior or event either at a rather abstract (e.g., animal; conservative attitude) or a rather specific level (e.g., my neighbor's dog; voting against Kerry in the 2004 US election to prevent legislation of gay marriage). Quite obviously, the level of abstractness is flexible and context-dependent, and both representations may have their advantages and disadvantages. The available evidence suggests, though, that individuals' affective states may play a crucial role in this regulation of abstractness in thinking.

Isen (1984) posited that positive affect results in increased integrative complexity, in "an organization of cognitive material, such that either more or broader, more integrated categories are used" (p. 535). This assumption was supported by the finding that happy participants were more likely than neutral-mood participants to assign atypical exemplars to a category (e.g., "cane" as a member of the category "clothing"). Similarly, happy participants sorted stimuli into fewer groupings than participants in a neutral-mood control condition (Isen & Daubman, 1984).

A more integrative, abstract representation of incoming information is also reflected in happy individuals' tendency to cluster information into larger chunks. For example, Bless, Hamilton, and Mackie (1992) presented participants in a happy, neutral, or sad mood with 28 behavioral descriptions pertaining to 4 different trait categories (e.g., intelligence, friendliness). Neutral-mood participants showed higher clustering (Roenker, Thompson, & Brown, 1971) when the instructions encouraged clustering rather than not (i.e., when an impression-formation set rather than a memory set was induced; Hamilton, Katz, & Leirer, 1980). However, independently of the instructional set, happy participants showed a very high level and sad participants a very low level of spontaneous clustering (for similar findings see Isen, Daubman, & Gorgoglione, 1987). Murray, Sujan, Hirt, and Sujan (1990) also reported evidence for an increased flexibility of categorization processes under happy mood.

The general assumption that happy moods are linked to more abstract levels of representations is also reflected in the relation between mood and language. Based on the linguistic category model (Semin & Fiedler, 1988), a general framework for assessing linguistic abstractness of language use, Beukeboom (2003) investigated the influence of mood on language use. In a series of studies, happy participants provided more abstract descriptions than sad participants. Again it seems as if individuals' mood regulates the abstractness of thinking. Similar conclusions can be drawn about nonlinguistic task materials, as suggested in recent research by Gasper and Clore (2002). The participants were presented with a perception task (geometrical figures). When a happy mood had been induced, the perceptual focus was on more global features than when a sad mood had been induced, which led to a focus on more local features (for the notion that narrower categorizations are more likely under sad moods, see also Sinclair, 1988).

Although not directly addressing the impact of mood, research on action identification theory (Vallacher & Wegner, 1986) provides converging evidence for the notion that different affective states are linked to different levels of abstractness. This theory holds that successful actions are represented on a more general level whereas unsuccessful actions are represented on more specific levels. Assuming that unsuccessful actions tend to be evaluated negatively and that successful actions tend to be positive, these assumptions converge with the reported evidence on the relation between affective state and the level of abstraction. While much of the evidence pertains to the encoding of new information, there is also some evidence suggesting that mood may also influence the abstractness of information retrieved from memory. Bless, Mackie, and Schwarz (1992) found that happy participants were more likely to retrieve a global representation of a persuasive message whereas sad participants were more likely to retrieve a specific representation.

As concrete representations stick to the contextualized stimulus world whereas abstract representations are mediated by the individuals' decontextualized conceptual knowledge, the former reflect accommodation whereas the latter reflect assimilation. Therefore, the consistently obtained finding of more abstract representations resulting from happy than sad mood fits into the general interpretation that good mood supports assimilative regulation whereas bad mood serves an accommodative adaptive function.

Elaboration Depth

A fair amount of research has addressed the question whether mood regulates the degree and depth of elaboration. In particular, it was hypothesized that happy moods are more strongly associated with heuristic processing strategies than sad moods. Much of this research has been conducted within the domains of persuasion and person perception. We will first address these two domains, before we turn to theoretical explanations for these findings.

Mood and Persuasion   To investigate the impact of mood on persuasion, researchers have typically applied dual-process models of persuasion (Chaiken, 1980, 1987; Petty & Cacioppo, 1986; see Eagly & Chaiken, 1993). In a number of studies, participants who had undergone a mood treatment were subsequently exposed to a persuasive message that included either strong or weak arguments. In general, participants in sad moods reported more favorable attitudes toward the advocated position when they had been presented with strong rather than weak arguments. In contrast, participants in happy moods were less influenced by the message quality; they were equally persuaded by strong and weak arguments. Equivalent findings were obtained for recipients' cognitive responses, reflecting differential sensitivity to message quality under sad and neutral but not under happy-mood conditions. This general pattern of findings has been replicated in a number of studies using a range of different mood inductions and attitudinal issues (for examples, see Bless, Bohner, Schwarz, & Strack, 1990; Bless et al., 1992; Bohner, Crow, Erb, & Schwarz, 1992; Innes & Ahrens, 1991; Mackie & Worth, 1989; Sinclair, Mark, & Clore, 1994; Wegener & Petty, 1994; Worth & Mackie, 1987). These findings have been complemented by the observation that attitudes of recipients in positive but not in neutral moods are responsive to heuristic cues, as distinguished from argument contents (Mackie & Worth, 1989; Worth & Mackie, 1987; see, however, Bohner et al., 1992, for an opposite view). Within the framework of dual-process models, the decreased effect of message quality and the increased impact of peripheral cues under happy-mood conditions suggests that happy moods are associated with heuristic processing strategies, whereas sad moods are associated with a systematic elaboration of the information that is presented (for overviews see Bohner, Moskowitz, & Chaiken, 1995; Mackie, Asuncion, & Rosselli, 1992; Schwarz, Bless, & Bohner, 1991;Wegener & Petty, 1996). This account, to be sure, is consistent with the interpretation of the systematic processing of stimulus contents as an accommodative function and the heuristic reliance on internalized rules of thumb, which are detached from the validity of the stimulus input, as an assimilative function.

Person Perception   Similar to attitude formation and change, judgments of other persons may reflect different processing strategies. When based on a more heuristic, assimilative strategy, they reflect the perceiver's general knowledge about categories to which the target belongs (i.e., implications of stereotypes). Alternatively, judgments may be primarily based on a systematic, accommodative account of the available individuating information about a specific target person, thereby attenuating the impact of the stereotype (cf. Brewer, 1988; Fiske & Neuberg, 1990). A number of studies explored whether and how individuals' mood states influence their reliance on stereotypes in impression formation. For example, Bodenhausen, Kramer, and Süsser (1994; see also Bodenhausen, 1993) presented

participants in different mood states with descriptions of alleged student miscon-
duct and asked them to evaluate the target's guilt. Happy participants judged the
offender to be more guilty when he was identified as a member of an ethnic group
that is stereotypically associated with the described offence than when this was not
the case. This impact of the stereotype, however, was not observed for participants
in a sad-mood state. The heightened impact of stereotypes on the processing by
happy individuals was replicated in a series of experiments that additionally demonstrated the complementary increased impact of individuating information on the
processing of sad individuals (Bless, Schwarz, & Wieland, 1996). Edwards and
Weary (1993) reported similarly converging evidence based on naturally depressed
moods. Nondepressed participants were more likely to rely on category membership information than depressed participants, who were more strongly influenced
by individuating information.

If we equate reliance on category membership information with reliance on
peripheral cues (assimilation), and reliance on individuating stimulus information
with reliance on the presented arguments (accommodation), these findings converge
with those obtained for persuasion and other domains. In combination, these findings suggest that individuals in a happy mood are more likely to rely on heuristics or
stereotypes, whereas individuals in a sad mood are more likely to attend to the specific information provided. The conclusion that happy individuals are more likely to
rely on heuristic processing strategies is not restricted to domains of persuasion and
person perception. As Ruder and Bless (2003) have demonstrated recently, happy
individuals were more likely to apply the availability heuristic, basing their judgments
on the ease with which information came to mind, than sad participants, whose judgments were better predicted by the activated information content and the situational context (for similar evidence, see Isen, Means, Patrick, & Nowicki, 1982).

Theoretical Accounts   Given that social cognition research has consistently
demonstrated that individuals' processing motivations and capacities have a pronounced impact on the use of heuristic processing strategies (e.g., Eagly &
Chaiken, 1993; Fiske & Neuberg, 1990; Fiske & Taylor, 1991; Petty & Cacioppo,
1986), it comes as no surprise that various accounts have proposed that happy
individuals' reliance on heuristic cues reflects a reduction in the amount of cognitive processing, reflecting either capacity deficits or motivational deficits as the
likely cause.

Processing Capacity   Within an associative network memory approach (see
Eich & Macaulay, this volume), assuming that mood states activate links to related
memory contents, it has been argued that being in a happy mood limits processing
capacity due to the activation of a large amount of interconnected positive material
stored in memory (e.g., Isen, 1987; Mackie & Worth, 1989), because more positive
than negative information is assumed to be stored in memory (Matlin & Stang,
1979). Due to such a capacity shortage, people in happy moods may have to
engage in less taxing heuristic strategies, rather than more demanding
systematic processing.

Cognitive Tuning   Extending the mood-as-information hypothesis (Clore & Storbeck, this volume; Schwarz & Clore, 1983), it has been proposed that affective states may inform the individual about the nature of the current situation (Schwarz & Clore, 1996; see also Frijda, 1988). Thus, individuals usually feel good in situations that are characterized by positive outcomes and/or in situations that do not threaten their current goals. In contrast, individuals usually feel bad in situations that threaten their current goals, because of the presence of negative outcomes or the lack of positive outcomes. If different situations result in different affective states, individuals may consult their affect as a usually valid and quick indicator as to the nature of the current psychological situation. Specifically, positive affective states may inform the individual that the current situation poses no problem, whereas negative affective states signal that the current situation is problematic. Based on such affective cues, individuals in a bad mood are more motivated to engage in detail-oriented systematic processing strategies, which are typically adaptive in handling problematic situations. In contrast, individuals in a good mood may see little reason to engage in strenuous processing strategies, unless this is called for by another goal. Note that reduced processing under happy moods is but one implication of the cognitive tuning perspective, which also implies high flexibility of cognitive processes under happy moods (see Schwarz, 1990; Schwarz & Clore, 1996, for more detailed discussions)—all indicative of clearly assimilative functions.

Rather direct evidence supporting the role of the informational value provided by individuals' moods is reported in the study by Sinclair et al. (1994). In this study, sad individuals differentiated between messages comprising either strong or weak arguments, while happy individuals did not, replicating the pattern of previous studies reported above. This differential pattern for happy versus sad recipients was eliminated, however, when recipients attributed their mood to the weather. Such an external attribution undermines the diagnostic value of good mood as a situational cue that signals heuristic processing as an appropriate strategy.

Mood Management   Different accounts entail the hypothesis, implicitly or explicitly, that individuals are motivated to maintain positive affective states and to enhance negative affective states (Isen, 1987; Wegener & Petty, 1994; Wegener et al., 1995). Starting from the assumption that strenuous cognitive processes interfere with the goal of maintaining positive-mood states, researchers have argued that individuals in happy moods are less motivated to invest cognitive effort than sad individuals. As a consequence of such reduced motivation, happy individuals should be more likely to rely on heuristic processing while sad individuals should be more likely to engage in systematic processing. This effect may be overridden, however, if the task promises to maintain or even enhance individuals' positive moods (Wegener et al., 1995). Other researchers questioned the strong belief in individuals' motivations to improve their moods. In many situations, individuals may pursue more long-term benefits at the costs of immediate mood management effects (for a discussion of the hedonic view and related evidence see Erber, 1996, 2001; Erber et al., 1996; see also Schwarz and Clore, 1996, for a discussion of the empirical evidence).

Reconsidering the Evidence for Reduced Processing under Happy Moods
All theoretical approaches discussed so far share the notion that happy individuals' reliance on heuristics reflects a processing deficit, either in motivation or in capacity. It is interesting that, with very few exceptions, support for the various positions is mostly based on the demonstration that happy individuals' reliance on heuristics can be overridden by additional manipulations. For example, happy individuals' failure to differentiate in their attitude judgments between strong and weak arguments, or their use of stereotypes, could be overcome by (1) informing people that processing the content would make them feel happy (Wegener et al., 1995); (2) providing unlimited processing time (Mackie & Worth, 1989); (3) instructing recipients to focus on the specific message content (Bless et al., 1990); or (4) introducing an accountability manipulation (Bodenhausen et al., 1994). However, the demonstration that one manipulation "x" can override the impact of another manipulation "y" does not constitute a cogent proof of the claim that the former reflects the same underlying cause as the latter. Thus, even when manipulations that reduce a deficit can undo heuristic processing, this does not imply that heuristic processing is entirely due to a cognitive deficit.

The underlying dual-process models also presuppose that a reduction in processing capacity and/or processing motivation increases the reliance on heuristics or stereotype information. Through backward inference from heuristic processing to motivational or capacity deficits, reduced motivation and capacity are typically considered the only sensible factors underlying the enhanced reliance on heuristics (see also Bless & Schwarz, 1999). Interestingly enough, though, rather few attempts have been made to directly measure capacity and resource restrictions, or the amount of processing, under different mood states. There are good reasons, therefore, to consider an alternative account, which will be offered in the next section on the regulation of top-down versus bottom-up processing.

The quality of the evidence for moods delimiting motivation or capacity becomes important as other accounts question the proposed link between mood and amount of processing. Working from the mood-as-input model (Martin, 2001; Martin & Stoner, 1996; Martin, Ward, Achee, & Wyer, 1993; see also Hirt, Melton, McDonald, & Harackiewicz, 1996), Martin argued that moods may both increase or decrease cognitive effort. This assumption was corroborated by the finding that happy people invested more effort in a task than sad participants when instructed to continue as long as they enjoyed the task. However, when participants were instructed to continue until they were satisfied with their performance, happy participants invested less effort than sad participants (Martin et al., 1993). Thus, when satisfaction with one's performance was the judgment criterion, happy people were presumably more satisfied and refrained from investing additional effort. In contrast, when enjoyment with the task itself was the judgment criterion, happy participants felt more enjoyment than sad participants, which in turn increased their motivation to continue the task.

Regulation of Top-Down Versus Bottom-Up Processing

If heuristics are defined as the application of general knowledge structures to specific information (Nisbett & Ross, 1980), the research on mood and heuristic processing we have just discussed is nicely matched with other research directly addressing the impact of mood on prior general knowledge. Indeed, numerous studies confirm the general notion that prior general knowledge is more influential when individuals are in a happy rather than a sad mood (Bless, 2001). In this respect, research addressing the role of scripts (Bless, Clore, Schwarz, Golisano, Rabe, & Wölk, 1996), prior trait judgments (Bless & Fiedler, 1995), stereotypes (Bless et al., 1996; Bodenhausen et al., 1994; Krauth-Gruber & Ric, 2000), constructive memory effects in eyewitness memory (Forgas, Laham, & Vargas, 2005), inference making in recognition decisions (Fiedler, Nickel, Muehlfriedel, & Unkelbach, 2001), enhanced memory for self-generated information (Fiedler et al., 2003), and general attitude representations (Bless et al., 1992) provides a consistent pattern of evidence. Individuals' affective states regulate the relative contributions of top-down processes, facilitated in positive mood, and bottom-up processes, supported by negative mood states. As top-down and bottom-up processes can be clearly identified as assimilative versus accommodative functions, respectively, this regular pattern matches the general explanatory principle.

Mood and General Knowledge   Given that top-down processing serves an economical function by reducing the amount of memory load, one may argue that happy individuals' top-down processing is identical to the assumption that happy mood reduces cognitive effort and depth of elaboration, as discussed above. Casting this interpretation into doubt, Bless' (1997, 2001) mood-and-general-knowledge assumption says that happy individuals' reliance on heuristics and general knowledge structures may not be mediated by mood-dependent restrictions in cognitive resources, motivation, or capacity. This approach does adopt the notion that positive affective states may inform the individual that the current situation poses no problem, whereas negative affective states may signal that the current situation is problematic. It is argued, however, that the key effect of these affective signals is not, or not only, motivational. Instead their key function may indeed lie in triggering the adaptive use of pre-existing general knowledge structures (Bless, 2001; Bless et al., 1996). Specifically, if being in a positive mood informs individuals that the present situation poses no big problem, this "business-as-usual" signal may increase the likelihood that they rely on general knowledge structures, which usually serve them well. In contrast, if being in a negative mood signals a problematic situation, reliance on defaults and general knowledge structures may not be adaptive and individuals may be more likely to attend to the specifics of the information at hand. These different weights given to old and new information may often be associated with unequal effort or amount of processing. However, according to the mood-and-general-knowledge assumption, reduced effort is the *consequence* of using economical heuristics and schemas, rather than a *cause* that enforces heuristic strategies, as if resources were too restricted to allow for other strategies (for a more detailed discussion see Bless & Schwarz, 1999).

Given that the mood-and-general-knowledge approach on one hand and the mood-and-reduced-resources approaches on the other lead to many parallel predictions, an important theoretical question is how to disentangle the different explanations. At least two aspects allow for such a differentiation. First, if happy moods reduce processing motivation or capacity, they should not only impair performance on the primary task, but also performance on a secondary task. In contrast, if happy moods elicit reliance on general knowledge structures pertaining to the primary task, the primary task should be less taxing and performance on a secondary task should improve. In support of the latter position, Bless et al. (1996) found that happy participants were more likely than sad participants to apply pre-existing knowledge in the form of scripts when encoding new information. However, when provided with a secondary task during encoding, happy participants outperformed sad participants. Such increased performance on the secondary task is hardly compatible with the assumption of a capacity deficit as a cause of script-based top-down processing. Conversely, using an economical script seemed to save the cognitive resources for the secondary task, as evident in the additional finding that no improvement was observed on the secondary task when it was the only task, in the absence of a primary task involving scripts.

A second aspect pertains to the impact of information that is inconsistent with the implications of the script, or general knowledge structure. If happy moods reduce processing motivation or capacity, any observations that are unexpected or inconsistent with the knowledge structure should be likely to go unnoticed and to be lost during encoding. In contrast, if happy moods elicit reliance on general knowledge structures, inconsistent information should be particularly salient and should therefore have a strong impact on subsequent judgments and inferences. Consistent with the latter possibility, experimental evidence showed that happy participants' increased use of stereotypes was accompanied by an enhanced impact of stereotype-inconsistent information on judgments (Bless et al., 1996) and by improved recall for the stereotype-inconsistent information (Dovidio, Gaertner, & Loux, 2000; for a direct test of this assumption see Krauth-Gruber & Ric, 2000). Granting that elaboration on inconsistent information calls for the allocation of additional resources (Stangor & McMillan, 1992), these findings render it unlikely that the primary cause of happy individuals' use of general knowledge structures lies in an absolute shortage of mental resources. At the same time, these findings support the contention that the interplay between top-down and bottom-up components of cognitive activities is regulated by affective experience, in accordance with the general principle that positive mood fosters assimilation (knowledge-driven, top-down inferences) whereas negative mood supports accommodation (stimulus-driven, bottom-up processes).

Temporal Regulation

The taxonomy of Table 4.1 suggests some further modes of regulation that past research has hardly ever investigated in relation to affective states. However, they deserve to be considered in future research. As the assimilation–accommodation distinction is clearly applicable to these regulation modes, the pertinent working hypotheses suggest themselves.

Temporal regulation, to begin with, can be conceived in terms of the temporal distance from which behaviors are planned and behavioral goals are represented. Trope and Liberman's (2003) temporal-construal theory provides a well-elaborated framework for describing and investigating such temporal-regulation processes. Accordingly, behaviors and goals in the far future are normally construed more abstractly, in terms of their intrinsic meaning and desirability, whereas actions in the present or near future are represented in more detail, with reference to their feasibility and external constraints. No doubt, far-distance construal involves a high degree of assimilation whereas near-distance construal calls for accommodation. An obvious prediction, therefore, is that positive mood should induce a more distant mode of temporal regulation than negative mood.

Promotion Focus and Prevention Focus

Higgins' (1997, 1998) regulatory-focus theory is based on a distinction between two basic motivational states: promotion focus or the success-oriented motive to win, and prevention focus or the failure-oriented motive not to lose. In spite of the popularity of this approach, instigating a large number of pertinent experiments, systematic evidence on the influence of mood on this motivational dimension is missing. One plausible hypothesis is that when the focus is on promotion or exploration, people might place more weight on assimilation, and less weight on accommodation, than when the focus is on prevention or avoidance. Another, slightly different, hypothesis would be that when there is regulatory fit—between the individual's current focus and the requirements of the task—assimilation should increase and accommodation should increase. The theoretical predictions about the impact of mood have to be adapted accordingly. However, in any case, it should be evident that the current approach to affect and behavior regulation is of both explanatory and predictive value.

CONCLUDING REMARKS

In summary, the presented findings indicate that individuals' affective states have pronounced effects on cognitive and behavioral regulation on a large variety of dimensions. This conclusion raises the question *why* affective states may serve such regulation functions. From the present perspective, at least two answers suggest themselves, both of which refer to the adaptive value of affective states and emotions.

First, in line with other theorizing, we assume that affective states very often reflect the meaning of an ecological situation and thus can be conceptualized as a sort of "summary" of the nature of the situation (see Clore & Storbeck, this volume, for a more extensive discussion of this aspect; Frijda, 1988; Schwarz, 1990; see also Nowlis & Nowlis, 1956 or Pribram, 1970). It is important to note that although individuals can become at least potentially aware of their affective state, this does not hold for the information that caused the affective state. Individuals may, or may not, be aware of the representations that led to their affective states. Thus, affective states may potentially provide *more* information than individuals can access directly.

Given this advantage, affective states may provide a better basis for regulatory processes than the mere content of activated and accessible representations. This advantage, however, comes with the disadvantage that the situation underlying an affective state may sometimes be misinterpreted (see Clore & Storbeck, this volume; e.g., Schwarz & Clore, 1983) and, consequently, individuals may derive the wrong implications for the regulation of their cognitive processes and behaviors.

Second, individuals need to have direct access to variables that function as regulators. If the mechanisms involved in regulation were too complex and strenuous, fast and smooth adjustment would be impossible. Affective states—at least at the coarse level of the positive versus negative distinction—are easy to read off. Individuals may have problems determining the causes of their affective state, but they can usually tell without difficulty whether they feel happy or sad. This simple, binary cue can then serve an important adaptive function in the organism's interaction with the social and physical environment. Feeling good suggests assimilating the environment to the organism's internal state. Feeling bad suggests accommodating the internal state to the requirements of a problematic external state. From such a cognitive-ecological perspective, it is no coincidence that the two complementary components of all adaptation, assimilation and accommodation, afford an integrative account of the role of mood in cognitive and behavioral regulation.

Individuals' tendency to trust the diagnostic value of their affective states may thus be considered a multiply adaptive mechanism. Returning to our example in the "Introduction", we therefore believe that Captain Kirk may be better equipped for dealing with a complex environment than Mr. Spock. Skeptics who recall that Mr. Spock may have sometimes had the better insights and solutions should consider that Mr. Spock is in fact not only half-Vulcanian but also half-human and may thus have access to affective experiences as well.

ACKNOWLEDGMENTS

This research was supported by the Sonderforschungsbereich 504 "Rationalitätskonzepte, Entscheidungsverhalten und ökonomische Modellierung" at the University of Mannheim, Germany, and by the German Federal Ministry of Education and Research (BMFT) within the framework of the German-Israeli Project Cooperation (DIP).

REFERENCES

Bentham, J. (1789). *An introduction to the principles of morals and legislation*. Oxford, England: Clarendon.

Beukeboom, C. (2003). *How mood turns on language*. Doctoral dissertation, Free University of Amsterdam.

Bless, H. (1997). *Stimmung und Denken: Ein Modell zum Einfluß von Stimmungen auf Denkprozesse* [Affect and cognition]. Bern: Huber.

Bless, H. (2001). The relation between mood and the use of general knowledge structures. In L. L. Martin & G. L. Clore (Eds.), *Mood and social cognition: Contrasting theories* (pp. 9–29). Mahwah, NJ: Lawrence Erlbaum Associates, Inc.

Bless, H., Bohner, G., Schwarz, N., & Strack, F. (1990). Mood and persuasion: A cognitive response analysis. *Personality and Social Psychology Bulletin, 16,* 331–345.

Bless, H., Clore, G. L, Schwarz, N., Golisano, V., Rabe, C., & Wölk, M. (1996). Mood and the use of scripts: Does happy mood make people really mindless? *Journal of Personality and Social Psychology, 63*, 585–595.

Bless, H., & Fiedler, K. (1995). Affective states and the influence of activated general knowledge. *Personality and Social Psychology Bulletin, 21*, 766–778.

Bless, H., Fiedler, K., & Strack, F. (2004). *Social cognition: How individuals construct social reality*. Philadelphia: Psychology Press.

Bless, H., Hamilton, D. L., & Mackie, D. M. (1992). Mood effects on the organization of person information. *European Journal of Social Psychology, 22*, 497–509.

Bless, H., Mackie, D. M., & Schwarz, N. (1992). Mood effects on encoding and judgmental processes in persuasion. *Journal of Personality and Social Psychology, 63*, 585–595.

Bless, H., & Schwarz, N. (1999). Sufficient and necessary conditions in dual process models: The case of mood and information processing. In S. Chaiken & Y. Trope (Eds.), *Dual process theories in social psychology* (pp. 423–440). New York: Guilford Press.

Bless, H., Schwarz, N., & Wieland, R. (1996). Mood and stereotyping: The impact of category and individuating information. *European Journal of Social Psychology, 26*, 935–959.

Bodenhausen, G. V. (1993). Emotions, arousal, and stereotype-based discrimination: A heuristic model of affect and stereotyping. In D. M. Mackie & D. L. Hamilton (Eds.), *Affect, cognition, and stereotyping: Interactive processes in group perception* (pp. 13–35). San Diego, CA: Academic Press.

Bodenhausen, G. V., Kramer, G. P., & Süsser, K. (1994). Happiness and stereotypic thinking in social judgment. *Journal of Personality and Social Psychology, 66*, 621–632.

Bohner, G., Crow, K., Erb, H.-P., & Schwarz, N. (1992). Affect and persuasion: Mood effects on the processing of message content and context cues. *European Journal of Social Psychology, 22*, 511–530.

Bohner, G., Moskowitz, G. B., & Chaiken, S. (1995). The interplay of heuristic and systematic processing of social information. In W. Stroebe & M. Hewstone (Eds.), *European review of social psychology* (Vol. 6, pp. 33–68). Chichester: Wiley & Sons.

Bower, G. H. (1981). Mood and memory. *American Psychologist, 36*, 129–148.

Brewer, M. A. (1988). A dual model of impression formation. *Advances in Social Cognition, 1*, 1–35.

Chaiken, S. (1980). Heuristic versus systematic information and the use of source versus message cues in persuasion. *Journal of Personality and Social Psychology, 39*, 752–766.

Chaiken, S. (1987). The heuristic model of persuasion. In M. P. Zanna, J. M. Olson, & C. P. Herman (Eds.), *Social influence: The Ontario symposium* (Vol. 5, pp. 3–39). Hillsdale, NJ: Lawrence Erlbaum Associates, Inc.

Cialdini, R. B., & Kenrick, D. T. (1976). Altruism as hedonism: A social development perspective on the relationship of negative mood state and helping. *Journal of Personality and Social Psychology, 34*, 907–914.

Dovidio, J. F., Gaertner, S. L., & Loux, S. (2000). Subjective experiences and intergroup relations: The role of positive affect. In H. Bless & J. P. Forgas (Eds.), *The message within: The role of subjective experience in social cognition and behavior* (pp. 340–371). Philadelphia: Psychology Press.

Eagly, A. H., & Chaiken, S. (1993). *The psychology of attitudes*. Fort Worth, TX: Harcourt Brace Jovanovich.

Edwards, J. A., & Weary, G. (1993). Depression and the impression-formation continuum: Piecemeal processing despite the availability of category information. *Journal of Personality and Social Psychology, 64*, 636–645.

Erber, R. (1996). The self-regulation of moods. In L. L. Martin & A. Tesser (Eds.), *Striving and feeling: Interactions among goals, affect, and self-regulation* (pp. 251–275). Mahwah, NJ: Lawrence Erlbaum Associates, Inc.

Erber, R. (2001). Mood and processing: A view from a self-regulation perspective. In L. L. Martin & G. L. Clore (Eds.), *Mood and social cognition: Contrasting theories* (pp. 63–84). Mahwah, NJ: Lawrence Erlbaum Associates, Inc.

Erber, R., & Erber, W. E. (2000). The self-regulation of moods: Second thoughts on the importance of happiness in everyday life. *Psychological Inquiry, 11,* 142–148.

Erber, R., Wegner, D. M., & Therriault, N. (1996). On being cool and collected: Mood regulation in anticipation of social interaction. *Journal of Personality and Social Psychology, 70,* 757–766.

Fiedler, K. (1991). On the task, the measures, and the mood in research on affect and social cognition. In J. P. Forgas (Ed.), *Emotion and social judgments* (pp. 83–104). Cambridge: Cambridge University Press.

Fiedler, K., Nickel, S., Asbeck, J., & Pagel, U. (2003). Mood and the generation effect. *Cognition and Emotion, 17,* 585–608.

Fiedler, K., Nickel, S., Muehlfriedel, T., & Unkelbach, C. (2001). Is mood an effect of genuine memory or response bias? *Journal of Experimental Social Psychology, 37,* 201–214.

Fiske, S. T., & Neuberg, S. L. (1990). A continuum of impression formation from category-based to individuating processing: Influences of information and motivation on attention and interpretation. In M. P. Zanna (Ed.), *Advances in experimental social psychology* (Vol. 23, pp. 1–74). Orlando, FL: Academic Press.

Fiske, S. T., & Taylor, S. E. (1991). *Social cognition.* New York: McGraw-Hill.

Forgas, J. P. (1998). Asking nicely: Mood effects on responding to more or less polite requests. *Personality and Social Psychology Bulletin, 24,* 173–185.

Forgas, J. P. (1999). On feeling good and being rude: Affective influences on language use and request formulations. *Journal of Personality and Social Psychology, 76,* 928–939.

Forgas, J. P. (2000). Introduction: The role of affect in social cognition. In J. P. Forgas (Ed.), *Feeling and thinking: The role of affect in social cognition* (pp. 1–28). New York: Cambridge University Press.

Forgas, J. P., & Bower, G. H. (1987). Mood effects on person-perception judgments. *Journal of Personality and Social Psychology, 53,* 53–60.

Forgas, J. P., & Ciarrochi, J. V. (2002). On managing moods: Evidence for the role of homeostatic cognitive strategies in affect regulation. *Personality and Social Psychology Bulletin, 28,* 336–345.

Forgas, J. P., & Fiedler, K. (1996). Mood effects on intergroup discrimination: The role of affect in reward allocation recisions. *Journal of Personality and Social Psychology, 70,* 28–40.

Forgas, J. P., Laham, S. M., & Vargas, P. T. (2005). Mood effects on eyewitness memory: Affective influences on susceptibility to misinformation. *Journal of Experimental Social Psychology, 41,* 574–588.

Frijda, N. H. (1988). The laws of emotion. *American Psychologist, 43,* 349–358.

Gasper, K., & Clore, G. L. (2002). Attending to the big picture: Mood and global versus local processing of visual information. *Psychological Science, 13,* 34–40.

Hamilton, D. L., Katz, L. B., & Leirer, V. O. (1980). Cognitive representation of personality impressions: Organizational processes in first impression formation. *Journal of Personality and Social Psychology, 39,* 1050–1063.

Hertel, G., & Fiedler, K. (1994). Affective and cognitive influences in a social dilemma game. *European Journal of Social Psychology, 24,* 131–145.

Higgins, E. T. (1997). Beyond pleasure and pain. *American Psychologist, 52*, 1280–1300.

Higgins, E. T. (1998). Promotion and prevention: Regulatory focus as a motivational principle. In M. P. Zanna (Ed.), *Advances in experimental social psychology* (Vol. 30, pp. 1–46). San Diego, CA: Academic Press.

Hirt, E. R., Melton, R. J., McDonald, H. E., & Harackiewicz, J. M. (1996). Processing goals, task interest, and the mood-performance relationship: A mediational analysis. *Journal of Personality and Social Psychology, 71*, 245–261.

Innes, J. M., & Ahrens, C. R. (1991). Positive mood, processing goals, and the effects of information on evaluative judgment. In J. Forgas (Ed.), *Emotion and social judgment* (pp. 221–239). Oxford: Pergamon.

Isen, A. M. (1984). Toward understanding the role of affect in cognition. In R. S. Wyer, Jr. & T. K. Srull (Eds.), *Handbook of social cognition* (Vol. 3, pp. 179–236). Hillsdale, NJ: Lawrence Erlbaum Associates, Inc.

Isen, A. M. (1987). Positive affect, cognitive processes, and social behavior. In L. Berkowitz (Ed.), *Advances in experimental social psychology* (Vol. 20, pp. 203–253). San Diego, CA: Academic Press.

Isen, A. M., & Daubman, K. A. (1984). The influence of affect on categorization. *Journal of Personality and Social Psychology, 47*, 1206–1217.

Isen, A. M., Daubman, K. A., & Gorgoglione, J. M. (1987). The influence of positive affect on cognitive organization. In R. Snow & M. Farr (Eds.), *Aptitude, learning and instruction: Affective and conative processes* (Vol. 3). Hillsdale, NJ: Lawrence Erlbaum Associates, Inc.

Isen, A. M., Johnson, M. M. S., Mertz, E., & Robinson, G. (1985). The influence of positive affect on the unusualness of word association. *Journal of Personality and Social Psychology, 48*, 1413–1426.

Isen, A. M., Means, B., Patrick, R., & Nowicki, G. (1982). Some factors influencing decision making strategy and risk-taking. In M. S. Clark & S. T. Fiske (Eds.), *Affect and cognition: The 17th annual Carnegie Mellon symposium on cognition* (pp. 241–261). Hillsdale, NJ: Lawrence Erlbaum Associates, Inc.

Isen, A. M., Shalker, T. E., Clark, M. S., & Karp, L. (1978). Affect, accessibility of material in memory, and behavior: A cognitive loop? *Journal of Personality and Social Psychology, 36*, 1–12.

Krauth-Gruber, S., & Ric, F. (2000). Affect and stereotypic thinking: A test of the mood-and-general-knowledge-model. *Personality and Social Psychology Bulletin, 26*, 1587–1597.

Mackie, D. M., Asuncion, A. G., & Rosselli, F. (1992). The impact of positive affect on persuasion processes. In M. S. Clark (Ed.), *Review of personality and social psychology* (Vol. 14, pp. 247–270). Beverly Hills, CA: Sage.

Mackie, D. M., & Worth, L. T. (1989). Cognitive deficits and the mediation of positive affect in persuasion. *Journal of Personality and Social Psychology, 57*, 27–40.

Manucia, G., Baumann, D. J., Cialdini, R. B. (1984). Mood influences on helping: Direct effects or side effects? *Journal of Personality and Social Psychology, 46*, 357–364.

Martin, L. L. (2001). Moods don't cause effects, people do: A mood as input look at mood effects. In L. L. Martin & G. L. Clore (Eds.), *Mood and social cognition: Contrasting theories* (pp. 135–157). Mahwah, NJ: Lawrence Erlbaum Associates, Inc.

Martin, L. L., & Stoner, P. (1996). Mood as input: What people think about how they feel moods determines how they think. In L. L. Martin & A. Tesser (Eds.), *Striving and feeling: Interactions between goals, affect, and self-regulation* (pp. 279–301). Hillsdale, NJ: Lawrence Erlbaum Associates, Inc.

Martin, L. M., Ward, D. W., Achee, J. W., & Wyer, R. S. (1993). Mood as input: People have to interpret the motivational implications of their moods. *Journal of Personality and Social Psychology, 64,* 317–326.

Matlin, M. W., & Stang, D. J. (1979). *The Pollyanna principle.* Cambridge, MA: Schenkman.

Morris, W. N. (1989). *Mood: The frame of mind.* New York: Springer.

Morris, W. N., & Reilly, N. P. (1987). Toward the self-regulation of mood: Theory and research. *Motivation and Emotion, 11,* 215–249.

Murray, N., Sujan, H., Hirt, E. R., & Sujan, M. (1990). The influence of mood on categorization: A cognitive flexibility interpretation. *Journal of Personality and Social Psychology, 59,* 411–425.

Nisbett, R., & Ross, L. (1980). *Human inference: Strategies and shortcomings in social judgment.* Englewood Cliffs, NJ: Prentice-Hall.

Nowlis, V., & Nowlis, H. H. (1956). The description and analysis of mood. *Annals of the New York Academy of Sciences, 65,* 345–355.

Petty, R. E., & Cacioppo, J. T. (1986). The elaboration likelihood model of persuasion. In L. Berkowitz (Ed.), *Advances in experimental social psychology* (Vol. 19, pp. 124–203). New York: Academic Press.

Piaget, J. (1954). *The construction of reality in the child.* New York: Free Press.

Pribram, H. H. (1970). Feelings as monitors. In M. Arnold (Ed.), *Feelings and emotions* (pp. 41–53). New York: Academic Press.

Raghunathan, R., & Trope, Y. (2002). Walking the tightrope between feeling good and being accurate: Mood as a resource in processing persuasive messages. *Journal of Personality and Social Psychology, 83,* 510–525.

Roenker, D. L., Thompson, C. P., & Brown, S. C. (1971). Comparison of measures for the estimation of clustering in free recall. *Psychological Bulletin, 76,* 45–48.

Ruder, M., & Bless, H. (2003). Mood and the reliance on the ease of retrieval heuristic. *Journal of Personality and Social Psychology, 85,* 20–32.

Schaller, M., & Cialdini, R. B. (1988). The economics of empathic helping: Support for a mood management motive. *Journal of Experimental Social Psychology, 24,* 163–181.

Schwarz, N. (1990). Feelings as information: Informational and motivational functions of affective states. In R. M. Sorrentino & E. T. Higgins (Eds.), *Handbook of motivation and cognition: Foundations of social behavior* (Vol. 2, pp. 527–561). New York: Guilford Press.

Schwarz, N., Bless, H., & Bohner, G. (1991). Mood and persuasion: Affective states influence the processing of persuasive communications. In M. Zanna (Ed.), *Advances in experimental social psychology* (Vol. 24, pp. 161–197). New York: Academic Press.

Schwarz, N., & Clore, G. L. (1983). Mood, misattribution, and judgments of well-being: Informative and directive functions of affective states. *Journal of Personality and Social Psychology, 45,* 513–523.

Schwarz, N., & Clore, G. L. (1996). Feelings and phenomenal experiences. In E. T. Higgins & A. Kruglanski (Eds.), *Social psychology: A handbook of basic principles* (pp. 433–465). New York: Guilford Press.

Semin, G. R., & Fiedler, K. (1988). The cognitive functions of linguistic categories in describing persons: Social cognition and language. *Journal of Personality and Social Psychology, 54,* 558–568.

Sinclair, R. C. (1988). Mood, categorization breadth, and performance appraisal: The effects of order of information acquisition and affective state on halo, accuracy, information retrieval, and evaluations. *Organizational Behavior and Human Decision Processes, 42*, 22–46.

Sinclair, R. C., Mark, M. M., & Clore, G. L. (1994). Mood-related persuasion depends on misattributions. *Social Cognition, 12*, 309–326.

Stangor, C., & McMillan, D. (1992). Memory for expectancy-congruent and expectancy-incongruent information: A review of the social and social developmental literatures. *Psychological Bulletin, 111*, 42–61.

Trope, Y., Ferguson, M., & Raghunathan, R. (2001). Mood as a resource in processing self-relevant information. In J. P. Forgas (Ed.), *Handbook of affect and social cognition* (pp. 256–274). Mahwah, NJ: Lawrence Erlbaum Associates, Inc.

Trope, Y., & Liberman, N. (2003). Temporal construal. *Psychological Review, 110*, 403–421.

Vallacher, R. R., & Wegner, D. M. (1986). What do people think they're doing? Action identification theory and human information processing. *Psychological Review, 94*, 3–15.

Wegener, D. T., & Petty, R. E. (1994). Mood management across affective states: The hedonic contingency hypothesis. *Journal of Personality and Social Psychology, 66*, 1034–1048.

Wegener, D. T., & Petty, R. E. (1996). Effects of mood on persuasion processes. In L. L. Martin & A. Tesser (Eds.), *Striving and feeling: Interactions among goals, affect, and self-regulation* (pp. 303–328). Mahwah, NJ: Lawrence Erlbaum Associates, Inc.

Wegener, D. T., Petty, R. E., & Smith, S. M. (1995). Positive mood can increase or decrease message scrutiny: The hedonic contingency view of mood and message processing. *Journal of Personality and Social Psychology, 69*, 5–15.

Williams, S., & Voon, Y. W. W. (1999). The effects of *mood* on managerial *risk* perceptions: Exploring affect and the dimensions of *risk*. *Journal of Social Psychology, 139*, 268–287.

Worth, L. T., & Mackie, D. M. (1987). Cognitive mediation of positive affect in persuasion. *Social Cognition, 5*, 76–94.

5

Emotion-Eliciting Appraisals of Social Situations

CRAIG A. SMITH, BIEKE DAVID, and LESLIE D. KIRBY

*T*here is a notable dialectic in current emotion theory and research. On the one hand, and as the contributions to this volume attest, emotions are highly social. One of the basic functions commonly ascribed to emotion (e.g., Scherer, 1984) is that of *social communication*. Through their observable, expressive manifestations (postural, facial, vocal, etc.) emotions are thought to communicate much to members of the social environment about the emotional person's thoughts, feelings, and likely behaviors—for instance, whether the person is likely to strike out in anger, to give up and withdraw in sadness, or to perceive a serious danger in fear. This information can then be used by the perceiver to regulate his or her actions to both the expressive individual and the affect-eliciting circumstances—to apologize to the angry person, to offer support and comfort to the sad one, or to become more vigilant to potential danger in the fear-inducing circumstances. In addition, as several contributions in this volume emphasize (e.g., Bless & Fiedler, this volume; Clore & Storbeck, this volume; Forgas, this volume; Huppert, this volume; Sedikides, Wildschut, Arndt, & Routledge, this volume), our own emotional states affect our perceptions and cognitions in ways that influence decision making (e.g., Baumeister, Vohs, & Tice, this volume), interpersonal behaviors (e.g., Ciarrochi & Blackledge, this volume; Holmes & Anthony, this volume), and a broad array of additional behaviors that have social implications.

On the other hand, within *appraisal theory*—currently the dominant theoretical perspective concerned with the antecedents of emotion—the elicitation of emotions is viewed as a largely *intrapersonal*, self-centered process. On this view, emotions are elicited by appraisals or evaluations of what one's circumstances imply for *personal* well-being (see Smith & Lazarus, 1990). How one's circumstances are appraised is hypothesized to determine one's emotional state, with different appraisals leading to the experience of different emotions. As reviewed below, much of the research conducted to date on appraisal theory has maintained the self-centered focus evident in the above definition of appraisal. Although the research on appraisal theory working from this self-centered focus has contributed greatly to our understanding of the antecedents of emotion, it seems likely that the value and applicability of appraisal theory would increase if the approach would more explicitly embrace the highly social nature of emotion.

Therefore, we have two distinct goals in this chapter. The first is to review the current status of appraisal theory—to outline the major assumptions of the theory, to indicate the main theoretical issues addressed by research on the theory, and to review the empirical status of the theory. The second is to discuss some ways in which appraisal theory is being, and might be further, developed to increase the degree to which the theory both reflects and can theoretically account for the highly social nature of emotion.

APPRAISAL THEORY, ITS MAJOR ASSUMPTIONS, THEORETICAL ISSUES, AND CURRENT STATUS

Since its inception (e.g., Arnold, 1960; Lazarus, 1966) a primary purpose of appraisal theory has been to explain the often large and readily observable individual differences in emotional response to highly similar sets of circumstances (see, e.g., Lazarus, 1991; Roseman & Smith, 2001). For instance, an upcoming exam might represent an anxiety-producing threat to one individual, an invigorating challenge to another, and a largely nonaffective chore to yet a third. To explain such variation, appraisal theory asserts that emotional reactions are not directly elicited by the circumstances (or stimulus situations) themselves, but rather are elicited by the results of an evaluation, or "appraisal" of what those circumstances imply for the individual's personal well-being. This evaluation is proposed to take into account not only the nature of the circumstances themselves, but also how those circumstances relate to the individual's personal goals, needs, and abilities (e.g., Lazarus, 1991; Smith & Lazarus, 1990). Thus, different individuals (having different goals, needs, and abilities) will often appraise the same set of circumstances quite differently, and thus will respond with quite different emotions.

The development and testing of appraisal theory has been directed toward translating this general postulate into a series of more specific models that could then be subjected to empirical test. Virtually all of the work on appraisal theory conducted to date can be conceptualized as contributing to the development and testing of three distinct types of appraisal models—structural, procedural, and relational—each of which we review in turn.

Structural Models

The vast majority of theoretical and empirical work on appraisal theory has been directed toward the development and testing of *structural models*. These models attempt to describe the appraisal conditions under which different emotions are evoked (e.g., Lazarus, 1991; Roseman, 1984; Scherer, 1984; Smith & Lazarus, 1990). In particular, they have been developed to describe the *contents* of appraisal: the specific evaluations made by the individual, as well as the outcomes of these evaluations, which are responsible for evoking different emotions.

Several such models have been proposed (e.g., Lazarus, 1991; Roseman, 1984, 1991; Scherer, 1984; Smith & Ellsworth, 1985; Smith & Lazarus, 1990). Although these models differ in several respects (e.g., in some of the specific appraisal dimensions proposed to differentiate emotional experience; see Scherer, 1988 for an in-depth comparison of some of these models), far more telling is the fact that, overall, they are highly similar in the appraisal dimensions they propose and in the ways that outcomes along these dimensions are hypothesized to differentiate emotional experience.

Thus, in one form or another, the existing structural models of appraisal include some sort of evaluation of how important or relevant the stimulus situation is to the person, and this evaluation is hypothesized to determine the strength or intensity of the resulting emotional reaction. They also include an evaluation of whether the situation is desirable or undesirable, which is hypothesized to differentiate pleasant or positive emotions (resulting from appraised desirable circumstances) from unpleasant or negative ones (resulting from appraised undesirable circumstances). Two additional dimensions of appraisal have generally been represented in the structural models to further differentiate among different forms of emotion associated with undesirable circumstances. First, most models include one or more dimensions reflecting the person's assessment of the degree to which he or she is able to cope, or contend, with the situation. The evaluation of coping ability is hypothesized to differentiate emotions such as sadness and fear (associated with appraised low coping ability) from states of calmness, challenge, and determination (associated with appraised high coping ability). Second, most models also include some sort of an evaluation of who or what caused, or is responsible for, the situation, typically represented as an evaluation of self- versus other-responsibility. This responsibility evaluation is hypothesized to differentiate between emotions of anger (appraised other-responsibility) and shame or guilt (appraised self-responsibility).

To date, a considerable body of research has been directed toward testing these models, and substantial evidence in support of them has accrued. In particular, many studies have now asked participants to report on both their appraisals and a wide array of emotions across a variety of contexts, including diverse retrospectively remembered experiences (Frijda, Kuipers, & ter Schure, 1989; Scherer, 1997; Smith & Ellsworth, 1985; Smith, Haynes, Lazarus, & Pope, 1993), and hypothetical vignettes (e.g., Roseman, 1991; Smith & Lazarus, 1993). The results of these studies have been highly supportive of the appraisal approach. In each of these studies, not only have the experiences of different emotions been consistently found to be reliably and systematically associated with different appraisals but also the specific relations observed between the appraisals and the emotions have largely been in line with the models being investigated. Thus, at the present time, there can be little question that the patterns of appraisal hypothesized by the structural appraisal models to elicit specific emotions are, by and large, strongly correlated with those emotions.

Much of the more recent work on the structural appraisal models has attempted to build on and test the documented relations between appraisal and emotion in one of two ways. First, there have been a number of attempts to address the methodological limitations of the existing work. As critiqued by Parkinson (1997; Parkinson & Manstead, 1992), virtually all of the research cited above has been strictly correlational, and it has been heavily dependent on the examination of either remembered or hypothetical events. Thus, there is considerable ambiguity as to whether appraisal is a causal antecedent of emotion as hypothesized, and there is some question as to whether the documented relations reflect actual linkages between appraisal and emotion, or whether they more directly reflect respondents' lay theories concerning those linkages (Russell, 1987). Although these methodological concerns have not yet been fully resolved, a number of more recent studies have begun to address them. In particular, a number of studies have examined appraisal–emotion relations in the context of meaningful, ongoing experiences (e.g., Griner & Smith, 2000; Kirby & Smith, in press; Roseman & Evdokas, 2004; Smith & Ellsworth, 1987), and in several of these studies efforts have been made to manipulate the appraisals to be examined either quasi-experimentally (Griner & Smith, 2000; Kirby & Smith, in press) or experimentally (Roseman & Evdokas, 2004). In each case, these methodologically stronger studies have also been highly supportive of the structural appraisal models being examined. Thus, evidence is mounting to indicate both that the documented relations between appraisal and emotion reflect genuine linkages rather than mere lay theories, and that appraisal serves a causal role in the elicitation of emotion.

In addition to these attempts to shore up appraisal theory, there have also been attempts to examine whether the appraisal patterns hypothesized for particular emotions are necessary and sufficient for the experience of those emotions, and the results of these studies suggest that the hypothesized links between appraisal and emotion may not be as invariant as hypothesized. For instance, Kuppens, Van Mechelen, Smits, and de Boek (2003) have provided data suggesting that, although appraisals of other-responsibility bear a strong relation to anger, they are neither necessary nor sufficient to evoke anger. Such studies, although currently rare, are important for the development of appraisal theory because they suggest important boundary conditions for the theory and present challenges that should help spur the theory's further development.

Procedural Models

The second class of appraisal models being developed and tested are *procedural* ones designed to describe the processes underlying the emotion-eliciting appraisals. That is, these models describe the cognitive operations by which appraisals are made. A primary theoretical motivation for these models has been to explain how appraisals can serve as elicitors of emotions when often the emotions seem to arise automatically, unbidden, and outside of the person's conscious awareness (Smith & Kirby, 2000). As critics of the appraisal approach to emotion have correctly noted (e.g., Izard, 1992; Zajonc, 1980), such quick and seemingly automatically elicited emotions are very difficult for appraisal theory to handle if appraisal is a conscious, volitional, largely verbally mediated process. From the beginning, appraisal theorists have been very consistent in maintaining that appraisals could be automatic, fast, and "intuitive" (e.g., Arnold, 1960), rather than necessarily being conscious and volitional (see Smith & Kirby, 2000). However, until recently, appraisal theorists have remained largely silent as to *how* appraisals might be made automatically and outside of awareness. A number of process models have now been proposed in an attempt to fill this explanatory void (e.g., Lazarus, 1991; Leventhal & Scherer, 1987; Scherer, 2001; Smith & Kirby, 2000, 2001; van Reekum & Scherer, 1997).

Although, as with the structural models, the proposed process models differ in a number of details, they are formally rather similar in that they each propose that appraisal involves at least two distinct levels of processing: a slow, deliberate, likely verbally mediated form of processing, often referred to as "conceptual processing" (Leventhal & Scherer, 1987) or "reasoning" (Smith & Kirby, 2000), and a fast, automatic, memory-based mode of processing involving such things as priming and spreading activation, often referred to as "schematic processing" (Leventhal & Scherer, 1987) or "associative processing" (Smith & Kirby, 2000). It is this latter mode of processing that enables appraisals to elicit emotions quickly, automatically, and outside of awareness. For instance, as proposed by Smith and Kirby (2000), as memories associated with particular emotional reactions and appraisals become activated (e.g., due to perceived similarities between the past experiences and one's present circumstances), the associated appraisals become activated as well, and when those appraisals become sufficiently activated the associated emotion will be automatically elicited.

Although the Leventhal and Scherer (1987) model was proposed some time ago, it is only fairly recently that concerted efforts to develop and test such models have been undertaken (e.g., Scherer, 2001; Smith & Kirby, 2000, 2001). Thus, although there is good support for the general plausibility of these models (e.g., Sloman, 1996; Smith & DeCoster, 2000), few data have yet directly tested them. Given that many critics of appraisal theory (e.g., Izard, 1992; Zajonc, 1980) have tended to assume that appraisal generally corresponds to reasoning or conceptual processing as described by the process models, the relatively little research that has been conducted has been directed toward documenting the existence of the more automatic mode of associative or schematic processing. For instance, in one series of studies, over the course of repeated trials in a video game van Reekum (2000) had participants quickly categorize spaceships differing in the sounds they emitted as friends or foes. Then, halfway through the game, participants were told to switch the contingencies, such that former "friends" were now "foes," and vice versa. Although at the time of the switch participants had explicit conceptual knowledge of the changed contingencies, reaction times were substantially slowed for several trials following the switch, which van Reekum interpreted as interference from an associatively conditioned expectation that had been established during the initial trials. This suggested that for a number of trials the spaceships were being appraised in opposite ways at the conceptual (reasoning) and associative levels of processing. In another study, Kirby, Edwards, and Smith (2004) have presented preliminary data that appraisals of coping ability can be incidentally primed, and that such primed appraisals can influence both one's emotional reactions and one's performance on a challenging problem-solving task. Specifically, primed appraisals of high coping ability, relative to ones of low coping ability, were associated with decreased feelings of resignation, and increased probability of solving the problem when attempting to solve a difficult math word problem.

Such initial findings are encouraging, but, obviously, the process models are in need of further development and testing. Current efforts in our lab are pursuing this end. First, to shore up the evidence for the existence of multiple levels of processing in appraisal, we are replicating and extending our initial appraisal priming study (Kirby et al., 2004) to examine the degree to which associative effects can be observed with subliminal priming. In addition, we are currently pursuing studies designed to explore the boundary conditions of both reasoning and associative processing, and to explore ways in which the various levels of processing interact.

Relational Models

A third class of appraisal models, *relational* ones, have also begun to be developed and tested. These models attempt to describe the relational antecedents of emotion-eliciting appraisals, or, in other words, to describe the information that is drawn on in making the appraisals. As reviewed above, a central tenet of appraisal theory is that emotion-eliciting appraisals represent evaluations of what a person's circumstances imply for his or her personal well-being *in relation to* his or her goals, needs, and abilities (Smith & Lazarus, 1990). In the work conducted on appraisal theory to date, however, relatively little attention has been devoted either to specifying the type of situational and personal information that is drawn on in making the appraisals, or how this information is combined to produce appraisal outcomes. For example, although there is now considerable research examining the degree to which appraisals of other-responsibility contribute to feelings of anger (e.g., Kuppens et al., 2003; Smith & Lazarus, 1993; Smith et al., 1993), there has been very little work examining the types of situational and/or dispositional information that are drawn on to determine whether and to what degree the other person is to be held accountable.

The goal of relational models of appraisal is to address this type of issue. Such models are potentially theoretically very important because they greatly increase the predictive utility of appraisal theory: by knowing both which features of the person and/or the situation are likely to be drawn on in appraising one's circumstances, and how those features are likely to be combined to produce specific appraisal outcomes, one gains the potential to predict how a particular individual is likely to appraise, and thus respond emotionally to, a particular set of circumstances. In fact, a theoretical emphasis on the relational nature of appraisal is a hallmark of appraisal theory that has been frequently discussed in the literature (e.g., Lazarus, 1966, 1991; Lazarus & Folkman, 1984; Lazarus & Launier, 1978; Smith & Lazarus, 1990), and described as one of the most important properties of appraisal. It is somewhat surprising, therefore, that relatively little research has been directed toward documenting the relational nature of appraisal.

In fact, to our knowledge, our research group has been the only one actively pursuing the development of relational models of appraisal. To date, we have initiated three distinct lines of inquiry, each examining the relational antecedents of a particular appraisal component included in our version of a structural appraisal model (i.e., that of Smith & Lazarus, 1990). Here we briefly review our initial progress along each of these three research lines.

First, we have investigated the antecedents of appraisals of *importance*. Smith and Pope (1992) hypothesized that the perceived importance of a situation would be a joint function of a person's concerns and the degree to which a situation was relevant to those concerns. To generate specific, testable hypotheses from this principle, they noted that individuals vary in the degree to which they are committed to, or motivated by, affiliative versus achievement concerns. They reasoned that when confronted with an achievement relevant situation, individuals high in achievement motivation would respond with higher appraisals of importance, and stronger emotion, than would individuals lower in achievement motivation. Conversely, for affiliative situations, individuals higher in affiliative motivation should respond with higher appraisals of importance and stronger emotion.

Using remembered experiences and hypothetical vignettes, Smith and Pope (1992) confirmed these hypotheses for achievement-relevant situations, but not for affiliative ones. However, in a subsequent study (Griner & Smith, 2000), involving a real-time interpersonal interaction (a teaching task), the hypotheses were supported within the affiliative domain as well: while anticipating the start of the task, affiliatively oriented individuals reported that they viewed the upcoming task as having more affiliative relevance, and in line with this they reported their appraisals of importance and their feelings of interest as being stronger than did less affiliative individuals. In combination, these studies provide considerable support to Smith and Pope's (1992) hypotheses regarding the antecedents of appraised importance.

In a parallel fashion, Smith and Pope (1992) proposed that appraisals of *coping ability* were a joint function of both the demands of the task confronting the individual and the individual's perceived abilities relevant to those demands. They reported on a pilot study in which individuals selected to be either more or less confident of their mathematical abilities reported on their appraisal and emotions while working on a difficult math task. As predicted, higher levels of perceived math ability were associated with higher levels of appraised coping ability, higher levels of felt challenge, and lower levels of resignation. These initial findings were replicated and extended in a subsequent study reported by Kirby and Smith (in press).

Finally, Smith and colleagues (e.g., Smith & Noser, 1998) have attempted to model the informational antecedents of appraisals of *self- versus other-responsibility* hypothesized to differentiate between the emotions of guilt and anger, respectively. In their analysis, Smith and Noser (1998) follow the lead of Smith and Lazarus (1990; Lazarus & Smith, 1988; Smith et al., 1993) and draw a distinction between attributions, such as that of causal locus as discussed by Weiner (1985), and appraisals, such as those of responsibility. In what they refer to as a "Heiderian" (Heider, 1958) attributional analysis, Smith and Noser (1998) argue that, all else being equal, attributed causal locus will determine appraised responsibility. However, several mitigating factors including evaluations of intentionality, foreseeability, and controllability can moderate this relationship through their influence on the perceived justifiability of the situation. Generally speaking, the extent to which the mitigating factors combine to increase the perceived justifiability of the perceived causal agent for the unwanted situation (whether oneself or someone else) will be held less responsible for the situation, resulting in reduced levels of anger or guilt.

Drawing on data involving both remembered experiences and learning one's grades on a midterm exam, Smith and Noser (1998) found considerable support for their account. Both justifiability and causal locus were found to contribute to appraisals of responsibility, and the influences of justifiability and causal locus on the relevant emotion (i.e., on anger and guilt) were mediated through the appraisals of responsibility, as hypothesized. In addition, any effects of the mitigating factors of controllability, foreseeability, and intentionality on responsibility, and hence anger or guilt, were mediated through the assessment of justifiability.

These initial developments are quite promising. In each case much has been learned about the nature of the antecedent information that is evaluated in making a particular type of appraisal. As noted above, such information is important for developing the theory to the point where it can be used to predict or explain a particular individual's specific emotional reactions to a certain set of circumstances. Although promising, these initial developments only scratch the surface of what needs to be done in developing relational models of appraisal. The antecedents of the full complement of appraisal dimensions contributing to emotion elicitation need to be modeled, and even for those that have been examined so far their antecedents need to be examined across a much broader range of contexts than has been the case to date.

ON INCREASING THE SOCIALITY OF APPRAISAL THEORY

At the outset we noted that there is an important theoretical tension in appraisal theory. Whereas emotions are highly social phenomena, emotion-eliciting appraisal, at least as depicted in current theory, is highly self-centered. Having reviewed the current state of development of appraisal theory, we would now like to turn our attention to briefly considering ways in which appraisal theory might be further developed and extended to better account for the social nature of emotion. Although we believe that the theoretical depiction of appraisal as self-centered is largely accurate, it is also clear that these appraisals do not occur in a social vacuum. For modern humans, many emotion-eliciting situations are social creations, and often highly interpersonal. Even deeply personal events, such as losing one's job or learning that one has a serious chronic illness, have important, wide-ranging interpersonal implications. Therefore, we believe that in its future development it is vital that appraisal theory more explicitly embrace the highly social nature of both appraisal and emotion. In exploring the ways that the sociality of appraisal might be better captured theoretically, we begin by considering how certain appraisals and emotions encompassed by the theory already are quite interpersonal. Then we consider several directions in which the theory might be profitably extended to increase its sociality.

Inherently Interpersonal Appraisals and Emotions Already Handled by Appraisal Theory: Anger and Guilt

At least two of the emotions commonly considered by appraisal theory—anger and guilt—are associated with appraisals that are inherently interpersonal. Both emotions are associated with an evaluation of who, either the self or someone else, is responsible for an undesired situation: if someone else is held responsible, then anger results, whereas if one holds oneself responsible, guilt results. The social nature of these two emotions and their antecedent appraisals are further highlighted if one considers the functions posited to be served by these emotions (e.g., Ellsworth & Smith, 1988; Izard, 1977; Plutchik, 1980; Smith & Lazarus, 1990; Tomkins, 1963). The function commonly proposed for anger is to remove an external source of harm (i.e., the person appraised as responsible for the problem) from the environment, and to undo the harm if possible; whereas in guilt the focus is on the self, who has been appraised as responsible, and the proposed function of guilt is to motivate the person to make reparations for harms that he or she has caused, and, more generally, to motivate pro-social behavior. In both cases, the appraisal of responsibility serves to identify a social target toward whom to direct one's emotion-related behaviors, whether it be to get someone else to stop their harmful behavior in anger, or toward oneself to make amends to others for perceived wrongs that one has committed.

Although we feel that appraisal theory has more of a social orientation than may at first appear to be the case, it is nonetheless true that appraisal models need to be extended to better take the social context of emotional experience into account. One way to accomplish this is to increase the range of emotions addressed by structural appraisal models.

Accounting for Differences among Guilt, Shame, Embarrassment: The Need to Extend Appraisal Models

Consider the emotions of guilt, shame, and embarrassment. All three emotions are often referred to as "self-conscious" emotions (e.g., Tangney, 1990, 1992), and all three arise in negative circumstances appraised as having been brought about by oneself. Thus, all three emotions share some strong "family resemblances." In fact, historically, shame and guilt have often been treated as synonyms referring to the same underlying emotion, and there is a long tradition of considering embarrassment to be a mild form of shame (e.g., Borg, Staufenbiel, & Scherer, 1988; Tomkins, 1987). However, although the exact differences among these emotions remain somewhat controversial, there is a growing theoretical consensus emerging regarding the key differences among them (e.g., Parkinson, Fischer, & Manstead, 2005; Sabini, Garvey, & Hall, 2001; Sabini & Silver, 1997; Tangney, 1990, 1992).

First, there is a fair degree of consensus that guilt focuses on a specific event or transgression committed by the person that violates internal standards (e.g., Tangney, 1990), whereas in shame the focus appears to be more on a more general problem regarding the self—often a perceived character flaw (e.g., Parkinson et al., 2005; Tangney, 1990). Second, in both shame and embarrassment there appears to be a focus on the evaluation of the (flawed) self by others that does not seem to characterize guilt (Parkinson et al., 2005; Sabini et al., 2001; Tangney, 1990). However, in shame the negative evaluation by others need not have occurred, but can be simply anticipated if others were to find out about the perceived flaw (Parkinson et al., 2005; Tangney, 1990). In contrast, in embarrassment actual public exposure of the perceived flaw is more central (Parkinson et al., 2005). In addition, in shame the person believes that the flaw he or she is concerned about revealing is real and reflects a true shortcoming in his or her character, whereas in embarrassment the person views the perceived flaw as something that might lower his or her esteem in the eyes of observers, but which in his or her own eyes does not reflect a true personal shortcoming (Sabini et al., 2001; Sabini & Silver, 1997). For example, a woman who trips while walking across a stage to receive an award will likely feel embarrassed, but not ashamed, because although worried that the audience might think she is clumsy, she knows this is not the case, but that it was a momentary distraction, not general clumsiness that led her to trip.

In general, as currently proposed, none of the current major appraisal models (i.e., Roseman, 1984, 1991, 2001; Scherer, 1984, 2001; Smith & Lazarus, 1990) do a terribly good job of capturing the differences among these three emotions. None of the models even consider embarrassment, and thus they have not attempted to differentiate it from shame and guilt. Moreover, the Smith and Lazarus (1990) model does not differentiate between shame and guilt, but rather hypothesizes that both emotions are associated with appraisal of holding oneself responsible for an undesirable situation. Although other appraisal models (e.g., Roseman, 1984, 1991, 2001; Scherer, 1984, 2001) do make some fairly minor distinctions between the appraisals associated with shame versus guilt, it appears that none of them have the available constructs needed to adequately capture the concern, seemingly central to both shame and embarrassment, that one may be, or is in the process of being, judged by others and that oneself is likely to be found lacking. We are not yet sure of the best way to build such an evaluation into any of these appraisal models without giving the models too much of an ad hoc feel. However, we believe that efforts to do so will reflect an important extension to appraisal theory that will increase the theory's ability to account for the social aspects of emotional experience, and we are currently pursuing this avenue ourselves.

Appraisal as a Social Process

A second way that appraisal theory can be extended to better take the social context of appraisal and emotion into account is to begin to consider appraisal as a social process, rather than as a purely intrapersonal one. Although consideration of the descriptions of existing appraisal models might lead one to suspect that most emotion-eliciting appraisals are made by lone individuals with little or no input from others in the social environment, this clearly is not the case. We are a gregarious species and we talk to one another about the important things that are happening in our lives (and which are likely to be accompanied by considerable emotion). The information we extract from such conversations very likely systematically influences and shapes the appraisals, and hence the emotions, we experience. Although, to our knowledge, appraisal theorists have not yet considered how input from the social environment might affect appraisal, we believe that it is important for appraisal theory to develop in this direction. Below we highlight three literatures we believe provide important leads as to how appraisals are likely to be influenced through social interaction.

First, *seeking social support* is a common coping response to stressful events (Carver, Scheier, & Weintraub, 1989; Dunkel-Schetter, Folkman, & Lazarus, 1987; Ptacek, Smith, & Dodge, 1994). In addition to seeking help, or instrumental support, individuals often also seek informational and emotional support. That is, they talk with their friends about the stressful events, gaining information about them that might change their appraisals of, and hence their emotional reactions to, the situation.

A very similar theme can be found in the literature on the *social sharing of emotion*, advanced by Rimé and colleagues (e.g., Luminet, Bouts, Delie, Manstead, & Rimé, 2000; Rimé, Mesquita, Philippot, & Boca, 1991). An extremely common, almost ubiquitous response to strong emotional experiences is to seek out opportunities to talk about the emotional experience with others in one's social environment. In these conversations the person will talk about the circumstances leading up to the emotional reaction, his or her feelings in the situation, and his or her reactions to the experience more generally. In reviewing their work on the social sharing of emotion, Rimé, Corsini, and Herbette (2002) note that this sharing appears to be related to a need to "search for meaning" and/or to come to terms with the emotional event. In other words, it appears that through this social sharing others in the social environment help the person to shape and validate his or her appraisals of emotionally significant events.

In the third literature, Snyder and colleagues (e.g., Snyder, 1989; Snyder & Higgins, 1988, 1997) have examined the role of excuses in a process that they refer to as *"reality negotiation."* They have found that when caught in a situation involving a personal transgression (i.e., a situation that should elicit guilt or shame), individuals will engage in a "negotiation" with others in the social environment, in which, through the use of excuses, they seek to minimize the negative impact of the situation on themselves. Notably, the excuses that are proffered are typically designed to reduce the perceived seriousness of the transgression (referred to as "valence-of-act" by the authors, but essentially the appraised motivational incongruence of the situation), or the person's perceived responsibility for the situation (referred to by the authors as "linkage-to-act"; e.g., Snyder & Higgins, 1997). Thus, through the excuses, the person who committed the transgression seeks to minimize the appraisals leading to shame or guilt. The investigators note that the persons in the social environment often serve as active co-conspirators in the reality negotiation process, and often work with the person to support the modified appraisals meant to be produced through the offered excuses (Snyder & Higgins, 1988).

Together, these three literatures indicate that emotional experiences are very social in a way that must strongly influence the person's appraisals of emotion-eliciting circumstances, however self-centered those appraisals may be. Whether it is conceptualized as support seeking, emotional sharing, or reality negotiation, individuals appear to talk extensively with others in their social environment about their emotional experiences, and it appears that these emotion-related discussions serve to help shape the person's appraisals of the emotion-eliciting event. Thus, it appears that a very important and promising direction for the development of appraisal theory is to make more meaningful contact with the literatures alluded to above, and to begin to explicitly model the influences of the social environment on the appraisal process.

Social Extensions to the Self and Self-Interest

Although, as we have been arguing thus far, both the contents and processes of appraisal are more socially oriented than current appraisal models suggest, it is still the case that, ultimately, we agree with the theoretical characterization of appraisal as highly self-centered, in that appraisal is an evaluation of what one's circumstances imply for *personal* well-being. However, in this final section, we want to argue that even this self-centeredness can be subject to considerable social influence.

First, our sense of self does not develop in a vacuum, but rather in a social context. We come to identify with certain individuals and groups and to differentiate ourselves from others. This identification process can have profound effects on our self-concept, and thus on how we appraise our social environment. It is now generally accepted that people's identities are shaped in part through their relationships with others (Aron & McLaughlin-Volpe, 2001; Hogg, 2001; Lancaster & Foddy, 1988; Sedikides & Brewer, 2001; Smith, Coats & Walling, 1999). As individuals enter into close relationships with others, these relationships help the individual to define his or her goals, values, and expectations in ways that help determine what the individual will appraise as important, what he or she will appraise as good or bad, what is blameworthy, and so on. And thus, by helping to shape the individual's identity and beliefs, these sources of social influence also help to shape the individual's personal appraisals and emotions.

Second, our self-interest is not purely about our own individual self. Instead, when we are in very close relationships, and when we strongly identify with another person or group, we can incorporate these others into our self-concept, such that their well-being becomes an extension of our own personal well-being. Specifically, it appears that the boundaries of one's self-concept can be expanded to incorporate certain others, such that their interests become one's own self-interest as well. As noted by Smith et al. (1999), "close relationships and group membership both involve some sort of merging of self and of other" and "this process may deeply influence cognition, affect, and behavior in relationships and group contexts" (p. 881). Aron and McLaughlin-Volpe (2001) noted that this merging of oneself with another entails that people to some degree assume their close other's motives and cognitions. Thus, in appraising the relevance of one's circumstances for personal well-being, the concerns of the other explicitly can be taken into account.

The boundaries of the self also can be extended to encompass others through the social roles we assume (Lancaster & Foddy, 1988). These roles are almost always connected to a significant *role-other*: mothers have children, husbands have a wife, graduate mentors have a graduate student, and so on. Often in the eyes of the social environment, due to the role relationship, the way in which the role-other behaves is in part perceived as the responsibility of the actor. For example, a young child's behavior in public is often seen as being the responsibility of the child's parents. Thus, when the child acts out in public (e.g., throwing a tantrum in a grocery store), the parent is often viewed with disapproval. Thus, it becomes part of the parent's direct self-interest to help the child to successfully navigate the particular public encounter. There are numerous social roles that a person might assume (parent, teacher, caregiver, etc.), in which by taking on the role the person becomes directly responsible for another's well-being. In such cases it is very natural and adaptive for the self-interests of the parties involved in the role relationships to become heavily merged.

Thus, it appears that the definition of the "self" that provides the basis of one's self-interest in appraisal is itself rather socially defined and quite interpersonal in nature. Expanding the scope of appraisal theory so that it more explicitly takes into account the social, interpersonal nature of the self represents an important future direction for appraisal theorists.

SUMMARY AND CONCLUSIONS

Appraisal theory represents an important and influential approach to understanding emotion. In fact, it appears to be the only contemporary theoretical approach that provides a viable account of *how* emotions are elicited. In this chapter we have reviewed the current status of appraisal theory, noted several directions in which the theory is currently being developed, and identified a new direction in which we think it is very important to begin extending the theory. As we have reviewed, there are a number of well-developed *structural appraisal models* that identify the specific appraisals hypothesized to elicit specific emotions, and the empirical data in support of such models are quite strong. By themselves, the existence of these well-validated structural models makes the appraisal approach a valuable one for understanding the elicitation of emotion. In addition, however, two additional classes of models are currently under development, and they promise to further strengthen the value of appraisal theory: *process models* that outline the cognitive operations underlying appraisal, and *relational models* that identify the situational and dispositional information that is combined in appraisal to produce the emotion-eliciting evaluations of what one's circumstances imply for personal well-being. In terms of appraisal theory's future development, we have highlighted the importance of extending the theory to better capture the social nature of appraisal. We have made the case that, although nominally focused on one's personal self-interest, appraisals are highly social in several respects: individuals often discuss with others their emotional experiences, and these discussions almost certainly help define the individual's appraisals of those experiences; one's self-concept is in part defined by significant others in the social environment; and the boundaries of the self-concept can be expanded to incorporate the interests and concerns of others who are sufficiently important to the person. As a result, however self-centered appraisals might be, they are often far from selfish.

Thus, it appears that appraisals, although based on one's self-interest, are, in fact, every bit as interpersonal and social as the emotions they elicit. If appraisal theory is to meet its full potential, such that it can be better integrated with theoretical perspectives that emphasize the social and interpersonal nature and functions of emotion (e.g., Bless & Fiedler, this volume; Forgas, this volume; Holmes & Anthony, this volume), it is crucial for the theory to better explain and account for the highly social nature of both appraisal and emotion. Efforts toward achieving this goal are under way in our lab, and we hope other appraisal theorists will expand their research lines to address these important issues as well.

REFERENCES

Arnold, M. B. (1960). *Emotion and personality* (2 vols.). New York: Columbia University Press.

Aron, A., & McLaughlin-Volpe, T. (2001). Including others in the self. In C. Sedikides & M. B. Brewer (Eds.), *Individual self, relational self, collective self* (pp. 89–108). Philadelphia: Psychology Press.

Borg, I., Staufenbiel, T., & Scherer, K. R. (1988). On the symbolic basis of shame. In K. R. Scherer (Ed.), *Facets of emotion: Recent research* (pp. 79–98). Hillsdale, NJ: Lawrence Erlbaum Associates, Inc.

Carver, C. S., Scheier, M. F., & Weintraub, J. K. (1989). Assessing coping strategies: A theoretically-based approach. *Journal of Personality and Social Psychology, 56,* 267–283.

Dunkel-Schetter, C., Folkman, S., & Lazarus, R. S. (1987). Correlates of social support receipt. *Journal of Personality and Social Psychology, 53,* 71–80.

Ellsworth, P. C., & Smith, C. A. (1988). From appraisal to emotion: Differences among unpleasant feelings. *Motivation and Emotion, 12,* 271–302.

Frijda, N. H., Kuipers, P., & ter Schure, E. (1989). Relations among emotion, appraisal, and emotional action readiness. *Journal of Personality and Social Psychology, 57,* 212–228.

Griner, L. A., & Smith, C. A. (2000). Contributions of motivational orientation to appraisal and emotion. *Personality and Social Psychology Bulletin, 26,* 727–740.

Heider, F. (1958). *The psychology of interpersonal relations.* New York: Wiley.

Hogg, M. A. (2001). Social identity and the sovereignty of the group: A psychology of belonging. In C. Sedikides & M. B. Brewer (Eds.), *Individual self, relational self, collective self* (pp. 125–146). Philadelphia: Psychology Press.

Izard, C. E. (1977). *Human emotions.* New York: Plenum.

Izard, C. E. (1992). Basic emotions, relations among emotions, and emotion-cognition relations. *Psychological Review, 99,* 561–565.

Kirby, L. D., Edwards, J. S., & Smith, C. A. (July 2004). *Priming appraisals: An early test of a process model of emotion elicitation.* New York: International Society for Research on Emotions.

Kirby, L. D., & Smith, C. A. (in press). Relational antecedents of appraised problem-focused coping potential and its associated emotions. *Cognition and Emotion.*

Kuppens, P., Van Mechelen, I., Smits, D. J. M., & de Boek, P. (2003). The appraisal basis of anger: Specificity, necessity, and sufficiency of components. *Emotion, 3,* 254–269.

Lancaster, S., & Foddy, M. (1988). Self-extensions: A conceptualization. *Journal for the Theory of Social Behavior, 18,* 77–94.

Lazarus, R. S. (1966). *Psychological stress and the coping process.* New York: McGraw-Hill.

Lazarus, R. S. (1991). *Emotion and adaptation.* New York: Oxford University Press.

Lazarus, R. S., & Folkman, S. (1984). *Stress, appraisal, and coping.* New York: Springer.

Lazarus, R. S., & Launier, R. (1978). Stress-related transactions between person and environment. In L. A. Pervin (Ed.), *Perspectives in interactional psychology* (pp. 287–327). New York: Plenum.

Lazarus, R. S., & Smith, C. A. (1988). Knowledge and appraisal in the cognition-emotion relationship. *Cognition and Emotion, 2,* 281–300.

Leventhal, H., & Scherer, K. R. (1987). The relationship of emotion to cognition: A functional approach to a semantic controversy. *Cognition and Emotion, 1,* 3–28.

Luminet, O., Bouts, P., Delie, R., Manstead, A. S. R., & Rimé, B. (2000). Social sharing of emotion following exposure to a negatively valenced situation. *Cognition and Emotion, 14,* 661–688.

Parkinson, B. (1997). Untangling the appraisal-emotion connection. *Personality and Social Psychology Review, 1,* 72–79.

Parkinson, B., Fischer, A. H., & Manstead, A. S. R. (2005). *Emotion in social relations: Cultural, group, and interpersonal processes.* New York: Psychology Press.

Parkinson, B., & Manstead, A. S. R. (1992). Appraisal as a cause of emotion. In M. S. Clark (Ed.), *Review of personality and social psychology: Vol. 13: Emotion* (pp. 122–149). Newbury Park, CA: Sage.

Plutchik, R. (1980). *Emotion: A psychoevolutionary synthesis.* New York: Harper & Row.

Ptacek, J. T., Smith, R. E., & Dodge, K. L. (1994). Gender differences in coping with stress: When stressor and appraisals do not differ. *Personality and Social Psychology Bulletin, 20,* 421–430.

Rimé, B., Corsini, S., & Herbette, G. (2002). Emotion, verbal expression, and the social sharing of emotion. In S. R. Fussell (Ed.), *The verbal communication of emotions: Interdisciplinary perspectives* (pp. 185–208). Mahwah, NJ: Lawrence Erlbaum Associates, Inc.

Rimé, B., Mesquita, B., Philippot, P., & Boca, S. (1991). Beyond the emotional event: Six studies on the social sharing of emotion. *Cognition and Emotion, 5,* 435–465.

Roseman, I. J. (1984). Cognitive determinants of emotion: A structural theory. In P. Shaver (Ed.), *Review of personality and social psychology: Vol. 5. Emotions, relationships, and health* (pp. 11–36). Beverly Hills, CA: Sage.

Roseman, I. J. (1991). Appraisal determinants of discrete emotions. *Cognition and Emotion, 5,* 161–200.

Roseman, I. J. (2001). A model of appraisal in the emotion system: Integrating theory, research, and applications. In K. R. Scherer, A. Schorr, & T. Johnstone (Eds.), *Appraisal processes in emotion: Theory, methods, research* (pp. 68–91). New York: Oxford University Press.

Roseman, I. J., & Evdokas, A. (2004). Appraisals cause experienced emotions: Experimental evidence. *Cognition and Emotion, 18*, 1–28.

Roseman, I. J., & Smith, C. A. (2001). Appraisal theory: Overview, assumptions, varieties, controversies. In K. R. Scherer, A. Schorr, & T. Johnstone (Eds.), *Appraisal processes in emotion: Theory, methods, research* (pp. 3–19). New York: Oxford University Press.

Russell, J. A. (1987). Comments on articles by Frijda and by Conway and Bekerian. *Cognition and Emotion, 1*, 193–197.

Sabini, J., Garvey, B., & Hall, A. L. (2001). Shame and embarrassment revisited. *Personality and Social Psychology Review, 27*, 104–117.

Sabini, J., & Silver, M. (1997). In defense of shame: Shame in the context of guilt and embarrassment. *Journal for the Theory of Social Behavior, 27*, 1–15.

Scherer, K. R. (1984). On the nature and function of emotion: A component process approach. In K. R. Scherer & P. Ekman (Eds.), *Approaches to emotion* (pp. 293–317). Hillsdale, NJ: Lawrence Erlbaum Associates, Inc.

Scherer, K. R. (1988). Cognitive antecedents of emotion. In V. Hamilton, G. H. Bower, & N. H. Frijda (Eds.), *Cognitive perspectives on emotion and motivation* (pp. 89–126). Dordecht, The Netherlands: Kluwer.

Scherer, K. R. (1997). Profiles of emotion-antecedent appraisal: Testing theoretical predictions across cultures. *Cognition and Emotion, 11*, 113–150.

Scherer, K. R. (2001). Appraisal considered as a process of multilevel sequential checking. In K. R. Scherer, A. Schorr, & T. Johnstone (Eds.), *Appraisal processes in emotion: Theory, methods, research* (pp. 92–120). New York: Oxford University Press.

Sedikides, C., & Brewer, M. B. (2001). Individual self, relational self and collective self: Partners, opponents or strangers? In C. Sedikides & M. B. Brewer (Eds.), *Individual self, relational self, collective self* (pp. 1–6). Philadelphia: Psychology Press.

Sloman, S. A. (1996). The empirical case for two systems of reasoning. *Psychological Bulletin, 119*, 3–22.

Smith, C. A., & Ellsworth, P. C. (1985). Patterns of cognitive appraisal in emotion. *Journal of Personality and Social Psychology, 48*, 813–838.

Smith, C. A., & Ellsworth, P. C. (1987). Patterns of appraisal and emotion related to taking an exam. *Journal of Personality and Social Psychology, 52*, 475–488.

Smith, C. A., Haynes, K. N., Lazarus, R. S., & Pope, L. K. (1993). In search of the "hot" cognitions: Attributions, appraisals, and their relation to emotion. *Journal of Personality and Social Psychology, 65*, 916–929.

Smith, C. A., & Kirby, L. D. (2000). Consequences require antecedents: Toward a process model of emotion elicitation. In J. Forgas (Ed.), *Feeling and thinking: The role of affect in social cognition* (pp. 83–106). New York: Cambridge University Press.

Smith, C. A., & Kirby, L. D. (2001). Toward delivering on the promise of appraisal theory. In K. R. Scherer, A. Schorr, & T. Johnstone (Eds.), *Appraisal processes in emotion: Theory, methods, research* (pp. 121–138). New York: Oxford University Press.

Smith, C. A., & Lazarus, R. S. (1990). Emotion and adaptation. In L. A. Pervin (Ed.), *Handbook of personality: Theory and research* (pp. 609–637). New York: Guilford.

Smith, C. A., & Lazarus, R. S. (1993). Appraisal components, core relational themes, and the emotions. *Cognition and Emotion, 7*, 233–269.

Smith, C. A., & Noser, K. A. (1998, Abstract). Attributional antecedents in anger and guilt. In A. Fischer (Ed.), *Proceedings of the Tenth Conference of the International Society for Research on Emotions* (pp. 322–325). Amsterdam: International Society for Research on Emotions.

Smith, C. A., & Pope, L. K. (1992). Appraisal and emotion: The interactional contributions of dispositional and situational factors. In M. S. Clark (Ed.), *Review of Personality and Social Psychology: Vol. 14. Emotion and Social Behavior* (pp. 32–62). Newbury Park, CA: Sage.

Smith, E. R., Coats, S., & Walling, D. (1999). Overlapping mental representations of self, in-group and partner: Further response time evidence and a connectionist model. *Personality and Social Psychology Bulletin, 25,* 873–882.

Smith, E. R., & DeCoster, J. (2000). Dual-process models in social and cognitive psychology: Conceptual integration and links to underlying memory systems. *Personality and Social Psychology Review, 42,* 108–131.

Snyder, C. R. (1989). Reality negotiation: From excuses to hope and beyond. *Journal of Social and Clinical Psychology, 8,* 130–157.

Snyder, C. R., & Higgins, R. L. (1988). Excuses: Their effective role in the negotiation of reality. *Psychological Bulletin, 104,* 23–35.

Snyder, C. R., & Higgins, R. L. (1997). Reality negotiation: Governing one's self and being governed by others. *Review of General Psychology, 1,* 336–350.

Tangney, J. P. (1990). Sharing shame and guilt: Another social clinical interface. *Contemporary Social Psychology, 14,* 83–88.

Tangney, J. P. (1992). Situational determinants of shame and guilt in young adulthood. *Personality and Social Psychology Bulletin, 18,* 199–206.

Tomkins, S. S. (1963). *Affect, imagery, consciousness: Vol. 2. The negative affects.* New York: Springer.

Tomkins, S. S. (1987). Shame. In D. Nathanson (Ed.), *The many faces of shame* (pp. 133–161). New York: Guilford.

van Reekum, C. M. (2000). *Levels of processing in appraisal: Evidence from computer game generated emotions.* Doctoral dissertation, University of Geneva, Switzerland.

van Reekum, C. M., & Scherer, K. R. (1997). Levels of processing for emotion-antecedent appraisal. In G. Matthews (Ed.), *Cognitive Science Perspectives on Personality and Emotion* (pp. 259–300). Amsterdam: Elsevier Science.

Weiner, B. (1985). An attributional theory of achievement motivation and emotion. *Psychological Review, 92,* 548–573.

Zajonc, R. B. (1980). Feeling and thinking: Preferences need no inferences. *American Psychologist, 35,* 151–175.

Part II

Affect and Social Cognition

6

Cognitive and Clinical Perspectives on Mood-Dependent Memory

ERIC EICH and DAWN MACAULAY

*T*his chapter considers the problem of *mood-dependent memory* (MDM) from three points of view. Before describing these perspectives, we should begin by defining what MDM means and why it is a problem.

Conceptually, mood dependence refers to the idea that what has been learned in a certain state of affect or mood is most expressible in that state. Empirically, MDM is commonly examined within the context of a 2 × 2 design, where one factor is the mood—usually either happy (H) or sad (S)—in which a person encodes a collection of to-be-remembered or target events, and the other factor is the mood—again, either H or S—in which retrieval of the targets is tested. If these two factors are found to interact, such that more events are recollected when encoding and retrieval moods match (conditions H/H and S/S) than when they mismatch (conditions H/S and S/H), then mood dependence is said to occur.

Why is mood dependence gingerly introduced here as "the problem?" The answer lies in the 25-year history of attempts to demonstrate MDM experimentally. Whereas most of the studies published in the 1970s succeeded in showing mood dependence, the majority of those reported in the 1980s failed to do so. Worse, attempts to replicate positive results rarely prevailed, even when undertaken by the same investigator using similar memory materials, encoding tasks, retrieval measures, and methods of mood modification (for reviews, see Bower, 1992; Eich, 1995a; Kenealy, 1997). So quick and complete was this turn of events that, in less than a decade, MDM went from being "a genuine phenomenon" (Bower, 1981, p. 134) to "an unreliable, chance event" (Bower & Mayer, 1989, p. 145) with the "properties of a will-o'-the-wisp" (Kihlstrom, 1989, p. 26) that "presents more problems than solutions" (Ellis & Hunt, 1989, p. 280).

Clearly, any effect as capricious as MDM deserves to be called a "problem." But is it a problem worth worrying about, and is it important enough to pursue?

Two considerations suggest that it is. In the first place, MDM has long been thought to play a major role in the memory impairments associated with chronic depression, bipolar illness, traumatic amnesia, dissociative identity disorder, and other clinical conditions (Johnson & Magaro, 1987; Schacter & Kihlstrom, 1989). Second, the occurrence of mood dependence is implied by many influential theories of learning and memory: examples include such classic contributions as McGeogh's (1942) interference theory of forgetting and the drive-as-stimulus views held by Hull (1943) and Miller (1950), as well as such modern innovations as Baddeley's (1982) distinction between interactive and independent and interactive contexts, Bower's (1981, 1992) network model of emotion, and Tulving's (1983) encoding specificity principle.

Given these considerations, it is important to continue to carry on with the search for insight into the circumstances under which mood dependence occurs and the mechanisms that enable its emergence. To these ends, several teams of investigators, including ours, have been pursuing two different but complementary approaches to the study of MDM.

The *cognitive approach* features laboratory studies involving exogenous or experimentally induced moods in healthy volunteers. The aim here is to identify variables or factors that are vital to finding clear and consistent evidence of mood dependence. This approach is called "cognitive" because it focuses on factors— such as cued versus uncued recall, or real versus simulated moods—that are familiar to students of mainstream cognitive psychology, social cognition, or cognition/emotion interactions.

The second perspective concentrates on endogenous or naturally occurring moods in select psychiatric samples. The key issue at stake in this *clinical approach* is whether it is possible to demonstrate MDM in people who experience marked shifts in mood as a consequence of a psychiatric disorder, such as rapid-cycling bipolar illness. The rest of this chapter focuses on work which we and others have done along both the cognitive and clinical fronts, mainly since the mid-1990s.

COGNITIVE PERSPECTIVES ON MOOD-DEPENDENT MEMORY

Research reflecting a cognitive approach to MDM has revealed several factors that play pivotal roles in the phenomenon's occurrence. Whereas some of these factors have to do with the nature of the encoding and retrieval tasks that participants are asked to carry out, others concern characteristics of the moods they experience while performing these tasks. Representatives of both types are reviewed below.

Nature of the Retrieval Task

The first factor of note is also the best supported and longest recognized, and it relates to the manner in which memory for the target events is tested. By several accounts, MDM is more apt to obtain when retrieval is mediated by "invisible" cues produced by the subject than by "observable" cues provided by the experimenter (see Bower, 1981; Eich, 1980). Thus, as a rule, free recall is a more sensitive measure of mood dependence than are either cued recall or recognition memory. This is why free recall has been the test of choice in most studies of MDM undertaken in the past 15 years (e.g., Eich & Metcalfe, 1989; Schramke & Bauer, 1997).

Though free recall, cued recall, and recognition memory seem to differ in their sensitivity to mood-dependent effects, all represent explicit, as opposed to implicit, measures of retention. As defined by Roediger (1990, p. 1043), explicit measures "reflect conscious recollection of the past," whereas implicit tests "measure transfer (or priming) from past experience on tasks that do not require conscious recollection for their performance." Given that prior MDM research has relied almost exclusively on explicit measures (for exceptions see Macaulay, Ryan, & Eich, 1993; Tobias, Kihlstrom, & Schacter, 1992), the question arises: Is it possible to demonstrate mood dependence using implicit tests of memory?

Novelty aside, the question is interesting inasmuch as it appears to admit two totally different answers. On the one hand, there are two good reasons for thinking that implicit measures should not show MDM. First, in cases of functional amnesia, it is common to find abnormally poor performance in explicit tests, such as recall or recognition, coupled with normal levels of priming in implicit tests, such as word fragment completion or perceptual identification (see Kihlstrom & Schacter, 1995; Schacter & Kihlstrom, 1989). As an example, most individuals diagnosed with multiple personality or dissociative identity disorder (DID) manifest interpersonality amnesia, such that events encoded by a particular personality state or identity are retrievable by that same identity but not by a different one. From one DID patient to the next, these identities can vary tremendously in number, complexity, periodicity, and other fundamental features including age, gender, handedness, emotional complexion, allergic reactions, and pain tolerance. In general, however, they can be construed as "highly discrete states of consciousness organized around a prevailing affect, sense of self (including body image), with a limited repertoire of behaviors and a set of state dependent memories" (Putnam, 1989, p. 103). It is for this reason that interpersonality amnesia has often been interpreted as an extreme example of mood dependence (see Bower, 1994; Eich, Macaulay, Loewenstein, & Dihle, 1997; Ludwig, Brandsma, Wilbur, Bendfeldt, & Jameson, 1972; Nissen, Ross, Willingham, MacKenzie, & Schacter, 1988). Given this interpretation, it is significant—vis-à-vis the prospects of demonstrating implicit mood dependence—that performance on at least some implicit tests is spared in cases of DID, even when the interpersonality amnesia profoundly impairs performance under explicit test conditions (Eich et al., 1997; Nissen et al., 1988).

The second reason for doubting the possibility of implicit MDM relates to a point made at the outset of this section; specifically, that MDM is more apt to occur when explicit recollection is tested in the absence than in the presence of overt reminders (such as the stimulus cues provided in a test of paired-associates recall, or the copy cues presented in a test of recognition memory). This point is pertinent to the present discussion because even though implicit measures, by definition, do not demand conscious recollection of past events, they do require that subjects respond to overt cues in the form of specific, tangible test stimuli. Thus, for example, implicit memory for a previously studied item such as *apple* might be assessed by asking subjects to (a) name the first word they think of that begins with *app*, (b) unscramble the anagram *eplap* to form a meaningful word, or (c) identify what they saw on a screen following the fleeting appearance of *apple*. Given their overtly cued nature, implicit tests such as stem completion, anagram solution, or perceptual identification would seem ill-suited to showing MDM.

On the other hand, there are two good reasons for thinking that implicit tests should show mood dependence. First, prior research has revealed that changes in contextual information—such as presentation modality, type font and orientation, and even environmental setting—from study to test attenuates priming on a variety of implicit tasks (see Roediger & McDermott, 1993). If mood is construed as a kind of internal contextual cue, then priming in at least some implicit tests may be susceptible to shifts in mood state.

The second source of support for the idea of implicit MDM stems from the work of Tobias and her associates (Tobias, 1992; Tobias et al., 1992), who hold that mood-dependent effects emerge when the cues afforded by the retention test are "impoverished" (as in free recall), but not when they are "rich" (as in cued recall or recognition memory). On this view, implicit tests entail the most impoverished cues of all—indeed, they do not even specify that the subject should try to retrieve a specific memory (see Kihlstrom, Eich, Sandbrand, & Tobias, 1998)—which implies that implicit tests should be especially sensitive to mood-dependent effects.

Tobias (1992) investigated this implication in her doctoral dissertation, the results of which are reviewed in Tobias et al., 1992. Her first study, comparing explicit stem-cued recall with implicit word-stem completion, revealed no evidence of MDM on either measure. However, her second study evinced a small but significant mood-dependent effect in a novel, ostensibly implicit test of free association, but—rather remarkably—no effect at all in an explicit test of free recall. Though the reliability and generality of Tobias' results remain to be determined, they strengthen the possibility that mood dependence may affect performance even on tasks that do not demand deliberate, conscious recollection of the past. Clearly, this is a matter that merits more attention.

Nature of the Encoding Task

The last section began with the observation that, in general, the odds of demonstrating MDM are improved by having subjects produce their own cues for retrieving the target events (as in an explicit test of free recall), rather than allowing them to rely on reminders provided by the experimenter (as in explicit tests of cued recall or recognition memory). The point to be made now is that these same odds are improved when the targets themselves are subject-produced rather than experimenter-provided.

To elaborate, Eich and Metcalfe (1989) found (in three out of four studies) a significantly greater mood-dependent effect in the free recall of verbal items (e.g., *gold* or *guitar*) that subjects had actively generated (e.g., *Name a precious stone that begins with G*), in contrast to items that the subjects had simply read (e.g., *A guitar is a musical instrument*). This pattern has been replicated (Beck & McBee, 1995) and it obtains whether the overall level of generate-item recall is higher or lower than that of read items (Eich & Metcalfe, 1989, Experiments 1 & 2). Moreover, and in line with remarks made earlier, the results of a test of old/new recognition memory, which was given shortly after free recall, showed no sign of MDM for either type of target (cf. Beck & McBee, 1995). Thus it appears that the more one must rely on internal resources, rather than on external aids, to generate both the cues required to effect retrieval of the target events *and* the events themselves, the more likely is one's memory for these events to be mood dependent.

This "do-it-yourself" principle was the impetus for a series of studies reported by Eich, Macaulay, and Ryan (1994). During the encoding session of one study (Experiment 2), university students recollected specific incidents, from any time in their personal past, that were called to mind by neutral-noun probes such as *candle* and *camera*; every participant recollected as many as 16 different events, each evoked by a different probe. After recounting the gist of a given event, subjects rated its original emotional valence—that is, whether the event was a positive, neutral, or negative experience when it occurred. We reasoned that this task would promote the occurrence of MDM, given that (1) events produced through internal mental processes such as reasoning, imagination, and reflection are more deeply colored by or closely connected to one's current mood than are those derived from external sources (see Johnson & Multhaup, 1992) and (2) generating autobiographical events should place a premium on internal mental processes.

Half of the subjects completed the task of *autobiographical event generation* while they were feeling happy (H) and half did so while sad (S). These affective states were induced using the *MCI technique*, whereby subjects are asked to contemplate mood-appropriate thoughts while mood-appropriate music plays softly in the background (for details, see Eich, Ng, Macaulay, Percy, & Grebneva, in press).

Periodically, subjects placed a checkmark on an *affect grid* (Russell, Weiss, & Mendelsohn, 1989) to indicate their current levels of pleasure/displeasure and high/low arousal—the two principal, bipolar dimensions of affective experience (Feldman Barrett & Russell, 1998; Russell, 2003). Predictably, subjects who had been induced to feel happy reported much higher levels of both pleasure and arousal than did their sad-mood peers, especially at the start than at the end of the generation task (owing, in part, to regression effects).

During the retrieval session, held 2 days after encoding, subjects were asked to recall—in any order and without benefit of any observable reminders or cues—the gist of as many of their previously generated, real-life experiences as possible, preferably by recalling their corresponding probes (such as *camera*). Subjects undertook this test of *autobiographical event recall* either in the same mood in which they had generated the events or in the alternative affective state, thus creating two conditions in which encoding and retrieval moods matched (H/H, S/S) and two in which they mismatched (H/S, S/H).

Results of the encoding session, in the form of mean numbers of positive, neutral, and negative events generated by happy and sad subjects, appear in the left panel of Figure 6.1. In comparison with their sad counterparts, happy subjects

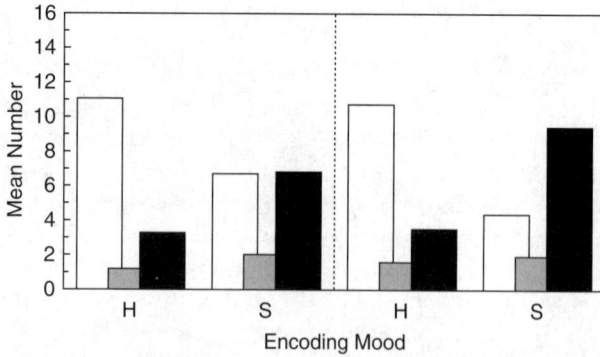

FIGURE 6.1   Positive (white), neutral (gray), and negative (black) events generated as a function of encoding mood (H = happy, S = sad). Data in the left panel reflect induced moods (Source: Eich et al., 1994, Experiment 2); those in the right panel reflect simulated moods (Source: Eich & Macaulay, 2000).

generated more positive events, fewer negative events, and about the same, small number of neutral events. This pattern replicates earlier experiments (e.g., Clark & Teasdale, 1982; Snyder & White, 1982), and it provides evidence of mood *congruent* memory—the "enhanced encoding and/or retrieval of material the affective valence of which is congruent with ongoing mood" (Blaney, 1986, p. 229).

Results of the retrieval session, shown in the left panel of Figure 6.2, provided evidence of MDM. Regardless of whether the recall probabilities for positive, neutral, and negative events were analyzed separately, or whether the data for all three types were averaged together to yield a single index of retention termed *all-event recall* (the dependent measure depicted in Figure 6.2), a reliable advantage in recall of matched over mismatched moods was obtained. Similar results were obtained in two other studies (Experiments 1 & 3 in Eich et al., 1994), suggesting that autobiographical event generation, when combined with autobiographical event recall, is a useful tool for exploring MDM under laboratory conditions. As will be seen later, this same pair of tasks works well in certain clinical settings as well.

Nature of the Encoding and Retrieval Moods

Our focus thus far has been on factors that determine the sensitivity of an encoding or a retrieval task to the detection of mood dependence. It stands to reason, however, that no matter how sensitive these tasks may be, the odds of demonstrating MDM are slim in the absence of an effective manipulation of mood. So, what makes a mood manipulation effective?

One consideration is mood strength. By definition, MDM demands a statistically significant loss of memory when target events are encoded in one mood and retrieved in another. It is doubtful whether anything less than a substantial shift in mood could produce such impairment. Indeed, the results of a meta-analysis by Ucros (1989) revealed that the greater the difference in moods—depression

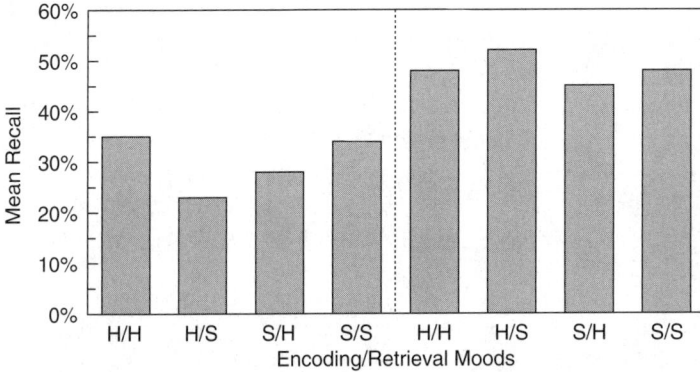

FIGURE 6.2   All-event recall as a function of encoding/retrieval moods (H = happy, S = sad). Data in the left panel reflect induced moods (Source: Eich et al., 1994, Experiment 2); those in the right panel reflect simulated moods (Source: Eich & Macaulay, 2000).

versus elation, for example, as opposed to depression versus a neutral affect—the greater the mood-dependent effect.

No less important than the strength of the moods is their stability over time and across tasks. In terms of demonstrating MDM, it does no good to engender a mood that evaporates as soon as the subject is given something to do, like memorize a list of words or recognize previously presented pictures. It is probable that some studies failed to find mood dependence simply because they relied on moods that were potent initially but paled rapidly (see Eich & Metcalfe 1989).

In our most recent studies, we have asked subjects to candidly assess (post-experimentally) whether the MCI method of mood induction (which involves combining music with thought) caused an authentic change in their mood. Nearly 90% of the participants rate the method as being at least moderately effective in this regard (a rating of 5 or higher on a 0–10 mood-genuineness scale), indicating a high degree of affective realism. Moreover, those who feel most genuinely "moved" tend to show the strongest mood dependence (Eich, 1995a). Thus, it seems that the odds of demonstrating MDM are improved by instilling affective states that have three important properties: strength, stability, and sincerity.

Induced versus Simulated Moods

A short step from mood sincerity leads to still another factor that seems to play a prominent role in MDM—whether the moods at encoding and retrieval are truly felt or merely faked.

To amplify, consider a study by Perrig and Perrig (1988) in which subjects were instructed to act as though they were either extremely happy or extremely sad while they memorized, and then immediately recalled, a mixed list of positive, neutral, and negative words (e.g., *graduation*, *grass*, and *guilt*). Though there was no difference between simulated-mood conditions in the recall of neutral words, subjects who feigned happiness recalled more positive words, and fewer negative words, than did pseudo-sad subjects. This is mood *congruent* memory—but in the absence of mood!

In a second study, the Perrigs again had subjects learn the same mixed list in simulated states of happiness or sadness. This time, however, subjects were tested for free recall in either their original or the alternative sham state. Though the Perrigs found no evidence of mood dependence—performance was the same under matched versus mismatched study/test conditions, they again found mood congruence—happy/happy subjects recalled more positive words, and fewer negative words, than did sad/sad subjects.

The results of these two studies lead to the remarkable conclusion that real moods are sufficient but not necessary for demonstrating mood congruent memory. Though it is tempting to attribute these results simply to task demands or expectation effects, Perrig and Perrig (1988) proposed that the data are better understood in terms of people's knowledge "about doing what they think they would do if they were actually in [a particular] mood" (p. 103).

The Perrigs' research prompted us to undertake a study (Eich & Macaulay, 2000) that aimed to answer three questions. First, do simulated states of happiness or sadness give rise to mood congruent effects in autobiographical event generation—a task that has already been shown to be acutely sensitive to actual moods induced via a combination of music and thought?

The second question, which presupposed an affirmative answer to the first, was whether the mood congruent effects evoked by simulated H and S states are qualitatively different from those elicited by induced H and S states? In the Perrigs' experiments, simulated happiness selectively enhanced the recall of positive words to the same extent as simulated sadness selectively elevated the recall of negative words—a pattern indicative of *symmetric* mood congruence. However, in studies involving induced moods, the typical finding has been one of *asymmetric* mood congruence—happy subjects remember more positive than negative items, but sad subjects remember roughly the same number of both types (see Blaney, 1986; Bower, 1981). A case in point is the previously described study by Eich et al. (1994, Experiment 2), the results of which appear in the left panel of Figure 6.1. Whereas the ratio of positive-to-negative events generated was roughly 3:1 among the induced-happy participants in that study, the corresponding figure for induced-sad subjects was about 1:1.

According to Isen (1984), at least some instances of asymmetric mood congruence are attributable to a process of mood repair—people try to feel better if they are feeling bad, but tend not to take themselves down if they are feeling up (also see Clark & Isen, 1982; Ellis & Hertel, 1993). Though this intuitively appealing account can be challenged (see Parrott, 1993), the important point is that the mood congruent effects elicited by simulated moods may differ qualitatively from those instilled by induced moods.

Given that this chapter is chiefly concerned with mood dependence, rather than mood congruence, the third question is the most critical: do induced moods have the power to produce mood-dependent effects in a test of autobiographical event recall? Though the Perrigs failed to find MDM with simulated moods, it is by no means certain that they would have succeeded had they used induced moods, given their choice of stimulus material and study task. Since we know, from the work reviewed earlier, that shifts in induced moods reliably reduce autobiographical event recall, it is logical to ask whether shifts in simulated moods do likewise.

Methodologically, the present study was similar to the one described earlier (Eich et al., 1994, Experiment 2). Thus, during the encoding session of either study, undergraduates recollected and recounted real-life events in response to neutral-noun probes, and rated each event in terms of its original affective valence (either positive, neutral, or negative). Two days later, during the retrieval session, subjects were asked to freely recall the gist of as many of their previously generated events as possible.

The crucial difference between the studies lay in the substitution of simulated for induced moods during the encoding and retrieval sessions. Subjects in the present study were instructed to perform a given task (either event generation or event recall) as if they were feeling happy or sad—a pretense that their counterparts in the original study did have to maintain, in as much as they had been induced into either affect through a combination of music and thought. Participants in the current study were also cautioned against letting their true feelings drift in the direction of the specified sham state.

The right panel of Figure 6.1 shows the mean numbers of positive, neutral, and negative events that subjects generated in simulated H and S moods. Recall from earlier discussion that the left panel contains comparable data culled from a study involving induced H and S moods (Eich et al., 1994, Experiment 2).

Comparison of the two panels suggests two conclusions. First, simulated moods, like induced moods, are capable of causing mood congruence: in either case, happy subjects generate more positive but fewer negative events than do sad subjects. Second, mood congruent effects elicited by simulated moods are qualitatively different from those incurred by induced moods—the former being symmetric in form, the latter, asymmetric. This difference makes sense in terms of Isen's (1984) idea that asymmetry arises as a consequence of affect-reducing control processes in the case of depression but not elation. But if the depression is merely feigned rather than truly felt, then there is no motive to engage in mood repair. Hence, when asked to recount experiences from their personal past, simulated-sadness subjects show a strong bias towards negative autobiographical events that is held in check by their induced-sadness counterparts.

Mean percentages of all-event recall (positive, neutral, and negative events averaged together) under simulated encoding/retrieval moods appear in the right panel of Figure 6.2, beside the results obtained for induced moods. Comparing the two panels, it is clear that the overall level of recall is considerably higher for simulated than for induced moods—about 37% higher, counting just the two matched mood conditions (H/H and S/S averaged together). A plausible explanation for this curious result is suggested by the research of Ellis and his associates (e.g., Ellis & Ashbrook, 1989; Seibert & Ellis, 1991). Their work implies that the experience of a mood—good or bad—begets two effects that can interfere with the performance of a cognitive task: a decrease in attentional resources and an increase in the production of stray or task-irrelevant thoughts. Provided they stay in a neutral state, subjects who simulate happiness or sadness are exempt from these effects, and hence they outperform their induced-mood peers.

Looking at Figure 6.2, it is also apparent that the robust mood-dependent effect revealed by induced-mood subjects is altogether absent among simulated-mood subjects. Though this fits with the finding, mentioned earlier, that strong MDM effects are associated with sincere moods, it raises the question of why subjects are able to simulate (at least passably) mood congruence but not mood dependence. Perhaps people have a better intuitive understanding of the former phenomenon than of the latter. Alternatively, it may be that they know full-well that a match between encoding and retrieval moods should enhance memory performance, but cannot put this knowledge into practice. Owing to its 2×2 factorial design, Eich and Macaulay's (2000) study allowed every subject to serve in only one of the four combinations of simulated encoding and retrieval moods. Even if a participant had a good grasp on the concept of MDM, he or she would have been hard pressed to predict how well subjects in any of the other encoding/retrieval conditions would have performed in the test of event recall. Consequently, it would have been difficult, perhaps impossible, for the simulated-mood subject to put his or her knowledge of MDM into practice, and act in a way that accurately mimicked the behavior of induced-mood individuals.

Whatever the reason, the essential point is that there seems to be something special about induced moods that gives them the power to produce mood dependence. A fundamental task for future, cognitively oriented investigations of MDM is to figure out just what this something is.

CLINICAL PERSPECTIVES ON MOOD-DEPENDENT MEMORY

Recall from the chapter's introduction that mood dependence has been implicated in a diverse array of psychiatric disorders. Though the MDM literature is replete with clinical conjectures, it is lacking in hard clinical data. Worse, the few pertinent results that have been reported are difficult to interpret.

Here we refer to a seminal study by Weingartner, Miller, and Murphy (1977), in which patients who cycled rapidly between states of mania and normal mood were observed over several months. Periodically, the patients generated 20 free associations to each of 2 common nouns, such as *river* and *radio*, and were tested for recall of all 40 associations 4 days later. When their mood at testing (either manic or normal) matched their mood at generation, the patients recalled 93% more associations than when their moods mismatched.

Though this result is striking, its interpretation is not straightforward. The problem arises from an ambiguity in the recall-test instructions. Though it is clear from Weingartner et al.'s account that participants were asked to recall their prior associations, it is unclear how the patients interpreted this request. One possibility is that they understood "recall" to mean that they should restrict their search to episodic memory (in effect, saying to themselves, "What associations did I produce the last time I saw *river*?"), in which case the results would seem to suggest mood-*dependent* memory. Alternatively, they may have taken "recall" as a cue to search semantic memory ("What comes to mind now when I think of *radio*, regardless of what I said four days ago?"), in which case the data may be more indicative of mood *congruent* memory. In short, while it is clear that Weingartner's results show something, it is unclear just what that something is: mood dependence, mood congruence, or perhaps a mixture of the two (see Blaney, 1986).

A study by Eich, Macaulay, and Lam (1997) sought to resolve this ambiguity and to investigate the impact of clinical mood shifts on the performance of several different tasks. Participants were 10 patients with rapid-cycling bipolar disorder, diagnosed according to DSM-IV criteria (American Psychiatric Association, 1994).

Every patient was seen on several occasions, the odd-numbered serving as encoding sessions and the even-numbered as retrieval sessions. Though the interval separating successive encoding and retrieval sessions varied from 2 to 7 days between patients, the interval remained constant within a given patient. Superimposed on these sessions was a 2 × 2 design, with mood at encoding—manic (or hypomanic) versus depressed—crossed with these same two moods at retrieval.

At the outset of each encoding session, patients rated their present levels of pleasure and arousal on an affect grid. Participants then undertook a series of cognitive tasks, two of which are of interest here. Though the same tasks were undertaken in every encoding session, the materials used in these tasks were systematically varied from one session to the next. The same applied to the tasks and materials involved in the retrieval session, which will be described shortly.

One encoding task was *autobiographical event generation*. Paralleling the procedures described earlier, patients recollected a maximum of 10 episodes, from any time in the personal past, that were called to mind by *candle, camera,* and other neutral-noun probes. After recounting the gist of a given event, patients rated the episode along several dimensions, including its original affective valence (positive, neutral, or negative).

A second encoding task was *letter association production*, whereby patients were asked to name aloud 20 words beginning with one letter of the alphabet (e.g., *E*) and 20 words beginning with a different letter (e.g., *S*).

As was the case at encoding, patients began the retrieval session by rating their current mood on the affect grid. The patients then went on to complete several tasks, one of which was *autobiographical event recall*—a task that shows strong MDM effects with experimentally induced moods.

A second retrieval task, *letter association retention*, was designed with a view to clarifying the results reported by Weingartner et al. (1977). As discussed earlier, they found that word associations produced in either a manic or normal mood were especially reproducible in that mood—a finding can be taken as evidence for either mood dependence or mood congruence.

Seeking to avoid this ambiguity, we divided the test of letter association retention into two phases, each with its own set of instructions. One phase involved *episodic instructions*: after reminding the patients that they had produced 20 words beginning with a particular letter (e.g., *E*) in the course of the last session, we asked them to freely recall aloud as many of these words as possible. Patients were dissuaded from guessing and cautioned against making intrusions. The other phase involved *semantic instructions*: patients were presented with the other letter to which they had previously responded in the immediately preceding session (e.g., S), and were asked to name aloud 20 words—any 20 words—beginning with that letter. Patients were explicitly encouraged to state the first responses that came to mind, and specifically told that they need not try to remember their prior associations.

The reasoning behind these instructions was that if memory is truly mood dependent, such that returning to the original mood helps remind subjects of what they were thinking about when last in that mood, then performance in the episodic task should show an advantage of matched over mismatched moods. In contrast, an analogous advantage in the semantic task could be construed as evidence of mood congruence.

Though plausible in principle, this reasoning did not pan out in practice: recall averaged about 30% irrespective of test instructions (episodic vs. semantic) and encoding/retrieval moods (matched vs. mismatched). Thus, whereas Weingartner et al. (1977) found an effect in word-association recall that could be construed as either mood congruence or mood dependence, we found no effect at all.

Though this discrepancy defies easy explanation, it is not because the participants experienced weak moods: ratings of both pleasure and arousal were markedly higher (125 and 115%, respectively) in (hypo)manic than in depressed states.

A more credible—but as yet untested—account concerns the fact that whereas we used letters to prime the production of associative responses, Weingartner et al. used words—stimuli that patients with clinical mood disturbance may interpret in different ways, depending on their current affective state (see Henry, Weingartner, & Murphy, 1971). It may be that associations made to letters allow less room for state-specific interpretive processes to operate, and this in turn may lessen the likelihood of detecting either mood congruent or mood-dependent effects (see Eich & Forgas, 2003; Nissen, Ross, Willingham, MacKenzie, & Schacter, 1988).

In contrast to letter association retention, both the generation and recall of autobiographical events showed statistically and theoretically significant results. Regarding the former task, positive outnumbered negative events when participants were in a manic (or hypomanic) state (means of 5.9 vs. 3.1), but the two types of events were generated with equal frequency when the patients were depressed (means 5 4.1 vs. 4.2). This pattern is identical to the one we came across earlier in connection with real—but not fake—moods that had been induced experimentally (compare the left and right panels of Figure 6.1), and it is indicative of asymmetric mood congruence in autobiographical event generation.

Regarding the recall task, events generated during depression were better remembered in a similar state than during mania or hypomania (means = 31 vs. 24%). By the same token, events generated during mania were more accessible for retrieval in the same than in the contrasting condition (means = 35 vs. 21%). In short, recall performance was higher when encoding and retrieval moods matched (33%) than when they mismatched (23%)—a clear demonstration of mood dependence in a clinically significant condition.

Because such demonstrations are rare, it is reasonable to ask whether Eich et al.'s (1997) findings with bipolar patients are a fluke, or whether they can be replicated using the same event generation and recall tasks but with a different mood disorder. Accordingly, we recently ran a study involving unipolar patients whose depression is reliably and robustly entrained to a diurnal cycle. For most of these patients, morning is the time of peak depression; later in the afternoon their moods are in the normal range (as assessed by the affect grid and other measures). A minority of patients experience the reverse cycle, with their relatively normal mood in the morning giving way to depression in the afternoon.

Fifteen patients recently completed all four encoding/retrieval conditions (viz. normal vs. depressed mood at encoding × these same two states at retrieval). The results are now being written up, and they provide more clinical evidence of mood dependence: on the standard test of autobiographical event recall, patients performed better when their encoding and retrieval moods matched (mean = 54%) than when they mismatched (means = 39%).

CONCLUDING COMMENTS

Two key conclusions can be drawn from this review of cognitive and clinical research on mood-dependent memory. First, mood dependence is not the erratic effect it was widely believed to be 15 or so years ago. Rather, it now appears that robust and reliable evidence of MDM emerges under conditions in which subjects (1) experience strong, stable, and sincere moods; (2) take responsibility for generating the target events themselves; and (3) also assume responsibility for generating the cues required to retrieve these events. Second, MDM occurs in concert not only with normal moods (such as happiness and sadness) that have been instilled in healthy volunteers, but also with abnormal states (such as mania and depression) that are endogenous in nature and characteristic of certain psychiatric conditions. Clinicians had been speculating for decades that this might be so; now their conjectures have some empirical support.

Taken together, these observations make a start toward demystifying MDM— but only a start. There is still much to do on both the cognitive and clinical fronts. Regarding the latter, it would be informative to know how far the clinical envelope around MDM extends. Is mood dependence implicated in, say, generalized anxiety (Lang, Craske, Brown, & Ghaneian, 2001) or seasonal affective disorder (aka winter depression; Lam, 2001)? Also, in cases of dissociative identity disorder, does *interpersonality amnesia*—the characteristic lack of information transfer across disparate identity states—reflect an extreme example of MDM, as some theorists have surmised (e.g., Bower, 1994; Kihlstrom & Schacter, 1995; Nissen et al., 1988), or are there other, simpler, better explanations for this remarkable form of memory pathology?

Regarding prospects for future cognitive research, it is worth noting that, to date, only a few factors have been examined for their role in MDM. Odds are that other factors of equal or greater importance exist, awaiting discovery. One possibility arises from a study by Salovery and Singer (1989), which showed that childhood memories are more resistant that recent memories to contextual factors like mood. Acording to these authors, memories of childhood experiences:

> ... are vivid, rehearsed repeatedly, rather unforgettable, and can take on "a life of their own." A contextual variable such as mood state has little impact on such memories; they have many more links to other memories in one's memorial network, and they are rarely the targets of memory searches. They reside in memory, instead, as self-contained wholes with dense and far reaching connections (p. 116).

If so, then recent memories should be especially sensitive not only to mood-congruent effects, but to mood-dependent effects as well. That is, a mismatch between the moods in which autobiographical events are (first) generated and (later) retrieved should bave a greater adverse impact on memory for events of the recent as opposed to the remote personal past.

Several other cognitively oriented issues seem particularly inviting. For instance, assuming that performance in any test of retention is a product of both controlled and automatic processes (Jacoby, 1991), are these processes differentially affected by a mismatch between encoding and retrieval moods? Relatedly, does a change in mood state impair one's ability to "remember" prior episodes or experiences without compromising the subjective sense of "knowing" that such-and-such event took place (Gardiner, 1988; Tulving, 1985)? And is it the case that how well information transfers from one pharmacological state to another (e.g., alcohol intoxication to sobriety), or from one physical environment to a different setting (e.g., a windowless office to a sunny courtyard), depend critically on how these drugs and places make you feel? Put another way, do both *drug*-dependent memory and *place*-dependent memory represent special—and rather subtle—cases of *mood*-dependent memory (Bower, 1981; Eich, 1995b). Answers to these and related questions would provide fresh insights into both the cognitive and affective foundations of mood dependence.

ACKNOWLEDGMENTS

Preparation of this chapter was aided by grants to the first author from the (Canadian) Natural Sciences and Engineering Research Council (37335) and the (American) National Institute of Mental Health (MH59636). We were privileged to work with a wonderful group of colleagues and students—Andrea Bull, Kirsten Campbell, Susan Carsky, Irina Grebneva, Meagan Hasek-Watt, Adam Margesson, Andrea Nelson, Joycelin Ng, Jim Russell, Lee Ryan, and Reiko West—and we gratefully acknowledge their many contributions. The advice and assistance provided by the late, great Sherry Eich are also deeply appreciated and will be long remembered.

REFERENCES

American Psychiatric Association. (1994). *Diagnostic and statistical manual of mental disorders* (4th ed.). Washington, DC: Author.

Baddeley, A. D. (1982). Domains of recollection. *Psychological Review, 89*, 708–729.

Beck, R. C., & McBee, W. (1995). Mood-dependent memory for generated and repeated words: Replication and extension. *Cognition and Emotion, 9,* 289–307.

Blaney, P. H. (1986). Affect and memory: A review. *Psychological Bulletin, 99,* 229–246.

Bower, G. H. (1981). Mood and memory. *American Psychologist, 36,* 129–148.

Bower, G. H. (1992). How might emotions affect learning? In S.-A. Christianson (Ed.), *Handbook of emotion and memory* (pp. 3–31). Hillsdale, NJ: Lawrence Erlbaum Associates, Inc.

Bower, G. H. (1994). Temporary emotional states act like multiple personalities. In R. M. Klein & B. K. Doane (Eds.), *Psychological concepts and dissociative disorders* (pp. 207–234). Hillsdale, NJ: Lawrence Erlbaum Associates, Inc.

Bower, G. H., & Mayer, J. D. (1989). In search of mood-dependent retrieval. *Journal of Social Behavior and Personality, 4,* 121–156.

Clark, D. M., & Teasdale, J. D. (1982). Diurnal variation in clinical depression and accessibility of memories of positive and negative experiences. *Journal of Abnormal Psychology, 91,* 87–95.

Clark, M. S., & Isen, A. M. (1982). Toward understanding the relationship between feeling states and social behavior. In A. H. Hastorf & A. M. Isen (Eds.), *Cognitive social psychology* (pp. 73–108). New York: Elsevier.

Eich, E. (1980). The cue-dependent nature of state-dependent retrieval. *Memory and Cognition, 8,* 157–173.

Eich, E. (1995a). Searching for mood dependent memory. *Psychological Science, 6,* 67–75.

Eich, E. (1995b). Mood as a mediator of place dependent memory. *Journal of Experimental Psychology: General, 124,* 293–308.

Eich, E., & Forgas, J. P. (2003). Mood, cognition, and memory. In A. F. Healy & R. W. Proctor (Eds.), *Experimental psychology* (pp. 61–83). Volume 4 in I. B. Weiner (Editor-in-Chief), *Handbook of psychology.* New York: Wiley.

Eich, E., & Macaulay, D. (2000). Are real moods required to reveal mood-congruent and mood-dependent memory? *Psychological Science, 11,* 244–248.

Eich, E., Macaulay, D., & Lam, R. W. (1997). Mania, depression, and mood dependent memory. *Cognition and Emotion, 11,* 607–618.

Eich, E., Macaulay, D., & Ryan, L. (1994). Mood dependent memory for events of the personal past. *Journal of Experimental Psychology: General, 123,* 201–215.

Eich, E., & Metcalfe, J. (1989). Mood dependent memory for internal versus external events. *Journal of Experimental Psychology: Learning, Memory, and Cognition, 15,* 443–455.

Eich, E., Ng, J. T. W., Macaulay, D., Percy, A. D., & Grebneva, I. (in press). Combining music with thought to change mood. In J. A. Coan & J. B. Allen (Eds.), *The handbook of emotion elicitation and assessment.* New York: Oxford University Press.

Ellis, H. C., & Ashbrook, P. W. (1989). The "state" of mood and memory research: A selective review. *Journal of Social Behavior and Personality, 4,* 1–21.

Ellis, H. C., & Hertel, P. T. (1993). Cognition, emotion, and memory: Some applications and issues. In C. Izawa (Ed.), *Cognitive psychology applied* (pp. 199–215). Hillsdale, NJ: Lawrence Erlbaum Associates, Inc.

Ellis, H. C., & Hunt, R. R. (1989). *Fundamentals of human memory and cognition* (4th ed.). Dubuque, IA: William C. Brown.

Feldman Barrett, L. A., & Russell, J. A. (1998). Independence and bipolarity in the structure of current affect. *Journal of Personality and Social Psychology, 74,* 967–984.

Gardiner, J. M. (1988). Functional aspects of recollective experience. *Memory and Cognition, 16,* 309–313.

Henry, G. M., Weingartner, H., & Murphy, D. L. (1971). Idiosyncratic patterns of learning and word association during mania. *American Journal of Psychiatry, 128*, 564–573.

Hull, C. L. (1943). *Principles of behavior*. New York: Appleton-Century-Crofts.

Isen, A. M. (1984). Toward understanding the role of affect in cognition. In R. S. Wyer & T. K. Srull (Eds.), *Handbook of social cognition* (Vol. 3, pp. 179–230). Hillsdale, NJ: Lawrence Erlbaum Associates, Inc.

Jacoby, L. L. (1991). A process dissociation framework: Separating automatic from intentional uses of memory. *Journal of Memory and Language, 30*, 513-541.

Johnson, M. H., & Magaro, P. A. (1987). Effects of mood and severity on memory processes in depression and mania. *Psychological Bulletin, 101*, 28–40.

Johnson, M. K., & Multhaup, K. S. (1992). Emotion and MEM. In S.-A. Christianson (Ed.), *Handbook of emotion and memory* (pp. 33–66). Hillsdale, NJ: Lawrence Erlbaum Associates, Inc.

Kenealy, P. M. (1997). Mood-state-dependent retrieval: The effects of induced mood on memory reconsidered. *Quarterly Journal of Experimental Psychology, 50A*, 290–317.

Kihlstrom, J. F. (1989). On what does mood-dependent memory depend? *Journal of Social Behavior and Personality, 4*, 23–32.

Kihlstrom, J. F., & Schacter, D. L. (1995). Functional disorders of autobiographical memory. In A. Baddeley, B. A. Wilson, & F. Watts (Eds.), *Handbook of memory disorders* (pp. 337–364). London: Wiley.

Kihlstrom, J. F., Eich, E., Sandbrand, D., & Tobias, B. A. (1998). Emotion and memory: Implications for self-report. In A. Stone & J. Turkkan (Eds.), The science of self-report: Implications for research and practice (pp. 81–99). Mahwah, NJ: Lawrence Erlbaum Associates, Inc.

Lam, R. W. (2001). Evidence-based management of Seasonal Affective Disorder: Focus on light therapy. *Directions in Psychiatry, 21*, 55–66.

Lang, A. J., Craske, M. G., Brown, M., & Ghaneian, A. (2001). Fear-related state dependent memory. *Cognition and Emotion, 15*, 695–703.

Ludwig, A. M., Brandsma, J. M., Wilbur, C. B., Bendfeldt, F., & Jameson, D. H. (1972). The objective study of a multiple personality. *Archives of General Psychiatry, 26*, 298–310.

Macaulay, D., Ryan, L., & Eich, E. (1993). Mood dependence in implicit and explicit memory. In P. Graf & M. E. J. Masson (Eds.), *Implicit memory: New directions in cognition, development, and neuropsychology* (pp. 75–94). Hillsdale, NJ: Lawrence Erlbaum Associates, Inc.

McGeogh, J. A. (1942). *The psychology of human learning*. New York: Longmans, Green.

Miller, N. E. (1950). Learnable drives and rewards. In S. S. Stevens (Ed.), *Handbook of experimental psychology* (pp. 435–472). New York: Wiley.

Nissen, M. J., Ross, J. L., Willingham, D. B., MacKenzie, T. B., & Schacter, D. L. (1988). Memory and awareness in a patient with multiple personality disorder. *Brain and Cognition, 8*, 21–38.

Parrott, W. G. (1993). Beyond hedonism: Motives for inhibiting good moods and for maintaining bad moods. In D. M. Wegner & J. W. Pennebaker (Eds.), *Handbook of mental control* (pp. 278–305). Englewood Cliffs, NJ: Prentice-Hall.

Perrig, W. J., & Perrig, P. (1988). Mood and memory: Mood-congruity effects in absence of mood. *Memory and Cognition, 16*, 102–109.

Putnam, F. W. (1989). *Diagnosis and treatment of multiple personality disorder*. New York: Guilford Press.

Roediger, H. L. (1990). Implicit memory: Retention without remembering. *American Psychologist, 45*, 1043–1056.

Roediger, H. L., & McDermott, K. B. (1993). Implicit memory in normal human subjects. In F. Boller & J. Grafman (Eds.), *Handbook of neuropsychology* (Vol.8, pp. 63–131). Amsterdam: Elsevier.

Russell, J. A. (2003). Core affect and the psychological construction of emotion. *Psychological Review, 110*, 145–172.

Russell, J. A., Weiss, A., & Mendelsohn, G. A. (1989). Affect grid: A single-item scale of pleasure and arousal. *Journal of Personality and Social Psychology, 57*, 493–502.

Salovey, P., & Singer, J. A. (1989). Mood congruency effects in recall of childhood versus recent memories. *Journal of Social Behavior and Personality, 4*, 99–120.

Schacter, D. L., & Kihlstrom, J. F. (1989). Functional amnesia. In F. Boller & J. Grafman (Eds.), *Handbook of neuropsychology* (Vol. 3, pp. 209–230). New York: Elsevier.

Schramke, C. J., & Bauer, R. M. (1997). State-dependent learning in older and younger adults. *Psychology and Aging, 12*, 255–262.

Seibert, P. S., & Ellis, H. C. (1991). Irrelevant thoughts, emotional mood states, and cognitive task performance. *Memory and Cognition, 19*, 507–513.

Snyder, M., & White, P. (1982). Moods and memories: Elation, depression, and the remembering of the events of one's life. *Journal of Personality, 50*, 149–167.

Tobias, B. A. (1992). *Mood effects on explicit and implicit memory.* Unpublished doctoral dissertation, University of Arizona.

Tobias, B. A., Kihlstrom, J. F., & Schacter, D. L. (1992). Emotion and implicit memory. In S.-A. Christianson (Ed.), *Handbook of emotion and memory* (pp. 67–92). Hillsdale, NJ: Lawrence Erlbaum Associates, Inc.

Tulving, E. (1983). *Elements of episodic memory.* Oxford: Oxford University Press.

Tulving, E. (1985). Memory and consciousness. *Canadian Psychologist, 26*, 1–12.

Ucros, C. G. (1989). Mood state-dependent memory: A meta-analysis. *Cognition and Emotion, 3*, 139–167.

Weingartner, H., Miller, H., & Murphy, D. L. (1977). Mood-state-dependent retrieval of verbal associations. *Journal of Abnormal Psychology, 86*, 276–284.

7

Affect as Information about Liking, Efficacy, and Importance

GERALD L. CLORE and JUSTIN STORBECK

S unny Spring days are associated with reports of greater life satisfaction (Schwarz & Clore, 1983), greater agreement with persuasive arguments (Sinclair, Mark, & Clore, 1994), and even greater profits from stocks and bonds (Saunders, 1993). Indeed, stock trades from 26 exchanges around the world between 1982 and 1997 showed that profits were up 24.8% on unseasonably sunny days compared to cloudy days (Hirshleifer & Shumway, 2003). Unseasonably sunny weather appears to elicit positive affect, which is then reflected in positive judgments. In this chapter, we discuss such findings from the standpoint of the affect-as-information approach (Clore, Schwarz, & Conway, 1994).

Affective reactions, in this view, provide embodied information about value, that is, about goodness and badness (Clore, Wyer, Dienes, Gasper, Gohm, & Isbell, 2001). Through the lens of positive affect, stocks, life satisfaction, and other objects of judgment seem more positive, and our sense of efficacy on tasks seems higher. In addition, the experience of affective arousal makes situations seem more important. The flashes of affective feeling that we experience thus govern our attitudes, provide red and green lights for different thinking styles, and guide attention and memory.

In our view, these affective influences are functional (Clore, 2005), in contrast to the prevailing view of affect as a source of irrationality and bias in the judgment and decision-making literature. Several other lines of work (e.g., Barrett, Mayer, & Salovey, 2003; Damasio, 1994; Haselton & Ketelaar, this volume) also suggest the adaptive value of affect as information for making judgments and decisions.

This review is organized into three sections devoted to recent investigations of affective influences on judgment, processing, and memory. We focus on new research from this perspective on judgment (see Forgas, this volume), processing (see Bless & Fiedler, this volume), and memory (see Eich & Macaulay, this volume).

AFFECT AND JUDGMENT

Mood influences our judgments of consumer products (Adaval, 1997), political candidates (Ottati & Isbell, 1996), risks (Gasper & Clore, 1998), and life satisfaction (Schwarz & Clore, 1983), as well as many other kinds of evaluations (e.g., Esses & Zanna, 1995; Forgas, Bower, & Krantz, 1984; Forgas & Moylan, 1991; Keltner, Locke, & Audrain, 1993). To determine whether such evaluations really reflect the influence of affect rather than of cognitive content, investigators often use films, music, and other techniques to vary feelings independently of thoughts about the object of judgment. The results show that affect does influence evaluative judgment quite readily, even when objectively irrelevant to the object of judgment. Since affective feelings usually are reactions to something in particular, affect that has no salient object (e.g., mood) tends to be experienced as a reaction to whatever is in mind at the time, a process that Clore et al. (2001) referred to as the immediacy principle. Of course, such affective promiscuity (in which objectless affect attaches itself to substitute objects) was also a cornerstone of Freud's (1959/1915) theory.

Affect-as-Information

The affect-as-information approach (e.g., Clore et al., 2001; Schwarz & Clore, 1983, 1988, 1996) rests on the idea that affective processes mainly occur outside of awareness. As a result, we are "strangers to ourselves" (Wilson, 2002), and the experience of affect is therefore crucial for providing us with conscious information about our unconscious appraisals. Affective feelings thus allow us to learn about our own implicit judgments and decisions.

Traditionally, investigators of judgment and decision-making emphasized the role of accessible information about objects of judgment and decision alternatives. Such stimulus information is important, of course, but it has gradually become apparent that the proximal factor in judgments and decisions is really a person's actual and anticipated affective reactions to that information (e.g., Baumeister et al., this volume; Schwarz & Clore, in press).

Integral Affect   The widespread acceptance of the role of affect means that it is no longer mandatory to induce irrelevant moods in order to vary affect independently of cognitive content. Thus, some studies now focus on integral, as opposed to incidental, affect (e.g., Harber, 2005; Pham, 2004). Does the affect-as-information position apply to integral affect studies, since they involve neither irrelevant mood nor misattribution? It does, because the theory is not really about mood, but is rather a general account of affective influences. Mood manipulations have simply provided investigators with a convenient source of unassigned affect. The larger idea is simply that when making evaluative judgments, people often attend to their feelings as if asking themselves, "How do I feel about it?" (Schwarz & Clore, 1988). When they do, they generally like what they feel good about and dislike what they feel bad about. But the link between affect and liking ultimately depends on its information value. The information value depends in turn on tacit attributions about the source and apparent meaning of the affect (Schwarz & Clore, 1983). In addition, it depends on the context, so that sad affect during a sad movie, for example, would be expected to increase rather than decrease evaluation of the film (Martin, 2001).

Heuristics Following the "How do I feel about it?" heuristic suggested by Schwarz and Clore (1988), Slovic, Finucane, Peters, and MacGregor (2003) proposed a similar "affect heuristic," and Monin (2003) proposed a "warm glow heuristic." Slovic et al. suggest that the affect heuristic leads to "probability neglect." That is, when potential outcomes are highly emotionally desirable or undesirable, people tend to ignore information about how probable or improbable they are, as illustrated by the rush to buy lottery tickets when large jackpots are announced.

Monin's (2003) "warm glow" heuristic, on the other hand, concerns the mere exposure effect. The mere exposure effect involves liking after familiarization, but Monin found that people also judge attractive faces and other liked stimuli as familiar. Using the affect-as-information approach, Monin suggested that people sometimes attribute the warm glow of positive feelings from liking as due to familiarity.

In a related way, various other investigators also assume that the attributional processes outlined in the feelings-as-information approach govern the construction of a variety of kinds of judgment situations. These include the impact of value from regulatory fit (Higgins, Idson, Freitas, Spiegel, & Molden, 2003), the role of ease of retrieval in belief and attitude judgment (Schwarz, 1998), and the influence of affect from processing fluency in mere exposure and other situations (Winkielman, Schwarz, Fazendeiro, & Reber, 2003). To illustrate the wide applicability of such affective processes, we consider next affective influences on perception.

Research

Perception In the 1950s, investigators of what was called the "New Look" (Bruner, 1957) proposed that perception was not a passive registration of external reality, but an adaptive process reflecting internal expectations and motivations. Fifty years later, research is again examining how internal factors, including emotion, have an impact on perception of the physical world. For example, research shows that when people are elderly, tired, or are simply wearing a heavy backpack, they perceive hills as steeper and distances as farther (e.g., Proffitt, Creem, & Zosh, 2001; Witt, Proffitt, & Epstein, 2004). In addition, some research has examined how negative affect can also cause people to make mountains out of molehills. For example, Riener, Stefanucci, Proffitt, and Clore (2003) had participants listen to happy or sad music as they stood at the base of a relatively steep hill and made multiple judgments of the degree of incline. They discovered that sad mood led people to overestimate steepness when it was assessed verbally and visually, but not when assessed haptically, through the use of a paddle board that participants adjusted by feel rather than by sight. Affective feelings thus appear to inform explicit, but not implicit, measures of perception.

Specific Emotions   In addition to studies of happy and sad mood, investigators are also increasingly examining specific emotions (e.g., Tiedens & Linton, 2001). For example, Lerner, Small, and Loewenstein (2004) found that disgust eliminates the endowment effect (the tendency to put a higher selling price on something one owns than one would have been willing to pay for it initially). The phenomenon indicates that mere ownership confers value. Feelings of disgust, however, appeared to *contaminate* the object, since both sellers and buyers reduced their prices.

Disgust has also been a focus of work by Haidt (2001) on morality. He proposed that moral judgments reflect emotional responses rather than deliberative moral reasoning, as assumed since Kohlberg (1969). In his studies of "moral dumbfounding," Haidt asks students to consider a variety of odd behaviors, such as siblings having sex or a person eating his pet dog after it is killed in an accident. Participants find such acts immoral, but they are unsure why. Haidt suggests that the judgments of immorality are based on reactions of disgust, and that the reasons people give for their judgments are really afterthoughts. Evidence comes from two experiments by Schnall, Haidt, and Clore (2005) who found that inducing feelings of disgust led to more severe moral judgments among people who routinely attend to their own bodily cues. For example, disgust was induced by having participants work in a dirty environment (e.g., sitting at a dirty desk next to an overflowing garbage can, etc.). Results showed that, at least for individuals who attend to their bodily cues, feelings of disgust were experienced as moral indignation, suggesting that moral judgments may indeed be based on affect.

The effects of fear and anger on judgments have also been examined in studies of attitudes toward outgroups (Mackie, Devos, & Smith, 2000). Different emotions mediated different reactions in that groups that were feared tended to be avoided, whereas groups that made people angry tended to elicit aggressiveness. Similarly, DeSteno, Dasgupta, Bartlett, and Cajdric (2004) found that anger increased implicit prejudice toward an outgroup, whereas sadness and neutrality did not.

Fear and anxiety have been the focus of research on risk (e.g., Butler & Mathews, 1987; Gasper & Clore 1998). Indeed, Loewenstein, Weber, Hsee, and Welch (2001) proposed a "risk-as-feeling model," which is quite similar to affect-as-information approaches. They suggest that risk estimates are more often guided by internal feelings than by objective evidence about risks and probabilities. For example, when deciding whether to get insurance against floods or earthquakes, people tend to overestimate the likelihood of such events if they are exposed to vivid examples that elicit affect.

Individual Differences   The pervasiveness of such influences leads one to ask whether all evaluative judgments and decisions are based on affect and emotion. Some investigators seem to assume that they are (e.g., Cabanac, Guillaume, Balasko, & Fleury, 2002; Loewenstein, 1996; Pham, 2004). But studies of mood and political choice (Isbell & Wyer, 1999; Ottati & Isbell, 1996) found mood effects on candidate evaluations mainly for individuals with little political knowledge. Mood effects were not found among those who were more politically informed. Individual differences in emotional intelligence also play a role (for a review of relevant scales see Gohm & Clore, 2000). For example, people who attend to their feelings, compared to those who do not, show mood effects (Gasper & Clore, 2000), as do people high in self-esteem, compared to those low in self-esteem (Harber, 2005). For example, Harber (2005) asked respondents to rate how distressed infants seemed to be during a circumcision operation on the basis of their recorded cries. He found that only high-esteem individuals relied on their own affective reactions as information about the distress of the infants.

Unconscious Processes   We have emphasized the role of experienced affective cues, but it turns out that similar effects can be found with primed concepts. For example, Winkielman, Zajonc, and Schwarz (1997) found that subliminally exposed happy or angry faces influenced liking for novel Chinese ideographs presented immediately afterward. Clore and Colcombe (2003) also reported mood-like effects after unconscious priming with happy and sad words. Such studies show that affective stimuli outside of awareness can influence judgment in a manner similar to that of affective feelings.

The parallel effects of affective mood and unconscious affective primes could have several meanings. They could mean that mood effects are generally mediated by mood-congruent conceptual primes (Bower, Monteiro, & Gilligan, 1978; Forgas & Bower, 1988; Isen, Shalker, Clark, & Karp, 1978). The findings could also mean the reverse, namely, that affective priming is effective because it elicits unconscious affect (Bargh, 1997; Winkielman et al., 1997). However, we favor a different possibility. Induced mood and subliminal affective primes have similar effects simply because both are compelling forms of affective information (Clore & Colcombe, 2003). The contribution of the affect-as-information perspective lies in the discovery that it is not affective feeling per se, but the compelling nature of the evaluative information that such feeling conveys. However, when confronted with an attitude object, we can also be informed by the emergence of positive or negative thoughts or inclinations toward it as a result of conceptual priming. The critical element is whether or not such feelings, thoughts, and inclinations are experienced as spontaneous reactions to the object of judgment. We construct our explicit attitudes by being visited by such affective information. These considerations raise larger issues about the role of conscious and unconscious processes more generally, a topic that we touch upon next.

Consciousness   If we need affective feelings to inform us about what we like and dislike, then it would seem to follow that the liking and disliking itself must occur out of awareness. If so, then feelings may only be correlated with, and not necessarily causal in, the formation of (implicit) liking. The role of consciousness of attitude objects and feelings would then mainly serve to ensure that explicit judgments are consistent with already formed implicit judgments. If so, *implicit* liking may be thought of as an unconscious association between some hormonal (e.g., dopamine) release in response to a neural representation of an attitude object. *Explicit* liking would then be the conscious association of the experience of that affect and the experience of the attitude object.

Crick and Koch (1998) have speculated about the basis and function of consciousness. They note that part of the brain acts like a zombie by producing motor output from visual input without being able to say what was seen. For example, lore has it that tennis players can react to a fast serve before they can see the ball, and that the seeing might come afterward. They suggest, however, that we are probably not guided merely by a collection of unconscious, specialized zombie systems for specific tasks, because that would be an inefficient arrangement. Instead, they proposed that our single, conscious representation of visual scenes has the benefit of reducing hesitation as the brain chooses among possible plans for action.

Does the same logic hold for emotion? Since most emotional processing is unavailable to awareness, could emotional tasks be handled by an unconscious affective zombie system? No, we suggest that the conscious feelings that do accompany emotions too are important as they motivate attention and action, influence choice, and alert us about what is of value.

Summary

We noted that the general acceptance of affective influences has led to an increase in studies relying on integral affect, and that the affect-as-information approach is equally applicable to instances of incidental and integral affect. The general applicability of the approach has led to the postulation of similar heuristics and to its use in a wide variety of social cognitive explanations. We reviewed research on the influence of sad affect on perception of the inclines of hills (Riener et al., 2003), and reviewed a variety of studies of specific emotions with judgment outcomes, including disgust, fear, and anger. For example, some findings indicate that anger leads to different orientations toward outgroups than does fear (Mackie et al., 2000) or sadness (DeSteno et al., 2004). In other research, disgust was shown to lower the desirability of associated objects (Lerner et al., 2004), but to heighten the sensitivity to moral infractions (Schnall et al., 2005). Anxiety was also found to elevate risk estimates (Loewenstein et al., 2001). Some research shows individual differences in affect use. For example, Harber (2005) suggested that low-esteem individuals tend not to base their judgments on their feelings, because they do not find their feelings to be a credible source of information. But individuals who habitually attend to their feelings appear especially likely to use them in judgment (Gasper & Clore, 2000).

We next discussed unconscious factors in affective influences on judgment (e.g., Winkielman et al., 1997). We examined the parallel results of unconscious affective priming and conscious mood manipulations, suggesting that each reflects the activation of affective meanings that are compelling and easily misattributed (Clore & Colcombe, 2003). We noted that the reason one needs the information conveyed in one's affective reactions in the first place is that the actual processes of liking and attitude formation are unconscious. We suggested that implicit liking reflects unconscious affective reactions, but explicit liking is a construction that relies on the conscious experience of affect (Clore, Storbeck, Robinson, & Centerbar, 2005). We turn next to a consideration of the influence of affect on styles of information processing.

AFFECT AND COGNITIVE PROCESSING

Positive and negative feelings are essentially our attitude toward whatever is in focus at the time. The basic rule of affect in judgment is, "If it feels good, it is good." But when we are focused on a task instead of an object of judgment, then our positive affect may be experienced as feelings of efficacy instead of as feelings of liking. Such positive feedback promotes reliance on one's own beliefs, expectations, and inclinations. The basic rule of affect in problem-solving tasks, therefore, is, "If it feels good, just do it." Depending on one's focus of attention, affective valence can provide information that an object of judgment is good or bad or that one's knowledge, expectations, and inclinations are adequate or inadequate for a task. In that case, rather than conveying attitude, affect guides how we process information. Positive affect promotes interpretive or "relational" processing; negative affect leads to detailed, stimulus-bound, or "referential" processing.

The general idea is that everyday information processing involves a constant interplay of perception and cognition. Neisser (1976) characterized this as a "perceptual cycle." In this cycle, he proposed that whatever schema is active guides information search, information search then provides new data, and new data in turn modifies the active schema, and so on. Piaget (1954/1981) also proposed that the developing child both assimilates incoming information to existing schemas and accommodates new information by changing existing schemas. Visual perception too is assumed to involve a constant interplay of top-down and bottom-up processes (e.g., Palmer, 1975).

The influence of affect can be thought of as privileging one or the other of these processes. For example, positive affective cues appear to trigger assimilation, top-down, or theory-driven processing, whereas negative affect elicits accommodation, bottom-up, or data-driven processing (e.g., Clore et al., 2001; Fiedler, 2001). Other related characterizations emphasize that affect conveys information about task situations as benign or as problematic, which elicits cognitive tuning (Schwarz & Clore, 1996). In that view, when positive affect signals a benign situation, people engage in heuristic processing, whereas when negative affect signals a problematic situation, people engage in more systematic processing. A variation is to suggest that positive affect, but not negative affect, results in reliance on general knowledge structures (Bless, Clore, Golisano, Rabel, & Schwarz, 1996). Our own current view is that positive affect leads to "relational" processing, and negative affect to "referential" or item-specific processing (Storbeck & Clore, 2005). These accounts make generally similar predictions. One phenomenon explained by these accounts is the influence of affect on global versus local processing, to which we turn next.

Research

Global versus Local Processing   Gasper and Clore (2002) found that individuals in happy moods were more likely than those in sad moods to match geometric figures on the basis of global rather than local similarities. In addition, Gasper (2004) found that as happiness increases, people also become faster at making global matches, whereas increases in sad mood speed-up local matches. This finding is interesting, because one might have expected sad moods to slow instead of speed-up reaction times. In addition, Gasper (2004) manipulated attributions and showed that, consistent with expectations from the affect-as-information approach, the effects of mood on global versus local focus depend on the apparent information value of the happy and sad feelings.

Other experiments also suggest that mood affects global and local attention. For example, Isbell, Burns, and Haaar (2005) demonstrated that affect influences the extent to which individuals select global versus specific social information when forming impressions. They found that happy participants were more likely to form impressions of others by examining global information (e.g., traits) before they looked at more specific information (e.g., behaviors). The results suggest that affect influences the types of information that individuals *seek out* when forming impressions of others.

Stereotypes The idea that positive affect elicits a focus on global rather than local stimuli can also be applied to the relationship between mood and stereotype use. Research has demonstrated that happy moods lead to increased stereotyping, while sad moods lead to reduced stereotyping (e.g., Bodenhausen, Kramer, & Süsser, 1994; Isbell, 2004). In addition, Bodenhausen, Sheppard, and Kramer (1994) showed that angry participants behaved like participants in happy moods. Both groups were more likely than sad participants to use an ethnic stereotype to convict a defendant in a mock trial situation. This result is somewhat surprising until one considers that both anger and happiness imply that one's own perspective is correct. Anger appears to be an emotion specifically concerned with asserting the rightness of one's own perspective. Indeed, angry individuals, even more than those in positive moods, may feel empowered to rely on their own beliefs, expectations, and inclinations.

Egalitarianism According to the affect-as-information approach, happy mood serves as a green light and sad mood as a red light for relying on accessible cognitions and inclinations. If so, the fact that stereotypes are so often accessible in the society at large suggests that individuals in happy (or angry) moods are likely to use stereotypes in everyday life. However, some research suggests that the effect of mood on stereotyping may depend critically on perceivers' goals.

Dunn and Clore (2004) reasoned that people who are chronically motivated to be egalitarian might exhibit less stereotyping in a happy mood, because positive mood promotes responding on the basis of one's accessible inclinations. If their inclination is to avoid stereotypical thinking, then positive feelings may act as a green light and negative affect as red light for that inclination. If so, then in contrast to the usual pattern, chronic egalitarians might show less stereotyping in happy moods and increased stereotyping in sad moods, as negative affect blocks their egalitarian inclinations. This is exactly what they found: chronic egalitarians in happy moods reduced stereotyping towards women in a lexical decision task, whereas controls in happy moods revealed more stereotyping of females in the same task. Thus, rather than exerting a direct influence on stereotyping, positive affect enhances dominant responses, which in the case of chronic egalitarians is to avoid stereotyping.

Priming Affect-as-information approaches have typically examined explicit processes, but the approach should also apply to implicit processes. To examine this possibility, Storbeck and Clore (2005) induced either positive or negative moods with music and then had participants complete either an evaluation-priming task, a categorization-priming task, or a lexical decision-priming task. They found that happy moods promoted the typical priming effects in each task, whereas sad moods inhibited priming. These effects were observed for all three priming tasks and for multiple prime presentation durations. Other researchers have found similar mood effects on priming and Stroop-like tasks (Corson, 2004; Hanze & Hesse, 1993; Hermsen, Holland, and van Knippenberg, 2004). Collectively, these studies suggest that mood may influence cognitive processes at an implicit, automatic level.

False Memory Effects The activation of implicit semantic associations observed in priming effects has also been proposed as the mechanism behind the Deese–Roediger–McDermott false memory paradigm (Roediger, Balota, & Watson, 2001). Based on this assumption, positive moods should promote such implicit associations and negative mood should impair implicit associations, thereby reducing false memory effects. Storbeck and Clore (2005) found support for this prediction. That is, when exposed to lists of words, each of which was associated with a different critical lure, individuals in happy moods recalled more critical lures, which had never been presented, compared to individuals in sad moods. For example, happy individuals were more likely to recall the word "sleep" (a critical lure) after studying associated words such as bed, pillow, awake, rest, wake, etc. Moreover, further experiments provided evidence suggesting that these effects were due to mood influences on encoding, rather than on retrieval processes.

Mood Effects Without Mood Before leaving the topic of affect and processing, it is important to note that sources of affective information other than mood often have similar influences. For example, evidence from Clore and Colcombe (2003) suggests that without changing people's moods, unconsciously primed affective thoughts can have mood-like effects on information processing. The same has been found for making happy and sad facial expressions (e.g., Schnall & Clore, 2002; Strack, Martin, & Stepper, 1988), and even for "happy" and "sad" colors (Soldat & Sinclair, 2001). Of course, unconscious priming, posed expressions, and related stimuli sometimes do affect mood, but in these instances their efforts were not mediated by mood. Hence, it appears that various different kinds of affective cues can have similar effects.

Similar effects can be expected to the extent that cues from diverse sources all convey information about goodness or badness (Clore & Colcombe, 2003).

Indeed, even in studies of felt mood, we assume that the active agent is not the feelings themselves, but their information value, as discussed earlier. The spontaneity and compellingness of the evaluative information are more important than whether the medium of the information consists of facial muscles, motor actions, visceral feelings, or thoughts. Thus, the influence of affective feedback on judgment and processing is not limited to feelings, because such affective information can be represented in multiple embodied media.

Relevant Neuroscience

Behavioral research by Gray (2001) found that positive moods increased performance on verbal working memory tasks, while negative moods decreased performance. A follow-up study done by Gray, Braver, and Raichle (2002) found that such mood and task manipulations led to changes within lateral prefrontal cortex, suggesting that moods paired with a task shifted processing to different neural areas. A study by Baker, Frith, and Dolan (1997) found that sad individuals performing a verbal fluency task showed reduced activation of areas relevant to verbal working memory. These findings are consistent with the neurological models proposed by Drevets (2000), George, Ketter, Parekh, Herscovitch, and Post (1996), and Mayberg et al. (1999). This brief look at activation patterns in the brain during positive and negative emotional states highlights some of the connections between emotional and cognitive areas (Drevets, 2000; Drevets & Raichle, 1998; Mayberg, 1997). In negative moods, one sees greater activation of limbic and emotional areas and less activation of areas relevant to working memory and attention. This pattern is consistent with the affect-as-information idea that sad mood leads to referential or item-specific processing. That is, individuals in sad moods tend to focus on perceptual data from the environment and are less concerned with cognitive associations in memory. In positive moods, the reverse is true. Limbic and emotional areas become less active, and the prefrontal areas associated with working memory and attention become more active. This pattern is consistent with the affect-as-information idea that happy moods lead to relational processing. That is, they are focused on relating incoming information to accessible cognitions in memory.

The neurological data might imply that the relationship between affect and processing is really a neuroanatomical rather than a psychological phenomenon. That is, perhaps good mood and relational processing occur together simply because they show the same neural address. The reality appears likely to be more complex, however, in part because attribution manipulations can so readily alter or reverse the mood-processing relationship. That is, awareness that one's affective feelings are irrelevant and do not represent efficacy feedback tends to reverse mood effects on processing (e.g., Dienes, 1996; Gasper, 2004; Isbell, 2004).

Summary

In this section, we discussed research on how affect influences cognitive processing. The research shows that processing strategies can be influenced by happy and sad moods (e.g., Schwarz & Clore, 1996), by specific emotions (e.g., Tiedens & Linton, 2001), by feedback from emotional expressions (e.g., Schnall, Clore, & Ryan, 2005), and even by engaging in approach and avoidance actions (e.g., Friedman & Förster, 2000). According to the affect-as-information perspective (e.g., Clore et al., 2001), these affective cues serve as feedback about the task (or one's efficacy on the task), which elicits cognitive processing tuned to the kind of situation signaled by the affect.

Specifically, positive moods promote processing of items relationally, which should increase priming, false memory effects, creative problem solving, and accessibility of automatic attitudes. On the other hand, negative moods should promote referential or item-specific processing, which should reduce effects that rely on relational processing, such as priming and the false memory effect. We reviewed imaging studies that find activation of different neural substrates for positive and negative moods. Those data show that positive moods increase activity relevant to verbal working memory and verbal associations, task switching, and error detection, whereas negative moods increase areas concerned with spatial working memory and visual attention. Such patterns are compatible with the behavioral results of mood on processing.

AFFECT AND MEMORY

Mood and Memory

Some of the most influential studies of affect and cognition were early studies by Bower et al. (1978) and by Isen et al. (1978). Both programs of work focused on the idea that mood activates valence-congruent material in memory. Bower (1981) suggested that moods act like nodes in memory that are capable of activating associated material in memory. Isen, who was focused more on judgment and behavior, suggested also that moods should activate mood-congruent material in memory, setting up a cognitive loop that would influence judgment (see also Eich & Macaulay, this volume).

An important difference between memory-based models and the affect-as-information approach lies in whether evaluative judgments are based on cognitive or affective factors. The memory-based models assume that affect operates through the concepts and beliefs that it brings to mind, whereas informational models assume that affect itself is often the critical stimulus. The issue is whether liking consists of having particular thoughts or particular feelings and inclinations?

One way to address the issue is to examine whether affect does activate affect-congruent material in memory. There is little doubt that feeling happy or depressed is often accompanied by similarly valenced thoughts. The question is whether such ideation is activated directly by affect or by cognitions about affect. A review of the mood and memory literature (Wyer, Clore, & Isbell, 1999) suggests caution in assuming that memory activation comes from the affect itself, as opposed to coming from cognitions inadvertently activated by mood induction procedures.

Of course focusing attention on one's feelings will result in feeling-congruent thoughts, just as focusing on a chair will result in chair-relevant thoughts. But this is an unremarkable claim. The issue is whether background feelings of mood themselves should automatically activate mood-congruent material in memory (rather than whether thoughts about mood would do so). A recent review by Storbeck, Robinson, and McCourt (in press) suggests that memory is organized in terms of descriptive categories (e.g., animals, places, etc.) rather than in terms of evaluations (e.g., good, bad).

Studies that have varied mood and the salience of mood-relevant concepts (e.g., Parrott & Sabini, 1990) suggest that mood itself may not be the active agent determining which memories come to mind. In addition, although mood does appear to govern priming generally (Storbeck & Clore, 2005), it does not lead to mood-congruent priming. Also, the asymmetry seen in mood effects on memory is not mirrored in mood effects on judgment, suggesting that mood effects on judgment may not be memory based. Indeed, a host of findings in the social cognition literature has long suggested that interpersonal judgments are surprisingly independent of the content of memories about people (for a review see Wyer & Srull, 1989). Thus, despite the popularity of the idea, it is not clear that mood effects on cognition are mediated by the activation of mood-congruent material in memory. However, new data do show that affective factors are crucial for understanding memory, as detailed below.

Arousal-as-Importance

From the affect-as-information perspective, the valence of affect provides information about goodness and badness and the arousal component provides information about importance (Clore & Schnall, 2005; Frijda, Ortony, Sonnemans, & Clore, 1992; Simon, 1967). Arousal draws attention to salient environmental stimuli, thereby influencing what gets consolidated into long-term memory. Arousal marks information as important both implicitly, through the action of adrenergic hormones, and explicitly, through the subjective experience of importance.

Research suggests that arousal will have its greatest influence on memory for events two days after encoding (see Christianson, 1984; McGaugh, 2004). Until recently, most relevant behavioral research has been limited to studies of arousal-congruent memory (e.g., Gilligan & Bower, 1984) and memory after relatively short delays (e.g., Varner & Ellis, 1998). Most of the relevant evidence comes from neuroscience data using rats, although some human data are beginning to appear.

Relevant Neuroscience

The implicit operation of arousal is mediated by the adrenergic hormonal system. Working with rats, McGaugh (2004) has found ample evidence that endogenous stress hormones directly and indirectly mediate amygdala activity. In turn, the amygdala then mediates the consolidation of long-term memories in the neocortex (e.g., hippocampus). Such a system presumably does not need the subjective experience of arousal to enhance memory (Cahill & Alkire, 2003). However, the activation of the amygdala by this system may be involved in drawing attention to stimuli in the environment. Back-projections from the amygdala to the visual cortex provide information about which features should be attended to and stored (Rolls, 1999).

The amygdala also modulates the long-term potentiation process that occurs in the hippocampus, which is necessary for the formation of declarative (experienced) memory (Abe, 2001). Consistent with such conclusions is the observation that patients with amygdala lesions fail to show enhanced memory for arousing stimuli (Adolphs, Cahill, Schul, & Babinsky, 1997). But amnesics with an intact amygdala do show enhanced memory for emotional stimuli (Hamann, Cahill, McGaugh, & Squire, 1997). Research in normal populations using imaging technology has also shown the amygdala to be involved in the enhanced memory for emotional stimuli (Cahill et al., 1996). Cahill et al. presented a series of affectively laden pictures and tested memory for the pictures 3 weeks later. They found an impressive correlation ($r = .93$) between amygdala activation during encoding and recall of those images (see Cahill, McGaugh, & Weinberger, 2001; Canli, Zhao, Brewer, Gabrieli, & Cahill, 2000; Guy & Cahill, 1999; Hamann, Ely, Grafton, & Kilts, 1999 for similar results).

In addition, Hamann et al. (1997, 1999) have observed similar memory enhancement effects for positive as well as negative images. Ashby, Isen, and Turken (1999) suggested a similar modulatory role for positive affect on memory via dopamine. They proposed that dopamine modulates the release of excitatory neurotransmitters vital for increased consolidation. Such considerations suggest that emotional memory enhancement is not limited to negative emotions.

Summary

Emotional arousal appears to act at both encoding (attention and elaboration) and consolidation (Hamann, 2001). Moreover, the effect can occur for various types of stimuli including emotional words, pictures, and stories (Cahill et al., 2001; Canli et al., 2000; Guy & Cahill, 1999; Hamann, 2001; Kleinsmith & Kaplan, 1963). We noted that arousal appears to be the critical factor, as evident in results reported by Cahill, Prins, Weber, and McGaugh (1994), who found that β-adrenergic blocking agents (which block adrenergic stress hormones) eliminate enhanced memory for emotional material. The experience of arousal may serve as information to the system about importance, guiding attention and thus selecting the material to be retained or consolidated into long-term memory.

REFERENCES

Abe, K. (2001). Modulation of hippocampal long-term potentiation by the amygdala: A synaptic mechanism linking emotion and memory. *Japanese Journal of Pharmacology, 86*, 18–22.

Adaval, R. (1997). Sometimes it just feels right: The differential weighting of affect-consistent and affect-inconsistent information. *Journal of Consumer Research, 28*, 1–17.

Adolphs, R., Cahill, L., Schul, R., & Babinsky, R. (1997). Impaired declarative memory for emotional material following bilateral amygdala damage in humans. *Learning and Memory, 4*, 291–300.

Ashby, F., Isen, A., & Turken, A. (1999). A neuropsychological theory of positive affect and its influence on cognition. *Psychological Review, 106*, 529–550.

Baker, S., Frith, C., & Dolan, R. (1997). The interaction between mood and cognitive function studied with PET. *Psychological Medicine, 27*, 565–578.

Bargh, J. A. (1997). The automaticity of everyday life. In R. S. Wyer (Ed.), *Advances in social cognition* (Vol. 10, pp. 1–61). Mahwah, NJ: Lawrence Erlbaum Associates, Inc.

Barrett, L. F., Mayer, J. D., & Salovey, P. (Eds.) (2003). *The wisdom of feelings: Processes underlying emotional intelligence.* New York: Guilford Press.

Bless, H., Clore, G. L., Golisano, V., Rabel, C., & Schwarz, N. (1996). Mood and the use of scripts: Do happy moods really make people mindless? *Journal of Personality and Social Psychology, 71*, 665–678.

Bodenhausen, G. V., Kramer, G. P., & Süsser, K. (1994). Happiness and stereotypic thinking in social judgment. *Journal of Personality and Social Psychology, 66*, 621–632.

Bodenhausen, G. V., Sheppard, L. A., & Kramer, G. P. (1994). Negative affect and social judgment: The differential impact of anger and sadness. *European Journal of Social Psychology, 24*, 45–62.

Bower, G. H. (1981). Mood and memory. *American Psychologist, 36*, 129–148.

Bower, G. H., Monteiro, K. P., & Gilligan, S. G. (1978). Emotional mood as a context of learning and recall. *Journal of Verbal Learning and Verbal Behavior, 17*, 573–585.

Bruner, J. S. (1957). Going beyond the information given. In J. S. Bruner, E. Brunswik, L. Festinger, F. Heider, K. F. Muenzinger, C. E. Osgood, & D. Rapaport (Eds.), *Contemporary approaches to cognition* (pp. 41–69). Cambridge, MA: Harvard University Press.

Butler, G., & Mathews, A. (1987). Anticipatory anxiety and risk perception. *Cognitive Therapy and Research, 11*, 551–565.

Cabanac, M., Guillaume, J., Balasko, M., & Fleury, A. (2002). Pleasure in decision-making situations. *BMC Psychiatry, 2*, 7. This article is available at http://www.biomed-central.com/1471-244X/2/7

Cahill, L., & Alkire, M. (2003). Epinephrine enhancement of human memory consolidation: Interaction with arousal at encoding. *Neurobiology of Learning and Memory, 79*, 194–198.

Cahill, L., Haier, R., Fallon, J., Alkire, M., Tang, C., Keator, D., Wu, J., & McGaugh, J. (1996). Amygdala activity at encoding correlated with long-term, free recall of emotional information. *Proceedings of the National Academy of Sciences of the United States of America, 93*, 8016–8021.

Cahill, L., McGaugh, J., & Weinberger, N. (2001). The neurobiology of learning and memory: Some reminders to remember. *Trends in Neurosciences, 24*, 578–581.

Cahill, L., Prins, B., Weber, M., & McGaugh, J. (1994). β-Adrenergic activation and memory for emotional events. *Nature, 371*, 702–704.

Canli, T., Zhao, Z., Brewer, J., Gabrieli, J., & Cahill, L. (2000). Event-related activation in the human amygdala associates with later memory for individual emotional experience. *Journal of Neuroscience, 20*, RC99.

Christianson, S. A. (1984). The relationship between induced emotional arousal and amnesia. *Scandinavian Journal of Psychology, 25*, 147–160.

Clore, G. L. (2005). For love or money: Some emotional foundations of rationality. *Chicago Kent Law Review, 80*, 1151–1165.

Clore, G. L., & Colcombe, S. (2003). The parallel worlds of affective concepts and feelings. In J. Musch & K. C. Klauer (Eds.), *The psychology of evaluation: Affective processes in cognition and emotion* (pp. 335–370). Mahwah, NJ: Lawrence Erlbaum Associates, Inc.

Clore, G. L., & Schnall, S. (2005). The influences of affect on attitude. In D. Albarracín, B. T. Johnson, & M. P. Zanna (Eds.), *Handbook of attitudes and attitude change.* Mahwah, NJ: Lawrence Erlbaum Associates, Inc.

Clore, G. L., Schwarz, N., & Conway, M. (1994). Affective causes and consequences of social information processing. In R. S. Wyer & T. Srull (Eds.), *The handbook of social cognition* (2nd ed., pp. 323–417). Mahwah, NJ: Lawrence Erlbaum Associates, Inc.

Clore, G. L., Storbeck, J., Robinson, M. D., & Centerbar, D. (2005). Seven sins of research on unconscious affect. In L. F. Barrett, P. Niedenthal, & P. Winkielman (Eds.), *Emotion: Conscious and unconscious.* New York: Guilford Press.

Clore, G. L., Wyer, R. S., Dienes, B., Gasper, K., Gohm, C., & Isbell, L. (2001). Affective feelings as feedback: Some cognitive consequences. In L. L. Martin & G. L. Clore (Eds.), *Theories of mood and cognition: A user's handbook* (pp. 27–62). Mahwah, NJ: Lawrence Erlbaum Associates, Inc.

Corson, Y. (2004). Effects of positive, negative, and neutral moods on associative and semantic priming. *Current Psychology of Cognition, 21,* 33–62.

Crick, F., & Koch, C. (1998). Consciousness and neuroscience. *Cerebral Cortex, 8,* 97–107.

Damasio, A. R. (1994). *Descartes' error: Emotion, reason, and the human brain.* New York: Avon.

DeSteno, D., Dasgupta, N., Bartlett, M. Y., & Cajdric, A. (2004). Prejudice from thin air: The effect of emotion on automatic intergroup attitudes. *Psychological Science, 15,* 319–324.

Dienes, B. P. A. (1996). *Mood as information: Affective cues for cognitive processing styles.* Unpublished doctoral dissertation, University of Illinois.

Drevets, W. (2000). Neuroimaging studies of mood disorders. *Biological Psychiatry, 48,* 813–829.

Drevets, W., & Raichle, M. (1998). Reciprocal suppression of regional cerebral blood flow during emotional versus higher cognitive processes: Implications for interactions between emotion and cognition. *Cognition and Emotion, 12,* 353–385.

Dunn, E. W., & Clore, G. L. (October 2004). *New light on mood and stereotyping.* Ft. Worth, TX: Society of Experimental Social Psychology.

Esses, V. M., & Zanna, M. P. (1995). Mood and the expression of ethnic stereotypes. *Journal of Personality and Social Psychology, 69,* 1052–1068.

Fiedler, K. (2001). Affective states trigger processes of assimilation and accomodation. In L. L. Martin & G. L. Clore (Eds.), *Theories of mood and cognition: A user's handbook* (pp. 85–98). Mahwah, NJ: Lawrence Erlbaum Associates, Inc.

Forgas, J. P., & Bower, G. H. (1988). Affect in social and personal judgments. In K. Fiedler & J. P. Forgas (Eds.), *Affect, cognition & social behavior* (pp. 183–208). Toronto: Hogrefe.

Forgas, J. P., Bower, G. H., & Krantz, S. E. (1984). The influence of mood on perception of social interactions. *Journal of Experimental Social Psychology, 20,* 497–513.

Forgas, J. P., & Moylan, S. (1991). Affective influences on stereotype judgments. *Cognition and Emotion, 5,* 379–395.

Freud, S. (1959). Instincts and their vicissitudes. In E. Jones (Ed.), *Sigmund Freud: Collected papers* (Vol. 4). New York: Basic Books. (Original work published 1915)

Friedman, R. S., & Förster, J. (2000). The effects of approach and avoidance motor actions on the elements of creative insight. *Journal of Personality and Social Psychology, 79(4)*, 477–492.

Frijda, N., Ortony, A., Sonnemans, J., & Clore, G. (1992). The complexity of intensity: Issues concerning the structure of emotion intensity. In M. Clark (Ed.), *Emotion. Review of personality and social psychology* (Vol. 13, pp. 60–89). Newbury Park, CA: Sage.

Gasper, K. (2004). Do you see what I see? Affect and visual information processing. *Cognition and Emotion, 18*, 405–421.

Gasper, K., & Clore, G. L. (1998). The persistent use of negative affect by anxious individuals to estimate risk. *Journal of Personality and Social Psychology, 74*, 1350–1363.

Gasper, K., & Clore, G. L. (2000). Do you have to pay attention to your feelings to be influenced by them? *Personality and Social Psychology Bulletin, 26*, 698–711.

Gasper, K., & Clore, G. L. (2002). Attending to the big picture: Mood and global vs. local processing of visual information. *Psychological Science, 13*, 34–40.

George, M., Ketter, T., Parekh, P., Herscovitch, P., & Post, R. (1996). Gender differences in regional cerebral blood flow during transient self-induced sadness or happiness. *Biological Psychiatry, 40*, 859–871.

Gilligan, S., & Bower, G. H. (1984). Cognitive consequences of emotional arousal. In C. Izard, J. Kagen, & R. Zajonc (Eds.), *Emotion, cognition, and behavior* (pp. 547–588). New York: Cambridge University Press.

Gohm, C. L., & Clore, G. L. (2000). Individual differences in emotional experience: Mapping scales to processes. *Personality and Social Psychology Bulletin, 26*, 679–697.

Gray, J. (2001). Emotional modulation of cognitive control: Approach-withdrawal states double-dissociate spatial from verbal two-back task performance. *Journal of Experimental Psychology: General, 130*, 436–452.

Gray, J., Braver, T., & Raichle, M. (2002). Integration of emotion and cognition in the lateral prefrontal cortex. *Proceedings of the National Academy of Sciences of the United States of America, 99*, 4115–4120.

Guy, S., & Cahill, L. (1999). The role of overt rehearsal in enhanced conscious memory for emotional events. *Consciousness and Cognition, 8*, 114–122.

Haidt, J. (2001). The emotional dog and its rational tail: A social intuitionist approach to moral judgment. *Psychological Review, 108*, 814–834.

Hamann, S. (2001). Cognitive and neural mechanisms of emotional memory. *Trends in Cognitive Sciences, 5*, 394–400.

Hamann, S., Cahill, L., McGaugh, J., & Squire, L. (1997). Intact enhancement of declarative memory for emotional material in amnesia. *Learning and Memory, 4*, 301–309.

Hamann, S., Ely, T., Grafton, S., & Kilts, C. (1999). Amygdala activity related to enhanced memory for pleasant and aversive stimuli. *Nature Neuroscience, 2*, 289–293.

Hanze, M., & Hesse, F. (1993). Emotional influences on semantic priming. *Cognition and Emotion, 7*, 195–205.

Harber, K. (2005). Self-esteem and affect as information. *Personality and Social Psychology Bulletin, 31*, 267–275.

Hermsen, B., Holland, R., & van Knippenberg, A. (2004). *The influence of mood on automatic evaluations.* Unpublished manuscript.

Higgins, E. T., Idson, L. C., Freitas, A. L., Spiegel, S., & Molden, D. C. (2003). Transfer of value from fit. *Journal of Personality and Social Psychology, 84*, 1140–1153.

Hirshleifer, D., & Shumway, T. (2003). Good day sunshine: Stock returns and the weather. *Journal of Finance*, 58(*June*), 1009–1032.

Isbell, L. M. (2004). Not all happy people are lazy or stupid: Evidence of systematic processing in happy moods. *Journal of Experimental Social Psychology*, 40(3), 341–349.

Isbell, L. M., Burns, K. C., & Haaar, T. (2005). *The role of affect on the selection of global versus specific target information*. Unpublished manuscript, University of Massachusetts.

Isbell, L. M., & Wyer, R. S. (1999). Correcting for mood-induced bias in the evaluation of political candidates: The roles of intrinsic and extrinsic motivation. *Personality and Social Psychology Bulletin*, 25, 237–249.

Isen, A. M., Shalker, T. E., Clark, M., & Karp, L. (1978). Affect, accessibility of material in memory, and behavior: A cognitive loop? *Journal of Personality and Social Psychology*, 36, 1–11.

Keltner, D., Locke, K. D., & Audrain, P. C. (1993). The influence of attribution on the relevance of negative feelings to personal satisfaction. *Personality and Social Psychology Bulletin*, 19, 21–29.

Kleinsmith, L. J., & Kaplan, S. (1963). Paired-associate learning as a function of arousal and interpolated interval. *Journal of Experimental Psychology*, 65, 190–193.

Kohlberg, L. (1969). Stage and sequence: The cognitive-developmental approach to socialization. In D. A. Goslin (Ed.), *Handbook of socialization theory and research* (pp. 347–480). Chicago: Rand McNally.

Lerner, J. S., Small, D. A., & Loewenstein, G. (2004). Heart strings and purse strings: Effects of specific emotions on economic transactions. *Psychological Science*, 15, 337–341.

Loewenstein, G. (1996). Out of control: Visceral influences on behavior. *Organizational Behavior and Human Decision Processes*, 65, 272–292.

Loewenstein, G. F., Weber, E. U., Hsee, C. K., & Welch, N. (2001). Risk as feelings. *Psychological Bulletin*, 127, 267–286.

Mackie, D. M., Devos, T., & Smith, E. R. (2000). Intergroup emotions: Explaining offensive action tendencies in an intergroup context. *Journal of Personality and Social Psychology*, 79, 602–616.

Martin, L. L. (2001). Mood as input: A configural view of mood effects. In L. L. Martin & G. L. Clore (Eds.), *Theories of mood and cognition: A user's guidebook* (pp. 135–157). Mahwah, NJ: Lawrence Erlbaum Associates, Inc.

Mayberg, H. (1997). Limbic-cortical dysregulation: A proposed model of depression. *Journal of Neuropsychiatry*, 9, 471–481.

Mayberg, H., Liotti, M., Brannan, S., McGinnis, S., Mahurin, R., Jerabek, P., Silva, J., Tekell, J., Martin, C., Lancaster, J., & Fox, P. (1999). Reciprocal limbic-cortical function and negative mood: Converging PET findings in depression and normal sadness. *American Journal of Psychiatry*, 156, 675–682.

McGaugh, J. (2004). The amygdala modulates the consolidation of memories of emotionally arousing experiences. *Annual Review of Neuroscience*, 27, 1–28.

Monin, B. (2003). The warm glow heuristic: When liking leads to familiarity. *Journal of Personality and Social Psychology*, 85, 1035–1048.

Neisser, U. (1976). *Cognition and reality*. San Francisco: W.H. Freeman & Co.

Ottati, V., & Isbell, L. (1996). Effects of mood during exposure to target information on subsequently reported judgments: An on-line model of misattribution and correction. *Journal of Personality and Social Psychology*, 71, 39–53.

Palmer, S. E. (1975). Visual perception and world knowledge: Notes on a model of sensory-cognitive interaction. In D. A. Norman, D. E. Rumelhart, & the LNR Research Group (Eds.), *Explorations in cognition*. San Francisco: Freeman.

Parrott, W. G., & Sabini, J. (1990). Mood and memory under natural conditions: Evidence for mood incongruent recall. *Journal of Personality and Social Psychology, 59*, 321–336.

Pham, M. T. (2004). The logic of feeling. *Journal of Consumer Psychology, 14*, 360–369.

Piaget, J. (1981). *Intelligence and affectivity: Their relation during child development*. Palo Alto, CA: Annual Reviews (original work published 1954).

Proffitt, D. R., Creem, S. H., & Zosh, W. (2001). Seeing mountains in mole hills: Geographical slant perception. *Psychological Science, 12*, 418–423.

Riener, C., Stefanucci, J. K., Proffitt, D. R., & Clore, G. (2003). *Mood and the perception of spatial layout*. Poster presented at the 44th Annual Meeting of the Psychonomic Society, Vancouver, BC.

Roediger, H., Balota, D., & Watson, J. (2001). Spreading activation and arousal of false memories. In H. L. Roediger, J. S. Nairne, I. Neath, & A. M. Surprenant (Eds.), *The nature of remembering: Essays in honor of Robert G. Crowder. Science conference series* (pp. 95–115). Washington, DC: American Psychological Association.

Rolls, E. T. (1999). *The brain and emotion*. Oxford, UK: Oxford University Press.

Saunders, E. M. J. (1993). Stock prices and wall street weather. *American Economic Review, 83*, 1337–1345.

Schnall, S., & Clore, G. L. (2002, June). *Enacted affect as information: How facial expressions influence recall of emotional events*. Paper presented at the meeting of the American Psychological Society, New Orleans, Louisiana.

Schnall, S., Clore, G. L., & Ryan, K. (2005). *Expression as information: How smiling enables priming*. Unpublished manuscript, University of Virginia.

Schnall, S., Haidt, J., & Clore, G. L. (2005). *Disgust as embodied moral judgment*. Unpublished manuscript, University of Virginia.

Schwarz, N. (1998). Accessible content and accessibility experiences: The interplay of declarative and experiential information in judgment. *Personality and Social Psychology Review, 2*, 87–99.

Schwarz, N., & Clore, G. L. (1983). Mood, misattribution, and judgments of well-being: Informative and directive functions of affective states. *Journal of Personality and Social Psychology, 45*, 513–523.

Schwarz, N., & Clore, G. L. (1988). How do I feel about it? The informative function of mood. In K. Fiedler & J. Forgas (Eds.), *Affect, cognition, and social behavior* (pp. 44–62). Toronto: C. J. Hogrefe.

Schwarz, N., & Clore, G. L. (1996). Feelings and phenomenal experiences. In E. T. Higgins & A. Kruglanski (Eds.), *Social psychology: A handbook of basic principle* (pp. 433–465). New York: Guilford Press.

Schwarz, N., & Clore, G. L. (in press). Feelings and phenomenal experiences. In E. T. Higgins & A. Kruglanski (Eds.), *Social psychology. A handbook of basic principles* (2nd ed.). New York: Guilford Press.

Simon, H. A. (1967). Motivational and emotional controls of cognition. *Psychological Review, 74*, 29–39.

Sinclair, R. C., Mark, M. M., & Clore, G. L. (1994). Mood-related persuasion depends on (mis)attributions. *Social Cognition, 12*, 309–326.

Slovic, P., Finucane, M., Peters, E., &. MacGregor, D. G. (2003). The affect heuristic. In T. Gilovich, D. Griffin, & D. Kahneman (Eds.), *Intuitive judgment: Heuristics and biases*. New York: Cambridge University Press.

Soldat, A. S., & Sinclair, R. C. (2001). Colors, smiles, and frowns: External affective cues can directly affect responses to persuasive communications in a mood-like manner without affecting mood. *Social Cognition, 19*, 469–490.

Storbeck, J., & Clore, G. L. (2005). *Affective triggers for cognitive priming.* Unpublished manuscript, University of Virginia.

Storbeck, J., & Clore, G. L. (2005). With sadness comes accuracy, with happiness, false memory: Mood and the false memory effect. *Psychological Science, 16*, 785–791.

Storbeck, J., Robinson, M. D., & McCourt, M. (in press). Semantic processing precedes affect retrieval: The neurological case for cognitive primacy in visual processing. *Review of General Psychology.*

Strack, F., Martin, L. L., & Stepper, S. (1988). Inhibiting and facilitating conditions of the human smile: A nonobtrusive test of the facial feedback hypothesis. *Journal of Personality and Social Psychology, 54*, 768–777.

Tiedens, L. Z., & Linton, S. (2001). Judgment under emotional certainty and uncertainty: The effects of specific emotions on information processing. *Journal of Personality and Social Psychology, 81*, 973–988.

Varner, L., & Ellis, H. (1998). Cognitive activity and physiological arousal: Processes that mediate mood-congruent memory. *Memory and Cognition, 26*, 939–950.

Wilson, T. D. (2002). *Strangers to ourselves: Discovering the adaptive unconscious.* Cambridge, MA: Belknap/Harvard Press.

Winkielman, P., Schwarz, N., Fazendeiro, T. A., & Reber, R. (2003). The hedonic marking of processing fluency: Implications for evaluative judgment. In J. Musch & K. C. Klauer (Eds.), *The psychology of evaluation: Affective processes in cognition and emotion.* Mahwah, NJ: Lawrence Erlbaum Associates, Inc.

Winkielman, P., Zajonc, R. B., & Schwarz, N. (1997). Subliminal affective priming resists attributional interventions. *Cognition and Emotion, 11*, 433–465.

Witt, J. K., Proffitt, D. R., & Epstein, W. (2004). Perceiving distance: A role of effort and intent. *Perception, 33*, 577–590.

Wyer, R. S., Clore, G. L., & Isbell, L. (1999). Affect and information processing. In M. Zanna (Ed.), *Advances in experimental social psychology* (Vol. 31, pp. 1–77). New York: Academic Press.

Wyer, R. S., & Srull, T. K. (1989). *Memory and cognition in its social context.* Hillsdale, NJ: Lawrence Erlbaum Associates, Inc.

8

Emotional Influences on Decision Making

ROY F. BAUMEISTER, KATHLEEN D. VOHS, and DIANNE M. TICE

A long tradition of folk wisdom assumes that emotions make for bad decisions. Being emotionally upset, in particular, is seen as causing people to do foolish, irrational things that they will likely regret later on. The legal system has accepted this view as valid, to the extent that crimes committed in the heat of passion are punished less severely than others (Averill, 1982). Even psychological research has provided some evidence that emotional states can cause people to make choices that lead to irrational or self-destructive outcomes (e.g., Leith & Baumeister, 1996).

Seemingly against this view, evidence has recently converged from multiple perspectives to argue that emotions can also be helpful for decision making (see Forgas, this volume). Perhaps the most dramatic evidence comes from studies of individuals who because of brain damage lack normal emotional reactions. The absence of emotion does not turn these people into paragons of wise, dispassionate, rational decision making. Au contraire, these individuals without emotions seem unable to make choices in a coherent manner or to learn from their mistakes (Damasio, 1994). The implication is that emotions serve some positive function for decision making.

This chapter will seek to provide a theoretical framework that can account for both the harm and the benefit to decision making that emotions can cause. That is, instead of taking one side of the debate as to whether emotions are good or bad for choosing, we will seek to reconcile the seemingly contradictory findings. In order to do that, however, we think it is useful to take a step back and ask why the link between emotion and decision making is generally investigated by exploring how the former affects the latter. Why not the reverse? That is, why do so few researchers ask about the effects of decision making on emotion? There are two easy and pretty good answers, but we think neither is ultimately satisfying.

The first answer is that decision making does not directly or necessarily cause any emotion. People may have plenty of emotions as a result of their decisions, but these emotions are in reaction to external events (how things fared as a result of the decision), not to the inner decision process itself. It is not surprising that little research looks for emotions arising directly from the decision process, because perhaps there is not generally much to find. Yet we think that the emotional reactions to outcomes that stem from decisions are a crucial part of the process.

The second answer is that emotional reactions to outcomes are often unsurprising and straightforward. If you make a decision that turns out well, you will be glad, whereas if your decision leads to disaster then you may be dismayed. These phenomena hardly seem to require years of painstaking laboratory verification. Moreover, if one were to conduct research to make those points, reviewers might well reject the findings as trivial and obvious. But we think that these outcomes, though perhaps trivial and obvious in some respects, when viewed from a more global perspective contain important clues to the link between emotion and decision making. Specifically, these pedestrian observations suggest that decisions may often be guided by the anticipation of the eventual emotional outcome.

This chapter builds on another project by Baumeister, Vohs, DeWall, and Zhang (2006), which addresses the fundamental question of how emotion is related to behavior. That work distinguished between automatic affect and conscious emotion (see below) and went on to propose that conscious emotion serves as a feedback system to facilitate learning. Emotion may have evolved initially for the sake of direct causation of behavior, but in humans there are multiple processes that can guide behavior, so emotion has become primarily a feedback system. Rather than emotion causing behavior, behavior may pursue emotion—which is to say that affect regulation is an important guiding principle behind much, even most, behavior (Baumeister et al., 2006). The present focus on decision making is a somewhat narrower and more specific version of the broader focus on behavior in general.

DUAL PROCESS THEORY OF EMOTIONAL PHENOMENA

Part of the difficulty of explaining the link between emotion and decision making is that there are quite different kinds of emotional phenomena, and the different kinds probably have different effects on decisions (see Baumeister, 2005). For present purposes, the most important distinction is between automatic affect and conscious emotion. (In contrast to other theorists, we use the terms "affect" and "emotion" in specific and noninterchangeable ways, and they are used here to represent the two types of processes of automatic and conscious feelings.) These correspond to the basic distinction between two kinds of cognitive processes, as is currently influential in psychology (see Chaiken & Trope, 1999). Automatic, largely nonconscious processes are highly influential and vital to nearly all forms of behavioral functioning. Conscious, controlled processes have a much more limited scope, but they vastly increase the flexibility and adaptability of human behavior (Bargh, 1994).

Conscious emotions are the full-blown experiences that correspond to what laypersons mean by the term emotions. They typically include a strong subjective feeling as well as some physical response such as arousal. From our experience with the scholarly review process, these features are widely regarded as important causes of behavior, and indeed many alternative explanations for research findings center on these emotions causing behavior. However, conscious emotions are at best a clumsy and inefficient means for guiding behavior, in part because they are slow to arise.

Automatic affects, in contrast, are essentially the rapidly arising evaluative reactions to stimuli and events. They may not even be experienced consciously at all, and if they are felt, they are likely to be nothing more than brief twinges of liking or disliking. They are felt swiftly in response to all sorts of events, and as such they may be useful for guiding behavioral decisions. Following one interpretation of Damasio (1994), Baumeister et al. (2006; also Baumeister, 2005) have speculated that one function of conscious emotion is to create residues that subsequently can give rise to automatic affects. That is, if a person performs an action and later comes to feel sad, or guilty, or regretful, then the next time a similar opportunity arises it is not necessary to re-experience the entire emotion. Rather, the residue of the earlier experience gives rise to an automatic affective reaction that, being unpleasant, helps remind and steer the person to eschew the sort of act that produced a bad outcome the last time.

Good emotions may also leave residues that can be automatically activated on future occasions and guide decisions. It seems likely, though, that the greater psychological power of bad events and negative reactions (than good) will entail that people are more strongly guided by them (Baumeister, Bratslavsky, Finkenauer, & Vohs, 2001). People probably have more tags for negative events and are more sensitive to them than to the good tags.

Obviously, the operation of such a feedback system is far from perfect or infallible. A decision that produced a bad outcome once will not necessarily do so again. If a young man offers to buy an attractive woman a drink at a bar and she rebuffs him, then he may feel a twinge of negative affect when he contemplates approaching another woman—but it is not certain that his offer would be rejected this time, and in fact it might be eagerly accepted. Learning to develop optimal strategies for making many complex decisions may be beyond the reach of the system of automatic affect. Then again, if one were to follow the general pattern of repeating decisions that have usually led to outcomes with positive feelings and avoiding those that produced negative feelings in the past, one will probably do much better than chance (and better than someone who lacks emotional inputs to the decision process).

CURRENTLY FELT VERSUS ANTICIPATED EMOTIONS

The assumption that similar decisions across different situations or points in time will produce largely similar emotional outcomes raises the point that decisions may be guided by anticipated emotion, rather than emotion felt at the time of the decision. This postulate is a second distinction that is important in describing how emotion affects decision making. The influence of anticipated emotion (with the emotion that one is going to experience in the future as the result of the decision signaled, perhaps, by automatically generated twinges of affect) may be quite different from the influence of current emotional states.

Anticipated emotion is linked to conscious emotion, in the sense that it is the conscious states that people anticipate. Automatic affect may thus contribute to the anticipation of future emotions. Anticipated emotion is probably one important subcategory of influential conscious experiences. As we shall elaborate, Baumeister (2005) has proposed that the advent of human consciousness has changed many motivational patterns. Whereas many animals are prompted directly by inner drives to perform certain actions, human action is often designed to pursue anticipated conscious experiences. The causation is thus less direct, more tentative and flexible, and more teleological.

Broadly, we propose that current emotional states may do more harm than good to the decision-making process, whereas the anticipation of emotional outcomes will do the opposite, which is to say have a generally beneficial effect. This argument is one of the most important and general principles about how emotions affect decision making. It emphasizes the role of emotion as a feedback system. To make a choice based on past emotional outcomes as well as anticipated future feedback will often be quite sensible and effective (provided that the feedback system is reasonably adaptive, which we think is a fair assumption). To let current emotions sway one's choosing may however disrupt the process and detract from the capacity for optimal choosing. This theme will be developed in the subsequent sections of this chapter.

One further caveat is in order, as indicated by the 2005 Sydney Symposium. Current emotions may have an adverse impact on judgments and decisions (see also Clore & Storbeck, this volume). It is possible that people may know this or at least may learn it via painful experience. Hence they could learn to escape from emotional states before making impactful decisions. Erber and Markunas (this volume) have argued persuasively that people sometimes escape from emotional states into neutral ones—even sometimes escaping from pleasant, positive emotional states—when to do so is functional. It could be that current emotion is generally detrimental to optimal decision making, and also that this fact is only a minor and occasional problem in everyday life, if people routinely or systematically attenuate their affective reactions before making important decisions.

OUTCOMES VERSUS PROBABILITIES

One further distinction that is relevant to understanding the impact of emotion on decision making is between the magnitude of outcomes and the probabilities. One broad principle appears to be that emotional phenomena (both conscious emotion and automatic affect) attune people strongly to the magnitude of possible outcomes but seem largely indifferent to shifts in probabilities, except for certainty.

An early demonstration of the emotional indifference to probabilities was provided by Monat, Averill, and Lazarus (1972). They showed that research subjects became physiologically aroused as they approached the moment at which they anticipated that a shock might be delivered to them. The arousal levels were essentially the same regardless of whether the probability of shock was high, medium, or low. Only if there was a zero percent chance of shock did people fail to become aroused.

The emotional insensitivity to probability was illustrated by Loewenstein, Weber, Hsee, and Welch (2001) in the following way. The difference between winning 10,000 versus 10 million dollars is quite appreciable, and presumably people would be willing to exert themselves more for the latter than the former. Although both outcomes are good, and either would bring a quick infusion of joy, ten million dollars would have a lasting impact on one's life in a way that ten thousand dollars could not. In simple terms, one can appreciate the difference emotionally. In contrast, the difference between a 1 in 10,000 chance versus a 1 in 10 million chance is emotionally negligible, even though the numerical difference is the same as that for the two rewards.

A vivid demonstration of the emotional blindness to probabilistic outcomes, in contrast to certain ones, was reported by Viscusi and Magat (1987; see also Loewenstein et al., 2001). The decision had to do with a pesticide that supposedly caused some risk and would cause poisoning to a small portion of human users. The researchers asked participants how much extra they would be willing to pay to reduce that risk from 15 in 10,000 to 5 in 10,000—or, alternatively, from 5 in 10,000 down to 0. Most participants were willing to pay significantly more for the latter improvement, even though the former was twice as powerful in saving lives. The implication is that zero risk has a special emotional appeal that elicits a much stronger reaction than a larger but merely probabilistic improvement that still left some degree of risk.

A more fully developed theory concerning the role that affect and cognition play in judgments that vary in scope has recently been proposed by Hsee and Rottenstreich (2004). The finding of this work is that people are insensitive to the scope (magnitude) of a judgment when the judgment activates the emotional system, whereas people are appropriately sensitive to scope when the judgment only calls into play cognition. In these (between subject) studies, people said they would give four times as much money to save four pandas as they would to save one panda—but only when the pandas were represented by abstract dots; when pandas were represented by pictures of cute, vulnerable, real animals people said they would give amounts of money that were somewhere in between the one and four panda amounts in the cognitive (dot) conditions. This pattern was replicated in other domains and suggested to explain the basic shape (concave) of most value judgments in the real world (which have elements of emotions in them and therefore are not linear). From these studies, we have another piece of supportive evidence for the notion that emotions do not lead to wise decisions. Decisions about how much money or other value of worth to attach to an object—or four objects—ought to vary with the number of objects on which the value will be distributed. Thus, this research supports the view that current emotional states make for less optimal decisions.

EFFECTS OF CURRENT EMOTIONAL STATE

There is no question that current emotions can alter decisions. There is substantial question, however, as to whether these effects are beneficial or detrimental. In our view, they are often detrimental—sufficiently so that the direct guidance of behavioral choices is not plausible as the main function of emotion. That is, we think current emotions cause bad decisions often enough that if directly dictating choices were the main function of emotional experience, natural selection would likely have phased emotions out of the human psyche (see Haselton & Ketelaar, this volume). Current emotional states do more harm than good to concurrent decision processes, and so people with fewer and fainter emotions would have survived and reproduced better than people with stronger and more frequent emotions.

Several studies have directly examined whether current emotional state can impair good decision making. Leith and Baumeister (1996) induced various emotions and then had participants choose among various lotteries that varied in risk and reward—and expected gain. The selections were deliberately engineered so that the high-reward lotteries were statistically less promising and therefore could reasonably be considered as foolish, self-defeating, high-risk behavior. The research asked, would people in emotional states be more or less likely to choose the correct, optimal, low-risk option? No emotions produced outcomes that were significantly better than the emotionally neutral control conditions (though some prior work has found a tendency for positive emotions to make people averse to risk generally; see Isen, Nygren, & Ashby, 1988). High-arousal negative emotions such as anger and embarrassment consistently caused people to choose the high-reward, high-risk lotteries. In other words, some forms of emotional distress moved people to take foolish risks.

Leith and Baumeister (1996) further found that this shift toward nonoptimal risk-taking was mediated by reduced cognitive processing. In one study, they replicated the effect that anger led people to select the nonoptimal, high-risk option—but the effect was eliminated in another condition by having similarly angry participants pause for a minute to write down the pros and cons of each option before making their selection. Thus, emotional distress cuts short the decision process (see also Keinan, 1987, on reduced cognitive processing and hence more mistakes as a result of stress). Such patterns are probably responsible for the stereotype that emotional states cause people to make irrational or destructive choices.

Negative emotions and the resultant effect on decision quality have been investigated in a series of studies by Luce (1998; see also Luce, Bettman, & Payne, 1997). In these studies, people's emotional states were manipulated by making the decision task that they must face either high or low in conflict between important and thus emotionally laden options. Note that this research tested the effect of task-specific (not ambient) emotion, insofar as the negative feelings were a direct result of the trade-off difficulties that people faced. These studies showed that people chose avoidant decision options considerably more often when they faced a choice that engendered negative emotion (the high difficulty trade-off condition, as opposed to the low difficulty trade-off condition). Specifically, participants who felt negative emotion selected the "easy" option as evidenced by higher likelihood of choosing (1) a status quo option (i.e., they relied on information that indicated that they had previously liked one of the options quite a lot, before seeing the other options), (2) an option that asymmetrically dominated another option (i.e., an option that was clearly better than one other option but still would involve making difficult trade-offs with the third option in the set), and (3) to prolong the search. Moreover, and in support of our second postulate that many behaviors are aimed at influencing future emotional states, Luce found that the choice of the "easy" option decreased negative emotion.

Whether these results extend to generalized negative emotion is unsure, but these results demonstrate that when negative emotions arise from having to make a tough choice, people will be more likely to make the easily justifiable choice—even if it is not the wisest one. The broad argument that emotions can impair information processing was proposed decades ago by Easterbrook (1959). He sought to explain the U-shaped effect of arousal on performance. Easterbrook proposed that the main impact of arousal is to narrow the range of information that is processed. A modicum of arousal may therefore be beneficial to perform-ance, because it helps screen out irrelevant information. Beyond a certain point, however, the irrelevant information has all been eliminated, and further arousal causes one to ignore task-relevant, potentially helpful information. Although Easterbrook was not specifically focused on emotion and decision making, that same analysis may be relevant, and it does fit the results of Leith and Baumeister (1996) and others. High-arousal states cause people to fail to take into account information that could help them make better decisions.

Thus, emotions can curtail information processing, which would be one path-way to making bad decisions (see also Kelly & Spoor, this volume). Another way that emotion can influence decisions, often for the worse, is that it shifts priorities toward feeling better in the immediate present. These impulses can distort a judg-ment process.

Intriguing evidence for the power of emotions to distort decisions to which they are properly irrelevant was provided by Lerner, Small, and Loewenstein (2004). These authors reasoned that some emotions, such as disgust and sadness, have evolutionary roots in the need to distance oneself from something and indeed to change one's circumstances. In their studies, Lerner et al. induced these emotions in participants and then instructed them to decide on the asking price for some item that they had to sell. They found that sad participants set relative-ly low prices, presumably because sadness creates a general orientation toward seeking change (and low prices will increase the likelihood of selling and thereby bringing about a change). However, sadness made people agree to buy the same object at a much higher price, presumably because sadness indicates a positive attitude toward change, and so a higher price increased the likelihood of change. This amounts to a reversal of the endowment effect, an effect that has been shown to be robust across many other manipulations. Disgust feelings led to a dampen-ing of buying and selling prices, so that they were statistically equal, a pattern that is also quite different from the typical effects.

Those findings are important because they show that current emotional states can alter and distort decisions to which they seemingly ought to be irrelevant. The emotional state appears to take priority over rationality and other considerations, including calculations of long-term self-interest and proper market value.

Further evidence about how emotion, especially negative emotions, can shift priorities toward the short run was provided by Knapp and Clark (1991). They showed that sadness impairs the capacity to delay gratification in the context of a social dilemma. Their procedure used a resource-management task involving a simulated fishing lake. The optimal strategy would be to harvest rather slowly and intermittently, allowing the pool to replenish its fish each time so that it could sustain one's profits over the long run, but short-sighted impulses prompt people to take their profits more rapidly, thereby depleting the resource and reducing the long-term gain. Knapp and Clark found that sad people were more likely than others to make that error. Thus, again, a current emotional state led to a pattern of decision making with a demonstrably less favorable outcome than a neutral state.

A subsequent study by Tice, Bratslavsky, and Baumeister (2001) confirmed that the nonoptimal, short-sighted decisions made by sad people were driven by assigning a higher priority to feeling better than to maximizing gains in the long run. They replicated the effects of Knapp and Clark (1991) but also showed that the bad effects of sadness could be eliminated by leading participants to believe that their emotional states were temporarily "frozen" (immune to change). Attempts to make oneself feel better are presumably useless if one's mood has been frozen. Thus, sadness impairs the ability to make decisions that favor long-term benefits over immediate gratification—but not if the mood is frozen. The implication is that sad people make decisions to favor immediate gratification only when they expect that gratification to improve their mood.

Indeed, one could further conclude that it is misleading, in a sense, to say sadness "impairs" the ability to make good decisions. The emotional state itself does not directly cause damage to the decision-making process or apparatus. Rather, sadness seems to change people's priorities. This fits our theme that the effects of emotion on decision making tend not to be strictly determined or direct effects. Instead, human decision making pursues emotional states in a flexible and teleological manner.

Mood-freezing manipulations have been shown to alter a variety of other apparent effects of bad moods. Sadness makes people helpful, but not in a mood-freeze condition (Manucia, Baumann, & Cialdini, 1984). Thus, sad people become helpful in order to make themselves feel better. Sadness does not directly create altruistic or helpful impulses, but rather sad people come to look upon helping as a possibly useful way to repair their mood. The tendency for sadness to prompt overeating of unhealthy foods is also apparently motivated by the desire to feel better, because sad people whose moods are ostensibly frozen do not indulge in such unhealthy eating (Tice et al., 2001). Even the tendency for anger to lead to aggression appears to be driven by the wish and expectation of feeling better: In a mood-freeze condition, angry people were no more aggressive than nonangered ones (Bushman, Baumeister, & Phillips, 2001).

These mood-freezing studies are important clues as to how emotions are involved in behavioral decisions. All those investigations began with established findings that seemed to indicate that emotional states exert a causal effect on behavior or decisions (e.g., sadness causes helping, anger causes aggression). Yet they showed that those effects of emotion vanished when participants were led to believe that their emotional state would remain fixed and unchangeable for about an hour. Thus, the emotion did not cause the behavior—rather, the behavior was designed to bring about a change in one's emotional state.

Evidence from the interpersonal realm also shows that when people feel bad as the result of an ego threat, they can behave in a manner that seeks to make themselves feel better but at the same time makes them less liked by others (Vohs & Heatherton, 2001). In this research, trait high self-esteem people were more likely to seek to make themselves feel better and consequently viewed themselves as better than others and behaved accordingly (Vohs & Heatherton, 2004). Ego threat brings about increased negative emotions, decreased positive emotions, and decreased state self-esteem, and among trait high self-esteem people leads to self-reparation attempts; the same state among low self-esteem people does not, however (Vohs & Heatherton, 2004). The reason for this difference appears to be the result of emotion regulation beliefs among high and low self-esteem people. High self-esteem people derogate others and elevate the self as ways to feel better after threat, whereas low self-esteem people do not see much benefit in engaging in such responses, given that they have little hope of feeling better.

In other words, many apparent effects of current emotional state on behavior can be reinterpreted as reflecting the view that emotion serves mainly as a feedback system. We have proposed (and will elaborate in the next section) that making decisions based on anticipated emotional outcomes is often a helpful, constructive way to decide. Some of these benefits are however lost if one's current emotional state distorts the calculations. It is not so much that emotion renders one unable to think or to make wise choices, as that concurrent emotion introduces a different set of priorities.

ANTICIPATED EMOTION

Thus far we have seen that concurrent emotional states can have an adverse impact on the decision process. In contrast, anticipated emotions can have beneficial effects on decisions. We think that choosing with the aim of maximizing one's emotional payoffs (that is, choosing the course of action that promises the most positive or least negative emotions) is likely to yield generally good results (see also Holmes & Anthony, this volume).

The reasoning is simple. Emotions evaluate outcomes. Positive emotions signify good outcomes, and negative outcomes recognize bad outcomes. Hence, almost by definition, if one makes choices that will maximize positive and minimize negative outcomes, these choices will be the same choices that will most likely yield good rather than bad outcomes.

The idea that choices are sometimes guided by anticipated emotional payoffs has been proposed by Mellers, Schwartz, and Ritov (1999). They argued that people do not simply make rational calculations of rational self-interest and maximal material gain but instead choose based on how they expect to feel. To confirm this, they demonstrated some departures from material rationality. These findings are important, because they show that the system of choosing based on emotional payoffs is not perfect. The departures are however relatively minor and subtle. By and large, the best pragmatic benefits will be associated with the best emotional outcomes.

A broader context for this has been suggested by Baumeister (2005). He noted that in order for humans to live in a complex, meaning-based culture, they would have to be able to make novel choices, including choices between options that have little in common (e.g., whether to spend the afternoon fishing, composing a song, or gossiping with friends). Even a very powerful computer could not easily make such a decision, because there is no obvious basis for comparing those options. Emotion serves as a "common currency" into which the possible outcomes of various options can be translated and compared.

Anticipated regret has probably been studied more than the anticipation of other emotions. People make decisions so as to avoid doing something they will regret. These decisions are not necessarily perfectly optimal, but it takes a cleverly designed dilemma in order to find an exception to optimal choosing. For example, Anderson (2004) offered participants a choice between two lotteries. One had a 90% chance of winning $60 and a 10% chance of winning $1. The second had a 90% chance of winning $40 and a 10% chance of winning $100. The former has the better-expected gain and so, strictly speaking, it is the superior choice. Many participants however would choose the latter option, despite the lower expected gain, because they anticipated how badly they would regret their choice if they took the former option and ended up with only the one measly dollar. These outcomes support the view of Mellers et al. (1999) and others, indicating that people choose by anticipated emotion rather than by dispassionate calculation.

Still, we regard such effects, in which anticipated regret leads to a nonoptimal selection, as relatively minor exceptions to what is a generally adaptive pattern. In Anderson's study, after all, even if most participants would end up with $40 rather than the $60, they would still have gained $40. In the main, if you went through life never doing anything about which you expected to be sorry or regretful, you would probably do quite well.

Another relevant point about the Anderson study is that it reflects the clumsiness of emotion with regard to probabilistic outcomes. The selection of the $40 lottery (the second choice, as listed above) was presumably driven by the wish to avoid the worst-case outcome, namely getting one dollar. Emotions are good at appreciating how one might feel about best- and worst-case scenarios—and not so good at adjusting those appraisals for the relatively small likelihood.

The main problem with choosing based on anticipated emotion is that anticipations may not be accurate. We focus on two well-documented inaccuracies. How serious are they?

The first concerns affective forecasting (Wilson & Gilbert, 2003; see also Dunn & Laham, this volume). Researchers have shown that people err systematically in predicting their emotional reactions. Specifically, they predict longer duration and deeper intensity for their emotional responses than is justified by actual events. Thus, when predicting how they would feel if they lost their job or were rejected by their loved ones, people predict they would be upset for a very long time, whereas when people actually experience such things their emotions dissipate relatively quickly.

Do these errors represent a problem for the view that people choose based on anticipated emotions? We think not (see also Baumeister et al., 2006). In the first place, predictions are not randomly inaccurate. People do seem able to predict correctly which emotions they would feel. (Thus, they are correct in predicting that they would be happy to get promoted, sad and disappointed to be fired, and angry to be treated unjustly; see Dunn & Laham, this volume.) The errors lie specifically in the duration of the emotional response, and in this too their errors are not random but rather indicate overestimation of the duration.

Overestimating the duration of response is far more compatible than underestimating with the view that people choose based on anticipated emotion. If people systematically underestimated their future emotional reactions to a particular event, then anticipated emotions would not be very helpful at choosing. To illustrate, suppose a person were contemplating a risky venture and were mainly deterred by the anticipation of regret if the risk turned out badly. If the person underestimated how much regret he or she would feel, then the regret would not be an effective deterrent. After all, why change one's plans based on a mere whisper of anticipated regret? In contrast, overestimating potential regret would be much more powerful and effective at giving pause. You would not want to do something that you would regret strongly for years.

Ultimately, it is not necessary that one actually feel intense regret for years. To help make a wise, safe decision, it is enough to anticipate that one might feel that much regret. Thus, the pattern of distortion in affective forecasting seems quite compatible with the view that people choose based on anticipated emotion.

The other problem with anticipated emotional outcomes is the so-called hot-cold empathy gap (Bouffard, 2002; Loewenstein, Nagin, & Paternoster, 1997). When people are not in an emotional state, they fail to anticipate how they would act in some future circumstance when they would be in the grip of emotion. For example, Ariely and Loewenstein (in press) asked male participants to rate the likelihood that they would engage in various socially controversial or even immoral sexual behaviors. They were asked to rate how appealing they would find having sex with a child or old woman, an extremely fat partner, or a woman they hated, and to rate their arousal in response to deviant sex acts such as spanking, bondage, and urination. They were also asked whether they might ever try to obtain sex by falsely declaring love for a woman, getting her drunk, or persisting in seductive efforts after she said no. Further questions asked whether they would take risks such as having unprotected sexual intercourse.

The independent variable was the arousal state of the respondent. All respondents answered the questions once in a neutral, dispassionate state and once in an aroused state (i.e., while they were masturbating and had reached a self-reported arousal level of at least 75 out of a maximum 100). With very few exceptions, male participants reported greater willingness to perform all the actions and greater appeal of all the stimuli when they were aroused than when they were calm. (The only exceptions were having sex with the lights on and having sex with another man, and even the latter showed a trend in the predicted direction.)

The implication of the hot-cold empathy gap is that people make errors in predicting how they will act in a very different emotional state. Strictly speaking, this is not an exception to the pattern of choosing by anticipated emotion, but rather it reflects yet another problem in how concurrent emotional state can influence decisions. Under the influence of intense emotions, people may make choices that are different from what they normally think they would and should make (i.e., concurrent emotional states lead to intertemporal choice problems).

The inability to anticipate how such states will bias one's choosing may cause various problems in precommitment and other preliminary decisions. For example, a man might fail to bring a condom along when going drinking in the company of a woman he dislikes or finds unattractive, on the assumption that he would not want to have sex with her anyhow, but if he became aroused he might well start to find her more appealing and, if she were receptive, he could end up having unprotected sex. (Failing to anticipate the regret one would have over an unwanted pregnancy or a sexually transmitted disease is probably an important instance in which choosing by anticipated emotion would have been better than of short-term hedonic payoffs!)

EMOTIONS AND LEARNING

We have suggested that a central function of conscious emotion (as opposed to automatic affect) is to facilitate learning. The delayed aspect of conscious emotion—that is, the fact that emotions often develop too slowly to be useful in guiding behavior on-line—is not a problem for the purpose of facilitating learning. Indeed, the slowness of emotion may be helpful in keeping attention focused on what has just happened. A robot or computer might turn its cognitive processes to each new situation as soon as an event ends, but human emotion can keep the mind focused on ruminating about recent events, so as to improve the chances of selecting the appropriate lesson from the variety of possible interpretations. Animals who live in a simple world of relatively unambiguous outcomes and who, after all, cannot verbally ruminate about multiple interpretations might not need to remain focused on recent events in order to learn from them. But human beings live in culture, which is a meaning-based form of social life. Most human events and outcomes can be interpreted in multiple ways and hence can support thinking about how to understand what happens. Conscious emotion may be instrumental in promoting learning under those complex, specifically human conditions (Baumeister, 2005).

One sign that negative emotion (in particular) serves this function is that it stimulates counterfactual thinking (Roese, 1997). Thus, emotion causes people to review recent events and think about how they might have turned out differently. Counterfactual thinking can facilitate learning from events by stimulating people to think about how they might have produced a different, possibly better outcome by acting in a different manner. Clearly this would also be beneficial for improving decision making. When a decision turns out badly, the human mind can learn by thinking about why the wrong decision was made and how a different decision might have yielded better outcomes, such as if one had used a different criterion or given more weight to a dimension that one neglected.

The importance of emotion for learning was demonstrated in an influential study by Bechara, Damasio, Damasio, and Lee (1999). In their research, participants drew cards from any of four decks and gained or lost money depending on the card. Two of the decks contained cards that brought large losses (as well as others that conferred gains). People with normal emotional responses would sample from the various decks but, once they incurred those large losses, would avoid the dangerous decks and concentrate on the decks that were predominantly benign. This pattern corresponds to a basic and presumably adaptive form of learning: One avoids repeating decisions that bring seriously bad outcomes. Unfortunately, one category of participants never seemed to learn in that way (and so they ended up losing money as compared to other participants). These were the ones who lacked emotional reactions as a result of brain damage they had suffered. Thus, without emotions, people seem unable or less able to learn from their bad experiences.

Among the various emotions, guilt may be particularly easy to recognize as a source of retrospective interpretation for the sake of learning. People feel guilty when ruminating over prior events that involve their misdeeds, and many people report avoiding acts that they anticipate will make them feel guilty (see Baumeister, Stillwell, & Heatherton, 1994, for review). Does guilt then lead to learning lessons and changing behavior?

One set of studies asked participants to furnish accounts of events in which another person objected to what they had done and after which they did, versus did not, feel guilty (Baumeister, Stillwell, & Heatherton, 1995). Comparing the two sets of stories, they found that feeling guilty was associated with greater reports of learning a lesson and changing one's behavior. These findings are particularly relevant because they illustrate how people describe past experiences. Thus, if the past experience involved feeling guilty, the account was likely to contain a statement of a lesson or moral that the person had learned, but such lessons were absent when guilt was absent too. The broader implication is that the emotional feeling of guilt stimulates people to reflect on the event that gave rise to the feeling and to extract positive lessons about what they did wrong and how to avoid such problems (and the guilt associated with them) in the future.

DECISIONS AND BEHAVIOR

The relevance of emotion for learning brings up the question of how behavior is actually guided. After all, theories of state-specific learning (Eich, 1977; see also Eich & Macaulay, this volume) might say that emotional learning is likely to be useless in most cases, because what is learned via emotion will mainly be remembered when the person is in the same emotional state. Assuming that most of the time the person is in a different emotional state or perhaps not feeling any particular emotion, would the lessons still be valid?

We think that conscious emotion can produce generally valid learning that is not limited to future episodes of the same emotion. It is not necessary for the full-blown conscious emotion to be experienced the next time in order for the lesson to be remembered. Rather, all that is needed is a twinge of affect. The automatic system can probably retain the memory of the emotion and send up an associated ping of liking or disliking whenever it recognizes circumstances that produced the full-blown emotion previously. We think these twinges may be what Damasio (1994) meant by *somatic markers*, though there are several ways of interpreting his theory and we lack confidence that ours is the sole or correct one. Regardless of whether the interpretation of Damasio is correct, the idea seems useful: Emotional experiences leave residues that are associated in memory with information about the circumstances that caused them. When the person encounters similar circumstances again, the information is retrieved—along with the affective trace that helps to guide the decision this time, especially for avoiding repeating a seeming mistake.

An idealized model of behavioral decision making would have people pause at each choice point, reflect on the various options and their outcomes, freely make a decision based on enlightened self-interest as indicated by the cost/benefit analysis, and then implement that decision. Alas, all too few human actions seem to follow that procedure, not least because making effortful decisions after careful conscious deliberation is psychologically costly and consumes a limited resource that people mainly seek to conserve for when it is needed most (e.g., Vohs, Baumeister, Twenge, Schmeichel, & Tice, 2006; see also Fiske & Taylor, 1991).

Instead, a more common pathway to behavior may be that at the choice point, the person automatically consults preset guidelines for how to act and simply does what those dictate. The fact that most behaviors follow directly from automatic processes has led some influential thinkers to conclude that conscious, controlled processing is largely irrelevant to behavior and serves little or no useful function (e.g., Bargh, 1997; Wegner, 2002). Our theory of emotion suggests that even if all behavior is the direct result of automatic processes, conscious processes—including consciously felt emotional states—can play an important role by altering the preset programs that the automatic system follows. And even if these alterations are often too slow to guide on-line behavior, they can be decisive in the long run, because each act of learning makes the person better able to behave effectively the next time around.

CONCLUDING REMARKS

Explaining human emotion has proven difficult, and indeed psychology's understanding of emotion lags far behind its understanding of cognition and performance. One reason for the difficulty is likely rooted in evolution. Emotional responses probably began to evolve long before humans were around, but it is quite possible that they have taken on different forms and functions in humans. Among the crucial differences are that humans have a much more thorough conscious dimension of experience than other animals, they use language-based meaning to interpret their experiences (including emotions) much more extensively than other animals, and they can respond to events far beyond their immediate stimulus environment, unlike most other animals.

Our main approach invokes the premise that humans evolved to live in culture (Baumeister, 2005). As such, they face far more complex and rewarding decisions than other animals. Most animals respond only to the here and now (Roberts, 2002; cf. Vohs & Schmeichel, 2003), and emotions may mainly be useful as direct guides of immediate behavior. Humans live in an expanded now and indeed can interpret complex links between present decisions and distant past and future events. In that context, in which past, present, and future are meaningfully intertwined, emotion can operate in ways it could not in simpler minds.

Moreover, consciousness has altered human behavior at least by transforming the nature of motivations: People direct their behavior to seek and avoid conscious experiences. Animals may become hungry and seek to ingest the nutrients they need to survive, and humans do too, but in humans the consumption of food is saturated with the quest for particular conscious experiences consisting of precise tastes, prepared and mixed in a certain way, enjoyed in special surroundings, and often shared with pleasing companions. Likewise, much has been written about how the human sex drive is a product of evolution and shares many behavioral features with our animal forebears, but the human desire for sex is also marked by the wish to enjoy a particular conscious experience shaped by characteristics of the setting, partner, and acts. If you got all your nutrients via intravenous injection and reproduced via test tube, your biological needs might be saturated, but you would have missed out on something—namely, the conscious experience that to many people is the main point.

In the same way, conscious emotion in humans becomes the goal of behavior. People make decisions based on how they expect to end up feeling.

Anger may have evolved to cause animals to fight, and there is still a significant link between anger and aggression in humans. But the link is tenuous and complicated. Not all anger leads to aggression, and not all aggression follows from anger. Moreover, angry people mainly aggress out of the expectation that aggressing will make them feel better, and when that expectation is removed, anger does not stimulate aggression (Bushman et al., 2001).

Hence making choices based on one's current emotional state may be maladaptive for humans, even if that is what works best for animals. Animals do not face decisions of the complexity that humans do, and in particular the blindness of emotional states to probabilities is not something that animals (who mainly respond to concrete events in the immediate present and could not calculate estimated gains or other statistical subtleties even if they wanted to do so) could appreciate. But choosing based on the emotion-facilitated lessons from past experiences and anticipated emotional states may be a highly adaptive and effective form of human decision making.

REFERENCES

Anderson, C. J. (2004). Inaction inertia is a rational choice: Regret, self-regulation, and the problem of the non-referential reference. Presented to the Society for Judgment and Decision Making, Minneapolis, MN.

Ariely, D., & Loewenstein, G. (in press). The heat of the moment: The effect of sexual arousal on sexual decision making. *Journal of Behavioral Decision Making*.

Averill, J. (1982). Anger and aggression: An essay on emotion. New York: Springer-Verlag.

Bargh, J. A. (1994). The four horsemen of automaticity: Awareness, intention, efficiency, and control in social cognition. In R. S. Wyer, Jr., & T. K. Srull (Eds.), *Handbook of social cognition* (pp. 1–40). Hillsdale, NJ: Lawrence Erlbaum Associates, Inc.

Bargh, J. A. (1997). The automaticity of everyday life. In R. S. Wyer, Jr. (Ed.), *The automaticity of everyday life: Advances in social cognition* (Vol. 10, pp. 1–61). Mahwah, NJ: Lawrence Erlbaum Associates, Inc.

Baumeister, R. F. (2005). *The cultural animal: Human nature, meaning, and social life.* New York: Oxford University Press.

Baumeister, R. F., Bratslavsky, E., Finkenauer, C., & Vohs, K. D. (2001). Bad is stronger than good. *Review of General Psychology, 5*, 323–370.

Baumeister, R. F., Stillwell, A. M., & Heatherton, T. F. (1994). Guilt: An interpersonal approach. *Psychological Bulletin, 115*, 243–267.

Baumeister, R. F., Stillwell, A. M., & Heatherton, T. F. (1995). Personal narratives about guilt: Role in action control and interpersonal relationships. *Basic and Applied Social Psychology, 17*, 173–198.

Baumeister, R. F., Vohs, K. D., DeWall, C. N., & Zhang, L. (2006). Does emotion cause behavior, or vice versa? Toward a dual process thery of emotion. Manuscript submitted for publication, Florida State University.

Bechara, A., Damasio, H., Damasio, A., & Lee, G. P. (1999). Different contributions of the human amygdala ventromedial prefrontal cortex to decision-making. *The Journal of Neuroscience, 19*, 5473–5481.

Bouffard, J. (2002). The influence of emotion on rational decision making in sexual aggression. *Journal of Criminal Justice, 30*, 121–134.

Bushman, B. J., Baumeister, R. F., & Phillips, C. M. (2001). Do people aggress to improve their mood? Catharsis beliefs, affect regulation opportunity, and aggressive responding. *Journal of Personality and Social Psychology, 81*, 17–32.

Chaiken, S., & Trope, Y. (Eds.) (1999). *Dual-process theories in social psychology.* New York: Guilford.

Damasio, A. (1994). *Descartes' error: Emotion, reason, and the human brain.* New York: Grosset/Putnam.

Easterbrook, J. A. (1959). The effect of emotion on cue utilization and the organization of behavior. *Psychological Review, 66*, 183–201.

Eich, J. E. (1977). State-dependent retrieval of information in human episodic memory. In E. M. Burnbaum & E. S. Parker (Eds.), *Alcohol and human memory*. Hillsdale, NJ: Lawrence Erlbaum Associates, Inc.

Fiske, S. T., and Taylor, S. E. (1991). *Social cognition.* New York: McGraw-Hill.

Hsee, C. K., & Rottenstreich, Y. (2004). Music, pandas, and muggers: On the affective psychology of value. *Journal of Experimental Psychology: General, 133*, 23–30.

Isen, A. M., Nygren, T. E., & Ashby, F. G. (1988). Influence of positive affect on the subjective utility of gains and losses: It is just not worth the risk. *Journal of Personality and Social Psychology, 55*, 710–717.

Keinan, G. (1987). Decision making under stress: Scanning of alternatives under controllable and uncontrollable threats. *Journal of Personality and Social Psychology, 52*, 639–644.

Knapp, A., & Clark, M. S. (1991). Some detrimental effects of negative mood on individuals' ability to solve resource dilemmas. *Personality and Social Psychology Bulletin, 17*, 678–688.

Leith, K. P., & Baumeister, R. F. (1996). Why do bad moods increase self-defeating behavior? Emotion, risk taking, and self-regulation. *Journal of Personality and Social Psychology, 71*, 1250–1267.

Lerner, J. S., Small, D. A., & Loewenstein, G. (2004). Heart strings and purse strings. Carryover effects of emotions on economic decisions, *Psychological Science, 15*, 337–341.

Loewenstein, G., Nagin, D., & Paternoster, R. (1997). The effect of sexual arousal on expectations of sexual forcefulness. *Journal of Research in Crime & Delinquency, 34*, 443–473.

Loewenstein, G. F., Weber, E. U., Hsee, C. K., & Welch, N. (2001). Risk as feelings. *Psychological Bulletin, 127*, 267–286.

Luce, M. F. (1998). Choosing to avoid: Coping with negatively emotion-laden consumer decisions. *Journal of Consumer Research, 24*, 409–433.

Luce, M. F., Bettman, J. R., & Payne, J. W. (1997). Choice processing in emotionally difficult decisions. *Journal of Experimental Psychology: Learning, Memory, and Cognition, 23*, 384–405.

Manucia, G. K., Baumann, D. J., & Cialdini, R. B. (1984). Mood influences on helping: Direct effects or side effects? *Journal of Personality and Social Psychology, 46*, 357–364.

Mellers, B., Schwartz, A., & Ritov, I. (1999). Emotion-based choice. *Journal of Experimental Psychology: General, 128*, 332–345.

Monat, A., Averill, J. R., & Lazarus, R. S. (1972). Anticipatory stress and coping reactions under various conditions of uncertainty. *Journal of Personality and Social Psychology, 24*, 237–253.

Roberts, W. A. (2002). Are animals stuck in time? *Psychological Bulletin, 128*, 473–489.

Roese, N. J. (1997). Counterfactual thinking. *Psychological Bulletin, 121*, 133–148.

Tice, D. M., Bratslavsky, E., & Baumeister, R. F. (2001). Emotional distress regulation takes precedence over impulse control: If you feel bad, do it! *Journal of Personality and Social Psychology, 80*, 53–67.

Viscusi, K., & Magat, W. (1987). *Learning about risk.* Cambridge, MA: Harvard University Press.

Vohs, K. D., & Heatherton, T. F. (2001). Self-esteem and threats to self: Implications for self-construals and interpersonal perceptions. *Journal of Personality and Social Psychology, 81*, 1103–1118.

Vohs, K. D., & Heatherton, T. F. (2004). Ego threat elicits different social comparison processes among high and low self-esteem people: Implications for interpersonal perceptions. *Social Cognition, 22*, 168–190.

Vohs, K. D., & Schmeichel, B. J. (2003). Self-regulation and the extended now: Controlling the self alters the subjective experience of time. *Journal of Personality and Social Psychology, 85*, 217–230.

Vohs, K. D., Baumeister, R. F., Twenge, J. M., Schmeichel, B. J., & Tice, D. M. (2006). Decision fatigue exhausts self-regulatory resources. Manuscript submitted for publication.

Wegner, D. M. (2002). *The illusion of conscious will.* Cambridge, MA: MIT Press.

Wilson, T. D., & Gilbert, D. T. (2003). Affective forecasting. In M. Zanna (Ed.), *Advances in experimental social psychology* (Vol. 35, pp. 345–411). New York: Elsevier.

9

Emotions as Moral Intuitions

DACHER KELTNER, E. J. HORBERG,
and CHRISTOPHER OVEIS

With a few notable exceptions, scholars have largely ignored the role of emotions in moral judgment, which are judgments concerning matters of right, wrong, and virtue. More typically, it has been assumed that emotions are antithetical to the reasoned, deliberate, principled qualities of our judgments in the moral realm (for review, see Haidt, 2001). The reasons for this are several, and stem from the age-old dichotomy between passion and reason. Moral judgments are thought by many to be achieved through complex cognitive processes, such as Rawls' ideas about a prior-to-society perspective, and assumed to be inclusive and universal, applying to all people and all relevant contexts. Emotions, in contrast, often occur as the result of relatively rapid, automatic appraisals, and are highly subjective and context-bound (Smith, David, & Kirby, this volume).

Yet emotions may represent a solution to certain difficulties encountered in the study of morality. One such difficulty is the cultural variation in moral judgment that is apparent in both empirical studies and informal observations. For example, Richard Shweder's work on the moral judgments of people in Eastern India documents that Indian participants find it morally wrong for a child to cut his hair after the death of his father, for a woman to eat with her husband's elder brother, and for upper-caste individuals to come into physical contact with lower-caste individuals (Shweder, Much, Mahapatra, & Park, 1997). People of different cultures often differ in the moral prioritization they give to matters concerning individual rights, freedoms, duties, and purity (e.g., Haidt, Koller, & Dias, 1993; Miller, 1984; Vasquez, Keltner, Ebenbach, & Banaszynski, 2001).

Just as striking is the ebb and flow of how social issues are moralized, that is, within-culture temporal variation in the moral significance of social issues. For instance, within US culture, the moral significance attached to various issues—cigarette smoking, animal welfare, the death penalty, abortion, and gay marriage as obvious examples—has shifted over time.

Between- and within-culture variation in moral judgment reveals difficulties in identifying universal moral standards and cognitive rules. One way to understand these kinds of variation in moral judgment is to turn to the emotions. The aim of this chapter is to review recent discoveries concerning how specific emotions figure in moral judgments. Our central claim will be that distinct emotions such as compassion, disgust, anger, or gratitude provide critical input into evaluations of right and wrong. That is, emotions often serve as moral intuitions (e.g., Haidt, 2001). To set the stage for this analysis, we first will review claims regarding the social functions of emotions, which suggest the highly moral nature of many emotions. Drawing upon studies of the effects of specific emotions upon social cognition, we will propose six ways in which emotions figure in moral judgment, reviewing relevant evidence when possible.

EMOTIONS AS SOCIAL COMMITMENTS

Moral judgments emerged, many have claimed (e.g., de Waal, 1996; Fiske, 1991; Haidt, 2001), to govern the complex social relations that make up human sociality. Moral concerns address many of the problems of social living—the allocation of resources, punishment, the justification of hierarchical arrangements, and so on. To understand how specific emotions contribute to moral judgment, one must first consider the highly social nature of emotions (see Smith et al., this volume).

In considering the social functions of emotions, we have found a useful answer in commitment-based analyses of emotion and relationships (Frank, 1988, 2002; Gonzaga, Keltner, Londahl, & Smith, 2001; Haselton & Ketelaar, this volume; Nesse, 1990). The long-term relationships crucial to human survival—pair bonding, parent–child bonds, cooperative alliances, group memberships—often require that individuals devote costly resources to others, and avoid self-interested behaviors that could harm social partners. These commitment-related problems implicate moral concerns (e.g., that people be good to others) and are met by certain emotions. These emotions, then, motivate courses of action that enhance long-term bonds, such as the devoted care of vulnerable offspring or submissive, conciliatory acts that defuse aggressive encounters (Frank, 1988, 2002). Emotions also serve as signals to others of long-term commitment. For example, displays of love and gratitude are reliable indicators of commitment to marital bonds and cooperative alliances, respectively (see Haselton & Ketelaar, this volume).

Emotions motivate commitments related to two general kinds of social problems. In intimate relationships, emotions address *problems of reproduction*, more specifically, procreation and the raising of offspring to the age of reproduction (Bowlby, 1979; Shaver, Morgan, & Wu, 1996). Sexual desire facilitates the identification of promising sexual partners and the establishment of reproductive relations, whereas love is one component of psychological attachment between romantic partners (Diamond, 2003; Ellis & Malamuth, 2000; Gonzaga et al., 2001; Hazan & Shaver, 1987). Jealousy motivates one to protect a mate from rivals, preserving both the mate's investment in current offspring and the opportunity to reproduce with the mate in the future (Buss & Schmidt, 1993). Filial love, a component of psychological attachment, motivates young and vulnerable offspring to stay close to protective adults. A complementary emotion, compassion, motivates parents to nurture and protect offspring (Shiota, Campos, Keltner, & Hertenstein, 2004).

A second realm in which emotions act as social commitments is related to the *problem of cooperation*, which lies at the heart of moral concerns about reciprocity and fairness (e.g., Gouldner, 1960; Trivers, 1971). Gratitude at others' altruistic acts is a signal that one recognizes the value of a benefit received and intends to repay in some form in the future (Trivers, 1971). Guilt occurs following one's own violations of reciprocity and is expressed in apologetic, remedial behavior (Keltner & Buswell, 1996; Tangney, 1992). Anger motivates the punishing of individuals who have violated rules of reciprocity, and accompanies moral concerns that emerge out of reciprocal relations, such as the concepts of equality and individual rights. Envy motivates individuals to derogate others whose favorable status is unjustified, thus helping to preserve equal relations (Fiske, 1991). Disgust is integral to the socialization of group members (Rozin, Haidt, & McCauley, 1999a) and may lead to the condemnation of individuals who behave in a deviant manner that threatens the group's sense of civility (Haidt, 2003; Miller, 1997; Rozin et al., 1999a).

Cooperation within large groups requires the distribution of labor and resources. Social hierarchies provide a useful heuristic for this process, and are negotiated, in part, through emotions related to dominance and submission (de Waal, 1996; Keltner, Gruenfeld, & Anderson, 2003; Öhman, 1986). Pride is experienced and displayed by individuals who have accomplished some socially valued task, and it projects the expectation of increased social status (Tiedens, Ellsworth, & Mesquita, 2000; Tracy & Robins, 2004). Embarrassment and shame appease dominant individuals and signal submissiveness (Keltner & Buswell, 1996; Miller & Leary, 1992). Contempt is defined by feelings of superiority and dominance vis-à-vis inferior others. Awe is experienced when one senses the presence of an entity greater than the self, and endows powerful individuals with respect, reverence, and authority (Fiske, 1991; Keltner & Haidt, 2003).

The extant literature on the ultra-social nature of emotions hints at the moral implications of emotional reactions. Many emotions and moral concerns, such as justice, harm, and sexual purity, are intertwined. Emotions, as Lutz and White (1986) observed, are a primary means of negotiating the place of the self in a social-moral order. In the remainder of this chapter we detail several different ways that emotions figure into moral judgment.

EMOTION–COGNITION INTERACTIONS FROM AN APPRAISAL TENDENCY PERSPECTIVE

Studies within the past 30 years have documented robust and systematic effects of affective states upon numerous cognitive processes, including selective attention, memory, causal attribution, life satisfaction judgments, use of heuristics, and risk perception (e.g., Baumeister, Vohs, & Tice, this volume; Bless, Clore, Schwarz, Golisano, Rabe, & Wolk, 1996; Bower, 1981; Eich & Macaulay, this volume; Forgas, 1995, 2001, this volume; Lerner & Keltner, 2000, 2001; Mineka & Sutton, 1992; Schwarz & Clore, 1983). In our own work, we have investigated the effects of specific emotions, such as compassion and anger, on social judgment, drawing upon what we have come to call an appraisal tendency framework (Keltner, Ellsworth, & Edwards, 1993; Lerner & Keltner, 2000, 2001; Oveis, Horberg, & Keltner, 2005). This perspective is guided by a simple set of assumptions. The first is that each distinct emotion is defined by a core appraisal or meaning analysis of the situation. Research on emotion-related appraisals (e.g., Lazarus, 1991; Ortony, Clore, & Collins, 1988; Smith & Ellsworth, 1985; Smith et al., this volume) has revealed the distinct appraisal profiles of many emotions, as well as the notion that each emotion is defined by a core appraisal theme. For example, anger is associated with appraisals of others' responsibility and injustice, fear with uncertainty, and compassion with another's suffering.

The second assumption of appraisal tendency perspectives is that specific emotions influence judgments in a manner consistent with the appraisal tendency. In functional terms, the appraisal tendency accompanying the emotional episode guides cognitive processes to features of the environment related to the problem or opportunity that elicited the emotion. For example, the appraised uncertainty that is central to fear should lead fearful individuals to consistently interpret elevated levels of uncertainty in their environments.

Finally, appraisal tendency perspectives produce clear claims about the domain specificity of the effects of distinct emotions upon judgment. The influence of emotion is limited to spheres of judgment related to the emotion's appraisal. Thus, fear will influence judgments of certainty, risk, and harm, judgment domains most tightly related semantically to its underlying appraisal tendency, but not judgments of blame or fairness, which are domains more closely related to anger (see Lerner & Keltner, 2000, for a fuller treatment of these claims).

As we now turn to the study of the relationship between emotion and moral judgment, we will have several occasions to draw upon studies conducted within an appraisal tendency perspective. This framework points to four questions that have warranted empirical attention. The first concerns the association between emotions and moral appraisals, such as appraisals of harm, rights violations, or impurity.

SOME EMOTIONS HAVE MORAL APPRAISALS

Early appraisal theorists implicitly acknowledged the relations between emotion and moral concerns. Lazarus (1991), for example, highlighted several moral themes, such as injustice, harm, and responsibility, in his analysis of the core-relational themes of the distinct emotions. Scherer (1984), in his componential analysis of the stages of emotion-related appraisal, argued that emotion-eliciting events are in part appraised for their relevance to moral standards.

In what more specific ways, then, are emotions associated with distinct moral appraisals? We provide a preliminary answer to this question, focusing on select emotions and select moral concerns that have been the focus of scholars interested in mapping the moral realm—namely harm, rights, status, purity, and reciprocity. Our suppositions derive from two sources. The first is the emotion-appraisal literature, which has begun to detail connections between moral concerns such as justice, fairness, harm, and different emotions (e.g., Larazus, 1991; Scherer, 1984; Smith & Ellsworth, 1985). The second is a recent line of inquiry in which investigators have begun to document empirical linkages between emotions and established moral concerns, such as rights, purity, obligations, and reciprocity (e.g., Batson & Shaw, 1991; Eisenberg & Miller, 1987; Greene, Sommerville, Nystrom, Darley, & Cohen, 2001; Haidt, 2001, 2003; Haidt et al., 1993; McCullough, Kilpatrick, Emmons, & Larson, 2001; Moll et al., 2002; Rozin, Lowery, Imada, & Haidt, 1999b; Skoe, Eisenberg, & Cumberland, 2002; Vasquez et al., 2001). These studies typically ask participants to report associations between moral rules or transgressions and emotion categories captured with words or facial expressions. Guided by these two traditions, we suggest in Table 9.1 the following connections between emotions and moral appraisals (see Haidt, 2003, for a similar analysis).

We expect harm to be associated with compassion, which motivates actions that reduce harm, need, and suffering (e.g., Batson & Shaw, 1991; Eisenberg et al., 1989). Violations of rights and freedoms, such as the right to free speech or freedom of action, should be associated with anger (e.g., Vasquez et al., 2001). Actions that are interpreted as impure and contaminating are associated with disgust (Rozin et al., 1993, 1999a, 1999b). Appraisals of actions that bolster reciprocity accompany gratitude (McCullough et al., 2001). The perceived failure of others to adhere to role requirements or the established hierarchy may be linked to the experience of contempt (Rozin et al., 1999b). Appraisals that one has violated a moral code or ethic, in particular by inflicting harm to others, are associated with guilt (Baumeister, Stillwell, & Heatherton, 1994; Higgins, 1987; Keltner & Buswell, 1997; Tangney, Wagner, Hill-Barlow, Marschall, & Gramzow, 1996), while shame emerges from the perception that one is fundamentally flawed (e.g., Haidt, 2003; Tangney, 1992). Finally, appraisals of others' moral virtue elicit other-praising emotions such as elevation and awe (Haidt, 2003; Keltner & Haidt, 2003; McCullough et al., 2001).

But what makes these particular appraisals *moral*, that is, imbued with the sense that they reflect inarguable truths about right and wrong that must be abided by (i.e., are obligatory and binding across context and culture)? In part, the

TABLE 9.1 Emotions and their Associated Moral Concerns

Emotion	Moral Concern
Anger	Rights, freedoms
Compassion	Harm, need
Contempt	Duties, obligations
Disgust	Purity, both sexual and spiritual
Gratitude	Reciprocity, equality
Guilt	Own transgression
Shame	Own characterological flaws
Awe, elevation	Other's virtue

answer to this question resides in the content of the appraisals. Concerns about harm, rights, reciprocity, and purity are essential to establishing enduring, cooperative relations within social collectives. The experience of the specific emotion is likewise likely to impart a sense of morality to the underlying appraisal. Subjective feelings of emotions such as anger, compassion, or awe feel involuntary, beyond strategic manipulation, and absolute (e.g., Frijda, 1986). The underlying appraisal, for example, that harm or injustice has occurred will therefore also be felt as truthful and right.

With these empirically established relations between moral concern and emotion as a backdrop, we now turn to ways in which emotions figure in moral judgment.

INTEGRAL EMOTIONS CAN COLOR MORAL COGNITION

Our second claim concerns the integral effects of emotions, or the extent to which an emotion elicited by a cause will trigger moral judgments about that causal event or action. Whereas it is widely assumed, particularly within moral psychology, that emotions play a minor role in moral judgment (for review, see Haidt, 2001), we are proposing that emotional reactions make powerful and direct contributions to various facets of moral judgments (see also Damasio, 1994).

Numerous studies show that participants rely on their emotions to reach moral judgments about actions portrayed in hypothetical scenarios. In one study, participants were presented with a series of harmless but offensive moral dilemmas (Haidt, 2001). As an example, one scenario depicts a man who has sex with a sterilized dead chicken, then cooks and eats it. Participants were asked to make moral evaluations of the scenarios, which, not surprisingly, overwhelmingly involved moral condemnation. When asked to justify this decision, participants formulated elaborate explanations of how an action could be harmful to a particular individual. However, after the experimenter discounted the harm-based justifications through a rehashing of the story's facts, participants most commonly concluded that they knew the action was "just wrong" despite not being able to provide a convincing cognitive rationale. Participants' emotional reactions had formulated their enduring moral evaluation.

In another study, Haidt et al. (1993) presented harmless but offensive acts to participants in the US and Brazil. An interesting cultural difference emerged that illustrates the role of emotion in moral judgment: Brazilian participants were more inclined than the US participants, especially upper SES US participants, to punish individuals portrayed as engaging in impure, offensive behaviors. Germane to the current argument about the integral effects of emotion on moral judgment, individuals who viewed the acts as morally wrong showed a high association between punitive tendencies and feelings of disgust and upset in response to the scenarios.

This research demonstrates that people will often rely on their feelings of discomfort to judge and punish offensive, contaminating, and impure actions. The work by Weiner, Graham, and Reyna (1997) indicates that emotions are integral to punitive judgments of different moral transgressions. They have studied participants' emotional reactions of anger and sympathy to various kinds of moral transgressions and assessed participants' inclination to punish in retributive fashion, seeking pain that would match the crime, or utilitarian fashion, seeking to reduce the likelihood that the criminal would commit such a crime in the future. Individuals angered by moral transgressions prefer the most vengeful form of punishment—retributive punishment. In contrast, participants who feel sympathy in response to the same crime prefer less severe forms of punishment, ones that protect the criminal and society, namely utilitarian punishment. In short, anger and sympathy contribute directly to one index of moral judgment: preferred forms and severities of punishment.

These initial studies suggest that moral judgments of right and wrong, and the punishments deemed appropriate for different moral transgressions, are shaped by integral emotion—that is, emotion triggered by the morally relevant action itself. Further studies are needed to explore other emotions and different moral judgments. For example, we would expect compassion and gratitude to shape moral judgments related to harm and reciprocity, respectively. Feelings of contempt, we further hypothesize, should contribute to the sense that violations of status-based roles are morally wrong. We now turn to our third claim that derives from an appraisal tendency perspective: emotions unrelated to the event to be judged—that is, incidental emotions—can shape moral judgments.

INCIDENTAL EMOTIONS CAN COLOR MORAL COGNITION

The incidental effects of emotions on social judgment have been documented by numerous investigators (Baumeister et al., this volume; Clore & Storbeck, this volume; Forgas, 2001, this volume; Isen, Daubman, & Nowicki, 1987; Schwarz & Clore, 1983, 1996). Emotions elicited by one source—a sunny day or disturbing film, for example—shape judgments in seemingly unrelated domains such as how satisfied one is with a political leader's policy making or the likelihood of positive life outcomes in the future. This literature has fairly striking implications for the study of emotion and moral cognition: evanescent emotions elicited by the most trivial of sources can profoundly shape the content of moral judgments, which have been considered by many to be fairly impervious to contextual influences.

We anticipate two different routes by which emotions will have incidental effects upon moral judgments. The first is by shaping constituent cognitive processes that underlie moral judgment. That is, moral judgments of right and wrong hinge critically upon judgments of the harm produced by an action, the intentionality of the actor, the fairness of the act, and so on. Several studies carried out within an appraisal tendency framework have shown that emotions influence these cognitive processes in distinct fashion. Thus, affective states influence attributional processes in dramatic fashion (Forgas, 1994).

With respect to specific emotions, anger heightens the sense that other individuals have intentionally caused negative and positive outcomes that are unrelated to the elicitor of the emotion. In one test of these ideas, Keltner et al. (1993) induced participants to experience anger by imagining being the victim of an unfair action on the part of a teaching assistant. When judging an ambiguous social event, angry participants, as opposed to sad participants, attributed greater responsibility to a protagonist in the story (see also Feigenson, Park, & Salovey, 2001; Lerner, Goldberg, & Tetlock, 1998; Quigley & Tedeschi, 1996). Anger thus heightens the salience of the intention behind others' actions, and increases judgments of moral wrongdoing of individuals who have committed harm.

Fear, in contrast, appears to amplify individuals' perceptions of threat associated with events unrelated to the original cause of fear. For example, people who have been induced to experience fear provide higher estimates of the likelihood of risky, harmful events in the future compared to angry participants (Lerner & Keltner, 2001). We would expect people experiencing fear, therefore, to judge threatening or harmful acts to the self as more immoral because of the documented sensitivity to these issues.

Finally, more recent work suggests that compassion and pride exert different influences upon an important component of certain moral judgments: perceived similarity between self and others (Oveis et al., 2006). The perceived similarity between self and other is central to the calculus of whether one engages in prosocial action (Sober & Wilson, 1998). In the research of interest, participants were induced to experience compassion or pride through exposure to images depicting harm (e.g., a malnourished child) or sources of pride (e.g., pictures of the participants' university). After the emotion manipulation, individuals rated how similar they were to a wide variety of social groups, including groups presumably very similar to the participant (e.g., young adults, US citizens) and those presumed to be very different from the participant (e.g., the elderly, citizens of other countries). Individuals induced to experience compassion displayed elevated perceptions of similarity to the set of groups overall.

Taken together, these studies indicate that emotions elicited by one cause influence important cognitive processes that are involved in moral judgments of right and wrong, namely judgments of intentionality, harm, and similarity between self and other. We would also expect emotions to influence moral judgments in a second incidental fashion, by contributing directly to moral judgments of right or wrong, and fairness or unfairness, of events unrelated to the elicitor of the emotion. In one of the few demonstrations of this effect, Keltner et al. (1993) led participants to move four facial muscles in ways that led to the configuration of an anger expression. Configuring the face in this fashion leads participants to report feeling anger, and these participants later judged a series of policy-related events as less fair compared to sad participants. Here, emotion induced through a physical event—moving facial muscles—altered a central dimension of moral judgment—perceptions of fairness. Other emotions should also influence moral judgments of events and objects unrelated to the cause of the emotion. Compassion, for example, should amplify judgments of right and wrong of harm- and need-related actions; disgust should amplify judgments of the moral appropriateness of violations of purity. These speculations assume that the effects of emotions are domain specific, and that they are most robust in certain moral domains (e.g., harm, rights, purity), a theme to which we now turn.

EMOTIONS WILL HAVE DOMAIN-SPECIFIC EFFECTS UPON MORAL COGNITION

The fourth claim deriving from an appraisal tendency perspective is that the effects of specific emotions on judgment are bounded (see also Forgas, 1995, this volume, for a fuller discussion of moderators of effects of moods upon cognition). We have claimed that the influence of a specific emotion is limited to spheres of judgment related to the emotion's appraisal theme. In a relevant work, it was found that fear only influenced risk perception of events that were ambiguous with respect to certainty and controllability (Lerner & Keltner, 2001). In a similarly motivated work, DeSteno, Petty, Wegener, and Rucker (2000) asked people feeling anger or sadness to estimate the likelihood of thematically "sad" events (of the 60,000 orphans in Romania, how many will be malnourished?) and "angry," unfair events (of the 20,000 violent criminals put on trial in the upcoming year, how many will be set free because of legal technicalities?). Angry participants judged the anger-inducing events to be more likely, whereas sad participants judged the sadness-inducing events to be more likely. Sadness and anger, however, did not influence estimates of all negative events, only those related to the underlying appraisal themes of loss and injustice, respectively.

The notion of domain-specific influences of emotions on judgment generates numerous predictions that await empirical attention. As simple examples, we would expect gratitude to influence moral judgments in the realm of reciprocity, but not harm, and the converse to be true of compassion. We would expect anger to shape moral judgments in the realm of rights and justice, but not purity, and the converse to be true of disgust. In a recent work, we have documented that compassion heightens a sense of similarity to other groups and individuals, but, importantly, only to those groups or individuals who are vulnerable and in need, consistent with our analysis of domain specificity (Oveis et al., 2006). More specifically, people feeling compassion indicated a stronger sense of connection to groups perceived as relatively weak (e.g., orphaned children), but less connection to groups perceived as relatively strong (e.g., corporate lawyers). Thus, we expect future studies to show that specific emotions guide moral judgments in domain-specific ways.

MORALIZATION: EMOTIONAL INTUITIONS AND VARIATION IN MORAL JUDGMENT

We began our chapter by posing a conundrum. On the one hand, moral judgments are thought to be universal, absolute, and binding across context and time. On the other hand, empirical studies find that moral judgments vary across culture and time and within individuals. We proposed that considering the emotional intuitions that guide moral judgments may help resolve this problem, and in the first part of this chapter endeavored to show how emotions guide moral judgments.

In this final part of the chapter, we will offer a more speculative answer to the question of how actions, objects, or issues acquire moral significance within individuals and cultures, in other words, how they are *moralized*. Salient examples include the moralization of cigarette smoking and vegetarianism over the past century. Currently, these issues are considered moral by many, though not all, individuals in the US (Fessler, Arguello, Mekdara, & Macias, 2003; Rozin, Markwith, & Stoess, 1997; Rozin & Singh, 1999). How does moralization work within the emotions as a moral intuitions perspective?

We suggest that moralization occurs when the moral frame of an action or issue—for example, harm, rights, purity, or obligation—matches a pre-existing emotional tendency related to that moral framing. For example, an individual that currently or dispositionally experiences compassion will deem issues and events (such as animal rights or the death penalty) as moral when they are framed in terms of harm to vulnerable entities.

Consider an illustrative study that speaks about the process of moralization. DeSteno, Petty, Rucker, Wegener, and Braverman (2004) induced participants to feel either sadness or anger by reading evocative hypothetical newspaper stories. Participants were then presented with one of two persuasive messages about raising taxes—a moral issue for many American citizens. One of the messages was sadness framed, and emphasized how increasing taxes would help special needs infants and the elderly. The other message was anger framed, and emphasized how increasing taxes would keep criminals from getting off on legal technicalities and would prevent aggravating traffic jams. Sad people indicated stronger moral attitudes toward raising taxes when presented with the sadness-framed message, whereas angry people indicated stronger moral evaluations of taxation when given the anger-framed message. A match between moral frame of an action and pre-existing emotion produced moralization of the issue. This analysis in part resembles Rozin's account of moral disgust, in which conceptions of purity, the natural order, and contamination acquire moral status through recruitment of a simpler emotional distaste system (e.g., Rozin, 1996; Rozin et al., 1999a; see also Marzillier & Davey, 2004), as well as Miller's (1997) observation that disgust broadens the moral domain to indiscriminately include objects of impurity and pollution, despite their amoral status accorded by principles of justice and fairness.

This account of moralization helps illuminate individual differences in moral judgment, an issue that has gained currency in the field in part thanks to Damasio and colleagues' research on patients who have suffered damage to the ventromedial prefrontal cortex, and who show many deficits in the social-moral realm. We would expect people prone to a particular emotion, say disgust or compassion, to moralize issues when they are framed according to the moral concerns—purity or harm in our examples—most closely intertwined with the emotion. A recent study conducted by Horberg and Keltner (2006) lends credence to this claim. In this research, disgust-prone individuals indicated the inclination to punish behaviors that violated a sense of purity and reward behaviors that upheld purity; they were not, however, inclined to punish or reward behaviors unrelated to purity, the moral appraisal of disgust.

Our emotional account of moralization also helps make sense of certain cultural variations in moral judgment. For example, several recent studies suggest that cultures vary quite significantly in which moral concerns—rights, purity, or duties and obligations—are salient (Rozin et al., 1999b; Shweder et al., 1997; Vasquez et al., 2001). To the extent that a moral concern is salient in a particular culture, as the violation of rights is in the US, then one would expect especially strong linkages between the moral concern and emotion within that realm. A recent study conducted in the United States and Republic of Philippines supports this prediction (Vasquez et al., 2001). College students in the two cultures were presented with violations of moral rules related to rights, purity, and obligation, and asked to label how they would feel in response to such a violation with one of several facial expressions, including ones depicting anger, disgust, contempt, or sadness. Across the two cultures, violations of rights were more likely to be labeled with anger than with contempt or disgust expressions, consistent with our earlier claims about hypothesized relations between moral concerns and specific emotions. Consistent with our moralization hypothesis about rights and anger in the US, American college students were more likely to label violations of rights in terms of anger than were Filipino students, and less likely to use the anger expression to label violations of purity or duties and obligations. As moral concerns become salient in a culture, they form tighter linkages with specific emotions.

CONCLUSION

As the study of the effects of affect and cognition has matured, it has become clear that many judgments, such as causal attribution, risk perception, or loss aversion, once thought to be universal regularities of the mind, are in fact swayed profoundly by fleeting emotions and moods. In this chapter we have argued that this is also true for moral judgment.

We have drawn extensively upon an appraisal tendency perspective, which posits that distinct emotions influence specific realms of judgment according to the underlying meaning of appraisal associated with the emotion. We extended this literature to the study of distinct emotion and moral judgment. This extension generated six predictions that we evaluated. We reviewed evidence concerning relations between moral appraisals and emotion, which are fairly robust for three moral concerns—rights/freedoms, duties/obligations, and purity—and three emotions—anger, contempt, and disgust. We examined studies of the effects of integral emotion upon moral judgment and punishment. We considered the effects of incidental emotion upon cognitive processes underlying moral judgment, such as perceptions of intentionality or harm, and moral judgments of right and wrong themselves. And in a more speculative vein, we proposed how emotional intuitions contribute to the moralization of issues, when a pre-existing emotion or emotional tendency matches the moral framing of an issue, thus giving rise to the subjective sense that the issue is a matter of absolute right and wrong. We think this approach to moralization helps account for individual and cultural differences in moral judgment—both empirical facts that have proven to be thorny issues in the study of moral judgment.

As empirical studies increasingly illuminate the contribution of distinct emotions to moral judgment, several opportunities await. This line of inquiry will shape the understanding of moral judgment, as we have suggested in this review.

Relevant studies will necessarily explore emotions such as gratitude, compassion, envy, and awe, which have long been on the margins of affective science. As researchers continue to explore the central nervous system correlates of moral judgment (e.g., Damasio, 1994; Greene et al., 2001), a focus on distinct emotions could reveal more precise relations between central nervous system structure and facets of moral judgment. And in terms of broader conceptualization, the study of the roles of emotions within moral judgment will inform the claim that emotions, once thought to be largely irrational and intrapsychic phenomena, are in fact principled elements of the social-moral order.

REFERENCES

Batson, C. D., & Shaw, L. L. (1991). Evidence for altruism: Toward a pluralism of prosocial motives. *Psychological Inquiry, 2,* 107–122.

Baumeister, R. F., Stillwell, A. M., & Heatherton, T. F. (1994). Guilt: An interpersonal approach. *Psychological Bulletin, 115,* 243–267.

Bless, H., Clore, G. L., Schwarz, N., Golisano, V., Rabe, C., & Wolk, M. (1996). Mood and the use of scripts: Does a happy mood really lead to mindlessness? *Journal of Personality and Social Psychology, 71,* 665–679.

Bower, G. H. (1981). Mood and memory. *American Psychologist, 36,* 129–148.

Bowlby, J. (1979). *The making and breaking of affectional bonds.* London: Tavistock.

Buss, D. M., & Schmidt, D. P. (1993). Sexual strategies theory: An evolutionary perspective on human mating. *Psychological Review, 100,* 204–232.

Damasio, A. R. (1994). *Descartes' error: Emotion, reason, and the human brain.* New York: G.P. Putnam.

DeSteno, D., Petty, R. E., Rucker, D. D., Wegener, D. T., & Braverman, J. (2004). Discrete emotions and persuasion: The role of emotion-induced expectancies. *Journal of Personality and Social Psychology, 86,* 43–56.

DeSteno, D., Petty, R. E., Wegener, D. T., & Rucker, D. D. (2000). Beyond valence in the perception of likelihood: The role of emotion specificity. *Journal of Personality and Social Psychology, 78,* 397–416.

de Waal, F. B. M. (1996). Conflict as negotiation. In W. C. McGrew, L. F. Marchant, & T. Nishida (Eds.), *Great ape societies* (pp. 159–172). New York: Cambridge University Press.

Diamond, L. M. (2003). What does sexual orientation orient? A biobehavioral model distinguishing romantic love and sexual desire. *Psychological Review, 110,* 173–192.

Eisenberg, N., Fabes, R. A., Miller, P. A., Fultz, J., Shell, R., Mathy, R. M., & Reno, R. R. (1989). Relation of sympathy and personal distress to prosocial behavior: A multimethod study. *Journal of Personality and Social Psychology, 57,* 55–66.

Eisenberg, N., & Miller, P. A. (1987). The relation of empathy to prosocial and related behaviors. *Psychological Bulletin, 101,* 91–119.

Ellis, B. J., & Malamuth, N. M. (2000). Love and anger in romantic relationships: A discrete model. *Journal of Personality, 68,* 525–556.

Feigenson, N., Park, J., & Salovey, P. (2001). The role of emotions in comparative negligence judgments. *Journal of Applied Social Psychology, 31,* 576–603.

Fessler, D. M. T., Arguello, A. P., Mekdara, J. M., & Macias, R. (2003). Disgust sensitivity and meat consumption: A test of an emotivist account of moral vegetarianism. *Appetite, 41,* 31–41.

Fiske, A. P. (1991). *Structures of social life*. New York: Free Press.

Forgas, J. P. (1994). Sad and guilty? Affective influences on the explanation of conflict episodes. *Journal of Personality and Social Psychology, 66*, 56–68.

Forgas, J. P. (1995). Mood and judgment: The affect infusion model (AIM). *Psychological Bulletin, 117*, 39–66.

Forgas, J. P. (2001). The affect infusion model (AIM): An integrative theory of mood effects on cognition and judgments. In L. L. Martin & G. L. Clore (Eds.), *Theories of mood and cognition: A user's guidebook* (pp. 99–134). Mahwah, NJ: Lawrence Erlbaum Associates, Inc.

Frank, R. H. (1988). *Passions within reason: The strategic role of the emotions*. New York: W.W. Norton & Co.

Frank, R. H. (2002). Altruism in competitive environments. In R. J. Davidson & A. Harrington (Eds.), *Visions of compassion* (pp. 182–211). London: Oxford University Press.

Frijda, N. H. (1986). *The emotions*. Cambridge, England: Cambridge University Press.

Gonzaga, G. C., Keltner, D., Londahl, E. A., & Smith, M. D. (2001). Love and the commitment problem in romantic relations and friendship. *Journal of Personality and Social Psychology, 81*, 247–262.

Gouldner, A. W. (1960). The norm of reciprocity: A preliminary statement. *American Sociological Review, 25*, 161–178.

Greene, J. D., Sommerville, R. B., Nystrom, L. E., Darley, J. M., & Cohen, J. D. (2001). An fMRI investigation of emotional engagement in moral judgment. *Science, 293*, 2105–2108.

Haidt, J. (2001). The emotional dog and its rational tail: A social intuitionist approach to moral judgment. *Psychological Review, 108*, 814–834.

Haidt, J. (2003). The moral emotions. In R. J. Davidson, K. R. Scherer, & H. H. Goldsmith (Eds.), *Handbook of affective sciences* (pp. 852–870). London: Oxford University Press.

Haidt, J., Koller, S., & Dias, M. (1993). Affect, culture, and morality, or is it wrong to eat your dog? *Journal of Personality and Social Psychology, 65*, 613–628.

Hazan, C., & Shaver, P. (1987). Romantic love conceptualized as an attachment process. *Journal of Personality and Social Psychology, 52*, 511–524.

Higgins, E. T. (1987). Self-discrepancy: A theory relating self and affect. *Psychological Review, 94*, 319–340.

Horberg, E. J., & Keltner, D. (2006). *Disgust, compassion, and moralization*. University of California, Berkeley. Manuscript in preparation. .

Isen, A. M., Daubman, K. A., & Nowicki, G. P. (1987). Positive affect facilitates creative problem solving. *Journal of Personality and Social Psychology, 52*, 1122–1131.

Keltner, D., & Buswell, B. N. (1996). Evidence for the distinctness of embarrassment, shame, and guilt: A study of recalled antecedents and facial expressions of emotion. *Cognition and Emotion, 10*, 155–171.

Keltner, D., & Buswell, B. N. (1997). Embarrassment: Its distinct form and appeasement functions. *Psychological Bulletin, 122*, 250–270.

Keltner, D., Ellsworth, P. C., & Edwards, K. (1993). Beyond simple pessimism: Effects of sadness and anger on social perception. *Journal of Personality and Social Psychology, 64*, 740–752.

Keltner, D., Gruenfeld, D. H., & Anderson, C. (2003). Power, approach, and inhibition. *Psychological Review, 110*, 265–284.

Keltner, D., & Haidt, J. (2003). Approaching awe, a moral, spiritual, and aesthetic emotion. *Cognition and Emotion, 17*, 297–314.

Lazarus, R. S. (1991). *Emotion and adaptation*. London: Oxford University Press.

Lerner, J. S., Goldberg, J. H., & Tetlock, P. E. (1998). Sober second thought: The effects of accountability, anger, and authoritarianism on attributions of responsibility. *Personality and Social Psychology Bulletin, 24*, 563–574.

Lerner, J. S., & Keltner, D. (2000). Beyond valence: toward a model of emotion-specific influences on judgment and choice. *Cognition and Emotion, 14*, 473–493.

Lerner, J. S., & Keltner, D. (2001). Fear, anger, and risk. *Journal of Personality and Social Psychology, 81*, 146–159.

Lutz, C., & White, G. M. (1986). The anthropology of emotions. *Annual Review of Anthropology, 15*, 405–436.

Marzillier, S. L., & Davey, G. C. L. (2004). The emotional profiling of disgust-eliciting stimuli: Evidence for primary and complex disgusts. *Cognition and Emotion, 18*, 313–336.

McCullough, M. E., Kilpatrick, S. D., Emmons, R. A., & Larson, D. B. (2001). Is gratitude a moral affect? *Psychological Bulletin, 127*, 249–266.

Miller, J. (1984). Cultural diversity in the morality of caring: Individually oriented versus duty-based interpersonal codes. *Cross-Cultural Research: The Journal of Comparative Social Science, 28*, 3–39.

Miller, W. I. (1997). *The anatomy of disgust*. Cambridge, MA: Harvard University Press.

Miller, R. S., & Leary, M. R. (1992). Social sources and interactive functions of emotion: The case of embarrassment. In M. S. Clark (Ed.), *Emotion and social behavior: Review of personality and social psychology* (Vol. 14, pp. 202–221). Thousand Oaks, CA: Sage Publications.

Mineka, S., & Sutton, S. K. (1992). Cognitive biases and the emotional disorders. *Psychological Science, 3*, 65–69.

Moll, J., de Oliviera-Souza, R., Eslinger, P. J., Bramati, I. E., Mourao-Miranda, J., Andraiulo, P. A., & Pessoa, L. (2002). The neural correlates of moral sensitivity: A functional magnetic resonance imaging investigation of basic and moral emotions. *Journal of Neuroscience, 22*, 2730–2736.

Nesse, R. M. (1990). Evolutionary explanations of emotions. *Human Nature, 1*, 261–289.

Öhman, A. (1986). Face the beast and face the fear: Animal and social fears as prototypes for evolutionary analyses of emotion. *Psychophysiology, 23*, 123–145.

Ortony, A., Clore, G. L., & Collins, A. (1988). *The cognitive structure of emotions*. New York: Cambridge University Press.

Oveis, C., Horberg, E. J., & Keltner, D. (2005). Compassion as a moral intuition. Manuscript submitted for publication.

Quigley, B. M., & Tedeschi, J. T. (1996). Mediating effects of blame attributions on feelings of anger. *Personality and Social Psychology Bulletin, 22*, 1280–1288.

Rozin, P. (1996). Towards a psychology of food and eating: From motivation to module to model to marker, morality, meaning, and metaphor. *Current Directions in Psychological Science, 5*, 18–24.

Rozin, P., Haidt J., & McCauley, C. (1999a). Disgust: The body and soul emotion. In T. Dalgleish & M. J. Power (Eds.), *Handbook of cognition and emotion* (pp. 429–445). New York: John Wiley & Sons.

Rozin, P., Lowery, L., Imada, S., & Haidt, J. (1999b). The CAD triad hypothesis: A mapping between three moral emotions (contempt, anger, disgust) and three moral codes (community, autonomy, divinity). *Journal of Personality and Social Psychology, 76*, 578–586.

Rozin, P., Markwith, M., & Stoess, C. (1997). Moralization and becoming a vegetarian: The transformation of preferences into values and the recruitment of disgust. *Psychological Science, 8*, 67–73.

Rozin, P., & Singh, L. (1999). The moralization of cigarette smoking in the United States. *Journal of Consumer Psychology, 8*, 339–342.

Scherer, K. R. (1984). On the nature and function of emotion: A component process approach. In K. Scherer & P. Ekman (Eds.), *Approaches to emotion* (pp. 293–318). Hillsdale, NJ: Lawrence Erlbaum Associates, Inc.

Schwarz, N., & Clore, G. L. (1983). Mood, misattribution, and judgments of well-being: Informative and directive functions of affective states. *Journal of Personality and Social Psychology, 45*, 513–523.

Schwarz, N., & Clore, G. L. (1996). Feelings and phenomenal experiences. In E. T. Higgins & A. W. Kruglanski (Eds.), *Social psychology: Handbook of basic principles* (pp. 433–465). New York: Guilford Press.

Shaver, P. R., Morgan, H. J., & Wu, S. (1996). Is love a "basic" emotion? *Personal Relationships, 3*, 81–96.

Shiota, M. N., Campos, B., Keltner, D., & Hertenstein, M. J. (2004). Positive emotion and the regulation of interpersonal relationships. In P. Philippot & R. S. Feldman (Eds.), *The regulation of emotion* (pp. 127–155). Mahwah, NJ: Lawrence Erlbaum Associates, Inc.

Shweder, R. A., Much, N. C., Mahapatra, M., & Park, L. (1997). The "big three" of morality (autonomy, community, and divinity), and the "big three" explanations of suffering. In A. Brandt & P. Rozin (Eds.), *Morality and health* (pp. 119–169). New York: Routledge.

Skoe, E. E. A., Eisenberg, N., & Cumberland, A. (2002). The role of reported emotion in real-life and hypothetical moral dilemmas. *Personality and Social Psychology Bulletin, 28*, 962–973.

Smith, C. A., & Ellsworth, P. C. (1985). Patterns of cognitive appraisal in emotion. *Journal of Personality and Social Psychology, 48*, 813–838.

Sober, E., & Wilson, D. S. (1998). *Unto others: The evolution and psychology of unselfish behavior*. Cambridge, MA: Harvard University Press.

Tangney, J. (1992). Situational determinants of shame and guilt in young adulthood. *Personality and Social Psychology Bulletin, 18*, 199–206.

Tangney, J. P., Wagner, P. E., Hill-Barlow, D., Marschall, D. E., & Gramzow, R. (1996). Relation of shame and guilt to constructive versus destructive responses to anger across the lifespan. *Journal of Personality and Social Psychology, 70*, 797–809.

Tiedens, L. Z., Ellsworth, P. C., & Mesquita, B. (2000). Stereotypes about sentiments and status: Emotional expectations for high- and low-status group members. *Personality and Social Psychology Bulletin, 26*, 560–574.

Tracy, J. L., & Robins, R. W. (2004). Show your pride: Evidence for a discrete emotion expression. *Psychological Science, 15*, 194–197.

Trivers, R. L. (1971). The evolution of reciprocal altruism. *The Quarterly Review of Biology, 46*, 35–57.

Vasquez, K., Keltner, D., Ebenbach, D. H., & Banaszynski, T. L. (2001). Cultural variation and similarity in moral rhetorics: Voices from the Philippines and the United States. *Journal of Cross-Cultural Psychology, 32*, 93–120.

Weiner, B., Graham, S., & Reyna, C. (1997). An attributional explanation of retributive versus utilitarian philosophies of punishment. *Social Justice Research, 10*, 431–452.

10

Affective Forecasting: A User's Guide to Emotional Time Travel

ELIZABETH W. DUNN and SIMON M. LAHAM

*H*uman beings possess a unique ability to engage in emotional time travel, mentally fast forwarding through time to envision how much they will love their spouse 5 years later or how much they will enjoy a hot fudge sundae next Thursday. Emotional time travel is not without its pitfalls, however, as recent research has documented (e.g., Gilbert & Wilson, 2000). At the most obvious level, people may make inaccurate predictions about how they will feel in a situation because the situation unfolds differently than they expect. For example, if a vacationer imagines a week of swimming and surfing in Australia and arrives to find the beaches swarming with man-eating sharks and deadly jellyfish, her actual emotional experiences during the vacation are likely to diverge sharply from her original expectations. Yet, even if the situation people experience objectively matches the situation they imagined, people face a fundamentally different *psychological* situation when they experience an event than when they imagine it. The failure to recognize this basic point begets a wide variety of affective forecasting errors. Following a brief review of common forecasting errors, the present chapter addresses six major questions regarding the processes and consequences of emotional time travel.

TYPES AND SOURCES OF FORECASTING ERRORS

Experiencing an event is fundamentally different from imagining it because once an event occurs people are generally motivated to make the best of it. Upon finding herself sharing a beach with sharks and jellyfish, for example, our traveler might find pleasure in the opportunity to observe exotic wildlife in their natural habitat, though she probably would not have foreseen her own ability to reconstrue the situation in this way. Indeed, people are extremely adept at reconstrual, rationalization, and other mental transformations that take the sting out of unwanted events, but they are often blind to these tools of the "psychological immune system" (Gilbert, Pinel,

Wilson, Blumberg, & Wheatley, 1998, p. 617). As a result of this blindness, they often overestimate how miserable they will feel when faced with misfortune, exhibiting an *intensity bias* (Buehler & McFarland, 2001), as well as how long they will feel that way, exhibiting a *durability bias* (Gilbert et al., 1998; Wilson, Wheatley, Meyers, Gilbert, & Axsom, 2000). In practice, it is often difficult to distinguish the intensity bias from the durability bias, and the broader tendency to overestimate the power and persistence of emotional reactions to events is now commonly labeled the *impact bias* (Gilbert, Driver-Linn, & Wilson, 2002; Wilson & Gilbert 2003). The impact bias has been observed for positive events, as well as negative (e.g., Buehler & McFarland, 2001; Dunn, Wilson, & Gilbert, 2003; Gilbert et al., 1998; Wilson et al., 2000). After all, just as people make sense of negative events, so too they come to "ordinize" positive events, such that the Harvard acceptance letter that was once novel, unexpected, and emotionally riveting soon gets tucked away and neatly incorporated into the self-concept, diluting the enduring joy it was supposed to deliver (Wilson, Gilbert, & Centerbar, 2002).

Whether positive or negative, imagining an event is also very different from experiencing it because people tend to *imagine* focal events in isolation, whereas events are rarely *experienced* in a vacuum. For example, in imagining how happy he will feel on the day his first child is born, an expectant father is likely to focus on the miraculous arrival of his new baby, while forgetting that the taste of hospital food, the chatter of relatives, and the songs playing in the waiting room will serve as the background, at least temporarily distracting him from the main event. Thus, because people exhibit *focalism*, imagining focal events without regard to background distractions, they tend to overestimate their emotional reactions to both positive and negative events (Lam, Buehler, & McFarland, 2005; Wilson et al., 2000; see also Schkade & Kahneman, 1998).

The affective forecasting errors discussed above stem from almost ubiquitous differences in the psychological situations faced by forecasters versus experiencers, but other important differences may arise as well, further clouding forecasts. Forecasts are likely to be particularly inaccurate to the extent that one's visceral state at the time of forecasting differs from one's visceral state at the time of experiencing (Gilbert, Gill, & Wilson, 2002; Loewenstein, 1996; Loewenstein, Nagin, & Paternoster, 1997; Loewenstein, O'Donoghue, & Rabin, in press; Read & van Leeuwen, 1998; Van Boven, Dunning, & Loewenstein, 2000; Van Boven, Loewenstein, & Dunning, 2005). Visceral factors, which include hunger, pain, moods, sexual arousal, and other motivational or drive states, have powerful effects on cognition and behavior (see also Baumeister, Vohs, & Tice, this volume; Clore & Storbeck, this volume; Forgas, this volume). People often fail to appreciate the full influence of such visceral factors, however, creating an *empathy gap* between their current and future selves that interferes with successful forecasting (Loewenstein, 1996; Loewenstein & Schkade, 1999). For example, sated people have trouble predicting what snacks they will like best when they are later hungry (Read & van Leeuwen, 1998), and unaroused men have trouble predicting how they will feel and behave around a woman when sexually aroused (Loewenstein, et al., 1997). Thus, the more one's psychological state differs between the stages of forecasting and experiencing, the more one's forecasts are likely to prove inaccurate.

There are, of course, other sources and types of affective forecasting errors, but excellent taxonomies are available elsewhere (Gilbertet al., 2002; Gilbert & Wilson, 2000; Loewenstein & Schkade, 1999; Wilson & Gilbert, 2003). Therefore, in the pages that follow, we address six broader questions that we believe are relevant to understanding everyday emotional time travel. Because the importance of affective forecasts lies primarily in their capacity to drive behavior, we begin by considering how and when people's affective forecasts influence their decisions (Question I). To the extent that affective forecasts influence decisions, the quality of those decisions rests on the correspondence between forecasts and actual experiences; under Question II, then, we address how well forecasts predict later experiences. Next, we consider whether emotional time travel can be improved (Question III) and whether some people are better emotional time travelers than others (Question IV). Finally, we discuss the consequences of affective forecasting errors for the survival of the human species (Question V), as well as for individual well-being, interpersonal relationships, economic growth, and social justice (Question VI).

I. How Do Affective Forecasts Influence Decisions?

Most articles on affective forecasting highlight the importance of this topic by noting that people's anticipated emotions influence their decisions. Often, however, relatively little evidence is provided for this assumption, perhaps because it seems so reasonable. But like many reasonable assumptions, this one is both accurate and oversimplified.

Recent research supports the basic intuition that affective forecasts can often guide decision-making. In fact, when faced with a decision between gambles, people's anticipated emotions predict their choices above and beyond the economic utility of the gambles (Mellers, Schwarz, Ho, & Ritov, 1997; Mellers, Schwarz, & Ritov, 1999). People's anticipation of regret seems to play a particularly powerful role in shaping their decisions (e.g., Crawford, McConnell, Lewis, & Sherman, 2002; Mellers et al., 1999; Zeelenberg, 1999; Zeelenberg, Beattie, van der Plight, & de Vries, 1996). For example, when individuals anticipate that complying with a persuasion attempt will produce less regret than defying it, they typically choose to comply (Crawford et al., 2002). Decision-making is also strongly influenced by the fear and panic that people expect to feel when encountering a frightening situation (e.g., Cox & Swinson, 1994; Craske, Rapee, & Barlow, 1988). Among patients suffering from panic disorder with agoraphobia, avoidance of traveling and crowds is better predicted by patients' anticipated levels of panic than by actual experiences of panic (Cox & Swinson, 1994). Affective forecasts may not only influence problem-focused coping behaviors such as eschewing potentially regrettable decisions or frightening situations, but may also guide decisions about emotion-focused coping. When forecasters anticipated possible social rejection, they selected higher levels of a mood-enhancing drug than did experiencers who had actually encountered this rejection, reflecting forecasters' mistaken belief that the rejection would be quite painful (Wilson, Wheatley, Kurtz, Dunn, & Gilbert, 2004). Regardless of their accuracy, then, affective forecasts influence people's decisions about whether to approach or avoid situations and about how to deal with situations that cannot be avoided.

Yet, affective forecasts sometimes play a more limited role in decision-making. The degree of correspondence between forecasts and decisions may depend in part on the nature of the choice situation. When people choose an item for immediate consumption, they tend to select the item that they expect to enjoy most, whereas when they choose a group of items, some of which will only be consumed at a later time, they tend to include items in their selection that are expected to produce lower levels of enjoyment during consumption (Read, Loewenstein, & Kalyanaraman, 1999; Simonson, 1990). For example, when choosing a video to watch that day, people tend to select enjoyable, if forgettable, "lowbrow" movies (e.g., *Speed*), whereas when choosing a series of movies to watch in the future, people are more likely to select more memorable "highbrow" movies that they are less likely to enjoy (e.g., *Schindler's List*; Read et al., 1999). This suggests that people's affective forecasts influence their decisions more strongly when the chosen option is to be consumed sooner rather than later.

The degree to which affective forecasts influence decisions also depends on whether people view their feelings as appropriate guides for choice (Hsee, 1999; Hsee & Rottenstreich, 2004; Hsee, Zhang, Yu, & Xi, 2003). While it is unsurprising that people would place little weight on their affective responses in selecting utilitarian goods such as vacuum cleaners, people may also sometimes dismiss their affective preferences in choosing hedonic goods such as chocolate. When Hsee (1999) asked participants to predict whether they would feel better eating a small, 50-cent chocolate shaped like a heart, or a larger, $2 chocolate shaped like a roach, most reported that they would feel better eating the small heart, but most also reported that they would choose the large roach. This discrepancy between affective forecasts and decisions seems to emerge because people feel that they should choose higher-value items, even if these items are relatively unenjoyable. More broadly, people may try to base their decisions on factors that seem scientific or justifiable, while suppressing the seemingly "irrational" influence of their affective forecasts (Hsee et al., 2003).

When are people likely to underweight their affective forecasts in this way? If people are comparing multiple options at once (e.g., two laptops), they can easily base their decision on rational, scientific attributes (e.g., gigabytes and megahertz). But if people are simply choosing whether or not to accept a single option, such attributes may be difficult to assess meaningfully (Hsee & Zhang, 2004), potentially leaving more room for people's overall affective forecasts about the available option to shape their decisions. The influence of affective forecasts on decisions may be moderated not only by how the choice is framed, but also by people's frame of mind; after solving math problems, participants show less reliance on their feelings about a product than after answering questions about their affective responses to unrelated attitude objects (Hsee & Rottenstreich, 2004).

Summary   Existing research supports the widespread intuition that affective forecasts guide many of our decisions, sometimes overpowering more "reasonable" or utilitarian concerns. Yet, affective forecasts may play a surprisingly small role in shaping our decisions, even those that are intended to produce pleasure, when people (1) choose items that will only be consumed after a delay; (2) believe that there are more appropriate, rational factors available for consideration; or (3) are in an analytical, calculation-oriented state of mind.

II.   How Well Do Affective Forecasts Predict Experiences?

To the extent that affective forecasts influence decisions, the validity of those decisions rests on whether forecasts accurately predict later experiences (Kahneman & Snell, 1992). Upon scanning the affective forecasting literature, one might be left with the impression that decisions based on affective forecasts are likely to be rather poor; typically, studies in this area report the discrepancies between affective forecasts and actual experiences, thereby highlighting the shortcomings of forecasts. Yet, examining the correlations between forecasts and experiences paints a more optimistic picture, suggesting that people may have some degree of self-insight into their own emotional futures.

It is theoretically possible, after all, for forecasts and experiences to be highly discrepant but perfectly correlated (e.g., if all participants overestimated their post-break-up misery by 2 points, they would show both the impact bias and perfectly correlated forecasts and experiences). Indeed, a number of studies that report significant discrepancies between forecasts and experiences also report that forecasts and experiences are significantly correlated (e.g., Buehler & McFarland, 2001; Dunn et al., 2003; Rachman & Eyrl, 1989; Wirtz, Kruger, Napa Scollon, & Diener, 2003). This suggests that knowing how happy someone expects to be in a particular situation is often a valid predictor of how happy they will actually be relative to other participants, though not necessarily of how happy they will be in an absolute sense.

There is, however, substantial variability in the strength of forecast-experience correlations across studies. While it is rare to observe near-zero correlations between forecasts and experiences, correlations range from quite small (e.g., .15; Klaaren, Hodges & Wilson, 1994) to extremely high (e.g., .98; Mellers et al., 1999). Variables such as the familiarity of the target situation and the amount of time between forecasts and experiences may moderate the degree of correspondence between forecasts and experiences, although the role of such moderating variables has not yet been directly examined.

Of course, even if forecasts and experiences are strongly correlated across a sample of participants, this does not necessarily reflect true self-insight on behalf of the participants, as a number of spurious factors can inflate forecast-experience correlations (e.g., response sets, stable individual differences in affect). For example, ice cream lovers are likely to predict and actually experience greater enjoyment of next Thursday's hot fudge sundae compared to ice cream haters. Rather than reflecting a real ability to peer into the future, the resulting correlation between forecasted and experienced sundae enjoyment may emerge because initial ice cream liking acts as a third variable, influencing both forecasts and experiences. In line with this idea, Kahneman and Snell (1992) found that participants' forecasts of how much they would like ice cream, yogurt, and music on a given day in the future typically predicted their actual liking on that day; there was, however, virtually no relationship between participants' predicted and actual *changes* in liking over the course of a week. This suggests that people may sometimes have little insight into how their affective reactions will differ in the future, and observed correlations between forecasts and experiences may occur largely because both are related to initial affect.

Still, even if people have little insight into the temporal dynamics of their specific tastes, they may be more adept at predicting shifts in their general mood. Using a within-subjects approach, Totterdell, Parkinson, Briner, and Reynolds (1997) found significant relationships between participants' forecasted and actual daily moods over a 2-week period. Still, forecasts explained no more than 10% of the variance in experiences. Some participants exhibited high correlations between forecasts and experiences across days while others exhibited low or even negative correlations, suggesting that there may be substantial individual differences in forecasting ability (see Question IV).

Summary   Although most studies emphasize discrepancies between forecasts and experiences and therefore highlight flaws in forecasting, it is important to recognize that forecasts and experiences are typically correlated. This means that if Aunt Rita expects to enjoy a vacation in Hawaii more than Uncle George, then it is a good bet that Rita will be happier in Hawaii than George (though neither may be as happy as they expected). It is not clear, however, whether such correspondence between forecasts and experiences reflects true knowledge about oneself and the temporal dynamics of affect. Thus, there is evidence that affective forecasts are often a useful, valid predictor of actual experiences, but future research must illuminate for whom, when, and why forecasts predict experiences.

III.   Can Emotional Time Travel Be Improved?

Although affective forecasts are rooted in reality, suggesting that emotional time travel is more than just a flight of fancy, there is clearly substantial room for improvement. Luckily, almost as fast as researchers have identified biases in affective forecasting, they have developed simple interventions that reduce these biases.

The impact bias is as pervasive as acne, and it may be as treatable. Simply priming people with the general concept of progression or change may lead them to recognize that their own affective responses will wear off quickly; when Igou (2004) exposed participants to a graph showing declining ozone levels (priming change), they predicted that their affective reactions would dissipate more quickly than when they saw a graph depicting stable ozone levels (priming continuity). The expected intensity of initial reactions to events may be reduced when people first think about their emotional responses to a wide range of similar past events (Buehler & McFarland, 2001; Morewedge, Gilbert & Wilson, 2005). It is not sufficient to think of just one similar past event, which may be the default strategy of people who bother to reflect on the past at all in predicting the future; when people think about just one relevant past event, they are likely to think of an extreme, atypical instance from their past, such as the Best Christmas Ever. Ironically, if it is only feasible to ask people to think of one past event, it may be best to ask specifically for an extreme, atypical instance. People normally recall this type of instance anyway, but explicitly labeling it as such underscores that the upcoming event is likely to be less extreme than the recalled event (Morewedge et al., 2005).

Just as taking a broad view of the past may help reduce the impact bias, so too may thinking more broadly about the future. People tend to make extreme forecasts about their emotional responses to a given upcoming event in part because they exhibit focalism, neglecting background distractions. Therefore, simply asking people to think about these background events and activities can reduce the extremity of their forecasts regarding a target event (Lam et al., 2005; Wilson et al., 2000). For example, college football fans made more moderate forecasts about how they would feel in the days following a win or loss by their team when they first described the other activities they would be engaged in during that time (e.g., studying, socializing; Wilson et al., 2000).

People's affective forecasts may be improved not only by drawing their attention to background events, but also by drawing their attention to features of the target event or outcome that they may typically overlook. When people are faced with a set of competing options, they typically focus on features that differentiate the outcomes, while neglecting features that are shared or similar across options. For example, in looking at colleges, students may focus on a few features that differentiate the colleges (e.g., location) while paying little attention to their many shared features (e.g., size, extracurriculars). Asking people to think about features that are similar or shared across outcomes can lead them to place increased weight on such features, which may be important for actual happiness but that otherwise would be neglected in forecasting (Dunn, Wilson, & Gilbert, 2003). An alternative to engaging in this kind of thought exercise may be to structure choice situations such that the options are not compared in side-by-side fashion, thereby reducing excessive focus on the options' differentiating features (Hsee & Zhang, 2004). This suggests that students who attend information sessions at three different schools in one day with notepad and pen clutched tightly in hand may make poorer affective forecasts than students who independently evaluate each school by spending a couple of days at each over several weeks.

Whereas the impact bias and related affective forecasting errors may be relatively easy to counteract, errors caused by empathy gaps may be harder to correct. Exhibiting an empathy gap, people fail to recognize that they will feel attached to an object once it becomes their own (the endowment effect; Loewenstein & Adler, 1995; Van Boven et al., 2000). Simple interventions such as monetary incentives for accuracy or classroom instruction on the endowment effect have failed to show promise in bridging this empathy gap (Van Boven et al., 2000). The best approach to reducing affective forecasting errors stemming from empathy gaps may lie in inducing the same type of visceral, emotional, or motivational state in forecasters that they are likely to experience at the relevant future time (Loewenstein et al., 1997; Van Boven et al., 2000). For example, there is indirect evidence that people may make more accurate forecasts about how they would feel and behave in a date rape scenario when they are in a state of heightened sexual arousal at the time of forecasting (Loewenstein et al., 1997).

While the strategies discussed above are targeted at combating specific sources of error in forecasting, recent evidence has revealed a single strategy that may effectively combat a broad range of forecasting errors. Because many forecasting errors stem from the biases inherent in mental simulation, accuracy may be improved when people generate forecasts not by imagining their own reaction to an event, but by learning about another person's response to the same event (Norwick, Gilbert, & Wilson, 2005). Indeed, Norwick et al. (2005) demonstrated that people's forecasts were more accurate when they relied on the actual experience of a single, randomly chosen individual than on their own mental simulation of the event.

Summary   There is strong evidence that one of the most prevalent pitfalls of emotional time travel, the impact bias, can be reduced by thinking about (1) images of change, (2) a range of relevant past experiences, or (3) background events that will serve as distractions from a focal event or outcome. Simple thought exercises may also be effective in drawing people's attention to important aspects of the focal event or outcome that are typically overlooked. Although affective forecasting errors stemming from empathy gaps may sometimes be more pertinacious, recent evidence suggests that relying on the experiences of others may allow forecasters to bypass a range of forecasting pitfalls, including empathy gaps.

IV.   Are Some People Better Emotional Time Travelers Than Others?

The interventions above suggest ways of reducing affective forecasting biases in the short term but are unlikely to produce long-term improvements in forecasting ability. Given that making consistently accurate, unbiased affective forecasts may have important intrapersonal and interpersonal benefits (see Question VI), it would be useful to know whether some people are consistently skillful at emotional time travel.

Although relatively little research has addressed this question, there are scattered indications that some people may be less prone than others to specific types of forecasting biases. Older people may be less susceptible to the durability bias because they come to recognize that even important events rarely have lasting emotional influence. Wilson, Gilbert, and Salthouse (2001) found some evidence that after age 60 people increasingly recognize how quickly the emotional power of events wears off (cited in Wilson & Gilbert, 2003). The tendency to overestimate the emotional power of events may also be less pronounced among East Asians than Westerners. Because East Asians are more likely to think holistically, recognizing the importance of contextual, background information, they may be less likely to fall into the trap of focalism when imagining their reactions to future events (Lam et al., 2005). When asked to imagine how they would feel on the first warm day of spring, Euro-Canadian students focused largely on the focal event of warm weather and therefore exhibited the impact bias, overestimating how happy they would be that day. In contrast, Asian students at the same university did not show the impact bias because they focused less heavily on the target event of warm weather.

Despite escaping the impact bias, Asians' forecasts were not especially accurate; when both forecasts and experiences were measured in a within-subjects design, the forecast-experience correlations were low for Asians and Euro-Canadians alike.

Moving beyond susceptibility to bias, then, do some people show an elevated correspondence between their forecasts and experiences? Interestingly, Riis and his colleagues found that end stage renal patients were significantly more accurate than healthy matched controls in making affective forecasts regarding their mood for the following week (Riis, Loewenstein, Baron, Jepson, Fagerlin, & Ubel, 2005). The patients' heightened accuracy seemed to emerge because they recognized that they would focus on their positive experiences, a common tendency that may be less transparent to those who have not encountered significant, enduring adversity. Of course, given that most people would not trade liver function for improved affective forecasting skills, it would be valuable to identify a more common trait that predicts forecasting ability.

Brackett, Dunn, and Schneiderman (2005) have found initial evidence that people who are high in emotional intelligence (EI) may make relatively accurate affective forecasts. Supporters of John Kerry who had previously completed an EI test were asked to predict how they would feel if George Bush won the 2004 American presidential election, and then they reported their actual feelings after Bush's win. Predicted and actual feelings were barely correlated among participants who were low or near average in EI, whereas predicted and actual feelings were strongly and significantly correlated among participants who were high in EI. Although this basic finding requires replication, it suggests that there may be predictable individual differences in forecasting accuracy.

Summary   The impact bias may be attenuated among older people and East Asians, although reducing the impact bias does not necessarily improve the correlation between forecasts and experiences. The correspondence between forecasts and experiences may be elevated among people who have encountered ongoing adversity and among people who are high in EI. These findings are recent and tentative, however, and examining individual differences in forecasting ability is a relatively new research area that is ripe for development.

V. Did Evolution Favor Affective Forecasting Biases?

Although affective forecasting biases may be reduced for some people in some situations, these biases are notable for their prevalence, spurring the question of whether the most common forecasting biases may somehow be functional on an evolutionary level. Indeed, the tendency to view cognitive and motivational biases in psychology as errors is shifting with the recent emergence of evolutionary psychological perspectives on decision-making and cognition (e.g., Cosmides & Tooby, 1994; Fox, 1992; Gigerenzer, 2000; Haselton & Buss, 2000, 2003; Haselton & Ketelaar, this volume; Pinker, 1997).

Evolutionary psychologists propose that evolution has produced a large number of domain-specific psychological mechanisms designed to solve particular kinds of problems (Buss, 1994; Symons, 1987; Tooby & Cosmides, 1992). Although the extent of the domain-specificity of evolved psychological mechanisms remains debatable, such an approach could nevertheless prove fruitful for forecasting research. There is evidence that people may possess adaptive biases in their actual affective reactions to specific stimuli, experiencing strong negative emotions that lead them to avoid possible threats to reproductive fitness, such as snakes (Tomarken, Mineka, & Cook, 1989) and potentially dangerous foods (Rozin & Fallon, 1987; Rozin, Markwith, & Ross, 1990). Do such adaptive biases also emerge in affective *forecasts* about evolutionarily recurrent threats to reproductive fitness? Does one not only fear snakes, but also overpredict fear of snakes? We would expect such biased predictions to be selected for if they have had an impact on behaviors that influenced fitness over evolutionary history.

Research on the prediction of fear and pain lends some support to our speculations. People generally overestimate how frightened they will be in the face of fear-provoking situations (Arntz & van den Hout, 1988; Rachman, 1990, 1994; Rachman & Bichard, 1988; Rachman, Lopatka, & Levitt, 1988). Such overpredictions have been demonstrated for fear of confined spaces, snakes, spiders, and panic episodes to name a few, and these findings are obtained in clinical as well as normal populations, in both field and laboratory settings (see Rachman, 1994 for a review). Predictions of pain show a similar trend. In predictions of dental (Arntz, van Eck, & Heijmans, 1990), arthritic (Rachman & Lopatka, 1988), and menstrual pain (Rachman & Eyrl, 1989), people show a consistent tendency to overestimate the intensity of their painful experiences. Insofar as such overestimations of fear and pain lead people away from aversive experiences that threaten reproduction and survival (fear of snakes and spiders are of particular note here), inaccuracies of this kind may be adaptive. In uncertain judgment situations in which the costs of affective underestimation (not fearing the snake and potentially being bitten) outweigh those of affective overestimation, forecasting inaccuracies may indeed have been selected for over evolutionary history (see Haselton & Ketelaar, this volume for a similar analysis of biases in mating behavior).

These suggestions are purposefully speculative and stand as examples of how evolutionary theory might inform affective forecasting research. Although these examples are consistent with an evolutionary approach to affective forecasting, they are readily encompassed by the mainstream social-cognitive explanatory framework of forecasting biases; the instances noted above may simply be the consequences of focalism or other such domain-general mechanisms. An evolutionary approach to forecasting biases gains unique explanatory power when it predicts novel effects contrary to more general social-cognitive explanations. Further, we would expect forecasts to confer evolutionary advantages only in domains that impact reproductive fitness such as those mentioned above, as well as mate choice and kin investment, for example. We are currently unaware of any specific instances in which evolutionary theory has been used to generate unique hypotheses regarding affective forecasts, but this focus may indeed provide a new perspective on affective forecasting in certain domains.

Summary   Although we may indeed be biased forecasters, some biases may not be disadvantageous from an evolutionary perspective. In particular, errors of overestimation may not necessarily be bad for human survival and may in fact be evolutionarily functional in many instances. More generally, taking an evolutionary approach to affective forecasting may not only reveal when forecasting biases prove functional, but can also yield interesting and novel predictions about when underestimation in affective predictions may occur.

VI. Do Affective Forecasting Errors Matter?

While affective forecasting errors may not impair or may even promote the survival of our species, these errors have important consequences for individuals and societies. Of course, many affective forecasting studies demonstrate that people mispredict their future feelings by just 1 to 2 points on 7–9 point scales (e.g., Buehler & McFarland, 2001; Dunn et al., 2003; Lam et al., 2005; Wilson et al., 2000). Yet, the shortcomings of emotional time travel revealed by these systematic errors have important implications for happiness, health, public policy, economics, and interpersonal relationships.

Clearly, errors in emotional time travel may interfere with the pursuit of happiness. As discussed by Gilbert and Wilson (2000), people often "miswant," leading them to seek out things that will not increase their happiness or to fervently avoid things that will not decrease their happiness. Interestingly, people may fall into these traps of emotional time travel even when they consciously recognize what matters for their happiness. For example, while realizing that climate is relatively unimportant for well-being, people expect living in California to increase happiness significantly (Schkade & Kahneman, 1998). And while realizing that the quality of a house's physical features matter less than the quality of the other human beings inside it, people readily neglect the latter and focus on the former (Dunn et al., 2003). Thus, the pitfalls of emotional time travel may frequently throw people off course, leading them to pursue goals that, if achieved, may produce little happiness.

Affective forecasting errors also have important implications for both physical and mental health. People may delay getting tested for serious health problems in part because they anticipate lasting misery if the test reveals unwanted results. Yet, such dire forecasts may be inaccurate; Sieff, Dawes, and Loewenstein (1999) found some evidence that people overestimate the extremity of their long-term reactions to receiving positive or negative HIV-test results. Similarly, people seem to overestimate how unhappy they would be while undergoing treatment for a serious disorder (Riis et al., 2005), suggesting that people may sometimes resist medical treatment because they fail to recognize how readily they will adapt to it. Blindness to the power of the psychological immune system may also lead people to seek out both legal and illegal mood-enhancing drugs. As already discussed, forecasters bracing themselves for rejection sought out greater quantities of a mood-enhancing drug than did experiencers who had already faced the rejection (Wilson et al., 2004), suggesting that people may underestimate their own ability to cope successfully without drugs.

Beyond interfering with one's own health and happiness, affective forecasting errors have important interpersonal consequences. When faced with the challenge of understanding how another person feels in a given situation, people typically begin by predicting how they themselves would feel in the situation and then adjust for differences between themselves and others (Van Boven et al., 2000; Van Boven & Loewenstein, 2003; Van Boven, Loewenstein, & Dunning, 2005; Van Boven, Loewenstein, & Dunning, 2003; Van Boven & Loewenstein, 2005). Therefore, to the extent that people mispredict their own feelings, they may also misunderstand others' feelings and their corresponding behaviors. For example, because people fail to foresee that owning an object will increase their own affection for it, they also fail to anticipate that others will show this endowment effect (Van Boven et al., 2000; Van Boven et al., 2003). As a result, buyers systematically underestimate how much owners will demand for an object, while owners overestimate how much buyers would willingly pay (Van Boven et al., 2000; Van Boven et al., 2003). This interpersonal empathy gap has serious economic consequences in that fewer successful transactions can be achieved. Negative social consequences may arise as well. If people fail to understand others' emotions, then the behaviors corresponding to these unpredicted emotions are likely to seem inappropriate and may be viewed as evidence of undesirable personality traits; when owners and buyers were asked why their transaction had failed, they typically attributed the failure to the other person's greed, rather than recognizing that the endowment effect might be responsible for the gap in object valuation between owners and buyers (Van Boven et al., 2000).

On a broader level, interpersonal empathy gaps may hinder successful policymaking. If policymakers fail to predict how they themselves would feel if they were in the position of a struggling single mother, a heroin addict, or a juvenile delinquent, they may wrongly infer that behaviors exhibited by members of these groups reflect undesirable personality traits and may create policies that treat members of these groups unfairly (Loewenstein, 1996; Van Boven & Loewenstein, 2005). Ordinary citizens may also fall into this trap when serving as jurors. Woodzicka and LaFrance (2001) found that women tend to mispredict how they would feel and behave in response to sexual harassment; whereas women expect to feel angry and to confront the harasser, they were more likely to experience fear and therefore avoid confrontation. If jurors mispredict how boldly they themselves would respond to sexual harassment, then they may take a negative view of a plaintiff who claims she was sexually harassed but feared confronting her harasser. Thus, to the extent that people fail to predict their own emotional reactions to events, they may have difficulty understanding how a "reasonable woman" or "reasonable person" would behave, casting doubt on the validity of these standards in legal cases.

Affective forecasting errors may also impede successful contact between members of different social groups. Mallett (2005) found evidence that people typically overestimate the amount of stress they would experience during intergroup interactions, leading to overly negative affective forecasts regarding such interactions. This suggests that inaccurate affective forecasts may be partially responsible for the common tendency to avoid interactions with members of other social groups—a tendency that curtails opportunities for prejudice-reducing intergroup contact.

This is not to say that affective forecasting errors always have negative consequences. Dunn and Finn (2005) found that people who overestimated the emotional benefits of interacting with their romantic partner exhibited strong relationship stability a year later, controlling for initial relationship satisfaction. Though correlational, this finding suggests that optimistic forecasting errors may sometimes promote successful relationships (see also Holmes & Anthony, this volume). In a similar vein, Gilbert, Brown, Pinel, and Wilson (2000) found that people's blindness to the power of their own psychological immune systems led them to attribute unexpected happiness to the benevolent intervention of an omniscient external agent. According to Gilbert et al. (2000), this blindness may support people's comforting belief that their world is guarded by a powerful and caring god. Thus, affective forecasting errors may contribute to both relationship stability and divine belief.

Summary   Affective forecasting errors can interfere with both intrapersonal and interpersonal functioning. Falling into the traps of emotional time travel may impair individuals' health and happiness and may lead them to misunderstand others' feelings and behaviors. Interpersonal misunderstandings that stem from poor emotional time travel may also undermine successful economic transactions, policymaking, and intergroup harmony. Yet, affective forecasting errors may also have important positive consequences, which future research may help to further identify.

CONCLUSIONS

The research reviewed in this chapter underscores the importance of everyday emotional time travel. People's predictions about how they will feel in the future shape many of their decisions, though under certain conditions people place surprisingly little weight on their affective forecasts in decision-making. Supporting the validity of decisions that are based on affective forecasts, most studies suggest that forecasts do reliably predict experiences, though we know relatively little about when, why, and for whom the relationship between forecasts and experiences is stronger or weaker. We do know that specific biases in forecasting can be readily eliminated, and there is a smattering of recent evidence that some people may be better forecasters than others. Finally, while common forms of affective forecasting errors may not interfere with the survival of our species, the shortcomings of emotional time travel have important ramifications for individual, interpersonal, and societal well-being.

Thus, the burgeoning body of research on affective forecasting stands to make an essential contribution to the study of hearts and minds. While most affect research examines the influence of *current* feelings on cognition and behavior (e.g., Forgas, this volume), emerging research on affective forecasting suggests that *anticipated* emotions may be just as important in understanding human behavior.

REFERENCES

Arntz, A., & van den Hout, M. (1988). Generalizability of the match-mismatch model of fear. *Behavior Research and Therapy, 28,* 249–253.

Arntz, A., van Eck, M., & Heijmans, M. (1990). Predictions of dental pain: The fear of any expected evil is worse than the evil itself. *Behavior Research and Therapy, 28,* 29–41.

Brackett, M. A., Dunn, E. W., & Schneiderman, E. (2005). Emotional intelligence and affective forecasting. Unpublished raw data, Yale University.

Buehler, R., & McFarland, C. (2001). Intensity bias in affective forecasting: The role of temporal focus. *Personality and Social Psychology Bulletin, 27,* 1480–1493.

Buss, D. M. (1994). *The evolution of desire: Strategies of human mating.* New York: Basic Books.

Cosmides, L., & Tooby, J. (1994). Better than rational: Evolutionary psychology and the invisible hand. *American Economic Review, 84,* 327–332.

Cox, B. J., & Swinson, R. P. (1994). Overprediction of fear in panic disorder with agoraphobia. *Behaviour Research & Therapy, 32,* 735–739.

Craske, M. G., Rapee, R. M., & Barlow, D. H. (1988). The significance of panic expectancy for individual patterns of avoidance. *Behavior Therapist, 19,* 577–592.

Crawford, M. T., McConnell, A. R., Lewis, A. C., & Sherman, S. J. (2002). Reactance, compliance and anticipated regret. *Journal of Experimental Social Psychology, 38,* 56–63.

Dunn, E. W., & Finn, S. M. (2005). Misunderstanding the affective consequences of everyday social interactions: The hidden benefits of putting one's best face forward. Unpublished manuscript, University of Virginia.

Dunn, E. W., Wilson, T. D., & Gilbert, D. T. (2003). Location, location, location: The misprediction of satisfaction in housing lotteries. *Personality and Social Psychology Bulletin, 29,* 1421–1432.

Fox, R. (1992). Prejudice and the unfinished mind: A new look at an old failing. *Psychological Inquiry, 3,* 137–152.

Gigerenzer, G. (2000). *Adaptive thinking: Rationality in the real world.* London: Oxford University Press.

Gilbert, D. T., Brown, R. P., Pinel, E. C., & Wilson, T. D. (2000). The illusion of external agency. *Journal of Personality and Social Psychology, 79,* 690–700.

Gilbert, D. T., Driver-Linn, E., & Wilson, T. D. (2002). The trouble with Vronsky: Impact bias in the forecasting of future affective states. In L. Feldman-Barrett & P. Salovey (Eds.), *The wisdom of feeling* (pp. 114–143). New York: Guilford.

Gilbert, D. T., Gill, M. J., & Wilson, T. D. (2002). The future is now: Temporal correction in affective forecasting. *Organizational Behavior and Human Decision Processes, 88,* 690–700.

Gilbert, D. T., Pinel, E. C., Wilson, T. D., Blumberg, S. J., & Wheatley, T. P. (1998). Immune neglect: A source of durability bias in affective forecasting. *Journal of Personality and Social Psychology, 75,* 617–638.

Gilbert, D. T., & Wilson, T. D. (2000). Miswanting: Some problems in the forecasting of future states. In J. P. Forgas (Ed.), *Feeling and thinking: The role of affect in social cognition* (pp. 178–197). Cambridge: Cambridge University Press.

Haselton, M. G., & Buss, D. M. (2000). Error management theory: A new perspective on biases in cross-sex mind reading. *Journal of Personality and Social Psychology, 78,* 81–91.

Haselton, M. G., & Buss, D. M. (2003). Biases in social judgment: Design flaws or design features? In J. P. Forgas, K. D. Williams, & W. von Hippel (Eds.), *Social judgments: Implicit and explicit processes* (pp. 23–43). Cambridge: Cambridge University Press.

Hsee, C. K. (1999). Value seeking and prediction-decision inconsistency: Why don't people take what they predict they'll like the most? *Psychonomic Bulletin & Review*, 6, 555–561.

Hsee, C. K., & Rottenstreich, Y. (2004). Music, pandas, and muggers: On the affective psychology of value. *Journal of Experimental Psychology: General*, 133, 23–30.

Hsee, C. K., & Zhang, J. (2004). Distinction bias: Misprediction and mischoice due to joint evaluation. *Journal of Personality and Social Psychology*, 86, 680–695.

Hsee, C. K., Zhang, J., Yu, F., & Xi, Y. (2003). Lay rationalism and inconsistency between predicted experience and decision. *Journal of Behavioral Decision Making*, 16, 257–272.

Igou, E. R. (2004). Lay theories in affective forecasting: The progression of affect. *Journal of Experimental Social Psychology*, 40, 528–534.

Kahneman, D., & Snell, J. (1992). Predicting a change in taste: Do people know what they will like? *Journal of Behavioral Decision Making*, 5, 187–200.

Klaaren, K. J., Hodges, S. D., & Wilson, T. D. (1994). The role of affective expectations in subjective experience and decision making. *Social Cognition*, 12, 77–101.

Lam, K. C. H., Buehler, R., & McFarland, C. (2005). Cultural differences in affective forecasting: The role of focalism. *Personality and Social Psychology Bulletin*, 31, 1296–1309.

Loewenstein, G. (1996). Out of control: Visceral influences on behavior. *Organizational Behavior and Human Decision Processes*, 65, 272–292.

Loewenstein, G., & Adler, D. (1995). A bias in the prediction of tastes. *The Economic Journal*, 105, 929–937.

Loewenstein, G., Nagin, D., & Paternoster, R. (1997). The effect of sexual arousal on sexual forcefulness. *Journal of Research in Crime and Delinquency*, 34, 443–473.

Loewenstein, G., O'Donoghue, T., & Rabin, M. (in press). Projection bias in predicting future utility. *Quarterly Journal of Economics*.

Loewenstein, G. F., & Schkade, D. (1999). Wouldn't it be nice? Predicting future feelings. In D. Kahneman, E. Diener, & N. Schwartz (Eds.), *Well-being: The foundations of hedonic psychology* (pp. 85–105). New York: Russell Sage Foundation.

Mallett, R. K. (2005). Cloudy crystal balls: Mis-predicting the nature of future intergroup experiences. Unpublished manuscript, University of Virginia.

Mellers, B. A., Schwarz, A., Ho, K., & Ritov, I. (1997). Decision affect theory: Emotional reactions to the outcomes of risky options. *Psychological Science*, 8, 423–429.

Mellers, B. A., Schwarz, A., & Ritov, I. (1999). Emotion-based choice. *Journal of Experimental Psychology: General*, 128, 332–325.

Morewedge, C. K., Gilbert, D. T., & Wilson, T. D. (2005). The least likely of times: How remembering the past biases forecasts of the future. *Psychological Science*, 16, 626–630.

Norwick, R. J., Gilbert, D. T., & Wilson, T. D. (2005). Surrogation: An antidote for errors in affective forecasting. Unpublished manuscript, Harvard University.

Pinker, S. (1997). *How the mind works*. New York: Norton.

Rachman, S. (1990). *Fear and courage* (2nd ed.). New York: W. H. Freeman.

Rachman, S. (1994). The overprediction of fear: A review. *Behavior Research and Therapy*, 32, 683–690.

Rachman, S., & Bichard, S. (1988). The overprediction of fear. *Clinical Psychology Review*, 8, 303–313.

Rachman, S., & Eyrl, K. (1989). Predicting and remembering recurrent pain. *Behavior Research and Therapy*, 27, 621–635.

Rachman, S., & Lopatka, C. (1988). Accurate and inaccurate predictions of pain. *Behavior Research and Therapy*, 26, 291–297.

Rachman, S, Lopatka, C., & Levitt, K. (1988). Experimental analyses of panic: Panic patients. *Behavior Research and Therapy*, 26, 33–40.

Read, D., & van Leeuwen, B. (1998). Predicting hunger: The effects of appetite and delay on choice. *Organizational Behavior and Human Decision Processes*, 76, 189–205.

Read, D, Loewenstein, G., & Kalyanaraman, S. (1999). Mixing virtue and vice: Combining the immediacy effect and the diversification heuristic. *Journal of Behavioral Decision Making*, 12, 257–273.

Riis, J., Loewenstein, G., Baron, J., Jepson, C., Fagerlin, A., & Ubel, P. A. (2005). Ignorance of hedonic adaptation to hemodialysis: A study using ecological momentary assessment. *Journal of Experimental Psychology: General*, 34, 3–9.

Rozin, P., & Fallon, A. E. (1987). A perspective on disgust. *Psychological Review*, 94, 23–41.

Rozin, P., Markwith, M., & Ross, B. (1990). The sympathetic magical law of similarity, nominal realism, and neglect of negatives in response to negative labels. *Psychological Science*, 1, 383–384.

Schkade, D. A., & Kahneman, D. (1998). Does living in California make people happy? A focusing illusion in judgments of life satisfaction. *Psychological Science*, 9, 340–346.

Sieff, E. M., Dawes, R. M., & Loewenstein, G. (1999). Anticipated versus actual reaction to HIV test results. *American Journal of Psychology*, 112, 297–311.

Simonson, I. (1990). The effect of purchase quantity and timing on variety-seeking behavior. *Journal of Marketing Research*, 27, 150–162.

Symons, D. (1987). If we're all Darwinians, what's all the fuss about? In C. B. Crawford, M. F. Smith, & D. L. Krebs (Eds.), *Sociobiology and psychology: ideas, issues and applications* (pp. 121–146). Hillsdale, NJ: Lawrence Erlbaum Associates, Inc.

Tomarken, A. J., Mineka, S., & Cook, M. (1989). Fear-relevant selective associations and co-variation bias. *Journal of Abnormal Psychology*, 98, 381–394.

Tooby, J., & Cosmides, L. (1992). The psychological foundations of culture. In J. Barkow, L. Cosmides, & J. Tooby (Eds.), *The adapted mind* (pp. 19–136). New York: Oxford University Press.

Totterdell, P., Parkinson, B., Briner, R. B., & Reynolds, S. (1997). Forcasting feelings: The accuracy and effects of self-predictions of mood. *Journal of Social Behavior & Personality*, 12, 631–650.

Van Boven, L., & Loewenstein, G. (2003). Social projection of transient drive states. *Personality and Social Psychology Bulletin*, 29, 1159–1168.

Van Boven, L., & Loewenstein, G. (2005). Cross-situational projection. In M. D. Alicke, D. Dunning, & J. Krueger (Eds.), *The self in social judgment*. New York: Psychology Press.

Van Boven, L., Dunning, D., & Loewenstein, G. (2000). Egocentric empathy gaps between owners and buyers: Misperceptions of the endowment effect. *Journal of Personality and Social Psychology*, 79, 66–76.

Van Boven, L., Loewenstein, G., & Dunning, D. (2003). Mispredicting the endowment effect: Underestimation of owners' selling prices by buyer's agents. *Journal of Economic Behavior & Organization*, 51, 351–365.

Van Boven, L., Loewenstein, G., & Dunning, D. (2005). The illusion of courage in social predictions: Underestimating the impact of fear of embarrassment on other people. *Organizational Behavior and Human Decision Processes*, 96, 130–141.

Wilson, T. D., & Gilbert, D. T. (2003). Affective forecasting. In M. P. Zanna (Ed.), *Advances in experimental social psychology* (Vol. 35, pp. 346–412). San Diego: Academic Press.

Wilson, T. D., Gilbert, D. T., & Centerbar, D. B. (2002). Making sense: The causes of emotional evanescence. In J. Carillo & I. Brocas (Eds.), *Economics and psychology* (pp. 209–233). Oxford: Oxford University Press.

Wilson, T. D., Gilbert, D. T., & Salthouse, T. (2001). Predicted emotional reactions across the adult life span. Unpublished raw data, University of Virginia.

Wilson, T. D., Wheatley, T., Kurtz, J., Dunn, E., & Gilbert, D. T. (2004). When to fire: Anticipatory versus postevent reconstrual of uncontrollable events. *Personality and Social Psychology Bulletin, 30,* 1–12.

Wilson, T. D., Wheatley, T. P., Meyers, J. M., Gilbert, D. T., & Axsom, D. (2000). Focalism: A source of the durability bias in affective forecasting. *Journal of Personality and Social Psychology, 78,* 821–836.

Wirtz, D., Kruger, J., Napa Scollon, C., & Diener, E. (2003). What to do on spring break? The role of predicted, on-line, and remembered experience in future choice. *Psychological Science, 14,* 520–524.

Woodzicka, J. A., & LaFrance, M. (2001). Real versus imagined gender harassment. *Journal of Social Issues, 57,* 15–30.

Zeelenberg, M. (1999). Anticipated regret, expected feedback and behavioral decision-making. *Journal of Behavioral Decision Making, 12,* 93–106.

Zeelenberg, M., Beattie, J., van der Plight, J., & de Vries, N. K. (1996). Consequences of regret aversion: Effects of expected feedback on risky decision making. *Organizational Behavior and Human Decision Processes, 65,* 148–158.

Part III

Affect and the Social Self

11

Affect and the Self

CONSTANTINE SEDIKIDES, TIM WILDSCHUT, JAMIE
ARNDT, and CLAY ROUTLEDGE

I magine you are walking through your neighborhood on a breezy spring afternoon and you see a child running excitedly after a ball tossed from a friend.
You begin to think about your own childhood and perhaps bask in the glow
of the bygone days of frivolous play and exuberance. What are the cognitive
abilities that enable, and the psychological functions served by, such nostalgic
reflection? More broadly, what is the relationship between affective states and
self-processes? In entertaining such questions, one may be surprised to learn that
contemporary social psychological discourse offers few answers. The purpose of
the present chapter is to provide a broad overview of the relationship between
affective states and the self, and then illustrate the interplay of affect and self-
processes through a special kind of self-related affective state, nostalgia.

We will first review literature on the relation between mood states and self-
focused attention. Second, we will discuss the relation between mood states and
the valence of self-views. Third, we will briefly couch the link between self and
affect in terms of self-related emotions and note those that have been the primary
subject of empirical scrutiny: shame, guilt, and embarrassment. Finally and most
importantly, we will discuss a relatively neglected self-related emotion, nostalgia,
to illustrate the interdependence between self and affect. We will also discuss the
similarities and differences between nostalgia and other self-related emotions.

THE INTERPLAY BETWEEN SELF AND AFFECT: MOOD AND SELF-FOCUSED ATTENTION, MOOD AND SELF-DESCRIPTION, AND SELF-RELATED EMOTIONS

Mood States and Self-Focused Attention

A persistent focus of the literature on self and affect has been the interplay
between mood states and self-focused attention. One of the initial observations of
this connection emerged from classic work on self-awareness theory (Duval &
Wicklund, 1972). According to theory and research from this perspective,

increased self-focus instigates regulatory processes, often heightening awareness of discrepancies between self and evaluative standards, and thus engendering feelings of negative affect (e.g., Scheier & Carver, 1977; see Fejfar & Hoyle, 2000 for a review). A considerable literature has also been guided by the reciprocal question: "What mood states lead to which kind of attentional focus?" (Sedikides & Green, 2000). The mood states of sadness and happiness attracted the bulk of empirical efforts. Further, attentional focus was conceptualized as falling on a bipolar continuum: directed either internally (i.e., to the self) or externally (e.g., to other persons).

In line with appraisal theories of emotion (Smith, David, & Kirby, this volume; Smith & Kirby, 2001), sadness was hypothesized to induce self-focused attention. Sadness is elicited by a setback or loss, is accompanied by the perception that the unfortunate event is rather uncontrollable and inevitable, and is associated with or leads to inaction, resignation, passivity, and withdrawal. Sadness instigates an avoidance orientation toward the outside world and an inclination to turn inward and clarify the implications of the unfortunate event for one's goals and behavioral options. On the other hand, happiness is characterized by an expansive, exploratory, and affiliative orientation. Happiness is linked with stimulation seeking and the facilitation of adaptive or approach behaviors. As such, happiness was hypothesized to induce other-focused attention.

The empirical findings were consistent with these hypotheses. Compared to neutral mood, sadness induces self-focused attention (Sedikides, 1992a), whereas happiness induces external-focused attention (Green, Sedikides, Saltzberg, Wood, & Forzano, 2003). Moreover, the causal relation between sadness and self-focused attention is not reciprocal: Sadness directly elicits self-focused attention, but the reverse pattern does not hold. Instead, the effects of self-focused attention on sadness are moderated by self-concept valence. Self-focused attention induces sadness only among individuals with chronically negative self-views (Sedikides, 1992b).

More recently, however, the literature moved beyond sadness and happiness by taking into account another, orthogonal, affective dimension: orientation. In particular, (negative or positive) mood states can be either reflective or social. Examples of reflective mood states are sadness and contentment, whereas examples of social mood states are anger and happiness. Reflective states should elicit stronger self-focused attention than social states, a hypothesis that was empirically validated (Green & Sedikides, 1999). As we will discuss, one of the possibly unique features of nostalgia is that it is both a reflective and social emotion.

Mood States and Self-Concept Valence

Sad and happy mood states also have distinct consequences for self-concept valence. An early review (Sedikides, 1992c) captured these consequences with the mood-congruency principle: Sad mood increases the negativity of self-conceptions, whereas happy mood increases the positivity of self-conceptions. A comprehensive model on the relation between mood and social cognition, however, the affect infusion model (AIM: Forgas, 1995, 2002, this volume), offered theoretical insights that qualified the mood-congruency principle.

According to the AIM, affect is infused differentially into information processing strategies. In some strategies, such as the direct-access strategy (when processing is based on the cognitive retrieval of knowledge structures) and the motivated-processing strategy (when processing is goal-driven), affect infusion is low. In other strategies, such as heuristic processing (requiring an online judgment) or substantive processing (requiring an open information search and the transformation or creation of cognitive structures), affect infusion is high. The postulates of the AIM have clear implications for the influence of mood states on the self-concept. Affect will infuse the self-system and change the self-views in a mood-congruent manner only when these self-views are relatively uncertain or loosely formed. However, affect will have no influence on self-views that are crystallized and well-formed. The former (i.e., peripheral self-conceptions) are computed via an online judgment, whereas the latter (i.e., central self-conceptions) require the retrieval of a stored judgment. Thus, heuristic processing is involved in judgments of peripheral self-views, whereas direct-access processing is involved in judgments of central self-views.

The empirical evidence was consistent with these hypotheses. The mood-congruency effect was obtained for judgments pertaining to peripheral but not central self-conceptions (Sedikides, 1995). Notably, support for the AIM has been obtained in regards to other domains, such as individual differences (Sedikides & Green, 2001). For example, mood-congruency effects on self-conceptions are present for low, but not high, self-esteem persons. This is attributed to the fact that the self-views of low self-esteem persons are held with less certainty compared to the self-views of high self-esteem persons (Campbell, Trapnell, Heine, Katz, Lavallee, & Lehman, 1996).

The mood-congruency effect is also qualified by the temporal dimension: Initial mood-congruent influences on self-views are reversed by subsequent mood-incongruent influences. In particular, although immediately following sad-mood induction self-descriptions become more negative, over time this pattern is spontaneously reversed, with self-descriptions becoming increasingly positive (Forgas & Ciarrochi, 2002, Exp. 3; Sedikides, 1994). These results indicate the activation of mood-management or mood-repair processes (Bless & Fiedler, this volume; Erber & Markunas, this volume; Forgas, in press).

Self-Related Emotions

The relation between self and affect becomes more intricate when self-related emotions are taken into consideration. The self-related emotions that have received the lion's share in the literature are shame, guilt, and embarrassment (Keltner & Beer, 2005; Tangney, 2002).

Self-related emotions are instigated by self-evaluation or self-reflection. Individuals feel shameful when they perceive the failure to meet an important internal standard (i.e., goal or rule) as indicative of a deep and all-encompassing personality defect or character flaw. Individuals also feel guilty when they violate an important internal standard, but the focus is on the specific transgression and its consequences for self and other. Finally, individuals feel embarrassed when they engage in relatively minor infractions of social conventions in a public setting or merely when they become the public target of attention (e.g., "Happy Birthday" sung for them).

Shame, guilt, and embarrassment differ in terms of how painful they are, how they are regulated, and how they are expressed. Shame is more painful than guilt, which is more painful than embarrassment (Tangney, 2003). Furthermore, shame is linked with anger and aggression (which are attempts to protect the self) and may be more strongly tied to situations that focus attention internally (Arndt & Goldenberg, 2004), whereas guilt is linked with empathy. Both guilt and embarrassment, however, are linked with reparative action (e.g., apology). Moreover, shame and embarrassment have distinct nonverbal displays, whereas guilt does not. In particular, shame is expressed with coordinated gaze and downward head movement, whereas embarrassment is expressed through gaze aversion, smile control, a non-Duchenne smile, downward head movement, and, on some occasions, face touching (Keltner, 1995).

THE INTERPLAY BETWEEN SELF AND AFFECT: NOSTALGIA

The literature on self-related emotions, while generating important insights, has yet to consider the emotional consequences of peoples' concurrent capacity to reflect on the past. In particular, the capacity for self-focus and also the capacity for temporal thought (i.e., the ability to project oneself into the past, present, and future) may enable people to reflect on their past and draw from it emotions such as nostalgia. We will begin with a historical synopsis and proceed with a discussion of the various facets of the nostalgic experience, highlighting the psychological landscape and functional significance of the emotion. Our discussion will be informed by the scarce literature on nostalgia and our own preliminary findings.

A Historical Overview of Nostalgia

The term "nostalgia" was coined by the Swiss physician Johannes Hofer (1688/1934), although references to its meaning date back to Hippocrates, Caesar, and the Bible. Nostalgia is a compound term, derived from the Greek words nostos (*return*) and algos (*pain*). Thus, nostalgia connotes the psychological suffering induced by the yearning to return to one's place of origin.

In its conceptual and empirical trajectory, the term did not always carry the same meaning. Hofer (1688/1934) focused on Swiss mercenaries fighting away from home on behalf of European rulers and described the mercenaries as suffering from despondency, weeping, anorexia, and suicidal ideation. Hofer characterized nostalgia (or homesickness) "a cerebral disease of essentially demonic cause" (p. 387) which was caused by "the quite continuous vibration of animal spirits through those fibers of the middle brain in which impressed traces of ideas of the Fatherland still cling" (p. 384). Some decades later, the German-Swiss physician J. J. Scheuchzer maintained in 1732 that nostalgia was due to "a sharp differential in atmospheric pressure causing excessive body pressurization, which in turn drove blood from the heart to the brain, thereby producing the observed affliction of sentiment" (cited in Davis, 1979, p. 2). To make matters worse, it was believed that nostalgia was restricted to the Swiss, and military physicians offered the unremitting clanging of cowbells in the Alps as the cause of nostalgia. The noise, it was said, inflicted damage to the eardrum and brain, hence the emotional lability and behavioral symptoms (Davis, 1979). In the 18th and 19th centuries, however, it became clear that nostalgia was not just a Swiss curiosity, as soldiers fighting in the French armies and the American Civil War manifested similar symptoms (Rosen, 1975). Nevertheless, the definition of nostalgia as a neurological disease persisted.

By the end of the 19th and the beginning of the 20th century, nostalgia was regarded as a psychiatric disorder (Batcho, 1998; McCann, 1941). Symptoms included anxiety, sadness, fatigue, loss of appetite, and insomnia (Havlena & Holak, 1991). Indeed, following the psychodynamic tradition, nostalgia was consigned to the realm of disorders until the middle of the 20th century (Sohn, 1983). Nostalgia was labeled as arising from a subconscious yearning to return to one's fetal state, as a "mentally repressive compulsive disorder" (Fodor, 1950, p. 25), as a "monomaniacal obsessive mental state causing intense unhappiness" (Fodor, 1950, p. 25), and as "immigrant psychosis" (Frost, 1938, p. 801). By the late 1970s and early 1980s, nostalgia was considered as a form of depression, "a regressive manifestation closely related to the issue of loss, grief, incomplete mourning, and, finally, depression" (Castelnuovo-Tedesco, 1980, p. 100; see also Kaplan, 1987). Furthermore, nostalgia was equated with homesickness and confined to four populations: immigrants, first-year boarding or university students, soldiers, and seamen (Cox, 1988; Jackson, 1986).

More recently, the constructs of nostalgia and homesickness have gone their separate ways. Homesickness refers to psychological difficulties that accompany life transitions such as to boarding school or university (Brewin, Furhnam, & Howes, 1989; Fisher, 1989; Stroebe, van Vliet, Hewstone, & Willis, 2002; Van Tilburg, Vingerhoets, & van Heck, 1996). Nostalgia, on the other hand, is considered an experience with a wider frame of reference, often associated with the words "warm, old times, childhood, and yearning" (Davis, 1979). We conceptualize nostalgia as yearning for aspects of one's past (e.g., events, persons, places), and see it as an emotional experience that is relevant to people of all ages and is present throughout the life course (Sedikides, Wildschut, & Baden, 2004). Below, we further clarify our conceptualization of nostalgia while discussing the available theoretical and empirical work as well as our own preliminary findings.

Structure of Nostalgia

We will consider three structural features of nostalgia: its triggers, its objects, and the role of self.

Triggers of Nostalgia   What triggers the nostalgic experience? Although the experience of nostalgia critically depends on the capacity for self-directed and temporal attention, theorists have speculated that triggers (i.e., stimuli associated with one's past) can be either social (e.g., friends, family reunions, disco nights) or nonsocial (e.g., music, scents, possessions) (Havlena & Holak, 1991; Holak & Havlena, 1998; Holbrook, 1993, 1994). Davis (1979) suggested that nostalgia occurs in the context of "present fears, discontents, anxieties, and uncertainties" (p. 34), whereas Cully, LaVoie, and Gfeller (2001) emphasized dejected mood as a trigger of nostalgia.

We (Wildschut, Sedikides, Arndt, & Routledge, in press) asked participants to provide detailed descriptions of the circumstances that trigger nostalgia. Contrary to some previous speculation but consistent with Davis (1979) and Cully et al. (2001), we found that the most common nostalgia trigger is negative mood. One participant, for instance, wrote: "I think of nostalgic experiences when I am sad as they often make me feel better." Another participant wrote: "I think people would turn to nostalgia in unhappy, sad or lonely situations to make themselves smile." Among the negative mood states mentioned, loneliness was by far the most common, as is illustrated by the following quote: "If I ever feel lonely or sad I tend to think of my friends or family who I haven't seen in a long time." Thus, nostalgia can in certain contexts be seen as a mood-management strategy. Consistently with prior speculation, though, other common triggers included sensory inputs and social interactions. Relevant to the idea that sensory inputs can trigger nostalgia, one participant remarked that "the strongest triggers are smells and music" and another referred to "pictures, smells, sounds, even tastes" as triggers of nostalgia. Relevant to the idea that social interaction can trigger nostalgia, many commented on how, in the words of one astute participant, nostalgia can be triggered by "being in the company of the people concerned."

Objects of Nostalgia   What are the objects of the nostalgic experience? In our research (Wildschut et al., in press), the most common objects of nostalgia were close others (e.g., friends, family members). Consider, for instance, the mother who wrote of her son's birth: "I remember exactly how he looked and smelt the first time I held him in my arms." The second most common objects of nostalgia were momentous events (e.g., anniversaries, holiday gatherings). Tellingly, momentous events often involved the presence of close others and coders occasionally found it difficult to separate the two categories. Other frequently reported objects were places or settings.

Role of Self: Nostalgia as a Self-Related Emotion   We conceptualized nostalgia as a self-related emotion. We considered the self as the protagonist of the nostalgic encounter, although we reasoned that the self operates in social context (Sedikides et al., 2004). This proposal was supported by our empirical findings (Wildschut et al., in press). In the vast majority of nostalgic accounts, the self figured in an important role alongside close others.

Is Nostalgia a Positive Emotion?

Some researchers have classified nostalgia as positive emotion. According to Davis (1979), nostalgia is a "positively toned evocation of a lived past" (p. 18), a view echoed by Kaplan (1987) in his definition of nostalgia as a "warm feeling about the past" (p. 465). Other researchers have also argued that nostalgia is associated with positive affect (e.g., Batcho, 1995, 1998; Chaplin, 2000; Gabriel, 1993; Holak & Havlena, 1998). An alternative camp of researchers, however, has classified nostalgia as a negative emotion. According to Ortony, Clore, and Collins (1988), nostalgia is a loss or distress emotion, as it involves sadness or mourning for one's past. The view of nostalgia as a loss emotion is shared by Best and Nelson (1985), Hertz (1990), Holbrook (1993, 1994), and Peters (1985). Finally, a third camp of researchers cast nostalgia as an ambivalent emotion. Werman (1977) defined nostalgia as "a joy tinged with sadness" (p. 393), whereas both Fodor (1950) and Socarides (1977) proposed that nostalgia entails some degree of psychological pain. Finally, Johnson-Laird and Oatley (1989) emphasized the ambivalent nature of nostalgia, arguing that it involves both happiness and mild discontent. The ambivalence is the outcome of a contrast between a satisfying past and a grim present.

In our view, nostalgia is a predominantly positive emotion, albeit not without bittersweet elements (Sedikides et al., 2004). A study by Holak and Havlena (1998) provided preliminary support for this view. Participants' nostalgic accounts (as judged by coders) were characterized more by positive (e.g., warmth, joy, gratitude) than negative (e.g., sadness, irritation, fear) emotions. More to the point, our own research (Wildschut et al., in press) has obtained evidence that nostalgia is principally a positive emotion. Participants' nostalgic accounts (as judged by independent coders) reflect more positive than negative affect, and participants report that nostalgia has more desirable than undesirable features. In addition, participants report that they experience more positive than negative affect following written descriptions of nostalgic events.

Another way to address the issue of whether nostalgia is a positive or negative emotion is to examine its narrative sequence. McAdams and his colleagues (McAdams, Diamond, de St. Aubin, & Mansfield, 1997; McAdams, Reynolds, Lewis, Patten, & Bowman, 2001) distinguished between two narrative sequences of life stories. In the first, *redemption*, the individual progresses from a disadvantaged to a victorious position, with accompanying positive feelings (e.g., contentment, happiness). In the second, *contamination*, the individual progresses from a position of strength to one of weakness, with accompanying negative feelings (e.g., sadness, depression). In our research (Wildschut et al., in press), we found that nostalgic accounts more often follow a redemption than a contamination sequence. The high frequency of redemption sequences in nostalgic narratives reinforces our view that nostalgia is a predominantly positive emotion. These findings further support the notion that nostalgia is more likely to be emotionally positive in nature.

Do Self-Related Emotions such as Nostalgia Involve a Contrast Between Past and Present?

Davis (1979) set forth an interesting hypothesis: Nostalgia is an emotional reaction to discontinuity in one's life. Johnson-Laird and Oatley (1989) echoed the discontinuity hypothesis when they argued that nostalgia involves a contrast between one's past and present. According to Davis, sources of discontinuity include death of a loved one, health deterioration, relationship break-up, and occupational crises (e.g., lay-offs). In addition, discontinuity has emotional consequences, such as "fears, discontents, anxieties, or uncertainties" (Davis, 1979, p. 34).

A more concrete and testable form of the discontinuity hypothesis is that individuals who experience discontinuity in their lives (i.e., deteriorating life circumstances) will report higher degrees of nostalgia (i.e., will rate the past as more favorable) compared to those who experience continuity. Best and Nelson (1985) tested this proposition by analyzing data from four surveys which involved US national samples and were carried out in 1968, 1974, 1976, and 1980. In these surveys, participants responded to statements such as "You are as happy now as you were when you were younger," "People had it better in the old days," "I am as happy as when I was younger," "These are the best years of my life," and "In spite of what some people say, the lot of the average man is getting worse, not better." Responses to these statements were combined to form an index of nostalgia. Support for the discontinuity hypothesis was equivocal. On the one hand, deteriorating circumstances (e.g., health problems, divorce, death of a loved one) were related with increased nostalgia. On the other hand, occupational mobility, geographic mobility, and work interruption were not associated with nostalgia. The equivocal support for the discontinuity hypothesis, however, may be due to conceptual and data-analytic problems with this study. For example, the survey items (Best & Nelson, 1985) were rather poor indicators of nostalgia, and the data were underanalyzed.

Batcho's (1995) research is also relevant to the discontinuity hypothesis. She assessed nostalgia in a two-part survey. In the first part, respondents evaluated (as good or bad) the world at present, 20 years into the future, and in the past. In the second part of the survey, participants completed the *Nostalgia Inventory*, indicating the degree to which they missed each of 20 items (toys, your house, friends, the way society was, not knowing sad or evil things, not having to worry, etc.) from their youth. In the first part of the survey, support for the discontinuity hypothesis was weak. On the one hand, evaluations of the world across past, future, and present did not differ by age or gender. On the other hand, the overall nostalgia score, although uncorrelated with judgments of the present or the future, was correlated with judgments of the past. Also, when the upper and lower quartile of the respondents were examined, high (compared to low) nostalgics rated the world when they were younger as better. In general, nostalgia was not linked with substantial dissatisfaction with the present or anxieties about the future, but it was associated with the view that the past was better. In the second part of the survey, the discontinuity hypothesis was discredited. Age main effects were significant for 14 of the 20 items of the nostalgia inventory: friends, family, school, house, music, heroes/heroines, feelings, having someone to depend on, not knowing sad or evil things, holidays, toys, pets, not having to worry, and the way people were. However, on all but two (family, music) of these items, younger adults were more nostalgic than older ones. Because it seems reasonable that older adults would have experienced more discontinuity than younger adults, these results do not seem to follow from the discontinuity hypothesis.

In a recent study, we (Wildschut, Sedikides, Arndt, Routledge, & Hodgson, 2006) tested the discontinuity hypothesis in a sample of 38 adult participants (mean age = 48 years). Discontinuity was measured using a revised version of the Social Readjustment Rating Scale (SRRS; Holmes & Rahe, 1967). This version of the scale asked participants to indicate for each of 14 disrupting life events (e.g., death of a close family member, change in living conditions, change in financial situation, divorce) whether they had experienced it over the past 2 years. Nostalgia was measured using Batcho's nostalgia inventory. Consistent with the discontinuity hypothesis, results revealed a significant positive correlation between the number of disrupting life events experienced and nostalgia.

In conclusion, there is some support, albeit preliminary, for the discontinuity hypothesis. This support comes from correlational studies. We believe that experimental tests have greater potential to evaluate rigorously the hypothesis. Conceptually, the prior articulations of the hypothesis imply that nostalgia is simply a byproduct of discontinuity. Looked at from a different vantage point, however, one may construe discontinuity as a form of threat that should in turn evoke *more* nostalgia as people try to marshal positive coping resources. Does threat in the form of negative feedback (Sedikides, Campbell, Reeder, & Elliot, 1998) or the awareness of inevitable mortality (mortality salience; e.g., Arndt, Greenberg, Solomon, Pyszczynski, & Simon, 1997), for example, induce corresponding changes in the level of nostalgia? Given what we believe to be the functional significance of the emotion, there are reasons to think that it might. We are in the process of carrying out such tests.

What Are the Functions of Self-Related Emotions such as Nostalgia?

We propose that nostalgia serves four important psychological functions. First, nostalgia serves as a repository of positive affect. Second, nostalgia maintains and enhances self-positivity. Third, nostalgia fosters affiliation. Finally, nostalgia carries existential meaning, serving as a reservoir of memories and experiences that is helpful for coping with existential threat. We will review these functions in more detail, complementing them with our preliminary findings, and also highlight future directions for empirical study. In our research (Wildschut et al., in press), participants brought to mind and wrote about a nostalgic experience or, in the control condition, an ordinary event that occurred in the past week. Subsequently, they completed a battery of scales assessing affect, aspects of the self-concept, and feelings of affiliation.

The Positive Affectivity Function of Nostalgia
We proposed and found (Wildschut et al., in press) that nostalgia predominantly gives rise to positive affect. Kaplan (1987) speculated that the joy that nostalgia induces gives rise to "an expansive state of mind" (p. 465). In a similar vein, Fredrickson (2001) argued that positive emotions increase resourcefulness, as they broaden thought–action repertoires. Indeed, positive emotions offset the impact of not only negative

emotions (Fredrickson, Tugade, Waugh, & Larkin, 2003) but also negative feedback about the self (Aspinwall, 1998; Trope, Igou, & Burke, this volume; Trope & Pomerantz, 1998). We found (Wildschut et al., 2005) that participants who brought to mind or wrote about a nostalgic experience reported more positive affect than participants in the control condition, who brought to mind or wrote about an ordinary experience. Similarly, in a recent study we found that perceiving the past as positive is associated with increased nostalgia proneness (Routledge, Arndt, Sedikides, & Wildschut, 2006). Given that nostalgia is associated with positive affect and positive affect can assist people in dealing with negative emotions and stressors such as negative feedback (Trope et al., this volume), future research should further examine the potential for nostalgia to be employed to combat negative affect.

The Self-Positivity Function of Nostalgia   Individuals are motivated to protect, maintain, and enhance the positivity of the self-concept (Sedikides & Gregg, 2003; Sedikides & Strube, 1997). Self-protection and self-enhancement mechanisms are typically activated when feedback is perceived as self-threatening (Baumeister, 1998; Sedikides, Green, & Pinter, 2004; see also Baumeister et al., this volume). We propose that nostalgia constitutes an important mechanism through which individuals ward off threat and restore the positivity of the self-concept (Sedikides et al., 2004) or self-esteem (Gabriel, 1993; Kaplan, 1987). The effectiveness of nostalgia as a self-protection mechanism may be due to its potential to affirm the self (Steele, 1988) by rendering accessible other desirable aspects of one's personality. That is, by resorting through nostalgia to an idealized past, one may affirm oneself (Kleiner, 1977). We found that (Wildschut et al., in press) participants who brought to mind or wrote about a nostalgic experience reported higher self-esteem than participants in the control condition. This suggests that nostalgia can be a resource for responding to self-related threats (e.g., derogation of outgroups, Fein & Spencer, 1997), providing an outlet for socially positive self-affirmation.

The Affiliation Function of Nostalgia   Another important function of nostalgia is the strengthening of social connectedness and belongingness. Davis (1979) regarded nostalgia as a deeply social emotion, whereas Hertz (1990) noted that, in the nostalgic experience, "...the mind is 'peopled'" (p. 195). Symbolic connections with close others are re-established (Batcho, 1998; Cavanaugh, 1989; Kaplan, 1987; Mills & Coleman, 1994), and these close others come to be momentarily part of one's present. Such meaningful connections are particularly relevant during life transitions (e.g., graduation, relocation, new employment), when individuals are likely to feel socially isolated. Nostalgia, then, contributes to a sense of safety and secures attachment (Mikulincer, Florian, & Hirschberger, 2003). Participants who brought to mind and wrote about a nostalgic experience subsequently evidenced a more secure adult attachment style than participants in the control condition (Wildschut et al., in press). Future research should further explore the potential for nostalgia to help people cope with situations that foster feelings of isolation or disconnection from close others. Indeed, for deployed soldiers separated from family, some of the most desired luxuries are objects that remind them of friends and family at home (armytimes.com).

The Existential Function of Nostalgia   We are all too frequently confronted with the ephemeral nature of life and this fragility represents a major hurdle that people must cross in order to function with relative psychological equanimity. According to terror management theory (Pyszczynski, Greenberg, Solomon, Arndt, & Schimel, 2004; Solomon, Greenberg, & Pyszczynski, 1991), such anxieties stem, in part, from our awareness of inevitable mortality and are mitigated by maintaining a two-part anxiety buffer that consists of faith in a cultural worldview (shared beliefs about the nature of reality that imbue life with meaning) and self-esteem (the sense that one is personally fulfilling the standards of one's worldview). Recently, Mikulincer et al. (2003) have argued that secure attachment to others represents another fundamental means of buffering existential anxiety.

Self-related emotions such as nostalgia can bolster each of the psychological mechanisms by which people manage existential anxiety. Nostalgia may serve to enhance the positivity of the self-concept and may enhance connectedness to others, weaving the self into a meaningful social fabric. Nostalgia can also contribute an overall sense of enduring meaning to one's life. The passing of time can be threatening, for as time passes the certainty of one's inevitable demise draws closer (Routledge & Arndt, 2005). Nostalgia, however, provides an emotional mechanism by which the passing of time can be perceived as meaningful as one builds a positive warehouse of memories of bygone days, and by reinforcing the value of cultural traditions. This is achieved by revelling in past celebrations of cultural rituals, such as Thanksgiving dinners, school fares, or parades, or by collecting movie, sports, or war memorabilia. Through such practices, one restores the belief of living a purposeful life in a meaningful cultural context (Simon, Arndt, Greenberg, Pyszczynski, & Solomon, 1998).

We examined how nostalgia moderates the effects of mortality salience. For example, in one study we (Routledge et al., 2006) found that after being reminded of one's mortality (relative to an aversive control topic), the more one tends to perceive the past as positive, the more he or she perceives life as meaningful. In another study, we further found that after being reminded of mortality (relative to an aversive control topic), people who are more prone to nostalgia actually show less activation of death-related cognition. Both studies thus converge to suggest that nostalgia can provide an important resource for buffering existential threat.

In short, self-related emotions such as nostalgia may serve as an important resource for managing existential anxieties. That is, nostalgic engagement may affirm the self, and self-affirmation (e.g., writing about one's important values) reduces existential angst (Schmeichel & Martens, 2005). Given that terror management often has unfortunate consequences such as fostering intolerance, prejudice, and aggression (Greenberg, Solomon, & Pyszczynski, 1997), an important direction for future research is to uncover more benevolent means of maintaining such views and nostalgia is emerging as a prime candidate to this end.

Additional Issues Surrounding Nostalgia

We have argued that nostalgia is a universal and predominantly positive self-related emotion that involves reliving momentous events or bygone relationships with significant others. Nostalgia is typically triggered by negative mood but also sensory inputs and social interactions. Importantly, nostalgia fulfills four psychological functions: positive affectivity, self-positivity, affiliation, and buffering against existential terror.

Many interesting issues await empirical investigation. In the first section of this chapter," we covered the interplay between self and affect, and noted the connection between mood and self-focused attention, and the role of mood congruency and affect infusion in self-views. How does nostalgia interface with these ideas? Nostalgia is self-reflective, yet social. Thus, how might nostalgia affect or be affected by an internal focus of attention? It is positive yet at times tinged with bittersweet elements. Thus, what are the congruent or infused moods elicited?

Further, one might examine whether nostalgia proneness is associated with psychological well-being. Bryant, Smart, and King (2005) found that reminiscing about positive memories increases reports of happiness over a period of a week. As a predominantly positive emotion, nostalgia may also contribute to a broader thought–action repertoire (Fredrickson et al., 2003), fostering creative thinking and being associated with markers of well-being such as ability to grow, plan, and achieve (Bless & Fiedler, this volume; Huppert, this volume; Taylor, Lerner, Sherman, Sage, & McDowell, 2003a).

In addition, nostalgia may be associated with physical well-being (Danner, Snowdon, & Friesen, 2001). Positive emotionality in the handwritten diaries of elderly Catholic nuns, written when they were young adults, predicted survival rates approximately 60 years later. In another study (Emmons & McCullough, 2003), positive emotions (e.g., counting one's blessings, gratitude) predicted physical well-being. Finally, self-positivity—a crucial function of nostalgia—was found to be associated with healthy biological profiles (Taylor, Lerner, Sherman, Sage, & McDowell, 2003b).

Our discussion of functions was not meant to be exhaustive. For example, Davis (1979; see also Rosen, 1975) proposed that, in nostalgic reverie, the individual constructs identity continuity via such processes as "an appreciative stance toward former selves; excluding unpleasant memories; reinterpreting marginal, fugitive, and eccentric facets of earlier selves in a positive light; and establishing benchmarks in one's biography" (Davis, 1979, pp. 35–46). Brown and Humphreys (2002) and Milligan (2003) have also offered speculations on the continuity function of nostalgia. In addition, Davis (1979) proposed that nostalgia serves an accuracy function, as it is an authentic experience. In particular, "nostalgia purports to represent the true places, events, and moods of our past, even if our powers of historical reflection may cause us to question whether "it was indeed that way" (p. 47). We call for empirical verification of these continuity and accuracy functions of nostalgia.

What kind of person is more prone to nostalgia and susceptible to its consequences? Are neurotics more prone to nostalgic engagement when in negative than in positive mood? Research showing that high (compared to low) neurotics were faster in making evaluative judgments when in negative than in positive mood (Tamir & Robinson, 2004) would be consistent with this reasoning. Also, are high, compared to low, neurotics more likely to benefit from nostalgic reverie in terms of positive affectivity, self-positivity, affiliation, or existential soothing? Research showing that high neurotics are more vulnerable to stress in situations construed as threatening (Schneider, 2004) is in line with this reasoning. That is, nostalgic reverie may have more "emotional room" to operate among high than low neurotics. Alternatively, to the extent that neuroticism is marked by affective instability (Larsen & Ketelaar, 1991; Spangler & Palrecha, 2004) and belies a more ambivalent investment in systems of meaning (Arndt & Solomon, 2003), high neurotics may not be able to marshal mainly positive memories in the nostalgic reverie, and this may undermine the palliative effects of the emotion.

Another individual difference variable that is worth empirical attention is narcissism. High (compared to low) narcissists are self-centered, interpersonally manipulative, and unforgiving, while scoring low on agreeableness, empathy, and affiliation (Juola Exline, Baumeister, Bushman, Campbell, & Finkel, 2004; Sedikides, Rudich, Gregg, Kumashiro, & Rusbult, 2004). Given that nostalgia is a deeply social emotion, we would expect nostalgia proneness to be lower among narcissists than non-narcissists. Furthermore, we would expect that nostalgia would be more likely to serve a self-positivity than affiliation function for high narcissists, but serve an affiliation rather than a self-positivity function for low narcissists.

CONCLUDING REMARKS

We began by reviewing several literatures that have a bearing on the interplay between self and affect. These literatures concerned the relation between mood and self-focused attention, the relation between mood and self-concept valence, and the cluster of self-related emotions. In the second half of the chapter we concentrated on a neglected self-related emotion, nostalgia, that exemplifies the complexity of the self–affect interface. We reviewed the literature, introduced a reconceptualization of the construct, and presented new findings from our laboratories.

Nostalgia shares important similarities with shame, guilt, and embarrassment. It implicates strongly the self, has a motivational component (e.g., goal clarification), and likely has behavioral consequences as well (e.g., phoning a friend or family member after feeling nostalgic about them). Also, like guilt and embarrassment (but unlike shame), nostalgia is focused on a particular social episode and is relevant to a specific facet of one's self, although, like shame, nostalgia may spill over and overcome the person as whole.

At the same time, nostalgia differs from shame, guilt, and embarrassment in important ways. Nostalgia does not necessarily involve a moral element, although internal standards may be indirectly activated by bringing to mind a close other. Nostalgia is not a painful emotion; to the contrary, it is a positive emotion.

Nostalgia instigates affiliative, not reparative, action. Finally, unlike shame and embarrassment (but like guilt), nostalgia may not be associated with a distinct nonverbal display.

In conclusion, the emotion of nostalgia has long been neglected in the psychological literature. This is unfortunate: Nostalgia is universal, prevalent, and serves a host of critical psychological functions. We hope that future research will redress this empirical imbalance and give this fundamental human experience its proper place in the pantheon of emotions.

ACKNOWLEDGMENT

Constantine Sedikides and Tim Wildschut have been supported by British Academy Grant No. LRG-33566.

REFERENCES

Arndt, J., & Goldenberg, J. L. (2004). From self-awareness to shame-proneness: Evidence of a causal sequence among women. *Self and Identity, 3*, 27–37.

Arndt, J., Greenberg, J., Solomon, S., Pyszczynski, T., & Simon, L. (1997). Suppression, accessibility of death-related thoughts, and cultural world-view defense: Exploring the psychodynamics of terror management. *Journal of Personality and Social Psychology, 73*, 5–18.

Arndt, J., & Solomon, S. (2003). The control of death and the death of control: The effects of mortality salience, neuroticism, and worldview threat on the desire for control. *Journal of Research in Personality, 37*, 1–22.

Aspinwall, L. G. (1998). Rethinking the role of positive affect in self-regulation. *Motivation and Emotion, 22*, 1–32.

Batcho, K. I. (1995). Nostalgia: A psychological perspective. *Perceptual and Motor Skills, 80*, 131–143.

Batcho, K. I. (1998). Personal nostalgia, world view, memory, and emotionality. *Perceptual and Motor Skills, 87*, 411–432.

Baumeister, R. F. (1998). The self. In D. T. Gilbert, S. T. Fiske, & G. Lindzey (Eds.), *Handbook of social psychology* (4th ed., Vol. 1, pp. 680–740). New York: McGraw-Hill.

Best, J., & Nelson, E. E. (1985). Nostalgia and discontinuity: A test of the Davis hypothesis. *Sociology and Social Research, 69*, 221–233.

Brewin, C. R., Furhnam, A., & Howes, M. (1989). Demographic and psychological determinants of homesickness. *British Journal of Psychology, 80*, 467–477.

Brown, A. D., & Humphreys, M. (2002). Nostalgia and the narrativization of identity: A Turkish case study. *British Journal of Management, 13*, 141–159.

Bryant, F. B., Smart, C. M., & King, S. P. (2005). Using the past to enhance the present: Boosting happiness through positive reminiscence. *Journal of Happiness Studies, 6*, 227–260.

Campbell, J. D., Trapnell, P. D., Heine, S. J., Katz, I. M., Lavallee, L. F., & Lehman, D. R. (1996). Self-concept clarity: Measurement, personality correlates, and cultural boundaries. *Journal of Personality and Social Psychology, 70*, 141–156.

Castelnuovo-Tedesco, P. (1980). Reminiscence and nostalgia: The pleasure and pain of remembering. In S. I. Greenspan & G. H. Pollack (Eds.), *The course of life: Psychoanalytic contributions toward understanding personality development: Vol.*

III: Adulthood and the aging process (pp. 104–118). Washington, DC: US Government Printing Office.

Cavanaugh, J. C. (1989). I have this feeling about everyday memory aging .... *Educational Gerontology, 15*, 597–605.

Chaplin, S. (2000). *The psychology of time and death*. Ashland, OH: Sonnet Press.

Cox, J. L. (1988). The overseas student: Expatriate, sojourner or settler? *Acta Psychiatrica Scandinavica, 78*, 179–184.

Cully, J. A., LaVoie, D., & Gfeller, J. D. (2001). Reminiscence, personality, and psychological functioning in older adults. *The Gerontologist, 41*, 89–95.

Danner, D. D., Snowdon, D. A., & Friesen, W. V. (2001). Positive emotions in early life and longevity: Finding from the nun study. *Journal of Personality and Social Psychology, 80*, 804–813.

Davis, F. (1979). *Yearning for yesterday: A sociology of nostalgia*. New York: Free Press.

Duval, S., & Wicklund, R. A. (1972). *A theory of objective self-awareness*. New York: Academic Press.

Emmons, R. A., & McCullough, M. E. (2003). Counting blessings versus burdens: An experimental investigation of gratitude and subjective well-being in daily life. *Journal of Personality and Social Psychology, 84*, 377–389.

Fein, S., & Spencer, S. J. (1997). Prejudice and self-image maintenance: Affirming the self through derogating others. *Journal of Personality and Social Psychology, 73*, 31–44.

Fejfar, M. C., & Hoyle, R. H. (2000). Effect of private self-awareness on negative affect and self-referent attribution: A quantitative review. *Personality and Social Psychology Review, 4*, 132–142.

Fisher, S. (1989). *Homesickness, cognition, and health*. Hove, UK: Lawrence Erlbaum Associates Ltd.

Fodor, N. (1950). Varieties of nostalgia. *Psychoanalytic Review, 37*, 25–38.

Forgas, J. P. (1995). Mood and judgment: The Affect Infusion Model (AIM). *Psychological Bulletin, 117*, 39–66.

Forgas, J. P. (2002). Feeling and doing: Affective influences on interpersonal behavior. *Psychological Inquiry, 13*, 1–28.

Forgas, J. P. (in press). Mood management: A dual-process theory of affect regulation. *Psychological Inquiry.*

Forgas, J. P., & Ciarrochi, J. V. (2002). On managing moods: Evidence for the role of homeostatic cognitive strategies in affect regulation. *Personality and Social Psychology Bulletin, 28*, 336–345.

Fredrickson, B. L. (2001). The role of positive emotions in positive psychology: The broaden-and-build theory of positive emotions. *American Psychologist, 56*, 218–226.

Fredrickson, B. L., Tugade, M. M., Waugh, C. E., & Larkin, G. R. (2003). What good are positive emotions in crises?: A prospective study of resilience and emotions following the terrorist attacks on the United States on September 11th, 2001. *Journal of Personality and Social Psychology, 84*, 365–376.

Frost, I. (1938). Homesickness and immigrant psychoses. *Journal of Mental Science, 84*, 801–847.

Gabriel, Y. (1993). Organizational nostalgia: Reflections on "The Golden Age." In S. Fineman (Ed.), *Emotion in organizations* (pp. 118–141). London, England: Sage Publications, Inc.

Green, J. D., & Sedikides, C. (1999). Affect and self-focused attention revisited: The role of affect orientation. *Personality and Social Psychology Bulletin, 25*, 104–119.

Green, J. D., Sedikides, C., Saltzberg, J. A., & Wood, J. V., & Forzano, L.-A. B. (2003). Happy mood decreases self-focused attention. *British Journal of Social Psychology, 42*, 147–157.

Greenberg, J., Solomon, S., & Pyszczynski, T. (1997). Terror management theory of self-esteem and social behavior: Empirical assessments and conceptual refinements. In M. P. Zanna (Ed.), *Advances in Experimental Social Psychology* (Vol. 29, pp. 61–139). New York: Academic Press.

Havlena, W. J., & Holak, S. L. (1991). "The good old days": Observations on nostalgia and its role in consumer behavior. *Advances in Consumer Research, 18*, 323–329.

Hertz, D. G. (1990). Trauma and nostalgia: New aspects of the coping of aging holocaust survivors. *Israeli Journal of Psychiatry and Related Sciences, 27*, 189–198.

Hofer, J. (1934). Medical dissertation on nostalgia (C. K. Anspach, Trans.). *Bulletin of the History of Medicine, 2*, 376–391. (Original work published 1688)

Holak, S. L., & Havlena, W. J. (1998). Feelings, fantasies, and memories: An examination of the emotional components of nostalgia. *Journal of Business Research, 42*, 217–226.

Holbrook, M. B. (1993). Nostalgia and consumption preferences: Some emerging patterns of consumer tastes. *Journal of Consumer Research, 20*, 245–256.

Holbrook, M. B. (1994). Nostalgia proneness and consumer tastes. In J. A. Howard (Ed.), *Buyer behavior in marketing strategy* (2nd ed., pp. 348–364). Englewood Cliffs, NJ: Prentice-Hall.

Holmes, T. H., & Rahe, R. H. (1967). The social readjustment rating scale. *Journal of Psychosomatic Research, 11*, 213–218.

Jackson, S. W. (1986). *Melancholia and depression: From Hippocratic times to modern times*. New Haven: Yale University Press.

Johnson-Laird, P. N., & Oatley, K. (1989). The language of emotions: An analysis of semantic field. *Cognition and Emotion, 3*, 81–123.

Juola Exline, J., Baumeister, R. F., Bushman, B. J., Campbell, W. K., & Finkel, E. J. (2004). Too proud to let go: Narcissistic entitlement as a barrier to forgiveness. *Journal of Personality and Social Psychology, 87*, 894–912.

Kaplan, H. A. (1987). The psychopathology of nostalgia. *Psychoanalytic Review, 74*, 465–486.

Keltner, D. (1995). The signs of appeasement: Evidence for the distinct displays of embarrassment, amusement, and shame. *Journal of Personality and Social Psychology, 68*, 441–454.

Keltner, D., & Beer, J. S. (2005). Self-conscious emotion and self-regulation. In A. Tesser, J. V. Wood, & D. A. Stapel (Eds.), *On building, defending and regulating the self: A psychological perspective* (pp. 197–215). New York: Psychology Press.

Kleiner, J. (1977). On nostalgia. In C. W. Socarides (Ed.), *The world of emotions* (pp. 471–498). New York: International University Press.

Larsen, R., & Ketelaar, T. (1991). Personality and susceptibility to positive and negative emotional states. *Journal of Personality and Social Psychology, 61*, 132–140.

McAdams, D. P., Diamond, A., de St. Aubin, E., & Mansfield, E. (1997). Stories of commitment: The psychosocial construction of generative lives. *Journal of Personality and Social Psychology, 72*, 678–694.

McAdams, D. P., Reynolds, J., Lewis, M., Patten, A. H., & Bowman, P. J. (2001). When bad things turn good and good things turn bad: Sequences of redemption and contamination in life narratives and their relation to psychosocial adaptation in midlife adults and in students. *Personality and Social Psychology Bulletin, 27*, 474–485.

McCann, W. H. (1941). Nostalgia: A review of the literature. *Psychological Bulletin, 38,* 165–182.

Mikulincer, M., Florian, V., & Hirschberger, G. (2003). The existential function of close relationships: Introducing death into the science of love. *Personality and Social Psychology Review, 7,* 20–40.

Milligan, M. J. (2003). Displacement and identity discontinuity: The role of nostalgia in establishing new identity categories. *Symbolic Interaction, 26,* 381–403.

Mills, M. A., & Coleman, P. G. (1994). Nostalgic memories in dementia: A case study. *International Journal of Aging and Human Development, 38,* 203–219.

Ortony, A., Clore, G. L., & Collins, A. (1988). *The cognitive structure of emotions.* Cambridge, England: Cambridge University Press.

Peters, R. (1985). Reflections on the origin and aim of nostalgia. *Journal of Analytical Psychology, 30,* 135–148.

Pyszczynski, T., Greenberg, J., Solomon, S., Arndt, J., & Schimel, J. (2004). Why do people need self-esteem?: A theoretical and empirical review. *Psychological Bulletin, 130,* 435–468.

Rosen, G. (1975). Nostalgia: A "forgotten" psychological disorder. *Psychological Medicine, 5,* 340–354.

Routledge, C., & Arndt, J. (2005). Time and terror: Managing temporal consciousness and the awareness of mortality. In A. Strathman & J. Joireman (Eds.), *Understanding behavior in the context of time: Theory, research, and applications* (pp. 59–84). Mahwah, NJ: Lawrence Erlbaum Associates, Inc.

Routledge, C., Arndt, J., Sedikides, C., & Wildschut, T. (2006). A blast from the past: The terror management function of nostalgia. Unpublished manuscript. University of Southampton.

Scheier, M. F., & Carver, C. S. (1977). Self-focused attention and the experience of emotion: Attraction, repulsion, elation, and depression. *Journal of Personality and Social Psychology, 35,* 625–636.

Schmeichel, B. J., & Martens, A. (2005). Self-affirmation and mortality salience: Affirming values reduces worldview defense and death-thought accessibility. *Personality and Social Psychology Bulletin, 31,* 658–667.

Schneider, T. R. (2004). The role of neuroticism on psychological and physiological stress responses. *Journal of Experimental Social Psychology, 40,* 795–804.

Sedikides, C. (1992a). Mood as a determinant of attentional focus. *Cognition and Emotion, 6,* 129–148.

Sedikides, C. (1992b). Attentional effects on mood are moderated by chronic self-conception valence. *Personality and Social Psychology Bulletin, 18,* 580–584.

Sedikides, C. (1992c). Changes in the valence of the self as a function of mood. *Review of Personality and Social Psychology, 14,* 271–311.

Sedikides, C. (1994). Incongruent effects of sad mood on self-conception valence: It's a matter of time. *European Journal of Social Psychology, 24,* 161–172.

Sedikides, C. (1995). Central and peripheral self-conceptions are differentially influenced by mood: Tests of the differential sensitivity hypothesis. *Journal of Personality and Social Psychology, 69,* 759–777.

Sedikides, C., Campbell, W. K., Reeder, G., & Elliot, A. J. (1998). The self-serving bias in relational context. *Journal of Personality and Social Psychology, 74,* 378–386.

Sedikides, C., & Green, J. D. (2000). The rocky road from affect to attentional focus. In H. Bless & J. P. Forgas (Eds.), *The message within: The role of subjective experience in social cognition and behavior* (pp. 203–215). Philadelphia, PA: Psychology Press.

Sedikides, C., & Green, J. D. (2001). Affective influences on the self-concept: Qualifying the mood congruency principle. In J. P. Forgas (Ed.), *The Handbook of affect and social cognition* (pp. 145–160). Mahwah, NJ: Lawrence Erlbaum Associates, Inc.

Sedikides, C., Green, J. D., & Pinter, B. (2004). Self-protective memory. In D. R. Beike, J. M. Lampinen, & D. A. Behrend (Eds.), *The self and memory* (pp. 161–179). Philadelphia, PA: Psychology Press.

Sedikides, C., & Gregg, A. P. (2003). Portraits of the self. In M. A. Hogg & J. Cooper (Eds.), *Sage handbook of social psychology* (pp. 110–138). London: Sage Publications.

Sedikides, C., Rudich, E. A., Gregg, A. P., Kumashiro, M., & Rusbult, C. (2004). Are normal narcissists psychologically healthy?: Self-esteem matters. *Journal of Personality and Social Psychology, 87*, 400–416.

Sedikides, C., & Strube, M. J. (1997). Self-evaluation: To thine own self be good, to thine own self be sure, to thine own self be true, and to thine own self be better. In M. P. Zanna (Ed.), *Advances in experimental social psychology* (Vol. 29, pp. 209–269). New York: Academic Press.

Sedikides, C., Wildschut, T., & Baden, D. (2004). Nostalgia: Conceptual issues and existential functions. In J. Greenberg, S. Koole, & T. Pyszczynski (Eds.), *Handbook of experimental existential psychology* (pp. 200–214). New York, NY: Guilford Press.

Simon, L., Arndt, J., Greenberg, J., Pyszczynski, T., & Solomon, S. (1998). Terror management and meaning: Evidence that the opportunity to defend the worldview in response to mortality salience increases the meaningfulness of life in the mildly depressed. *Journal of Personality, 66*, 359–382.

Smith, C. A., & Kirby, L. D. (2001). Toward delivering on the promise of appraisal theory. In K. R. Scherer, A. Schorr, & T. Johnstone (Eds.), *Appraisal processes in emotion: Theory, methods, research* (pp. 121–138). New York: Oxford University Press.

Socarides, C. W. (1977). (Ed.). *The world of emotions: Clinical studies of affects and their expression*. New York: International University Press.

Sohn, L. (1983). Nostalgia. *International Journal of Psychoanalysis, 64*, 203–211.

Solomon, S., Greenberg, J., & Pyszczynski, T. (1991). A terror management theory of social behavior: The psychological functions of self-esteem and cultural worldviews. In L. Berkowitz (Ed.), *Advances in experimental social psychology* (Vol. 24, pp. 93–159). New York: Academic Press.

Spangler, W. E., & Palrecha, R. (2004). The relative contributions of extraversion, neuroticism, and personal strivings to happiness. *Personality and Individual Differences, 37*, 1193–1203.

Steele, C. M. (1988). The psychology of self-affirmation: Sustaining the integrity of the self. In L. Berkowitz (Ed.), *Advances in experimental social psychology* (pp. 261–302). Hillsdale, NJ: Lawrence Erlbaum Associates, Inc.

Stroebe, M., van Vliet, T., Hewstone, M., & Willis, H. (2002). Homesickness among students in two cultures: Antecedents and consequences. *British Journal of Psychology, 93*, 147–168.

Tamir, M., & Robinson, M. D. (2004). Knowing good from bad: The paradox of neuroticism, negative affect, and evaluative processing. *Journal of Personality and Social Psychology, 87*, 913–925.

Tangney, J. P. (2002). Self-conscious emotions: The self as a moral guide. In A. Tesser, D. A. Stapel, & J. V. Wood (Eds.), *Self and motivation: Emerging psychological perspectives* (pp. 97–117). Washington, DC: American Psychological Association.

Tangney, J. P. (2003). Self-relevant emotions. In M. R. Leary & J. P. Tangney (Eds.), *Handbook of self and identity* (pp. 384–400). New York: Guilford Press.

Taylor, S. E., Lerner, J. S., Sherman, D. K., Sage, R. M., & McDowell, N. K. (2003a). Portrait of the self-enhancer: Well adjusted and well liked or maladjusted and friendless? *Journal of Personality and Social Psychology, 84*, 165–176.

Taylor, S. E., Lerner, J. S., Sherman, D. K., Sage, R. M., & McDowell, N. K. (2003b). Are self-enhancing cognitions associated with healthy or unhealthy biological profiles? *Journal of Personality and Social Psychology, 85*, 605–615.

Trope, Y., & Pomerantz, E. M. (1998). Resolving conflicts among self-evaluative motives: Positive experiences as a resource for overcoming defensiveness. *Motivation and Emotion, 22*, 53–72.

Werman, D. S. (1977). Normal and pathological nostalgia. *Journal of the American Psychoanalytic Association, 25*, 387–398.

Wildschut, T., Sedikides, C., Arndt, J., & Routledge, C. D. (in press). Nostalgia: Content, triggers, functions. *Journal of Personality and Social Psychology.*

Wildschut, T., Sedikides, C., Arndt, J., Routledge, C., & Hodgson, A. (2006). *A test of Davis's (1979) discontinuity hypothesis.* Unpublished raw data, University of Southampton.

Van Tilburg, M. A. L., Vingerhoets, J. J. M., & van Heck, G. L. (1996). Homesickness: A review of the literature. *Psychological Medicine, 26*, 899–912.

12

Mood as a Resource in Structuring Goal Pursuit

YAACOV TROPE, ERIC R. IGOU, and CHRISTOPHER T. BURKE

*I*magine that you wake up one morning, look at yourself in the mirror, and notice that there is a little more of you there than you remember seeing just a few years ago. You know you have been less active in recent years, you have not been watching what you eat, and certainly you can blame your slowing metabolism for at least part of the change. Whatever the cause, you determine that it is time to lose some weight. However, before you begin, you know that you should see your doctor to find out how bad your situation is and what you can do to remedy it. You know that the doctor is not going to have good news for you, but you know that the diagnostic feedback provided by your doctor is important for successful pursuit of your goal to lose weight, as well as your long-term goals of good health and longevity. What factors will influence your decision to visit your doctor?

While the above passage sounds like the beginning of a chapter in a book on self-control, we suggest that this passage is very much relevant for a book on affect. The question we pose is, how would your decision be affected by your current mood state? Will you be more likely to visit your doctor if you are feeling good, or will your positive mood prevent you from making a decision that serves your long-term goals? From a theoretical standpoint, either outcome is plausible. However, empirical evidence suggests that, in situations such as this, positive mood serves as a resource and facilitates action in line with long-term goals at the expense of short-term pleasures.

In this chapter, we will first outline the relevant theoretical approaches to this type of decision. We will start with theories of positive affect that would predict avoiding the doctor, which we will refer to as hedonic theories or theories of positive mood as a goal. Then, we will turn to theories suggesting that positive mood will lead to adherence to long-term goals, which we will refer to as theories of positive mood as a resource. After reviewing the evidence that positive mood does in fact promote the pursuit of long-terms goals, we will introduce a broader theory of affect-dependent structure (ADS) meant to differentiate these effects. We will outline the predictions of ADS and the empirical evidence supporting this approach. Finally, we will discuss how ADS relates to other theories of positive affect.

THEORIES OF POSITIVE MOOD AS A GOAL

Theories of positive mood as a goal suggest that positive affect is a desirable end state in itself. These hedonic theories may have their psychological roots in Freud's (1930/1989) pleasure principle, which posits that people "strive after happiness. They want to become happy and remain so" through the "absence of pain and unpleasure" and the "experiencing of strong feelings of pleasure" (p. 25). In other words, people should be motivated to maximize their positive moods and minimize their negative moods (e.g., Isen, Shalker, Clark, & Karp, 1978; see Erber & Markunas, this volume; Erber & Erber, 2001).

One such theory of positive mood as a goal is Wegener and Petty's (1994) hedonic contingency hypothesis. The authors propose that individuals are motivated to engage in behaviors that will improve their mood. According to the hedonic contingency model, when a person is in a negative mood, most behavioral options will result in a better mood. Therefore, the person can be less selective about which behaviors to engage in. When a person is in a positive mood, however, most behavioral options will result in a worse mood. Thus, the person must be more selective and devote more resources to mood management. The result is that individuals in a negative mood should engage in a behavior without a careful evaluation of its hedonic consequences, while individuals in a positive mood should only engage in a behavior to the extent that improves their already good mood.

As an initial test of their hypothesis, Wegener and Petty (1994) conducted three experiments where they induced positive, neutral, or negative mood in participants, then asked participants to rank their preferences for viewing several videotapes. These tapes varied on three dimensions (ostensibly based on prior participants' evaluations), one of which was how good the tape would make them feel. Across all three studies, positive mood participants showed a greater preference for tapes that would make them feel good relative to neutral and negative mood participants. The results of these studies are consistent with the hypothesis that individuals in a positive mood attend more to the hedonic consequences of an activity in order to maintain their mood state (for automatic mood maintenance under positive mood see Handley, Lassiter, Nickell, & Herchenroeder, 2004).

An alternative hedonic perspective is the negative state relief hypothesis (Cialdini, Darby, & Vincent, 1973). According to Cialdini and his colleagues, negative mood states are aversive compared to neutral and positive mood states. Thus, individuals in a negative mood should be more motivated to engage in mood management strategies than those in a positive or neutral mood in order to escape the aversive state.

Work by Handley and Lassiter (2002) has attempted to resolve the apparent discrepancies between Wegener and Petty's (1994) hedonic contingency hypothesis and Cialdini et al.'s (1973) negative state relief hypothesis. Handley and Lassiter predicted that they could find support for both hypotheses in a single study, given the appropriate design. That is, they believed that individuals in both positive and negative moods would show sensitivity to the hedonic properties of an activity relative to those in a neutral mood. They used a measure called "unitization," whereby participants are asked to view a video clip and record all of the occurrences that they deem meaningful. As predicted, both sad and happy participants showed finer unitization rates (indicating deeper processing) for a positive clip compared to a neutral clip. Neutral mood participants showed equivalent unitization rates regardless of the valence of the clip.

To address why previous studies failed to find support for both hypotheses, Handley and Lassiter (2002) proposed that expectations about the affective quality of the upcoming activity (e.g., Wegener, Petty, & Smith, 1995) could be the key. Most previous mood management studies had provided participants with expectations about the affective consequences of provided information (e.g., persuasive arguments), while their first study did not. In a second study, looking at the processing of strong versus weak arguments that were either uplifting or depressing, they found that participants in a positive mood processed uplifting arguments more, regardless of affective expectation. A similar pattern emerged for sad individuals, but only when they were not informed about the affective consequences of processing the message content. If, however, affective expectations were induced in sad participants, elaboration of message content was relatively low. Handley and Lassiter (2002) argue that sad participants with affective expectations regarding the consequences of the message content may have thought that reading the message would not make them feel worse than their current mood state.

Taken together, these hedonic theories suggest that people are motivated to approach pleasure and avoid pain, in line with Freud's pleasure principle. While the hedonic contingency hypothesis (Wegener & Petty, 1994) suggests that people in a positive mood should carefully attend to the affective implications of an activity, the negative state relief hypothesis (Cialdini et al., 1973) suggests that people in a negative mood should be sensitive to an activity's hedonic consequences. The work by Handley and Lassiter (2002) provides some support for both of these hypotheses: both positive and negative mood individuals seem to be more attuned to the hedonic properties of an activity than those in a neutral mood. However, this seems to be the case for sad individuals only when they are not provided with expectations about the affective nature of the task.

The underlying assumption of hedonic theories of positive mood as a goal is that mood management is often among individuals' primary motives. That is, when engaging in an activity, mood management concerns take precedence over other concerns. However, it would seem that maximizing one's mood is not always the primary motive in a situation. Returning to the weight loss conflict described earlier, the primary motive in that situation should be one's future health, not simply avoiding the pain of the negative feedback from the doctor. Wegener et al. (1995) concede that "[o]ther goals could certainly take precedence over hedonic considerations for some people or situations" (p. 13). Similarly, Handley and Lassiter (2002) point to several empirical examples where positive mood individuals seem not to be driven by simple hedonic motives. What, then, are these other motives, and what role does mood play in acting on them?

THEORIES OF POSITIVE MOOD AS A RESOURCE

The other possibility is that under positive mood you will be more likely to visit the doctor and maintain your goals of losing weight and good health. Why might this be the case? This situation represents a self-control problem (Mischel, 1974; Trope, 1986), in which temptations or short-term pleasures threaten the pursuit of one's long-term goals. Trope and Neter (1994) discuss this type of self-control problem as competing self-evaluative motives. On the one hand, a person is motivated to see himself or herself accurately. On the other hand, a person is motivated to see himself or herself positively. They point out that, in terms of realistic self-assessment, negative feedback may be even more diagnostic than positive feedback, and therefore it is important to obtain such feedback in order to improve the self. Trope and Neter (1994) suggest that positive mood can help in these sorts of situations because it buffers the self against the short-term affective consequences of receiving negative feedback. In other words, it can serve as a resource for coping with immediate affective costs (e.g., diminished self-esteem, disconfirmation of a positive self-view).

In a first study, Trope and Neter (1994) gave participants success or failure feedback about their performance on a prior task. Control participants completed a different task designed with minimal emphasis on achievement. Later, participants were asked to rate their interest in receiving feedback about their strengths and weaknesses in another, unrelated domain. While participants in the prior failure and control conditions showed a slight, nonsignificant preference for strength feedback over weakness feedback, participants in the prior success condition showed a very strong preference for weakness feedback over strength feedback. In fact, they showed significantly higher interest in weakness feedback and significantly lower interest in strength feedback than control and failure participants. In an additional study, mood was manipulated via the recall of positive versus negative past experiences (e.g., Sullivan & Conway, 1989). In an affect control condition participants performed an affectively neutral similarity judgment task. Participants were then asked about their interest in feedback on their performance in an earlier administered social sensitivity test. Consistent with the results of the prior study, participants in a positive mood condition were more interested in weakness feedback than strength feedback, whereas participants in both the negative and the neutral mood conditions indicated a greater interest in strength than in weakness feedback.

Building on these findings, Trope and Pomerantz (1998) suggested a boundary condition as to when positive mood might promote interest in weaknesses. While the motive to view oneself positively may always be operating to some extent, the motive to see oneself accurately may be particularly salient for domains that are highly self-relevant. For a domain that is largely irrelevant to one's self-concept, a person might sacrifice realistic self-assessment concerns in order to maintain a positive view of the self. The results of two studies indicate that interest in both strength and weakness feedback about participants' occupation and life goals increases as self-relevance increases. Importantly, however, the results of a third study suggest that the relationship between feedback interest and self-relevance is a function of mood. Participants' mood was manipulated via feedback about prior success or failure in an irrelevant domain. For those who received failure feedback, the relationship between self-relevance and interest in feedback was stronger for strength feedback than for weakness feedback. For those who received success feedback, however, the correlation between self-relevance and interest tended to be stronger for weakness feedback than for strength feedback. This work by Trope and Pomerantz (1998) further demonstrates that positive mood facilitates overcoming short-term obstacles in service of long-term goals. For domains that are irrelevant to long-term goals, it seems that individuals make decisions more in line with the hedonic theories described above (Cialdini et al., 1973; Handley & Lassiter, 2002; Wegener & Petty, 1994).

Extending to a domain familiar to mood researchers, Raghunathan and Trope (2002) tested the mood as a resource hypothesis for people processing persuasive messages. In three studies, they had participants read an essay about caffeine consumption. The self-relevance of the essay was determined by participants' self-reported levels of caffeine consumption. In a later recall task, participants high in caffeine consumption (i.e., the high relevance group) recalled more positive than negative items from the essay when in a negative mood and more negative items than positive items when in a positive mood. The overall level of recall did not vary as a function of mood for the high relevance group. In contrast, those participants low in caffeine consumption (i.e., the low relevance group) recalled equal numbers of positive and negative items regardless of mood, with those in a negative mood recalling somewhat more information overall.

Consistent with the findings of the recall task, participants experienced a change in mood as a result of reading the essay. Those high in caffeine consumption showed an overall negative shift in mood when they were induced to have a positive mood and an overall positive shift in mood when they were induced to have a negative mood. Those low in caffeine consumption showed a smaller mood change as a result of reading the essay. The overall valence of recall was a significant, positive predictor of mood change, as one might expect. Consistent with the model, a mediational analysis revealed that the interaction effects of mood and self-relevance on mood change were partially mediated by the recall of positive versus negative information (Raghunathan & Trope, 2002).

In sum, these studies (Raghunathan & Trope, 2002; Trope & Neter, 1994; Trope & Pomerantz, 1998) paint a very different picture of the effects of positive mood than are suggested by theories of positive mood as a goal (e.g., Wegener & Petty, 1994). While the hedonic theories suggest that people are motivated to approach positive states and avoid negative states, the theory of mood as a resource suggests that people in a positive mood may actually seek out negative information to the extent that it is diagnostic about a self-relevant domain. Work from several other researchers corroborates and extends this more functional view of positive mood.

Much of the most influential work regarding the functionality of positive emotions has come from Fredrickson and her colleagues. She proposed her broaden-and-build theory of positive emotions (Fredrickson, 1998, 2001) as an answer to the question posed by the title of her paper: "What good are positive emotions?"

Unlike negative emotions, which are typically conceptualized as leading to specific action tendencies, Fredrickson (1998) proposed that positive emotions should lead to nonspecific thought–action tendencies. In other words, since particular negative emotions (e.g., fear or sadness) signal specific problems (often) with specific behavioral solutions, it is adaptive for them to lead to specific action tendencies. However, since particular positive emotions (e.g., contentment or interest) signal a more global sense that things are going well, reactions to them can be more varied and will not necessarily be behavioral. The result is that positive emotions facilitate the temporary broadening of one's "thought–action repertoire" and the building of one's personal physical, intellectual, and social resources (Fredrickson, 1998).

Of particular relevance to the present discussion of mood as a resource is the proposition that positive mood serves a resource-building function. According to the theory, the building of resources is a direct consequence of broadening. Moreover, while the thought–action broadening (like the emotion itself) is short-lived, the resources that it builds are predicted to endure and accumulate (Fredrickson, 2001). In turn, the building of resources increases the likelihood of experiencing positive emotions in the future—a process referred to as an "upward spiral" (Fredrickson & Joiner, 2002). More specifically, Fredrickson and Joiner found that (over the course of five weeks) those who reported more positive emotions initially experienced a significant increase in what they called broad-minded coping skills. Initial level of positive emotions also predicted later positive emotions, partially mediated by broad-minded coping. Similarly, initial broad-minded coping predicted later broad-minded coping, partially mediated by positive emotions. This research is consistent with the mood as a resource model insofar as it indicates long-term improvement as a function of positive experiences (see also Aspinwall, 2001).

In sum, in recent years many studies contributed to the impression that positive affective states are associated with self-regulation that serves long-term interests (for a discussion of this perspective on positive affective states see Aspinwall, 1998). Important in this respect is the tendency to elaborate on information that may be unpleasant but useful for the improvement of the self. How can this role of positive affective experiences be reconciled with other models suggesting that positive affect reduces interest in unpleasant information (e.g., Wegener & Petty, 1994)?

ADS IN SELF-REGULATION

Thus far, our discussion has focused on the influence of positive mood on self-regulation. Of particular interest has been the conflict between short-term affective consequences and long-term learning consequences of considering self-relevant information. The research literature suggests that, on the one hand, positive mood functions as a resource when negative information about the self is processed. On the other hand, positive mood can also function as a goal by directing attention toward positive information and away from negative information. In this section we introduce a new, integrative framework that accounts for both of these functions of mood in self-regulation. This framework focuses on the influence of mood on the *structure* of means–goals relationships in cognitive goal representations.

Consistent with the notion that motivation can be understood in cognitive terms, ADS theory focuses on cognitive goal representations (e.g., Bargh & Gollwitzer, 1994; Fitzsimons & Bargh, 2004; Kruglanski, 1996; Kruglanski, Shah, Fishbach, Friedman, Chun, & Sleeth-Keppler, 2002; Shah & Kruglanski, 2002, 2003). In addition to conceptualizing means and goals as cognitive elements, ADS builds on research that views goals and means as embedded in a hierarchical structure (e.g., Liberman & Trope, 1998; Vallacher & Wegner, 1987, 1989). A typical structure of goal representations may consist of means that are associated with subgoals, and subgoals that are in turn associated with a superordinate goal. In other words, elements are distinguished according to their level in a goal hierarchy (e.g., low- vs. high-level goal).

ADS posits that mood changes the structure of means–goals relationships in goal representations. Positive mood presumably attunes individuals to the instrumentality of means to their superordinate, high-level goals to a greater degree than neutral mood does. In positive mood, the "big picture," the representation of the available action alternatives as means for the attainment of one's superordinate, overarching ends, is more likely to emerge. Positive mood thus increases the ability to distinguish between central and peripheral elements in the situation. As a result, goal representations in positive mood emphasize features that are essential for the attainment of the high-level goal, and goal-irrelevant information is excluded. Importantly, by structuring goal representations, positive mood promotes *action* in accordance with individuals' high-level goals. The resulting structure of means–goals relationships and its impact on behavior is similar to the characteristics of high-level construals of action in construal level theory (Trope & Liberman, 2003).

The influence of mood on self-regulation is viewed as a constructive process. If the available action alternatives do not serve one's goal, alternative high-level goal representations are more likely to be formed under positive mood. Because individuals in positive mood are more sensitive to means–ends relationships, they are more likely to shift their goal orientation when the available means are more instrumental for an alternative goal. Changes in high-level goals, in turn, would then change the appeal of the available courses of action and actual behavior (see Trope & Liberman, 2000, 2003). In sum, due to their greater attunement to the instrumental value of the available courses of action with respect to increasingly higher level ends, individuals in a positive mood can more readily distinguish between primary and secondary goals, set clear priorities, and thus structure their goal pursuit.

MOOD AS A RESOURCE AND MOOD AS A GOAL: AN ADS PERSPECTIVE

According to the hedonic contingency model (Wegener & Petty, 1994), positive mood sensitizes individuals to the hedonic consequences of actions (i.e., their affective costs and benefits) and thus leads to the avoidance of unpleasant information.

According to the mood as resource model (e.g., Raghunathan & Trope, 2002), positive mood buffers against the anticipated short-term costs of considering negative self-relevant information. As a result, individuals in positive mood are more likely to seek and elaborate on negative but diagnostic self-relevant information. This, in turn, enables them to learn and improve themselves. But under what conditions does mood serve as a goal? And under what conditions does mood serve as a resource?

Seeking self-evaluative feedback can serve both learning and affective goals (see Sedikides & Strube, 1995; Trope, 1986). When the feedback is diagnostic of an important, but changeable skill, the learning benefits of receiving the feedback are long-term and general, whereas the affective value of the feedback is short-term and confined to the feedback situation (Freitas, Salovey, & Liberman, 2001; Trope, 1986). Being more attuned to this difference in the instrumental value of feedback, individuals in positive mood should be more likely than individuals in neutral mood to use the feedback primarily for its learning value. For example, individuals in positive mood are more likely to selectively seek out feedback about their weaknesses—feedback from which they can learn how to improve the diagnosed skill—as past research reviewed above has actually shown (see, e.g., Raghunathan & Trope, 2002; Trope & Neter, 1994; Trope & Pomerantz, 1998). However, when the feedback is nondiagnostic or the skill is unimportant or unchangeable, the feedback may have little or no instrumental value for learning goals. In this case, individuals in positive mood are more likely to recognize the alternative use of feedback for affective goals and unequivocally pursue them as their primary goals (cf. Wegener & Petty, 1994). For example, individuals in positive mood, relative to individuals in neutral mood, should be more likely to prefer feedback about their strengths to feedback about their weaknesses and, thereby, improve their affective state.

In a series of studies, we (Gervey, Igou, & Trope, in press) tested the ADS analysis of feedback seeking. We hypothesized that when the available means are useful for attaining learning goals, individuals in positive mood, more than individuals in neutral mood, would prefer weakness-focused feedback than strength-focused feedback. However, when the feedback is not useful for learning goals, the priorities of individuals in positive mood would shift, and they would prefer, more than individuals in neutral mood, strength-focused feedback to weakness-focused feedback.

The first study was designed to examine the influence of positive versus neutral mood on feedback seeking as a function of the usefulness of feedback for the achievement of a superordinate, high-level goal. Based on our assumption that positive mood attunes individuals to means–goals relationships, we predicted that when feedback was useful to achieve a superordinate goal, positive mood would increase interest in weakness feedback compared to strength feedback. However, we expected positive mood to increase the interest in strength feedback relative to weakness feedback, when the usefulness of feedback with regard to the superordinate goal was relatively low.

After manipulating participants' mood via a modified autobiographical memory procedure (see Trope & Neter, 1994), we told participants that they could receive feedback on their "preconscious relations abilities," which was ostensibly a measure they completed prior to this study. It was explained that the Preconscious Relations Abilities Scale consisted of two components: interpersonal abilities and intrapersonal abilities. We manipulated the importance of feedback by informing participants that one of these abilities served the global goal of life satisfaction whereas the other would be relatively unimportant for this goal. The feedback consisted of strengths and weaknesses for each of the two ability domains, and it was presented one piece at a time on a computer screen. To measure participants' interest in their weaknesses versus strengths, we assessed length of time spent viewing each type of feedback and self-reports of interest in additional feedback on their strengths and weaknesses.

For both measures we obtained the same pattern: When the ability was presented as important means for the global goal of life satisfaction, participants in the positive mood condition spent more time reading and expressed more interest in weakness feedback than strength feedback compared to participants in a neutral mood. But when the ability was not important for and thus *un*related to the global goal, participants in the positive mood condition spent more time reading and expressed more interest in strength than weakness feedback relative to participants in the neutral mood condition.

These results supported our hypotheses about the different roles that positive mood plays in self-evaluation. When feedback was important with respect to individuals' superordinate goal, positive mood enabled participants to focus on information with long-term learning benefits as opposed to information that made them feel better in the current situation. Therefore, under the condition when feedback was highly instrumental for the achievement of the superordinate goal, positive mood enhanced feedback seeking as means for learning goals, consistent with the mood as a resource model. When, in contrast, feedback was not important regarding individuals' superordinate goal, positive mood increased feedback seeking in accordance with short-term affective goals confined in the feedback situation. In other words, when learning from feedback was not instrumental for achieving the superordinate goal, positive mood served as a goal. The results of this study suggest that the role of positive mood in self-evaluation depends on the instrumentality of feedback for individuals' high-level goals, and this is consistent with our contention that positive mood attunes individuals to those means that are instrumental for the achievement of high-level goals.

A second study was designed to more directly examine the proposed impact of mood on the perception of means–goals relationships and how it accounts for feedback seeking. After manipulating participants' moods (e.g., Trope & Neter, 1994), we told participants that they could receive feedback on their social intelligence scores that were ostensibly measured in a mass testing session prior to this study. We manipulated feedback diagnosticity by suggesting that the measure was either new and its reliability unknown, or that it was well-established and reliable. Several measures were obtained: (1) participants' interest in viewing strength and weakness feedback along six dimensions of social intelligence, (2) their anticipated affect upon receiving such feedback, and (3) the perceived instrumentality of such feedback for self-improvement goals.

Similar to the first study, the influence of positive versus neutral mood on feedback seeking was moderated by the degree to which participants could learn from this feedback in order to achieve a superordinate, high-level goal. Positive mood promoted interest in weakness feedback when feedback was diagnostic of one's ability (i.e., social intelligence). However, positive mood increased interest in strengths when feedback was relatively nondiagnostic and thus not instrumental for assessing and improving the self.

When participants were in a positive mood, they evaluated the informational benefits of diagnostic weakness feedback higher than those of diagnostic strength feedback. The differential evaluation of the informational benefits of strength and weakness feedback was reduced when the diagnosticity of feedback was low. However, these evaluations were less a function of feedback diagnosticity when participants were in a neutral mood. Overall, participants anticipated more negative affective consequences from considering weakness feedback than from considering strength feedback. As expected, mood and feedback diagnosticity moderated this effect: When participants were in a neutral mood, the anticipated affective consequences were less influenced by feedback diagnosticity than when they were in a positive mood. More specifically, in the positive mood condition participants saw the greatest difference in affective consequences of weakness feedback versus strength feedback when feedback diagnosticity was low. However, when feedback diagnosticity was high, positive mood participants differentiated least between the affective consequences that would result from the consideration of feedback.

These results indicate that positive mood attuned participants to the informational benefits of feedback when feedback was diagnostic and thus instrumental for learning goals. However, positive mood increased the sensitivity to the affective consequences of considering feedback when instrumentality of feedback for learning goals was low. Importantly, the evaluation of the informational benefits of feedback and its affective consequences both partially mediated the effects of mood and feedback diagnosticity on feedback interest.

The first two studies demonstrate that positive mood promotes feedback seeking in accordance with learning goals when action alternatives for the pursuit of these goals are available. When, in contrast, action alternatives for the pursuit of these goals are not available, positive mood promotes a shift toward affective goals, leading to a preference of strength feedback to weakness feedback. Importantly, the second study supported our contention that these mood effects are mediated by the increase in sensitivity to means–goals relationships. Specifically, goal pursuit in a positive mood is influenced by a stronger attunement to the instrumentality of means to high-level ends than in a neutral mood.

In the first two studies we investigated goal pursuit as a function of mood and means–goals relationships by manipulating the instrumentality of feedback for a self-evaluative goal. A third study was designed to examine mood effects on feedback seeking by directly inducing either a learning goal or an affective goal. We predicted that positive mood increases feedback seeking in accordance with the high-level goal that was contextually induced. That is, relative to neutral mood, positive mood was expected to promote interest in weaknesses when participants held a learning goal, but positive mood was expected to promote interest in strengths when participants held an affective goal.

After manipulating participants' mood similar to the procedure in the first two studies, we told participants that they could receive feedback on their "preconscious relations abilities," which was ostensibly measured as part of a mass testing session prior to this study. Participants were told that they would be shown a sample of their feedback so that they would better understand what the earlier measurement assessed. After looking over sample feedback, they would be given the opportunity to indicate how interested they were in receiving additional feedback. To induce a learning goal, we asked participants to think about the study "as an opportunity to improve yourself and gain a more accurate appraisal of where you stand." To induce an affective goal, we told participants to think about the study "as an opportunity to just feel good about yourself" (see Taylor, Neter, & Wayment, 1995). Afterwards we measured participants' interest in weakness and strength feedback.

In both positive and neutral mood conditions, participants with a learning goal showed greater interest in weakness feedback than strength feedback, while participants with an affective goal showed greater interest in strength than weakness feedback. However, the influence of the induced self-evaluative goal on feedback interest was more pronounced in the positive mood condition relative to the neutral mood condition. Therefore, positive mood increased the consistency of feedback interest as a function of the high-level goal that was induced. These results support our contention that positive mood attunes individuals to feedback that serves the overarching goal in a self-evaluative situation. And, as a result of this attunement, positive mood promotes action in accordance with individuals' prioritized goal.

In these three studies, the influence of mood on feedback seeking was a function of specific means–goals relationships. In the first two studies, we manipulated the instrumentality of feedback for learning goals. In the third study, we directly varied whether participants held a learning goal or an affective goal. When individuals were motivated to learn from feedback in order to assess and improve the self, positive mood promoted interest in weakness feedback compared to strength feedback. However, when the instrumental value of feedback for learning goals was low or when individuals held an affective goal, positive mood enabled individuals to recognize the alternative use of feedback for affective goals, resulting in more interest in strength than in weakness feedback.

Taken together, our research identified conditions under which mood serves as a resource and under which conditions mood serves as a goal. Feedback interest in a positive mood can either be mood-congruent or mood-incongruent. When individuals hold learning goals and when feedback qualifies as means for these goals, positive mood promotes interest in mood-incongruent feedback (i.e., weaknesses) and thus serves as a resource (e.g., Raghunathan & Trope, 2002; Trope & Neter, 1994). When feedback's instrumentality for learning goals is low and when individuals are primarily motivated to feel good about themselves, positive mood increases interest in mood-congruent feedback (i.e., strengths) and thus serves affective goals (e.g., Wegener & Petty, 1994; Wegener et al., 1995; see also Isen et al., 1978).

RELATING ADS TO RESEARCH ON MOOD AND INFORMATION PROCESSING

ADS proposes that positive mood promotes goal representations that can be described in terms of high-level construals (e.g., Trope & Liberman, 2000, 2003). This proposal is related to several lines of research and theorizing on affect and cognition. Most relevant here, Bless and Fiedler (this volume) argue that positive mood increases the level of abstractness with which information is processed. Similarly, research by Isen and her colleagues suggests that positive mood produces an "upward drift" in mental representations (e.g., Isen & Daubman, 1984; Isen, Johnson, Mertz, & Robinson, 1985; for reviews see Isen, 1987, 2004). For example, Isen and Daubman (1984) found that in positive mood individuals use broader cognitive categories, suggesting that they adopt a more global perspective on the situation, compared to individuals in neutral or negative mood. More recently, research on mood and perception showed that induction of positive mood enhanced processing at the "global" (vs. "local") level (Gasper, 2004; Gasper & Clore, 2002). For example, participants in a positive mood tended to reconstruct visual images and classify figures in terms of their global (vs. local) features (Gasper & Clore, 2002). This abstract "level of focus" (e.g., Clore, Wyer, Dienes, Gasper, Gohm, & Isbell, 2001) in positive mood was also demonstrated in research on the effects of mood on language (see Bless & Fiedler, this volume) and impression formation (e.g., Bless, Hamilton, & Mackie, 1992; see Clore & Storbeck, this volume). In addition, the well-documented effects of positive mood on the use of general knowledge structures (e.g., scripts and stereotypes) in judgments and decisions (e.g., Bless, 2001; Bless, Clore, Schwarz, Golisano, Rabe, & Wolk, 1996; Bodenhausen, Kramer, & Süsser, 1994) may also reflect a focus on more abstract, global information under positive mood (see Clore & Storbeck, this volume). In sum, research findings on mood and cognition are consistent with our contention that, compared to neutral mood, positive mood promotes goal representations that are structured around overarching, high-level goals.

Central to ADS is the assumption that positive mood attunes individuals to the instrumentality of the available means for their high-level goals. This assumption is based on research on the influence of mood on the ability to detect the relatedness among cognitive elements. For example, Murray, Sujan, Hirt, and Sujan (1990) showed that positive mood increases the ability to detect similarities as well as differences among cognitive elements and "move freely across all levels in a categorical hierarchy" (p. 413). Similarly, Isen and her colleagues argued that positive mood increases the ability to "see" the relatedness among cognitive elements (e.g., Isen & Daubman, 1984; see also Ashby, Isen, & Turken, 1999) and, thereby, the formation of coherent cognitive representations (Isen, 1987, 2004; Isen & Means, 1983). For example, Isen and Means (1983) found that participants in a positive mood considered relevant information but discarded irrelevant information in a problem-solving task, resulting in more efficient decision making. This is consistent with findings in person perception research, which indicate that positive mood sensitizes individuals to information that is *inconsistent* with well-structured, abstract knowledge (e.g., Bless, Schwarz, & Wieland, 1996).

In ADS, the attunement to means–ends relationships under positive mood does not necessarily favor a particular type of information such as prior knowledge over new, incoming information (cf. Bless & Fiedler, this volume; Clore & Storbeck, this volume). In the constructive process of structuring goal pursuit, new incoming information may be highly influential under positive mood. Indeed, as described earlier, our research shows that individuals in positive mood flexibly redirect their goal pursuit in accordance with current changes in the instrumentality of the available means for a current high-level goal (Gervey et al., in press). ADS assumes that positive mood facilitates the representation of the input in terms of hierarchical means–ends structures, independent of whether those structures were previously formed or constructed on line. In this view, positive mood promotes the formation of structured (vs. unstructured) cognitive representations, rather than the utilization of old (vs. new) information. Moreover, specific information is not necessarily lost when individuals are in positive mood. Instead, it is more likely to be embedded within hierarchical, coherent representations.

Another relevant line of research focuses on the information that is primed by mood states and how this information influences judgment and behavior (e.g., Bower, 1981; Forgas, 1995, 2001; Isen et al., 1978). This approach would suggest that positive mood may prime positive information about the current self (e.g., "I have good social skills") and thus diminish interest in information that suggests otherwise (e.g., feedback regarding one's poor social skills). However, this approach may also suggest more complex possibilities. For example, due to the negative affective implication of weakness feedback, it may be difficult to form a clear evaluation of the informational benefits of this feedback relative to its affective costs. The affect infusion model (see, e.g., Forgas, 1995, 2001) predicts that under such circumstances individuals are likely to engage in an open, constructive information search that is influenced by accessible mood-congruent information. In feedback seeking situations, positive mood would lead to a more positive outlook, confidence, and approach behavior (e.g., Forgas, 1998a, 1998b). Under positive mood, the expected benefits of weakness feedback would then seem to outweigh its costs, leading to a stronger preference for this negative, mood-incongruent feedback. However, this process does not readily explain the current findings showing that positive mood shifts individuals' interest from weakness feedback to strength feedback when the former, negative feedback is no longer instrumental for the individuals' high-level learning goals (Gervey et al., in press).

NEGATIVE MOOD AND GOAL PURSUIT

We examined the influence of positive mood versus neutral mood on goal pursuit. Of particular interest was the role of positive mood as either a resource (e.g., Trope & Neter, 1994) or a goal (e.g., Wegener & Petty, 1994). We introduced ADS as a more general model that integrates both of these roles of positive mood. So far, however, we have not considered the impact of negative mood on goal pursuit relative to positive or neutral mood. From the present perspective, negative mood may be expected to impair individuals' ability to extract the structure underlying the available input. These individuals are less likely to organize the available information into coherent goal hierarchies and to be attuned to the instrumental value of available actions as means for the attainment of their higher level goals. In a negative mood state, individuals are therefore less likely to switch their goal orientations in accordance with changes in the instrumentality of means. It should be noted, however, that this effect may be counteracted by asymmetric effects of positive and negative moods on self-regulation (see, e.g., Erber & Markunas, this volume). For example, individuals may attempt to repair their negative mood by selectively attending to positive information in order to get out of a negative "cognitive loop" (e.g., Isen, 1984, 1987; Isen et al., 1978). This, in turn, may counteract any differences in processing style between individuals in positive and negative mood (see Isen & Daubman, 1984; see also Forgas, this volume; Handley & Lassiter, 2002; Haselton & Ketelaar, this volume). The present predictions regarding negative mood are therefore tentative and need to be tested in future research.

SUMMARY AND CONCLUSION

A considerable amount of research suggests that, on the one hand, positive mood functions as a resource enabling individuals to process unpleasant but diagnostic information about their weaknesses. On the other hand, positive mood can also operate as a goal by directing individuals' attention toward pleasant information and away from unpleasant information. This chapter introduces ADS as a theoretical framework that integrates both of these functions of positive mood. ADS posits that in positive mood individuals are more likely to "see the big picture," to represent the available action alternatives as means for the attainment of their superordinate, high-level goals. Positive mood thus attunes individuals to their high-level goals and to means that serve those goals.

ADS suggests that in situations where self-relevant feedback is available, the effect of mood states on feedback seeking and processing should depend on the instrumentality of the feedback for the attainment of the individuals' goals. Being more attuned to this difference in the instrumental value of feedback, individuals in a positive mood, more than individuals in a neutral mood, would therefore prefer weakness-focused feedback than strength-focused feedback when the available feedback is useful for learning purposes. However, when the feedback is not useful for learning purposes, the priorities of individuals in positive mood would shift, and they would prefer, more than individuals in neutral mood, strength-focused feedback to weakness-focused feedback.

Consistent with this analysis, our research (Gervey et al., in press) shows that when individuals have learning goals and when feedback qualifies as means for these goals, positive mood promotes interest in mood-incongruent feedback about ones' weaknesses and thus serves as a resource (e.g., Raghunathan & Trope, 2002; Trope & Neter, 1994). When the instrumentality of the feedback for learning goals is low or when individuals are primarily motivated to feel good about themselves, positive mood increases interest in mood-congruent feedback about one's strengths and thus serves affective goals (e.g., Wegener & Petty, 1994; Wegener et al., 1995; see also Isen et al., 1978).

At a more general level, these findings are consistent with the basic tenet of ADS that positive mood promotes a high-level construal of incoming information, namely, the embedding of the information within coherent, hierarchical goal representations that are structured around overarching, superordinate goals. The emerging high-level goal representations better distinguish between central and peripheral elements in the situation and are more sensitive to the instrumental value of different courses of action as means for the attainment of one's goals. Positive mood thus structures goal pursuit. This proposal is consistent with our research on feedback seeking and earlier work on perceptions of relatedness of cognitive elements (see Isen, 1987, 2004). It is also consistent with past research showing that positive mood enhances individuals' tendency to relate specific instances to more abstract, global categories (e.g., Bless, 2001; Gasper & Clore, 2002; Murray et al., 1990; see Bless & Fiedler, this volume; Clore & Storbeck, this volume). Together, these lines of research suggest that mood states can significantly influence self-regulation. If individuals in a positive mood are more attuned to the instrumental value of the available courses of action as means for the attainment of increasingly higher level ends, those individuals should more readily set clear priorities, flexibly select means according to those priorities, and thus engage in more structured goal pursuit. These predictions suggest interesting directions for future research on affect and self-regulation, which our research on mood and self-assessment has only started to explore.

REFERENCES

Ashby, F. G., Isen, A. M., & Turken, A. U. (1999). A neuropsychological theory of positive affect and its influence on cognition. *Psychological Review, 106,* 529–550.

Aspinwall, L. G. (1998). Rethinking the role of positive affect in self-regulation. *Motivation and Emotion, 22,* 1–32.

Aspinwall, L. G. (2001). Dealing with adversity: Self-regulation, coping, adaptation, and health. In A. Tesser & N. Schwarz (Eds.), *The Blackwell handbook of social psychology, intrapersonal processes* (Vol. 1, pp. 159–214). Malden, MA: Blackwell.

Bargh, J. A., & Gollwitzer, P. M. (1994). Environmental control over goal-directed action. *Nebraska Symposium on Motivation* (Vol. 41, pp. 71–124).

Bless, H. (2001). Mood and the use of general knowledge structures. In L. L. Martin & G. L. Clore (Eds.), *Theories of mood and cognition. A user's guidebook* (pp. 9–26). Mahwah, NJ: Lawrence Erlbaum Associates, Inc.

Bless, H., Clore, G. L., Schwarz, N., Golisano, V., Rabe, C., & Wolk, M. (1996). Mood and the use of scripts: Does a happy mood really lead to mindlessness? *Journal of Personality and Social Psychology, 71,* 665–679.

Bless, H., & Fiedler, K. (2006). Mood and the regulation of information processing and behaviour. In J. P. Forgas (Ed.), *Affect in social thinking and behavior* (pp. 65–84). New York: Psychology Press.

Bless, H., Hamilton, D. L., & Mackie, D. M. (1992). Mood effects on the organization of person information. *European Journal of Social Psychology, 22,* 497–509.

Bless, H., Schwarz, N., & Wieland, R. (1996). Mood and the impact of category membership and individuating information. *European Journal of Social Psychology, 26,* 935–959.

Bodenhausen, G. V., Kramer, G. P., & Süsser, K. (1994). Happiness and stereotypic thinking in social judgment. *Journal of Personality and Social Psychology, 66*, 621–632.

Bower, G. H. (1981). Mood and memory. *American Psychologist, 36*, 129–148.

Cialdini, R. B., Darby, B. L., & Vincent, J. E. (1973). Transgression and altruism: A case for hedonism. *Journal of Experimental Social Psychology, 9*, 502–516.

Clore, G. L., & Storbeck, J. (2006). Affect as information liking, efficacy, and importance. In J. P. Forgas (Ed.), *Affect in social thinking and behavior* (pp. 123–141). New York: Psychology Press.

Clore, G. L., Wyer, R. S., Dienes, B., Gasper, K., Gohm, C., & Isbell, L. (2001). Affective feelings as feedback: Some cognitive consequences. In L. L. Martin & G. L. Clore (Eds.), *Theories of mood and cognition. A user's guidebook* (pp. 27–62). Mahwah, NJ: Lawrence Erlbaum Associates, Inc.

Erber, R., & Markunas, S. (2006). Managing affective states. In J. P. Forgas (Ed.), *Affect in social thinking and behavior* (pp. 253–266). New York: Psychology Press.

Erber, R., & Erber, M. W. (2001). Mood and processing: A view from a self-regulation perspective. In L. L. Martin & G. L. Clore (Eds.), *Theories of mood and cognition. A user's guidebook* (pp. 63–84). Mahwah, NJ: Lawrence Erlbaum Associates, Inc.

Fitzsimons, G., M., & Bargh, J. A. (2004). Automatic self-regulation. In R. F. Baumeister & K. D. Vohs (Eds.), *Handbook of self-regulation, research, theory, and applications* (pp. 51–170). New York: Guilford Press.

Forgas, J. P. (1995). Mood and judgment: The affect infusion model (AIM). *Psychological Bulletin, 117*, 1–28.

Forgas, J. P. (1998a). On feeling good and getting it our way: Mood effects on negotiation strategies and outcomes. *Journal of Personality and Social Psychology, 74*, 565–577.

Forgas, J. P. (1998b). Asking nicely? The effects of mood on responding to more or less polite requests. *Personality and Social Psychology Bulletin, 24*, 173–185.

Forgas, J. P. (2001). The affect infusion model (AIM): An integrative theory of mood effects on cognition and judgments. In L. L. Martin & G. L. Clore (Eds.), *Theories of mood and cognition. A user's guidebook* (pp. 99–134). Mahwah, NJ: Lawrence Erlbaum Associates, Inc.

Forgas, J. P. (2006). Affective influences on interpersonal behavior: Understanding the role of affect in everyday interactions. In J. P. Forgas (Ed.), *Affect in social thinking and behavior* (pp. 269–289). New York: Psychology Press.

Fredrickson, B. L. (1998). What good are positive emotions? *Review of General Psychology, 2*, 300–319.

Fredrickson, B. L. (2001). The role of positive emotions in positive psychology: The broaden-and-build theory of positive emotions. *American Psychologist, 56*, 218–226.

Fredrickson, B. L., & Joiner, T. (2002). Positive emotions trigger upward spirals toward emotional well-being. *Psychological Science, 13*, 172–175.

Freitas, A. L., Salovey, P., & Liberman, N. (2001). Abstract and concrete self-evaluative goals. *Journal of Personality and Social Psychology, 80*, 410–424.

Freud, S. (1989). *Civilization and its discontents* (J. Strachey, Trans.). New York: W. W. Norton & Company. (Original work published 1930).

Gasper, K. (2004). Do you see what I see? Affect and visual information processing. *Cognition and Emotion, 18*, 405–421.

Gasper, K., & Clore, G. L. (2002). Attending to the big picture: Mood and global versus local processing of visual information. *Psychological Science, 13*, 34–40.

Gervey, B., Igou, E. R., & Trope, Y. (in press). The role of positive mood in pursuing primary self-evaluative goals. *Motivation and Emotion.*

Handley, I. M., & Lassiter, G. D. (2002). Mood and information processing: When happy and sad look the same. *Motivation and Emotion, 26,* 223–255.

Handley, I. M., Lassiter, G. D., Nickell, E. F., & Herchenroeder, L. M. (2004). *Journal of Experimental Social Psychology, 40,* 106–112.

Haselton, M. G., & Ketelaar, T. (2006). Irrational emotions or emotional wisdom? The evolutionary psychology of affect and social behavior. In J. P. Forgas (Ed.), *Affect in social thinking and behavior* (pp. 21–39). New York: Psychology Press.

Isen, A. M. (1984). Toward understanding the role of affect in cognition. In R. S. Wyer, Jr., & T. K. Srull (Eds.), *Handbook of social cognition* (Vol. 3, pp. 179–236). Hillsdale, NJ: Lawrence Erlbaum Associates, Inc.

Isen, A. M. (1987). Positive affect, cognitive processes, and social behavior. In L. Berkowitz (Ed.), *Advances in experimental social psychology* (Vol. 20, pp. 203–253). New York: Academic Press.

Isen, A. M. (2004). Some perspectives on positive feelings and emotions, positive affect facilitates thinking and problem solving. In A. S. R. Manstead, N. Frijda, & A. Fischer (Eds.), *Feelings and Emotions, The Amsterdam Symposium* (pp. 263–281). Cambridge: Cambridge University Press.

Isen, A. M., & Daubman, K. A. (1984). The influence of affect on categorization. *Journal of Personality and Social Psychology, 47,* 1206–1217.

Isen, A. M., Johnson, M. S., Mertz, E., & Robinson, G. F. (1985). The influence of positive affect on the unusualness of word associations. *Journal of Personality and Social Psychology, 48,* 1413–1426.

Isen, A. M., & Means, B. (1983). The influence of positive affect on decision-making strategy. *Social Cognition, 2,* 18–31.

Isen, A. M., Shalker, T. E., Clark, M. S., & Karp, L. (1978). Affect, accessibility of material in memory, and behavior: A cognitive loop? *Journal of Personality and Social Psychology, 36,* 1–12.

Kruglanski, A. W. (1996). Goal as knowledge structures. In P. M. Gollwitzer & J. A. Bargh (Eds.), *The psychology of action: Linking cognition and motivation to behavior* (pp. 599–618). New York: Guilford Press.

Kruglanski, A. W., Shah, J., Fishbach, A., Friedman, R., Chun, W., Y., & Sleeth-Keppler, D. (2002). A theory of goal systems. In M. Zanna (Ed.), *Advances in experimental social psychology* (Vol. 34, pp. 331–376). New York: Academic Press.

Liberman, N., & Trope, Y. (1998). The role of feasibility and desirability considerations in near and distant future decisions: A test of temporal construal theory. *Journal of Personality and Social Psychology, 75,* 5–18.

Mischel, W. (1974). Processes in delay of gratification. In L. Berkowitz (Ed.), *Advances in experimental social psychology* (Vol. 7, pp. 249–292). San Diego, CA: Academic Press.

Murray, N., Sujan, H., Hirt, E. R., & Sujan, M. (1990). The influence of mood on categorization: A cognitive flexibility interpretation. *Journal of Personality and Social Psychology, 59,* 411–425.

Raghunathan, R., & Trope, Y. (2002). Walking the tightrope between feeling good and being accurate: Mood as a resource in processing persuasive messages. *Journal of Personality and Social Psychology, 83,* 510–525.

Sedikides, C., & Strube, M. J. (1995). The multiply motivated self. *Personality and Social Psychology Bulletin, 21,* 1330–1335.

Shah, J. Y., & Kruglanski, A. W. (2002). Priming against your will: How accessible alternatives affect goal pursuit. *Journal of Experimental Social Psychology, 38,* 368–383.

Shah, J. Y., & Kruglanski, A. W. (2003). When opportunity knocks: Bottom-up priming of goals by means and its effects on self-regulation. *Journal of Personality and Social Psychology, 84*, 1109–1122.

Sullivan, M. J. L., & Conway, M. (1989). Negative affect leads to low-effort cognition: Attributional processing for observed social behavior. *Social Cognition, 7*, 315–337.

Taylor, S., Neter, E., & Wayment, H. (1995). Self-evaluation processes. *Personality and Social Psychology Bulletin, 21*, 1278–1287.

Trope, Y. (1986). Self-assessment and self-enhancement in achievement motivation. In R. M. Sorrentino & E. T. Higgins (Eds.), *Handbook of motivation and cognition: Foundations of social behavior* (Vol. 1, pp. 350–378). New York: Guilford Press.

Trope, Y., & Liberman, N. (2000). Temporal construal and time-dependent changes in preference. *Journal of Personality and Social Psychology, 79*, 876–889.

Trope, Y., & Liberman, N. (2003). Temporal construal. *Psychological Review, 110*, 401–421.

Trope, Y., & Neter, E. (1994). Reconciling competing motives in self-evaluation: The role of self-control in feedback seeking. *Journal of Personality and Social Psychology, 66*, 646–657.

Trope, Y., & Pomerantz, E. M. (1998). Resolving conflicts among self-evaluative motives: Positive experiences as a resource for overcoming defensiveness. *Motivation and Emotion, 22*, 53–72.

Vallacher, R. R., & Wegner, D. M. (1987). What do people think they are doing? Action identification and human behavior. *Psychological Review, 94*, 3–15.

Vallacher, R. R., & Wegner, D. M. (1989). Levels of personal agency: Individual variation in action identification. *Journal of Personality and Social Psychology, 57*, 660–671.

Wegener, D. T., & Petty, R. E. (1994). Mood management across affective states: The hedonic contingency hypothesis. *Journal of Personality and Social Psychology, 66*, 1034–1048.

Wegener, D. T., Petty, R. E., & Smith, S. M. (1995). Positive mood can increase or decrease message scrutiny: The hedonic contingency view of mood and message processing. *Journal of Personality and Social Psychology, 69*, 5–15.

13

Positive Emotions and Cognition: Developmental, Neuroscience, and Health Perspectives

FELICIA A. HUPPERT

INTRODUCTION

While psychologists across diverse specialties have tended to focus on problems and dysfunction, there have always been a few who were more interested in human thriving—that is, in people feeling good or functioning well (Argyle, 1987; Bradburn, 1969; Jahoda, 1958; Winnicott, 1982). In 1998, during his Presidency of the American Psychological Association, Martin Seligman launched the Positive Psychology movement that brought together researchers who had already been asking questions such as why some people are happier or more resilient than others; why some people age more successfully than others; or what are the social or biological processes associated with positive emotional states. Seligman had, in short, recognized a readiness and eagerness to understand and promote positive mental states and positive behaviours, and interest in positive psychology is growing at an unprecedented rate. With this new approach comes the possibility of improving the lives of ordinary people, and not just of those with disorder or dysfunction. This conceptual shift is based on the growing recognition that positive health or well-being is more than the absence of disorder, that its determinants might not simply be the absence of risk factors for disorder, and that it deserves to be studied in its own right. Within social psychology in particular, Michael Argyle (1987) in Oxford and Ed Diener (1984) in Illinois have done much to establish the study of positive affectivity as an important aspect of understanding everyday social behaviour.

This chapter reviews some of the recent developments in the field we now call positive psychology. It examines the causes and consequences of positive mental states from both the behavioural and neuroscience perspectives, and their implications for cognitive processes, including social thinking and social behaviour. The links between positive mental states, health, and survival are also explored, along with a consideration of the underlying mechanisms.

WHY THE RELATIVE NEGLECT OF POSITIVE EMOTIONS?

Much of psychology appears to have been influenced by the medical model prevailing in the Western world—that health is simply the absence of disease, and the related concept that good functioning is simply the absence of dysfunction. This view has been quite explicit in neuropsychology, where it was assumed that we would understand the normal functioning of the brain by studying brain disorders. Certainly much insight has been gained into the neural structures and processes underlying memory, language, motor skills, and the like by studying patients with amnesia, aphasia, and apraxia, but this approach has shed little light on the mechanisms underlying above-average or exceptional performance. Similarly, in the area of mental health and emotional behaviour, the volumes of research findings on the negative emotions such as anger, fear, depression, and anxiety tell us very little about happiness, love, contentment, or compassion.

The influence of evolutionary theory has been another reason for the relative neglect of positive emotions. Evolutionary theory is dominated by the concept of survival and this has led behavioural scientists to investigate negative behaviours such as fight and flight, with their concomitant negative emotions of anger and fear. The focus has been on environmental threats and the strong in-built reactions to them. It is believed that we are hard-wired to be permanently vigilant because in survival terms the failure to fight or flee could have such disastrous consequences. Despite the fact that most of us rarely encounter life-threatening situations, high levels of anxiety are commonplace in response to very mild forms of threat, and may result in clinically diagnosed anxiety disorders (Nesse, 2005). Our physiological and behavioural responses are, however, also governed by our evolution as highly social animals. Recent research shows that among humans, even fundamental physiological reactions to challenge and threat depend to a large degree on the social knowledge that individuals bring to a given situation (Blascovich & Mendes, 2000), and on the quality of our social relationships (e.g., Cohen, Doyle, Turner, Alper, & Skoner, 2003a).

But what about the evolutionary origins of positive emotions? It has been suggested that positive emotions are associated with situations which present opportunities rather than threats, and with a strategy of approach rather than avoidance (Fredrickson, 2005; Nesse, 2005; see also Haselton & Ketelaar, this volume). It has also been suggested that the display of positive emotions in an individual is a signal to others that there is no threat in the environment. Thus, positive emotions have evolutionary benefits, since by pursuing opportunities and signalling that it is safe to approach, individuals displaying the positive emotions become more attractive to other members of the species, thereby increasing their reproductive success. In her "broaden-and-build" theory of positive emotions, Fredrickson (2001) proposes that in contrast to negative emotions which narrow the individual's repertoire of thought and action (a valuable survival strategy), positive emotions such as joy, contentment, and interest have the effect of broadening the thought–action repertoire and of building cognitive resources for the future. Recent work by cognitive social psychologists also suggests that positive and negative affective states selectively trigger different information processing styles, consistent with evolutionary principles. Thus, positive affect facilitates the use of internalized strategies using knowledge structures (assimilative thinking), while negative affect promotes a focus on external, environmental information (accommodative thinking) (see Bless & Fiedler, this volume).

DEVELOPMENTAL ORIGINS OF POSITIVE EMOTIONS

While such explanations for the evolutionary origins of positive emotions are plausible, we are on firmer ground when examining the developmental origins of positive emotions. The basic question is why do individuals show such marked differences in their levels of emotional well-being? The extraordinarily protracted period of human brain development is the key to understanding such individual differences. Unlike the other major organs of our body, our brain undergoes most of its development postnatally, and appears to be exquisitely designed to respond to the environmental conditions in which a child happens to grow up. There appears to be a sensitive period in brain development up to around age 2 (e.g., Dawson, Ashman, & Carver, 2000), but major changes and reorganization continue until puberty (Huttenlocher, 1990). Moreover, the development of our frontal lobes, which are responsible for such high-level processes as planning and emotional control, continues until early adulthood (see Keverne, 2004, 2005).

In all mammalian species, later emotional well-being and cognitive capability appear to be profoundly influenced by the early social environment. Of particular importance is the closeness of the bond between mother and infant. Pioneering studies of mother–infant bonding showed that infants with secure attachment were more confident in exploring their environment and in responding to strangers than infants whose attachment was insecure (Ainsworth & Bell, 1970). The body of research of Ainsworth and later investigators (e.g., Maccoby & Martin, 1983) provides evidence that even in infancy positive emotions are associated with positive cognitive and social behaviour that may provide a basis for resilience throughout life.

An elegant series of studies by Meaney and colleagues has taken our understanding of these processes to a deeper level. Meaney and his collaborators, using laboratory rats, have shown that high levels of maternal licking, grooming, and nursing are associated with a permanent increase in the concentration of glucocorticoid receptors in the hippocampus and prefrontal cortex (PFC) of the brain (Liu, Diorio, Day, Francis, & Meaney, 2000; Liu, Diorio, Tannenbaum, Caldji, Francis, & Freedman, 1997). These changes in the circuitry of emotion regulation have the effect of decreasing responsiveness to stressors later in life. They are also associated with improved learning and memory throughout life, presumably reflecting the important role of the hippocampus in memory processes.

Such findings begin to underpin the observations that childhood and adult well-being are linked to the development of loving and trusting relationships early in life, while the absence of such relationships due to parental neglect or abuse is associated with later behavioural problems, psychiatric disorder, and substance abuse (Leverich, Perez, Luckenbaugh, & Post, 2002).

To establish whether the beneficial effects of good maternal care stemmed directly from the mother's behaviour or was a reflection of her genetic make-up, Meaney took advantage of natural variations in rodent maternal behaviour that can be seen across generations. He took the offspring of neglectful, emotionally reactive mothers and reared them with calm, stress-resistant mothers whose maternal behaviour is characterized by high levels of licking and grooming. As adults, these offspring resembled their adoptive mothers, not their biological mothers (Meaney, 2001). Further studies show that maternal behaviour during the early postnatal period serves to programme the developing brain, including endocrine and neurotransmitter function, as well as emotional and cognitive function, and that these effects can be lifelong (Brake, Zhang, Diorio, Meaney, & Gratton, 2004; Weaver, Diorio, Seckl, Szyf, & Meaney, 2004; Weaver, Grant, & Meaney, 2002).

In view of the strength of these findings, it is surprising that so many psychologists believe that individual differences in characteristics such as happiness and cognitive ability are primarily determined by our genes. This belief is based on heritability estimates that come from twin studies, which suggest that genes account for 50% or more of the variation in trait happiness (Lykken, 2000; Lykken & Tellegen, 1996). A detailed critique of the conclusions drawn from twin studies is provided by Huppert (2005). A major problem is that such studies tend to assume that both identical and nonidentical twins experience the same family environment; they neglect the effect of the child's behaviour (influenced by the child's genes) on the parents' behaviour. Because of their genetic and hence behavioural differences, nonidentical twins do not experience the same family environment. Nonidentical twins have different genes and different environments, while identical twins have the same genes and (virtually) the same environment. As a result, twin studies routinely underestimate the importance of parental behaviour and the child's environment in emotional, social, and cognitive development.

POSITIVE EMOTIONS AND COGNITION

An impressive body of cross-sectional survey data shows that happy people tend to function better in life than less happy people, are typically more productive, more socially engaged, and tend to have higher incomes (Diener, 2000; Judge, Thoresen, Bono, & Patton, 2001). Ryan and Deci (2001) point out that people high in happiness or subjective well-being tend to have attributional styles that are more self-enhancing and more enabling than those low in subjective well-being, suggesting that happiness can lead to positive cognitions which in turn contribute to further happiness. Certainly there is a great deal of observational data showing that characteristically happy people tend to construe the same experiences and life events more favourably than unhappy people (Lyubomirsky & Tucker, 1998) and are less responsive to negative feedback (Lyubomirsky & Ross, 1999).

Observational studies, particularly cross-sectional ones, cannot of course establish the direction of causality, so it is not clear whether positive cognitions and behaviours are the consequence of happiness or its cause, or whether both are influenced by a third factor such as temperament. Longitudinal research can go some way towards establishing causal relationships, but the most persuasive evidence comes from experimental studies. Research using mood induction techniques demonstrates unequivocally that positive mood states can enhance attention and problem solving. Compared with individuals in negative or neutral mood states, subjects in a positive mood state have a broader focus of attention (see the bigger picture) (Gasper & Clore, 2000) and generate many more ideas in problem-solving tasks (Fredrickson & Branigan, 2005). Experimental social psychology is full of examples showing that positive emotional experiences have beneficial effects on the way people perceive and interpret social behaviours and the way they initiate social interactions (e.g., Forgas, 2001; Isen, 1987). It has also been found that people experiencing positive affect evaluate themselves and others more positively, make more lenient attributions, and behave in a more confident, optimistic, and generous way in interpersonal situations (Forgas, 2002; Sedikides, 1995; see also Forgas, this volume). Thus, it is clear from the experimental research on induced mood that happiness or other positive emotions can have a direct effect on cognitive performance, cognitive appraisal, and social relationships. Such findings support Fredrickson's broaden-and-build theory of positive emotions which proposes that the frequent experience of positive affect broadens cognitive processes and builds enduring coping resources which lead to later resilience (Fredrickson, 2001, 2004, 2005). Trope and colleagues (Trope, Igou, & Burke, this volume; Trope, Ferguson, & Raghunathan, 2001) have also suggested that positive emotions can act as a resource or buffer when we have to confront unpleasant tasks or information.

Positive emotions can be the consequence of certain cognitive/behavioural processes, as well as their cause. Extensive research on goal pursuit shows that enhanced subjective well-being is associated with goals being intrinsic, i.e., self-generated (e.g., Kasser & Ryan, 1996), with progress towards a valued goal (Sheldon & Kasser, 1998), the pursuit of approach goals rather than avoidance goals (Elliot, Sheldon, & Church, 1997), and the pursuit of goals congruent with personal values (Brunstein, Schultheiss, & Grassman, 1998; Sheldon & Elliot, 1999). In addition, a large body of work shows that active participation in social activities and involvement in one's community are associated with high levels of happiness and life satisfaction (Argyle, 1987; Helliwell, 2003; Helliwell & Putnam, 2004, 2005; Putnam, 2000). Taken together, the findings suggest that positive emotions lead to positive cognitions, positive behaviours, and increased cognitive capability, and that positive cognitions, behaviours, and capabilities in turn fuel positive emotions (Fredrickson & Joiner, 2002). The recognition of this upward spiral (and its reverse) forms the basis of cognitive therapy (Beck, 1979).

DO POSITIVE EMOTIONS HAVE A DOWN SIDE?

Most research on positive emotions emphasizes their beneficial effects for cognitive processes and interpersonal relationships, often contrasting these effects with the disadvantages of negative emotions. However, if we take an evolutionary perspective, we can assume that natural selection has shaped our capacities for both happiness and sadness, and that each is beneficial in certain situations, but may equally produce disbenefits in other situations. The evolutionary psychiatrist Randolph Nesse (2004, 2005) points out that by focussing almost exclusively on the disadvantages of negative states and the benefits of positive states, there has been a near total neglect of "diagonal psychology," which also considers the dangers of unwarranted positive emotions and the benefits of negative emotions in certain situations. His model is depicted in Figure 13.1.

Evidence in support of the off-diagonals (the shaded squares in Figure 13.1) comes from a number of sources. For example, positive affect is often inappropriate in situations of loss or bereavement, and may lead an observer to conclude that the person is insensitive or uncaring. Thus in some situations, negative affect is a more appropriate response, and experiencing disappointment, sadness, or grief may be beneficial for one's longer term well-being and social relationships.

There is also an extensive literature on affect as a source of information (Clore & Storbeck, this volume; Damasio, 1994), which suggests that recognizing our negative feelings is just as important as recognizing our positive feelings. For example, negative affect such as frustration or even mild depression can play a valuable role in signalling that a goal is unattainable and that it is time to pursue a different goal.

A variety of experimental studies using mood induction techniques provide important illustrations of the validity of considering a "diagonal psychology." As mentioned earlier, positive affect has many benefits for judgment and decision making, including seeing the bigger picture (Gasper & Clore, 2002; see Clore & Storbeck, this volume), in generating more ideas, and being more creative and

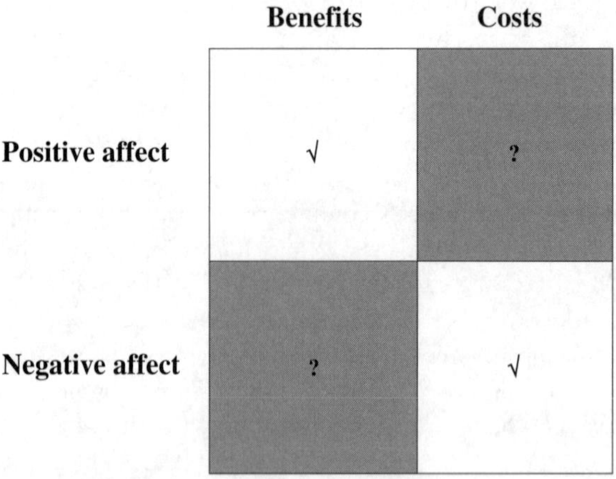

FIGURE 13.1 The concept of "diagonal psychology" (Nesse 2004, 2005), that is, the idea that we need to consider the benefits of negative affect and the costs of positive affect (shaded boxes) as well as the more commonly studied benefits of positive affect and costs of negative affect.

flexible in thinking (Ashby, Isen, & Turken, 1999; Bless, Mackie, & Schwarz, 1992; Fredrickson & Branigan, 2005; Murray, Sujan, Hirt, & Sujan, 1990). On the other hand, there is evidence that people in negative mood states are better at taking in the details of a stimulus or environment, and are more conforming and less likely to break rules (e.g., Forgas, 1998, 1999), although the latter applies to dysphoric mood states rather than anger (see Clore & Storbeck, this volume for a review of the effects of specific negative emotions).

In general, positive emotions and negative emotions appear to be associated with different styles of processing information. Fiedler contrasts these two approaches to information processing in terms of the Piggetian concepts of assimilation and accommodation. Assimilation involves imposing internalized structures onto the external world, whereas accommodation involves modifying internal structures in accordance with external conditions. Importantly, Fiedler proposes that both styles of information processing have their adaptive consequences, and that there are circumstances when it is more adaptive for an individual to be internally driven and other circumstances where it is more adaptable for them to be externally driven (see Bless & Fiedler, this volume).

An excellent illustration of the adaptive value of negative affect is seen in a recent series of experiments by Forgas, Laham, and Vargas (2005) which investigated the susceptibility to misinformation in studies of eyewitness memory, based on the well-known studies of Loftus (1979; Wells & Loftus, 2003). Loftus has shown that people are easily misled and report erroneous memories after being exposed to incorrect postevent information (Loftus, 1979), by being asked questions that contain misleading information about the original event. Following autobiographical mood induction tasks (positive, negative, or neutral) Forgas' subjects were asked a series of questions about complex photographic or naturalistic scenes that they had been exposed to earlier in the testing session. Forgas found that positive mood increased the tendency to incorporate misleading details into memory, while negative mood decreased this tendency. These data are consistent with evidence cited earlier that positive moods promote the kind of constructive, assimilative information processing style that facilitates the incorporation of misleading detail, while negative moods promote a stimulus-bound, accommodative style of information processing (Fiedler, Asbeck, & Nickel, 1991; see Bless & Fiedler, this volume). However, the importance of the Forgas study is its demonstration that negative affect has a beneficial effect on certain situations that are highly relevant to real life.

POSITIVE EMOTIONS AND PATTERNS OF BRAIN ACTIVATION

The emotion circuitry of the brain is complex, involving primarily structures in the prefrontal cortex (PFC), amygdala, hippocampus, anterior cingulated cortex, and insular cortex. These structures normally work together to process and generate emotional information and emotional behaviour. Research has particularly focussed on the PFC, since it shows very large differences in the activation of left and right sides in relation to positive and negative emotions. Davidson and his colleagues from Wisconsin are the most active researchers in this field. They have reported that induced positive and negative affective states shift the symmetry in prefrontal brain electrical activity; negative affect increases relative right-sided activation whereas positive affect increases relative left-sided activation (Davidson, 2005; Davidson, Chapman, Chapman, & Henriques, 1990). They have also reported large individual differences in baseline levels of asymmetric activation in PFC, which are related to dispositional affective style (trait affect). Individuals with a positive affective style show higher levels of left than right prefrontal activation at rest (using EEG or fMRI), while those with a negative affective style tend to show higher levels of right than left prefrontal activation at rest (Davidson, 1992; Tomarken, Davidson, Wheeler, & Doss, 1992). Further studies have shown that greater left than right prefrontal activation is associated with increased reactivity to positively valenced emotional stimuli (Tomarken, Davidson, & Henriques, 1990; Wheeler, Davidson, & Tomarken, 1993), increased ability to recover from negative affective challenge (Jackson et al., 2003), better voluntary suppression of negative affect (Jackson, Burghy, Hanna, Larson, & Davidson, 2000), and higher scores on scales measuring psychological well-being (Urry et al., 2004). Davidson has interpreted these findings as showing that the left and right PFC play differential roles in emotional processing. The recent paper by Urry et al. (2004) suggests that there are hemispheric differences in goal-directed tendencies (approach vs. avoidance) beyond those captured by positive or negative affect. They propose that the left PFC is active in response to stimuli that evoke the experience of positive affect because these stimuli induce a fundamental tendency to approach the source of stimulation.

Important links have also been reported between child development and the appearance of individual differences in patterns of brain activation. Although measures of baseline prefrontal asymmetry are stable in adults, Davidson and Rickman (1999) have shown that they are not stable during early childhood. In a cohort of around 65 children, they examined prefrontal activation asymmetry over an 8-year period from 3 to 11 years of age, and found little evidence of stability. This is a period during which high levels of plasticity are likely to occur in the brain's emotional circuitry, particularly in the PFC which is still undergoing important developmental changes at least until puberty (Huttenlocher, 1990). Life events, parental influences and other environmental factors are likely to play a crucial role during this period in establishing or shifting patterns of prefrontal activation. This is in accord with the rodent studies of Meaney and his co-workers referred to earlier, which demonstrate not only that aspects of the early postnatal environment have a profound influence on shaping the structure and function of the brain, but also that partial or even complete compensation for the damaging effects of adverse early environment is possible, following appropriate interventions around the time of puberty (Bredy, Grant, Champagne, & Meaney, 2003; Bredy, Zhang, Grant, Diorio, & Meaney, 2004; Francis, Diorio, Plotsky, & Meaney, 2002).

Of particular interest in the context of positive emotions and cognition is the neurobiological evidence that left and right frontal lobes play different roles in the processing of information. Spontaneous strategy production appears to depend critically on left PFC, while error-detection and checking processes appear to depend on right PFC (Shallice, 2004, 2006). Evidence for this differentiation, which is strikingly parallel to the processes of assimilation and accommodation referred to earlier, comes from both lesion studies and brain activation studies in normal adults. In a problem-solving task, patients with left or right prefrontal lesions were shown a series of cards containing geometric figures and asked to work out the rule governing the location of the different figures. Patients with left lateral frontal lesions were impaired in abstracting the relevant rule, while patients with right lateral prefrontal lesions showed normal performance on this task (Reverberi, Lavaroni, Gigli, Skrap, & Shallice, 2005). In a study of normal subjects, Rossi et al. (2001) used trans-cranial magnetic stimulation (TMS) to mimic the effects of cortical lesions. Subjects were asked to make recognition judgments for each of 96 magazine pictures, half of which they had been shown previously. Performance on this task is known to be determined by the effectiveness of strategies used at the time of encoding, and the ability to differentiate between old and new pictures at the time of retrieval. Consistent with the hypothesis that the left frontal cortex plays a crucial role in strategy production and the right frontal cortex is vital for checking and monitoring, the study found that performance was impaired if TMS was presented to the left frontal cortex at encoding or to the right frontal cortex at retrieval. Subjects made over 40% false positive responses when TMS was presented to the right frontal cortex at retrieval, suggesting that the criteria for recognition responses were excessively lax.

On the basis of the evidence available to date, a consistent picture is emerging which suggests a strong association between, on the one hand, positive emotions, internally driven behaviour, and left frontal activation; and on the other, negative emotions, externally driven behaviour, and right frontal activation. However, at present, studies tend to focus either on affect or on cognition, but future research will need to make more explicit links between affective and cognitive neuroscience. They will also need to develop a more detailed understanding of the affective/cognitive processes in distinct regions of the PFC (dorsolateral, ventromedial, orbitofrontal), as well as other brain areas.

POSITIVE EMOTIONS AND HEALTH

It has been known for a long time that negative emotions are related to a higher prevalence and severity of disease, but how strong is the evidence for a link between positive emotions and health? And if there is a link, what might be the pathways from positive emotions to health—biological, cognitive, social? In this section, when we refer to positive and negative emotions, we generally mean enduring or long-term emotional states, which we can regard as trait-like affect or affective style, although some of the research also examines the effects of affective states.

There are many large-scale correlational studies of the association between positive affect (questions about happiness or life satisfaction) and physical health status, but the latter is usually measured in terms of self-reported health rather than more objective measures of disease or functional ability. Although positive affect and self-reported health are highly positively correlated (e.g., Donovan & Halpern, 2002; Helliwell, 2003), these correlations may be spurious because there is evidence that people high in positive affect tend to under-report symptoms of illness (e.g., Cohen, Doyle, Turner, Alper, & Skoner, 2003b). Cross-sectional studies in general do not provide a firm basis for concluding that positive emotions influence health, because we cannot establish the direction of causality; in particular, an observed relationship could be predominantly the result of physical health influencing affective state. For this reason, the most persuasive evidence comes from longitudinal studies that examine the influence of affective traits on subsequent health outcomes, or from experimental studies that investigate the effect of affective states on physiological functioning.

In a prospective longitudinal study of a large, representative British population sample, Huppert and Whittington (2003) found that the probability of survival over a 7-year interval was related to positive well-being (positive emotions and attitude) at baseline 7 years earlier. Positive well-being was measured in terms of the number of positively worded items endorsed on the General Health Questionnaire (GHQ-30 of Goldberg, 1978), a widely used and well-validated mental health questionnaire. This relationship held even when adjustments were made for sociodemographic factors, baseline physical health and lifestyle, and baseline measures of blood pressure and respiratory function. Interestingly, scores on the negatively worded items were not strongly associated with subsequent survival. A similar separation between the effects of positive and negative mental states was reported by Ostir, Markides, Peek, and Goodwin (2001), who were examining the predictors of stroke in an elderly population sample. Using the positively worded items of a depression screening scale (the CES-D), they found that lower positive scores at baseline were associated with a greater risk of stroke over the 6-year follow-up, even when adjustments for other health-related conditions were made. The negatively worded items were not associated with the incidence of stroke, and controlling for scores on the negatively worded items did not reduce the association of positive well-being with stroke.

A related finding has been reported in the famous Nun Study (Danner, Snowdon, & Friesen, 2001). A group of ageing nuns had all written brief autobiographical sketches when they entered the convent (generally around age 20), and these sketches were recently found and categorized according to the number of positive statements they contained. It was reported that nuns in the lower half of the distribution of positive statements died on average 9 years sooner than those in the top category of positive statements. This finding is all the more remarkable because from their early twenties the lives of the nuns were as close to identical as human lives can be, so the difference in survival was not related to their lifestyle or circumstances in the intervening period but to their positive emotions six decades earlier.

It has been postulated that one of the physiological mediators underlying the relationship between positive affect and survival is the functioning of the immune system. For example, high levels or prolonged secretion of the stress hormone cortisol is damaging to immune function. Davidson and colleagues have shown that individuals with a positive affective style have a higher level of immune function than those with a negative affective style (Rosenkranz et al., 2003). They have gone on to demonstrate that an intervention that increases positive emotions is associated with enhanced functioning of the immune system (Davidson et al., 2003). This intervention involved training volunteers in the techniques of mindfulness meditation, then giving them an influenza vaccine and examining how strong an antibody response they mounted to the vaccine. Six months after vaccination, the meditation group had produced almost twice as many antibodies as the control group, providing strong support for the notion that positive emotional states can boost immune function.

Experimental studies have also confirmed that positive emotions can have a beneficial effect on physical health. For example, Cohen et al. (2003b) assessed several hundred healthy volunteers for their tendency to experience positive and negative emotions, and subsequently gave them nasal drops containing a cold virus, and monitored them in quarantine for the development of a common cold. They found that the higher the level of positive emotional style, the lower the risk of developing a cold. Negative emotional style was not associated with cold, and the association of positive style and cold was independent of negative style.

Most experimental studies however, manipulate emotions rather than disease. For example, Fredrickson, Mancuso, Branigan, and Tugade (2000) exposed volunteers to a stressful task (preparing to explain to a panel of judges "Why I am a good friend"), followed by a mood induction procedure. Measures of cardiovascular function such as heart rate and blood pressure revealed that subjects in a positive mood state showed a much more rapid recovery to baseline levels than those in a negative or neutral mood state. Prolonged reactivity to stress is known to be harmful, while a rapid recovery from stress is beneficial for health. A similar finding in a group of older adults has been reported by Levy, Hausdorff, Hencke, and Wei (2000), showing high levels of cardiovascular reactivity to stress following exposure to negative age stereotypes, but reduced stress reactivity with positive age stereotypes.

A recent, scholarly review of well-designed prospective and experimental studies (Pressman & Cohen, 2006) concludes that there is firm evidence for a beneficial effect of positive emotions on physical health and survival, and that this effect may be independent of the level of negative affect. However, this review also cites studies that show deleterious effects of positive emotions on physical health, which occur when the level of arousal is very high.

There are a number of pathways through which positive emotions can exert their beneficial effects on health. Evidence cited above supports the view that positive emotional states can have direct and usually beneficial effects on physiological, hormonal, and immune functions that in turn influence health outcomes. The magnitude and direction of these effects appear to be related to the level of affective arousal, such that very high levels of happiness or excitement can produce physiological effects which are comparable to those produced by negative affect (see Pressman & Cohen, 2006).

Behavioural and social factors may also mediate the link between positive emotions and health. Happier people tend to have healthier lifestyles (Watson, 1988), and in the social realm, they tend to have more friends and also more positive interpersonal experiences (Diener, Suh, Lucas, & Smith, 1999). Thus, the health benefits of positive emotional states may not be directly attributable to positive feelings, but to health practices or social factors (e.g., social support) that are known to have major effects on health and life expectancy.

An important conclusion that arises from reviewing studies of positive emotion and health is that there is a major gap in the research. While there is strong evidence for a relationship between positive emotions and the absence of disorder, or a reduced severity or duration of disorder, there appears to be a dearth of research on the relationship between positive emotions and good health. This is primarily because studies rarely attempt to measure positive health—being really well. For major advances in our understanding of positive emotions and their effects on health, we need to develop both survey measures and biological markers of good health. Measures of vitality are the closest things we have at present to survey measures of good health, but it is not clear whether vitality is primarily a measure of physical health or of psychological health. On the biological side, it is not yet known whether there are any specific patterns of physiological, hormonal, or immune responses that are characteristic of positive health rather than the absence of health problems, although it has been suggested that a particular diurnal pattern of secretion of the stress hormone cortisol (low on awakening, rapid but moderate rise in the morning, low in the evening) may prove to be a useful indicator of good health (Thorn, Hucklebridge, Esgate, Evans, & Clow, 2004).

CONCLUDING REMARKS

The positive psychology movement has been very effective in drawing the attention of the research community to the need to develop a better understanding of positive emotions, attitudes, appraisals, and values (Keyes, 2002a; Linley & Joseph, 2004; Seligman, 2002; Snyder & Lopez, 2001). However, within the domain of emotions, care must be taken to recognize that positive emotions are not always beneficial and that negative emotions are not always detrimental, and hence to pursue a diagonal psychology (Nesse, 2004, 2005).

More broadly, when examining the relationship between positive emotions and cognition, there is a need to establish whether specific positive emotions are associated with different forms of information processing, in the same way that different negative emotions are associated with different socio-cognitive processes and behaviours (Clore & Storbeck, this volume). In her elegant studies using induced mood techniques, Fredrickson routinely compares high and low arousal positive moods (joy, contentment) with high and low arousal negative moods (anger, sadness) and a neutral condition, but to date there are no reports of differential effects on cognitive processing of the different types of positive moods. In future studies of behaviour, health, and affective neuroscience, there is a case for paying more attention to possible differences in the role of energetic positive emotions such as happiness and joy, compared with low energy positive emotions such as tranquillity, relaxation, and contentment.

In relation to effects on physical health, it is difficult at present to make direct links between the cognitive effects of emotions and their health effects. However, the evidence for differences in underlying neurological activation for positive and negative emotions, and the information processing styles associated with them, may provide a mechanism for understanding the differential effects of positive and negative emotions on physical health. This is an area that is ripe for further investigation.

Most researchers and practitioners of positive psychology tend to take an individualistic approach, focussing on those attributes of an individual that are related to their subjective well-being (happiness, optimism, competence, self-realization). However, it is clear that the way in which an individual relates to others and to their society is a key component in their subjective well-being, and should accordingly play a larger role in mainstream positive psychology. This has been explicitly stated by Keyes (2002b). While the value of social connectedness and social support for physical and mental well-being has been known for a long time, further research is needed on the relative contribution of individual versus interpersonal characteristics to subjective well-being.

The crucial role that personal relationships and social networks play in establishing and maintaining a sense of well-being may be linked to an evolutionary perspective, pointing to the importance of sociability and acceptance in survival and reproduction. It has been suggested that the dominant focus of modern consumer societies on the fulfilment of individual needs and desires is at odds with the basic human need for a sense of belonging. Indeed, it could be argued that much consumption in modern industrialized societies is driven precisely by unsatisfied belongingness and identity needs, as more and more products are marketed not in terms of their real utility values, but in terms of their symbolic identity values. This is of course a futile enterprise, since material consumption ultimately cannot satisfy these deep-seated social needs, and this may account for the absence of increased well-being despite ever-increasing materialism and consumption.

REFERENCES

Ainsworth, M. D., & Bell, S. M. (1970). Attachment, exploration, and separation: Illustrated by the behaviour of one-year-olds in a strange situation. *Child Development, 41*, 49–67.

Argyle, M. (1987). *The psychology of happiness*. London: Methuen.

Ashby, F. G., Isen, A. M., & Turken, A. U. (1999). A neuropsychological theory of positive affect and its influence on cognition. *Psychological Review, 106(3)*, 529–550.

Beck, A. T. (1979). *Cognitive therapy and the emotional disorders*. New York: Penguin.

Blascovich, J., & Mendes, W. B. (2000). Challenge and threat appraisals: The role of affective cues. In J. Forgas (Ed.), *Feeling and thinking: The role of affect in social cognition* (pp. 59–82). Paris: Cambridge University Press.

Bless, H., Mackie, D. M., & Schwarz, N. (1992). Mood effects on encoding and judgmental processes in persuasion. *Journal of Personality and Social Psychology, 63*, 585–595.

Bradburn, N. M. (1969). *The structure of psychological well-being*. Chicago, IL: Alding Publishing Co.

Brake, W. G., Zhang, T. Y., Diorio, J., Meaney, M. J., & Gratton, A. (2004). Influence of early postnatal rearing conditions on mesocorticolimbic dopamine and behavioural responses to psychostimulants and stressors in adult rats. *European Journal of Neuroscience, 19(7)*, 1863–1874.

Bredy, T. W., Grant, R. J., Champagne, D. L., & Meaney, M. J. (2003). Maternal care influences neuronal survival in the hippocampus of the rat. *European Journal of Neuroscience, 18(10)*, 2903–2909.

Bredy, T. W., Zhang, T. Y., Grant, R. J., Diorio, J., & Meaney, M. J. (2004). Peripubertal environmental enrichment reverses the effects of maternal care on hippocampal development and glutamate receptor subunit expression. *European Journal of Neuroscience, 20(5)*, 1355–1362.

Brunstein, J. C., Schultheiss, O. C., & Grassman, R. (1998). Personal goals and emotional well-being: The moderating role of motive dispositions. *Journal of Personality and Social Psychology, 75*, 494–508.

Cohen, S., Doyle, W. J., Turner, R., Alper, C. M., & Skoner, D. P. (2003a). Sociability and susceptibility to the common cold. *Psychological Science, 14(5)*, 389–395.

Cohen, S., Doyle, W. J., Turner, R. B., Alper, C. M., & Skoner, D. P. (2003b). Emotional style and susceptibility to the common cold. *Psychosomatic Medicine, 65(4)*, 652–657.

Damasio, A. R. (1994). *Descartes' error: Emotion, reason and the human brain*. New York: Avon.

Danner, D., Snowdon, D., & Friesen, W. (2001). Positive emotions in early life and longevity: Findings from the Nun Study. *Journal of Personality and Social Psychology, 80(5)*, 804–813.

Davidson, R. J. (1992). Emotion and affective style: Hemispheric substrates. *Psychological Science, 3*, 39–43.

Davidson, R. J. (2005). Well-being and affective style: Neural substrates and biobehavioral correlates. In F. A. Huppert, N. Baylis, & B. Keverne (Eds.), *The science of well-being* (pp. 107–139). Oxford: Oxford University Press.

Davidson, R. J., Chapman, J. P., Chapman, L. P., & Henriques, J. B. (1990). Asymmetrical brain electrical activity discriminates between psychometrically-matched verbal and spatial cognitive tasks. *Psychophysiology, 27*, 238–543.

Davidson, R. J., Kabat-Zinn, J., Schumacher, J., Rosenkrantz, M., Muller, D., Santorelli, S. F., Urbanowski, F., Harrington, A., Bonus, K., & Sheridan, J. F. (2003). Alterations in brain and immune function produced by mindfulness meditation. *Psychosomatic Medicine, 65*, 564–570.

Davidson, R. J., & Rickman, M. (1999). Behavioral inhibition and the emotional circuitry of the brain: Stability and plasticity during the early childhood years. In L. A. Schmidt & J. Schulkin (Eds.), *Extreme fear and shyness: Origins and outcomes* (pp. 67–68). New York: Oxford University Press.

Dawson, G., Ashman, S. B., & Carver, L. J. (2000). The role of early experience in shaping behavioural and brain development and its implications for social policy. *Development and Psychopathology, 12*, 695–712.

Diener, E. (1984). Subjective well-being. *Psychological Bulletin, 95*, 542–575.

Diener, E. (2000). Explaining differences in societal levels of happiness: Relative standards, need fulfilment, culture and evaluation theory. *Journal of Happiness Studies, 1(1)*, 41–78.

Diener, E., Suh, E. M., Lucas, R. E., & Smith, H. L. (1999). Subjective well-being: Three decades of progress. *Psychological Bulletin, 125*, 276–302.

Donovan, N., & Halpern, D. (2002). Life satisfaction: The state of knowledge and implications for Government. Prime Minister's Strategy Unit. (http://www.strategy.gov.uk/2001/futures/attachments/ls/paper.pdf)

Elliot, A. J., Sheldon, K. M., & Church, M. A. (1997). Avoidance personal goals and subjective well-being. *Personality and Social Psychology Bulletin, 23,* 915–927.

Fiedler, K., Asbeck, J., & Nickel, S. (1991). Mood and constructive memory effects on social judgment. *Cognition and Emotion, 5,* 363–378.

Forgas, J. P. (1998). On feeling good and getting your way: Mood effects on negotiating strategies and outcomes. *Journal of Personality and Social Psychology, 74,* 565–577.

Forgas, J. P. (1999). On feeling good and being rude: Affective influences on language use and request formulations. *Journal of Personality and Social Psychology, 76,* 928–939.

Forgas, J. P. (2001). *The handbook of affect and social cognition.* Mahwah, NJ: Lawrence Erlbaum Associates, Inc.

Forgas, J. P. (2002). Feeling and doing: Affective influences on interpersonal behavior. *Psychological Inquiry, 13(1),* 1–28.

Forgas, J. P., Laham, S., & Vargas, P. (2005). Mood effects on eyewitness memory: Affective influences on susceptibility to misinformation. *Journal of Experimental Social Psychology, 41,* 574–588.

Francis, D. D., Diorio, J., Plotsky, P. M., & Meaney, M. J. (2002). Environmental enrichment reverses the effects of maternal separation on stress reactivity. *Journal of Neuroscience, 22(18),* 7840–7843.

Fredrickson, B. L. (2001). The role of positive emotions in positive psychology: The broaden-and-build theory of positive emotions. *American Psychologist, 56,* 218–226.

Fredrickson, B. L. (2004). Gratitude, like other positive emotions, broadens and builds. In R. A. Emmons & M. E. McCullough (Eds.), *The psychology of gratitude* (pp. 145–166). New York: Oxford University Press.

Fredrickson, B. L. (2005). The broaden-and-build theory of positive emotions. In F. A. Huppert, N. Baylis, & B. Keverne (Eds.), *The science of well-being* (pp. 217–238). Oxford: Oxford University Press.

Fredrickson, B. L., & Branigan, C. (2005). Positive emotions broaden the scope of attention and thought-action repertoires. *Cognition and Emotion, 19(3),* 313–332.

Fredrickson, B. L., & Joiner, T. (2002). Positive emotions trigger upward spirals toward emotional well-being. *Psychological Science, 13(2),* 172–175.

Fredrickson, B. L., Mancuso, R. A., Branigan, C., & Tugade, M. M. (2000). The undoing effect of positive emotions. *Motivation and Emotion, 24,* 237–258.

Gasper, K., & Clore, G. L. (2000). Do you have to pay attention to your feelings to be influenced by them? *Personality and Social Psychology Bulletin, 26,* 698–711.

Gasper, K., & Clore, G. L. (2002). Attending to the big picture: Mood and global versus local processing of visual information. *Psychological Science, 13,* 34–40.

Goldberg, D. P. (1978). *Manual of the general health questionnaire.* Windsor: NFER-Nelson.

Helliwell, J. F. (2003). How's life? Combining individual and national variations to explain subjective well-being. *Economic Modelling, 20,* 331–360.

Helliwell, J., & Putnam, R. D. (2004). The social context of well-being. *Philosophical Transactions of the Royal Society of London, series B, 359,* 1435–1446.

Helliwell, J., & Putnam, R. D. (2005). The social context of well-being. In F. A. Huppert, N. Baylis, & B. Keverne (Eds.), *The science of well-being* (pp. 435–459). Oxford: Oxford University Press.

Huppert, F. A. (2005). Positive mental health in individuals and populations. In F. A. Huppert, N. Baylis, & B. Keverne (Eds.), *The science of well-being* (pp. 307–340). Oxford: Oxford University Press.

Huppert, F. A., & Whittington, J. E. (2003). Evidence for the independence of positive and negative well-being: Implications for quality of life assessment. *British Journal of Health Psychology, 8*, 107–122.

Huttenlocher, P. R. (1990). Morphometric study of human cerebral cortex development. *Neuropsychologia, 28*, 517–527.

Isen, A. M. (1987). Positive affect, cognitive prcesses and social behaviour. In L. Berkowitz (Ed.), *Advances in experimental social psychology* (Vol. 20, pp. 203–253). New York: Academic Press.

Jackson, D. C., Burghy, C. A., Hanna, A. J., Larson, C. L., & Davidson, R. J. (2000). Resting frontal and anterior temporal EEG asymmetry predicts ability to regulate negative emotion. *Psychophysiology, 37*, S50.

Jackson, D. C., Mueller, C. J., Dolski, I., Dalton, K. M., Nitschke, J. B., Urry, H. L., Rosenkranz, M. A., Ryff, C. D., Singer, B. H., & Davidson, R. J. (2003). Now you feel it, now you don't: Frontal brain electrical asymmetry and individual differences in emotion regulation. *Psychological Science, 14*, 612–617.

Jahoda, M. (1958). *Current concepts of positive mental health.* New York: Basic Books.

Judge, T. A., Thoresen, C. J., Bono, J. E., & Patton, G. K. (2001). The job satisfaction-job performance relationship: A qualitative and quantitative review. *Psychological Bulletin, 127(3)*, 376–407.

Kasser, T., & Ryan, R. M. (1996). Further examining the American dream: Differential correlates of intrinsic and extrinsic goals. *Personality and Social Psychology Bulletin, 22*, 280–287.

Keverne, E. B. (2004). Understanding well-being in the evolutionary context of brain development. *Philosophical Transactions of the Royal Society of London, series B, 359*, 1349–1358.

Keverne, E. B. (2005). Understanding well-being in the evolutionary context of brain development. In F. A. Huppert, N. Baylis, & B. Keverne (Eds.), *The science of well-being* (pp. 35–56). Oxford: Oxford University Press.

Keyes, C. (2002a). *Flourishing: Positive psychology and the life well lived.* Washington, DC: American Psychological Association.

Keyes, C. (2002b). Promoting a life worth living. Human development from the vantage points of mental illness and mental health. In R. M. Lerner, F. Jacobs, & D. Wertlieb (Eds.), *Handbook of applied developmental science* (Vol. 4, Chap. 15, pp. 257–274). California: Sage Publications.

Leverich, G. S., Perez, S., Luckenbaugh, D. A., & Post, R. M. (2002). Early psychosocial stressors: Relationship to suicidality and course of bipolar illness. *Clinical Neuroscience Research, 2*, 161–170.

Levy, B. R., Hausdorff, J. M., Hencke, R., & Wei, J. Y. (2000). Reducing cardiovascular stress with positive self-stereotypes of aging. *Journals of Gerontology B Psychological Science and Social Science, 55(4)*, 205–213.

Linley, P. A., & Joseph, S. (Eds.) (2004). *Positive psychology in practice.* New Jersey: John Wiley & Sons.

Liu, D., Diorio, J., Day, J. C., Francis, D. D., & Meaney, M. J. (2000). Maternal care, hippocampal synaptogenesis and cognitive development in rats. *Nature and Neuroscience, 3(8)*, 799–806.

Liu, D., Diorio, J., Tannenbaum, B., Caldji, C., Francis, D., & Freedman, A. (1997). Maternal care, hippocampal glucocorticoid receptors and hypothalamic-pituitary-adrenal responses to stress. *Science, 277*, 1659–1662.

Loftus, E. F. (1979). *Eyewitness testimony*. Cambridge: Harvard University Press.

Lykken, D. (2000). *Happiness: The nature and nurture of joy and contentment*. New York: St Martin's Press.

Lykken, D., & Tellegen, A. (1996). Happiness is a stochastic phenomenon. *Psychological Science, 7(3)*, 186–189.

Lyubomirsky, S., & Ross, L. (1999). Changes in attractiveness of elected, rejected and precluded alternatives: A comparison of happy and unhappy individuals. *Journal of Personality and Social Psychology, 76*, 988–1007.

Lyubomirsky, S., & Tucker, K. L. (1998). Implications of individual differences in subjective happiness for perceiving, interpreting and thinking about life events. *Motivation and Emotion, 22*, 155–186.

Maccoby, E. E., & Martin, J. A. (1983). Socialization in the context of the family: Parent-child interaction. In P. H. Mussen (Ed.) & E. M. Hetherington (Vol. Ed.), *Handbook of child psychology: Vol. 4. Socialiation, personality, and social development* (4th ed., pp. 1–101). New York: Wiley.

Meaney, M. J. (2001). Maternal care, gene expression, and the transmission of individual differences in stress reactivity across generations. *Annual Reviews of Neuroscience, 21*, 1161–1192.

Murray, N., Sujan, H., Hirt, E. R., & Sujan, M. (1990). The influence of mood on categorization: A cognitive flexibility interpretation. *Journal of Personality and Social Psychology, 59*, 411–425.

Nesse, R. (2004). Natural selection and the elusiveness of well-being. *Philosophical Transactions of the Royal Society of London, series B, 359*, 1333–1348.

Nesse, R. (2005). Natural selection and the elusiveness of happiness. In F. A. Huppert, N. Baylis, & B. Kevernes (Eds.). *The science of well-being* (pp. 3–32). Oxford: Oxford University Press.

Ostir, G. V., Markides, K. S., Peek, M. K., & Goodwin, J. S. (2001). The association between emotional well-being and the incidence of stroke in older adults. *Psychosomatic Medicine, 63(2)*, 210–215.

Pressman, S. D., & Cohen, S. (2006). Does positive affect influence health? *Brain, Behavior, and Immunity, 20*, 175–181.

Putnam, R. D. (2000). *Bowling alone*. New York: Simon & Schuster.

Reverberi, C., Lavaroni, A., Gigli, G. L., Skrap, M., & Shallice, T. (2005). Specific impairments of rule induction in different frontal lobe subgroups. *Neuropsychologia, 43*, 460–472.

Rosenkranz, M. A., Jackson, D. C., Dalton, K. M., Dolski, I., Ryff, C. D., Singer, B. H., Muller, D., Kalin, N. H., & Davidson, R. J. (2003). Affective style and in vivo immune response: Neurobehavioral mechanisms. *Proceedings of the National Academy of Science, 100(19)*, 11148–11152.

Rossi, S., Cappa, S. F., Babiloni, C., Pasualetti, P., Miniussi, C., Carducci, F., Babiloni, F., & Rossini, P. M. (2001). Prefrontal cortex in long-term memory: An 'interference' approach using magnetic stimulation. *Nature Neuroscience, 9*, 948–952.

Ryan, R. M., & Deci, E. L. (2001). On happiness and human potentials: A review of research on hedonic and eudaimonic well-being. *Annual Reviews of Psychlogy, 52*, 141–166.

Sedikides, C. (1995). Central and peripheral self-conceptions are differentially influenced by mood: Tests of the differential sensitivity hypothesis. *Journal of Personality and Social Psychology, 69(4)*, 759–777.

Seligman, M. (2002). *Authentic happiness*. New York: Free Press.

Shallice, T. (2004). The fractionation of supervisory control. In M. S. Gazzaniga (Ed.), *The cognitive neurosciences III* (pp. 943–956). Cambridge, MA: MIT Press.

Shallice, T. (2006). Contrasting domains in the control of action: The routine and the non-routine. In Y. Munakata & M. Johnson (Eds.), *Attention and performance XXI: Processes of change in brain and cognitive development*. New York: Oxford University Press.

Sheldon, K. M., & Elliot, A. J. (1999). Goal striving, need satisfaction, and longitudinal well-being: The self-concordance model. *Journal of Personality and Social Psychology, 76*, 482–497.

Sheldon, K. M., & Kasser, T. (1998). Pursuing personal goals: Skills enable progress but not all progress is beneficial. *Personality and Social Psychology Bulletin, 24*, 1319–1331.

Snyder, C. R., & Lopez, S. J. (Eds.). (2001). *Handbook of positive psychology*. USA: Oxford University Press.

Thorn, L., Hucklebridge, F., Esgate, A., Evans, P., & Clow, A. (2004). The effect of dawn simulation on the cortisol response to awakening in healthy participants. *Psychoneuroendocrinology, 29(7)*, 925–930.

Tomarken, A. J., Davidson, R. J., & Henriques, J. B. (1990). Resting frontal brain asymmetry predicts affective responses to films. *Journal of Personality and Social Psychology, 59*, 791–801.

Tomarken, A. J., Davidson, R. J., Wheeler, R. E., & Doss, R. C. (1992). Individual differences in anterior brain asymmetry and fundamental dimensions of emotion. *Journal of Personality and Social Psychology, 62*, 676–687.

Trope, Y., Ferguson, M., & Raghunathan, R. (2001). Mood as a resource in processing self-relevant information. In J. P. Forgas (Ed.), *Handbook of affect and social cognition* (pp. 256–274). Mahwah, NJ: Lawrence Erlbaum Associates, Inc.

Urry, H. L., Nitschke, J. B., Dolski, I., Jackson, D. C., Dalton, K. M., Mueller, C. J., Rosenkranz, M. A., Ryff, C. D., Singer, B. H., & Davidson, R. J. (2004). Making a life worth living: Neural correlates of well-being. *Psychological Science, 15(6)*, 367–372.

Watson, D. (1988). Intraindividual and interindividual analyses of positive and negative affect: Their relation to health complaints, perceived stress and daily activities. *Journal of Personality and Social Psychology, 54(6)*, 1020–1030.

Weaver, I. C., Diorio, J., Seckl, J. R., Szyf, M., & Meaney, M. J. (2004). Early environmental regulation of hippocampal glucocorticoid receptor gene expression: Characterization of intracellular mediators and potential genomic target sites. *Annals of the New York Academy of Science, 1024*, 182–212. Review.

Weaver, I. C., Grant, R. J., & Meaney, M. J. (2002). Maternal behavior regulates long-term hippocampal expression of BAX and apoptosis in the offspring. *Journal of Neurochemistry, 82(4)*, 998–1002.

Wells, G. L., & Loftus, E. F. (2003). Eyewitness memory for people and events. In Goldstein, A. M. (Ed.), *Handbook of psychology: Forensic psychology* (Vol. 11, pp. 149–160). New York: John Wiley & Sons.

Wheeler, R. E., Davidson, R. J., & Tomarken, A. J. (1993). Frontal brain asymmetry and emotional reactivity: A biological substrate of affective style. *Psychophysiology, 30*, 82–89.

Winnicott, D. W. (1982). *Playing and reality*. London: Routledge.

14

Managing Affective States

RALPH ERBER and SUSAN MARKUNAS

*M*anaging affect is of key importance in everyday life. Consider the following two situations:

> Eddy is furious sitting on the bench for almost the entire third quarter. Sure, he missed an easy lay-up and then goofed up on defense to allow the opponent two easy scores. But for coach to yank him from the game and keep him—a first round NBA draft pick—on the bench was both ridiculous and humiliating. His teammates urge him to calm down, but Eddy ignores them, and instead alternates between angrily crushing empty Gatorade cups and sending hostile stares in the direction of the coaching staff.

> To say that the mood in the locker room was celebratory would be an understatement. Even though the final and deciding game of the NBA championship series ended almost half an hour ago, the players kept spraying each other with champagne while trying to smoke the really expensive cigars the team's owner had delivered. But the repeated knocks on the door signify that it was, at last, time for the league-mandated meeting with the reporters who had gathered outside. Michael walks over to his locker to take a long, mournful look at the picture of his father, who had been murdered 2 years ago.

Both of these scenes have played themselves out, if not exactly as we described, perhaps in a fashion that is reasonably close. Apart from revealing the enduring passion for basketball on the part of one of the authors, they illustrate a couple of fascinating instances of affect regulation. Eddy tried very hard to maintain his anger, perhaps to give him a competitive edge in the event if he ever gets back into the game. Michael tried equally hard to regain his sense of cool before facing the cameras and the millions of fans who were undoubtedly watching. Instances in which regulatory efforts are directed toward maintaining negative affect or getting rid of positive affect are in all likelihood not limited to those with enough athleticism and talent to play professional sports. Think about times when you held on to your grief over the loss of a loved one or your anger over being treated unfairly. Or think about times when you checked your feelings of happiness before entering a classroom to deliver a lecture about the implications of Bayesian Theorem. We agree that instances of affect regulation such as these may not be ubiquitous and perhaps not even typical. But we wholeheartedly disagree with those who claim that they represent "counterintuitive versions of affect regulation" that play little more than a "peripheral role" in terms of various regulation outcomes (Larsen & Prizmic, 2004).

THE RANGE OF REGULATORY TASKS

To suggest that affect regulation is primarily a matter of maintaining positive affect and repairing negative affect represents an oversimplification at best. It appears that to achieve a thorough understanding of how people manage their affective states requires consideration of the full range of regulatory tasks. This would suggest that we need to include the maintenance as well as the attenuation of positive and negative affective states as depicted in Figure 14.1 (Parrott, 1993).

To the extent that the management of affective states can be viewed as an instance of self-regulation, it is important to note that it is likely accomplished on several levels. Just like many other processes of self-regulation, affect regulation can operate in the absence of conscious awareness, intentions, and strategic goals (e.g., Forgas & Ciarrochi, 2002). Not surprisingly, then, there is evidence that sleep, especially REM sleep, and dreaming serve an affect-regulatory function (e.g., Perlis & Nielsen, 1994). Insufficient sleep has been linked to problems in the diurnal regulation of mood (Dahl & Lewin, 2003). There are also plenty of indications that affect regulation can be traced to specific structures in the brain. Specifically, it appears that the lateral prefrontal cortex (Paradiso, Chermerinski, Yazici, Tartaro, & Robinson, 1999), the hippocampus (Mintun, Sheline, Moerlein, Vlassenko, Huang, & Snyder, 2004), and the basal ganglia (Lacerda et al., 2003) form neural circuits involved in the management of affect. On the neural level, GABA neurons and their interactions with serotonin have also been implicated in affect regulation (Taylor, Bhagwagar, Cowen, & Sharp, 2003).

As fascinating as findings like these may be, for social psychologists those processes that occur with conscious awareness are of somewhat greater interest. How do people go about managing their affective states in a more volitional fashion? An early yet enduring answer to this question was initially provided by Alice Isen and her colleagues (Clark & Isen, 1982; Isen, 1984) who suggested that the management of affective states could primarily be understood in terms of *positive*

	Maintain	Attenuate
Positive Affect		
Negative Affect		

FIGURE 14.1 The range of affect regulation according to Parrott (1993).

affect maintenance and *negative affect repair*. The idea that affect management can be conceptualized in these terms is appealing because it capitalizes on lasting psychological ideas about pleasure and pain (Dollard & Miller, 1950; Thorndike, 1898). Most positive affective states are inherently pleasant and thus one should expect individuals experiencing such states to maintain them. At the same time, most negative affective states are inherently aversive and thus individuals experiencing them should mobilize available resources to repair them (Taylor, 1991). Some (e.g., Clark & Isen, 1982) have even claimed that this tendency was so strong that it would fail to manifest itself only when individuals suffer from a depletion of the cognitive and behavioral resources necessary to bring about affect repair.

If managing affective states were solely a matter of maintaining positive affect and repairing negative affect, one might be compelled to review the many strategies people employ in pursuit of these goals (Larsen & Prizmic, 2004), including, but not limited to, distraction (Larsen & Cowan, 1988), diet and exercise (Thayer, 2001), and perhaps mood-incongruent recall (Parrot & Sabini, 1990). However, as we mentioned earlier, the management of affective states is quite a bit more complicated because it can be the product of strategic goals that may override the simple desire to feel good. Parrott and Sabini (1990) were among the first to show that, under some conditions, people may be compelled to attenuate (or repair) their positive affect and maintain their negative affect. In one study, students in a large psychology class who had just received their grades on an exam were asked to recall three memories from their high school years. An inspection of the first memories recalled revealed some surprising results. Specifically, the first memory recalled by participants who had done better on the exam than expected (and thus were presumed to be in a good mood) was generally more negative than the first memory recalled by those who had done worse than expected (and thus were presumed to be in a bad mood). Analogous findings were obtained when the autobiographical memory task was administered to students entering a university library on a sunny day (when they were ostensibly happy) or a rainy day (when they were ostensibly unhappy).

The results of these field studies cannot easily be accounted for by confounds that may have contaminated the results because of the lack of random assignment. Two controlled laboratory studies (Parrott & Sabini, 1990; Studies 3 and 4) produced virtually identical results. Together, these findings pose an important challenge to the idea that people would always try to maintain positive moods and repair negative moods. Even though evidence for mood repair surfaced in all four studies, the hedonic view of affect regulation has difficulty accounting for the repeated observation that happy participants attempted to down-regulate their positive moods. After all, it proposes that the ultimate goal of individuals is to *maintain* positive affect and *repair* negative affect. The maintenance of positive affect results in the continuation of happy feelings (reward), whereas the repair of negative affect will result in the discontinuation of sad feelings (removal of the aversive situation). If nothing else, Parrott and Sabini's (1990) findings add to our suspicion that the management of positive and negative affect may not be primarily determined by simple principles of pleasure seeking and pain avoidance. Our suspicion is further supported by a sizable literature showing that sad participants frequently fail to repair their bad moods and that happy participants frequently fail to maintain their good moods.

MANAGING NEGATIVE AFFECT

Self-Esteem

Looking at the management of negative affect first, it appears that the extent to which individuals attempt to repair negative moods depends on a number of variables broadly related to the self. Smith and Petty (1995) provide a convincing case for the importance of self-esteem for negative affect regulation. In three studies employing different manipulations of sad mood, participants high in self-esteem consistently responded to a sad mood induction by recalling mood incongruent, that is, happy memories. However, participants low in self-esteem responded to a sad mood induction by recalling mood congruent (i.e., unhappy) memories. In fact, the more negative participants low in self-esteem were feeling, the more negative were the memories they recalled.

Of course, to demonstrate differences in the response patterns between participants low and high in self-esteem, by itself, does not explain why these differences exist in the first place. However, when Smith and Petty (1995, Study 3) presented participants with positive and negative material to be recalled, low self-esteem participants still recalled more negative items whereas high self-esteem participants recalled more positive items. In other words, low self-esteem participants failed to repair their mood even when the experimenter had provided them with the tools to accomplish just that. Thus, it appears that the different modes of responding among participants high and low in self-esteem can be traced to differences in motivation rather than ability.

It is important to note that high self-esteem provides no guarantee against the experience of negative affect. Although individuals high in self-esteem are very adept at employing mood incongruent recall in the service of managing negative affect, they are also uniquely vulnerable to the experience of intense negative affective states. The reason for their vulnerability is related to the way in which individuals high in self-esteem organize beliefs about the self into distinct positive and negative self-categories. When situational forces maintain the activation of negative self-aspects, compartmentalization of this sort can perpetuate a negative mood because of the relative inaccessibility of positive aspects of the self that could potentially aid in repairing it (Showers & Kling, 1996).

Expectancies

Regardless of self-esteem, there is evidence that individuals' ability to repair negative affective states may depend on their generalized expectancies for negative affect regulation. Catanzaro and Mearns (1990) developed a Negative Mood Regulation (NMR) scale to measure individual differences in people's expectancy that some behavior or cognitive activity will alleviate a negative mood. As expected, individuals scoring high on NMR reported fewer symptoms of depression than individuals with low scores and thus low expectancies for mood regulation. Presumably, strong expectations about one's ability to regulate negative mood aid in summoning effective strategies to repair a sad mood and help prevent the onset of depressive symptoms. Strong NMR expectancies also seem to serve as an important buffer for the emotional fallout following a relationship breakup, at least during the time immediately following the breakup (Mearns, 1991). Not surprisingly, NMR expectancies are not limited to regulating feelings of dysphoria but extend to anxiety and performance. In one study (Catanzaro, 1996), college students with weak NMR expectancies at the beginning of the semester performed more poorly in an exam than students with high NMR expectancies who seemed unaffected if not aided by their anxiety about the exam.

As with most individual differences, there is a question where they come from in the first place. It appears that NMR expectancies are related to differences in attachment (Bartholomew & Horowitz, 1991; Hazan & Shaver, 1987). In support of this link, Creasey (2003) reports that preoccupied individuals generally have less confidence in their NMR expectancies than secure and dismissing individuals. It may be that lowered NMR expectations among preoccupied individuals contribute to the increased psychological problems they report.

At any rate, NMR expectancies may be particularly important because of their propensity to offset the effects of rumination that are common for many negative affective states—dysphoria and depression included (Joorman & Siemer, 2004; Nolen-Hoeksema, 1993). One way to distinguish chronically depressed people from temporarily dysphoric people is by the inability of the former to turn their attention away from the symptoms, causes, and consequences of their depression and toward affectively neutral or even positive activities (Nolen-Hoeksema, 1993). As a result of repeated failures to employ regulatory strategies effectively, depressed people may well acquire lowered expectancies for the effective regulation of their profound negative affective state. Additionally, it may be that a focus on the events surrounding a negative affective state promotes the retrieval of mood congruent memories that would aid in the maintenance of the negative affect. In support of this idea, Rusting and DeHart (2000) found that sad mood participants with strong NMR expectancies were most likely to engage in mood incongruent retrieval when they were provided with an opportunity to recall positive memories. No such differences were observed among participants with weak NMR expectancies.

To the extent that mood congruent cognitions aid in the maintenance of negative affect while mood incongruent cognitions aid in its repair, healthy individuals may deploy them to manage fluctuations in their daily moods. In support of such a homeostatic notion of affect regulation, Forgas and Ciarrochi (2002) found that participants in whom either a happy or sad mood had been induced initially responded to a variety of tasks in a mood congruent fashion. However, over time, these initial responses became reversed and were eventually replaced by mood incongruent responses. Forgas and Ciarrochi (2002) interpret these findings as being due to an automatic decay in mood congruency followed by a motivated shift to mood incongruency ostensibly in the service of achieving an affective balance.

Emotional Intelligence

In light of findings that nondepressed individuals seem perfectly capable of managing fluctuations in their moods most of the time, one might well ask whether individuals high in emotional intelligence might be even better at it. By definition, emotional intelligence is "the capacity to reason about emotions, and of emotions to enhance thinking. It includes the abilities to accurately perceive emotions, to access and generate emotions so as to assist thought, to understand emotions and emotional knowledge, and to reflective regulate emotions so as to promote emotional and intellectual growth" (Mayer & Salovey, 1997; see also Ciarrochi & Blackledge, this volume).

But even though the regulation of affect is one of the four branches of emotional intelligence, "the exact manner in which emotions are managed with emotional intelligence is left open in the theory" (Mayer, 2001, p. 423). Given the lack of theoretical specificity that would link emotional intelligence to affect regulation, it is not surprising that virtually no attempt has been made to link the two empirically. The notable exception is a study by Gohm (2003), who reasoned that individuals' affective experience can be classified by the meta-emotion traits of clarity, attention, and intensity provided by emotional intelligence theory. Emotional clarity refers to the ability to identify and describe specific emotions. Attention to emotion reflects the tendency to recognize and value emotional experiences. Emotional intensity concerns the magnitude with which an individual typically experiences emotions.

Based on this analytic scheme, Gohm (2003) identified four types of individuals with distinct ways of responding to inductions of sad mood (hot, overwhelmed, cerebral, and cool). Both the hot and overwhelmed reported more intense feelings of negative affect than the cerebral and cool types. However, compared to the hot, the overwhelmed were more confused about the nature and meaning of their affective experience (i.e., lacked clarity). Not surprisingly, the mood induced in the cerebral and cool types decayed fairly rapidly while the mood of the hot remained intact. However, the mood of the overwhelmed improved over the course of the experimental session. To help account for this pattern of results, Gohm (2003, Study 3) provided participants with explicit instructions to avoid the influence of their mood for a subsequent task. As it turns out, the overwhelmed type was the only one to react to this cue by trying to actively attenuate his/her sad mood.

Should these findings be interpreted to suggest that those who experience intense negative affect but are confused about its meaning are superior affect managers? Perhaps not. What seems clear, though, is that the intensity of negative affect, by itself, is not sufficient for the initiation of regulatory efforts. Rather, it appears that efforts toward negative affect regulation are most likely to be initiated when the affect is intense *and* accompanied by confusion or uncertainty.

Regulatory Focus

Up to this point we have looked at the management of negative affect primarily in terms of avoiding versus maintaining pain. However, this may be a bit of an oversimplification. As Higgins (1997, 2001) has reminded us, there are many different forms of pain. Negative affect can stem from the absence of positive outcomes and may be experienced as dejection. Alternatively, negative affect can stem from the presence of negative outcomes and may be experienced as agitation. In addition to producing qualitatively different affective experiences, the absence of positive outcomes is characterized by a promotion focus involving a move toward a desired state. The presence of negative outcomes is related to a prevention focus involving a move away from an undesired state.

Self-regulatory focus theory is firmly tied to the principle of pleasure-seeking and pain avoidance. Thus, it does not allow us to predict when individuals will seek to repair or maintain negative affect. Rather, it suggests that how people go about it depends importantly on the nature of their affective experience. People saddened by the lack of friends may actively pursue avenues toward a more enriched social life; people saddened by negative performance-related feedback may try to prevent similar occurrences in the future. To the best of our knowledge no attempts have been made to empirically test hypotheses about the role of promotion versus prevention focus in the management of negative affect. However, one study (Hirt & McCrea, 2001) reports results that could be interpreted as showing that happy people maintain their happiness through employing strategies consistent with a prevention focus.

MANAGING POSITIVE AFFECT

Relative to the management of negative affect, the self-regulation of happiness, joy, and elation has received little attention. This makes a certain amount of sense. People are often troubled by feelings of anger, sadness, or irritation, and their performance often suffers as a result of being in these states. They rarely report being disturbed by prolonged and intense feelings of happiness, joy, and elation. Negative affect often signals that something may be terribly wrong or amiss while positive affect signals that everything is fine (e.g., McDougall, 1923). So why bother studying how people manage positive affect. And do they manage it at all?

One very good reason for studying positive affect management comes from the increasing recognition that positive affect can have profound effects on physical and mental health, and is especially important for the recovery from negative emotional experiences (Fredrickson, 1998). It is fortunate in that regard that humans appear to be amazingly adept at manufacturing happiness even out of misery (Gilbert, 2005). But manufacturing happiness is quite different from maintaining it. The path to maintaining happiness is littered with sharp objects that can cut into our happiness despite all intentions to maintain it.

In our daily lives these sharp objects often come in the form of tasks we have to undertake. Few of us can base their decisions on whether to go to work, write a paper, or file a tax return on the possible ramifications of such activities for our happiness. However, it is engaging in these types of activities that often absorbs our happiness and returns it to a state of affective neutrality. Erber and Tesser (1992) asked participants in happy moods to complete either a simple (additions and subtractions) or difficult math task (long division and multiplication) in 15 minutes. When they measured participants' moods at the end of the 15-minute period, those who had worked on the simple math task still felt happy. However, the mood of participants who had completed the difficult task was comparable to the moods of participants in the control (neutral mood) condition. Participants in the difficult task condition also recalled fewer details relating to the positive mood induction than participants in the simple task condition. Thus, it appears that the cognitive activity required for the difficult task provided a level of distraction that absorbed participants' moods.

There is reason to believe that people, at least implicitly, recognize the vulnerability of their happy moods and thus scrutinize the hedonic contingencies of their activities for their moods. To test this idea, Wegener and Petty (1994) presented participants in whom a happy, neutral, or sad mood was induced with a choice of different videotapes to watch for a second part of the experiment. All tapes had ostensibly been rated by other students in terms of their interest level and proclivity to induce happiness. Consistent with the hedonic contingency hypothesis, happy participants based their choices primarily on how happy they thought the tapes would make them feel. Sad and neutral mood participants did not submit the tapes to the same kind of hedonic scrutiny.

Close scrutiny of the affective consequences of our activities may be particularly important because the self-regulation of happiness is subject to paradoxical effects. According to the "pleasure paradox" (Wilson, Centerbar, Kermer, & Gilbert, 2005), many of the processes used to make sense of positive events can reduce the pleasure people receive from them. Some participants received an unexpected gift along with an index card that contained a seemingly arbitrary set of statements (e.g., "We like to promote random acts of kindness") that left the reasons for the gift relatively uncertain. Other participants received the gift with a card that provided a somewhat better explanation for the gift ("Why do we do this? We like to promote random acts of kindness"). Participants in both conditions were both surprised and happy about receiving the unexpected gift. However, happiness persisted longer for those with more uncertainty about the reason for the gift. Presumably, getting closure for the causes of one's happiness terminates the cognitive activity necessary to maintain it.

Paradoxical effects of a different sort have been observed among people who try not to experience happiness. Wegner, Erber, and Zanakos (1993) asked participants not to get into a happy mood as they were reminiscing about a happy event in their lives (something that would ordinarily make them happy). Some participants did the suppression task while they were under cognitive load while others did it without being burdened by load. As it turns out, the unburdened participants were pretty successful in controlling their happy mood. However, those who attempted to control their happiness while under load failed miserably, experiencing the very happiness they were trying so hard to control. As paradoxical as this finding may be, it makes perfectly good sense. We may try to regulate our happiness, but concurrent tasks in which we might engage not only prevent us from achieving our goals but instead produce ironic and counterintentional effects.

The preceding discussion may suggest that managing happiness and other positive affective states is primarily a matter of affect maintenance. If down-regulation of positive affect is observed, it appears to be a matter of self-regulation failure. However, there are many instances in which people deliberately choose to check their feelings of happiness. We discuss them in the context of the social constraints model of affect regulation.

THE SOCIAL CONSTRAINTS MODEL OF AFFECT REGULATION

We (Erber, 1996; Erber & Erber, 2000; Erber, Wegner, & Therriault, 1996) created the social constraints model of mood regulation (SCM) specifically to account for the full range of affect regulation, including the maintenance of negative affect and the "repair" of positive affect. Unlike the majority of affect regulation models, the SCM awards pleasure seeking and pain avoidance a minor role at best. Sure, given a choice most people would probably opt to be happy rather than sad. But the choices we make in this regard are often constrained by the unique demands of our social environment. In fact, there are social constraints that may dictate the down-regulation, or attenuation, of positive affect. For example, being happy is perfectly fine at one's birthday party yet wildly inappropriate at someone's funeral. The extent to which people may up-regulate their negative affect may similarly be influenced by the presence or absence of social constraints. Being sad may bother us little when we are alone in our room and may well remain unregulated. On the other hand, when our room is filled with guests helping us celebrate our birthday, that same sadness may be just as inappropriate as the happiness at the funeral.

From this perspective then, the actual, imagined, or implied presence of others may act as the major constraint on the kind of affect we can reasonably experience. Strangers in particular may place powerful constraints on our affective experience in part because we know little about how they are feeling and how they may evaluate us when we are feeling happy or sad. Consequently, the presence of others may motivate us to relinquish both sad and happy moods and may compel us to seek a state of relative affective neutrality.

Being Cool and Collected

To test our ideas about the power of others to attenuate our moods, we (Erber, Wegner, & Therriault, 1996) used an anticipation-of-interaction paradigm. We first made participants happy or sad through exposure to cheerful or depressing music. Subsequently, half the participants were led to believe that, following the main experiment, they would work on an unrelated (and unspecified) task either by themselves or with another participant across the hall. All participants were then asked to indicate their preference for a set of newspaper stories, identified by their headlines as uplifting, depressing, or affectively neutral. In line with our theoretical expectations, participants who expected to complete the second part of the experiment by themselves preferred mood congruent stories: happy participants indicated a preference for cheerful stories while sad participants preferred depressing stories. As expected, this pattern of preferences was reversed among participants who expected to complete the second part of the experiment with the stranger across the hall. In these conditions, happy participants preferred depressing stories whereas sad participants preferred cheerful stories.

This apparent predilection to be cool and collected when entering into an interaction with a stranger seems to be fairly robust as we were able to replicate it with different mood manipulations and different dependent measures.

Interestingly, participants' attempts at regulating their moods were aimed at neutralizing both their happy and sad moods. This was even the case when we told participants about how the stranger across the hall was ostensibly feeling. We found no evidence to suggest that participants regulated their mood in such a way as to match the other's mood. Attempts at attenuation were observed in all but one condition: Happy participants who expected to work with a stranger described as "somewhat depressed" attempted to bolster their mood prior to meeting him/her.

Affect Regulation in Response to Task Demands

As we alluded to earlier, our affective experience is often constrained by the tasks we carry out in our daily lives. As Gohm (2003) has shown, people have an implicit understanding that their affect may interfere with task performance. In an initial test of the idea that task demands may lead to the attenuation of both happy and sad moods, we (Erber & Erber, 1994) asked students enrolled in sections of the same introductory psychology course to recall either a happy or sad autobiographical memory. Half the participants completed this task at the beginning of class; the remainder completed it at the end of class. Following the initial recall task we asked all participants to recall a second autobiographical memory of their choice. Two independent judges then rated the content of the second memories in terms of their happiness or sadness. As we expected, anticipating the task of participating in class acted as an important constraint that motivated participants to regulate their moods in the direction of attenuation. Participants who initially recalled a sad memory generated happy memories whereas participants who initially recalled a happy memory recalled a sad memory. Participants who completed the task at the end of class faced no such constraints and thus recalled mood congruent memories the second time around.

Because the findings reported by Erber and Erber (1994) were based on a study conducted in a naturalistic setting, they are, of course, open to alternative explanations. Sad participants who recalled mood congruent memories when the task was administered at the end of class may have done so less because they had no reason to regulate their moods. They may simply not have bothered because they reasonably expected that their experience outside the classroom (e.g., lunch, meeting friends) would provide ample opportunities for mood regulation. However, we have reason to believe in the veracity of our preferred explanation based on recent research in which we varied task demands as part of a decision-making task.

Affect Regulation and Decision-Making

Affect is related to decision-making in a myriad of ways (see Baumeister, Vohs, & Tice, this volume), yet to date little is known about the extent to which people might strategically regulate their affect prior to making decisions. A few years ago, Alan Greenspan, chairman of the US Federal Reserve Bank, warned investors not to get carried away by irrational exuberance. In issuing this warning, Greenspan was obviously concerned that a large number of investors basing their decisions more on their affect than the value of the stock might have adverse, if not disastrous, consequences for the stock market, the economy, and possibly world peace. His concern was well-advised from the perspective of economic theory (Shiller, 2000). However, the SCM suggests that concerns with irrational exuberance may themselves be a bit irrational, particularly when it comes to previously induced positive affect that is carried over into a decision-making context (i.e., decision-irrelevant positive affect).

Specifically, the SCM predicts that irrational exuberance (and positive affect generally) might drive decisions primarily when the stakes are low. On the other hand, decisions with high stakes may act as a constraint that might motivate people to check their positive affect so as to be able to proceed in a cool and level-headed fashion. Again, the assumption is that people are aware of the potentially deleterious consequences of their positive affect, and are particularly mindful of them in situations that carry a high degree of risk.

To test the idea that people would attempt to set aside their moods prior to making a decision with high stakes, we (Erber, Erber, & Poe, 2004) asked participants in happy and sad moods to make decisions involving either low or high stakes. The experimental procedure was identical to the one used by Erber et al. (1996) with one exception. Instead of anticipating a subsequent task to be completed alone or with a stranger, participants who were required to earn a total of 5 research credits to pass the course anticipated making decisions that would lead to either small gains or losses (1 research credit) or larger losses (2 research credits) based on their performance. In other words, participants in the low stakes conditions believed that their performance would at best result in one additional research credit and at worst in having a credit taken away. In the high stakes conditions, the respective gains and losses amounted to nearly half the total credits required. As expected, participants led to believe that their performance would result in small gains or losses showed no evidence of mood regulation. However, when the stakes were high and participants believed that their performance might result in large gains or losses, happy participants preferred information that would decrease their happiness and sad participants preferred information that would decrease the sadness.

Implications of the Social Constraints Model

At the risk of sounding self-serving, we believe that the SCM provides a promising framework from which to understand the self-regulation of affect. It suggests that affect, by itself, may not serve as a primary motivational force that determines its maintenance and attenuation. Rather, it predicts that people are equally sensitive to the situational constraints that operate in their experience of affect. When social constraints are absent, positive and negative affect is maintained. It is primarily when social constraints are present that people make attempts to attenuate both positive and negative affect. As such, the model is helpful because it covers the full range of affect management expressed by Parrott's (1993) factorial mentioned at the beginning of this paper. It helps us make sense of Eddy's attempts at keeping his anger and Michael's attempts to diminish his happiness. Our research further indicates that the maintenance of negative affect and the attenuation of positive affect represent neither self-regulation failures nor instances of affect regulation that are counterintentional and peripheral as Larsen and Prizmic (2004) has claimed.

Finally, even though the focus of the SCM is on the influence of constraints that are social in nature, it can nonetheless help account for the myriad of variables that have been shown to influence the management of negative affect. We can look at self-esteem, expectancies, emotional intelligence, and regulatory focus as individual difference variables. Ultimately, however, they are part of the self. And the self does not exist in isolation from the social environment but is instead a part of it. Consequently, constraints originating from the self are ultimately social constraints as well.

REFERENCES

Bartholomew, K., & Horowitz, L. M. (1991). Attachment styles among young adults: A test of the four category model. *Journal of Personality and Social Psychology*, 61, 226–244.

Catanzaro, S. J. (1996). Negative mood regulation expectancies, emotional distress, and examination performance. *Personality and Social Psychology Bulletin*, 22, 1023–1029.

Catanzaro, S. J., & Mearns, J. (1990). Measuring generalized expectancies for negative-mood regulation: Initial scale development and implications. *Journal of Personality Assessment*, 54, 546–563.

Clark, M. S., & Isen, A. M. (1982). Toward understanding the relationship between feeling states and social behavior. In A. Hastorf & A. M. Isen (Eds.), *Cognitive social psychology* (pp. 73–108). New York: Elsevier.

Creasey, G. (2003). Psychological distress in college-aged women: Links with unresolved/preoccupied attachment status and the mediating role of negative mood regulation expectancies. *Attachment and Human Development*, 4, 261–277.

Dahl, R. E., & Lewin, D. S. (2003). Sleep and depression. In G. Stores & L. Wiggins (Eds.), *Sleep disturbance in children and adolescents with disorders of development: Its significance and management. Clinics in developmental medicine* (Vol. 155, pp. 161–168). New York: Cambridge University Press.

Dollard, J., & Miller, N. E. (1950). *Personality and psychotherapy*. New York:McGraw-Hill.

Erber, R. (1996). The self-regulation of moods. In L. L. Martin & A. Tesser (Eds.), *Striving and feeling: Interactions among goals, affect, and self-regulation*. Mahwah, NJ: Lawrence Erlbaum Associates, Inc.

Erber, R., & Erber, M. W. (1994). Beyond mood and social judgment: Mood incongruent recall and mood regulation. *European Journal of Social Psychology*, 24, 79–88.

Erber, R., & Erber, M. W. (2000). The self-regulation of moods: Second thoughts on the importance of happiness in everyday life. *Psychological Inquiry*, 11, 142–148.

Erber, R., Erber, M. W., & Poe, J. (2004). Mood regulation and decision-making: Is irrational exuberance really a problem? In I. Brocas & J. D. Carrillo (Eds.), *The psychology of economic decisions, Vol. II: Reasons and choices*. London, UK: Oxford University Press.

Erber, R., & Tesser, A. (1992). Task effort and the regulation of mood: The absorption hypothesis. *Journal of Experimental Social Psychology*, 28, 339–359.

Erber, R., Wegner, D. M., & Therriault, N. (1996). On being cool and collected: Mood regulation in anticipation of social interaction. *Journal of Personality and Social Psychology*, 70, 757–766.

Forgas, J. P., & Ciarrochi, J. V. (2002). On managing moods: Evidence for the role of home-ostatic cognitive strategies in affect regulation. *Personality and Social Psychology Bulletin, 28*, 336–345.

Fredrickson, B. L. (1998). What good are positive emotions? *Review of General Psychology, 2*, 300–319.

Gilbert, D. T. (2005, January 20). Four more years of happiness. *New York Times*.

Gohm, C. (2003). Mood regulation and emotional intelligence: Individual differences. *Journal of Personality and Social Psychology, 84*, 594–607.

Hazan, C., & Shaver, P. (1987). Romantic love conceptualized as an attachment process. *Journal of Personality and Social Psychology, 52*, 511–524.

Higgins, E. T. (1997). Beyond pleasure and pain. *American Psychologist, 52*, 1280–1300.

Higgins, E. T. (2001). Promotion and prevention experiences: Relating emotions to non-emotional states. In J. P. Forgas (Ed.), *Handbook of affect and social cognition* (pp. 186–211). Mahwah, NJ: Lawrence Erlbaum Associates, Inc.

Hirt, E. R., & McCrea S. M. (2001). Beyond hedonism: Broadening the scope of affect regulation. *Psychological Inquiry, 11*, 180–183.

Isen, A. M. (1984). Toward understanding the role affect in cognition. In R. S. Wyer, Jr. & T. Srull (Eds.), *Handbook of social cognition* (pp. 179–236). Hillsdale, NJ: Lawrence Erlbaum Associates, Inc.

Joorman, J., & Siemer, M. (2004). Memory accessibility, mood regulation, and dysphoria: Difficulties in repairing sad mood with happy memories? *Journal of Abnormal Psychology, 113*, 179–188.

Lacerda, A., Nicoletti, M. A., Brambilla, P., Sassi, R. B., Mallinger, A. G., Frank, E., Kupfer, D. J., Keshavan, M. S., & Soares, J. C. (2003). Anatomical MRI study of basal ganglia in major depressive disorder. *Psychiatry Research: Neuroimaging, 124*, 129–140.

Larsen, R. J., & Cowan, G. S. (1988). Internal focus of attention and depression: A study of daily experience. *Motivation and Emotion, 12*, 237–249.

Larsen, R. J., & Prizmic, Z. (2004). Affect regulation. In R. Baumeister & K. D. Vohs (Eds.), *Handook of self-regulation* (pp. 40–61). New York: Guilford.

Mayer, J. D. (2001). Emotion, intelligence, and emotional intelligence. In J. P. Forgas (Ed.), *Handbook of affect and social cognition*. Mahwah, NJ: Lawrence Erlbaum Associates, Inc.

Mayer, J. D., & Salovey, P. (1997). What is emotional intelligence? In P. Salovey & D. Sluyter (Eds.), *Emotional development and emotional intelligence: Educational implications* (pp. 3–31). New York: Basic Books.

McDougall, W. (1923). *Outline of psychology*. New York: Scribner.

Mearns, J. (1991). Coping with a breakup: Negative mood regulation expectancies and depression following the end of a romantic relationship. *Journal of Personality and Social Psychology, 60*, 327–334.

Mintun, M. A., Sheline, Y. I., Moerlein, S. M., Vlassenko, A. G., Huang, Y., & Snyder, A. Z. (2004). Decreased hippocampal 5-HT–sub(A) recepror binding in major depressive disorder: In vivo measurement with [-sup1-sup-8F] altanserin positron emission tomography. *Biological Psychiatry, 55*, 217–224.

Nolen-Hoeksema, S. (1993). Sex differences in control of depression. In D. M. Wegner & J. W. Pennebaker (Eds.), *Handbook of mental control* (pp. 306–324). Englewood Cliffs, NJ: Prentice-Hall.

Paradiso, S., Chermerinski, E., Yazici, K. M., Tartaro, A., & Robinson, R. G. (1999). Frontal lobe syndrome reassessed: Comparison of patients with lateral or medial frontal brain damage. *Journal of Neurology, Neurosurgery & Psychiatry, 67*, 664–667.

Parrott, W. G. (1993). Beyond hedonism: Motives for inhibiting good moods and for maintaining bad moods. In D. M. Wegner & J. W. Pennebaker (Eds.), *Handbook of mental control.* Englewood Cliffs, NJ: Prentice-Hall.

Parrott, W. G., & Sabini, J. (1990). Mood and memory under natural conditions: Evidence for mood-incongruent recall. *Journal of Personality and Social Psychology, 59,* 321–336.

Perlis, M. L., & Nielsen, T. A. (1994). Mood regulation, dreaming, and nightmares: Evaluation of a desensitization function for REM sleep. *Dreaming, 3,* 243–257.

Rusting, C. L., & DeHart, T. (2000). Retrieving positive memories to regulate negative mood: Consequences for mood-congruent memory. *Journal of Personality and Social Psychology, 78,* 737–752.

Shiller, R. J. (2000). *Irrational exuberance.* Princeton, NJ: Princeton University Press.

Showers, C. J., & Kling, K. C. (1996). Organization of self-knowledge: Implications for recovery from sad mood. *Journal of Personality and Social Psychology, 70,* 578–590.

Smith, S. M., & Petty, R. E. (1995). Personality moderators of mood congruency effects on cognition. The role of self-esteem and negative mood regulation. *Journal of Personality and Social Psychology, 68,* 1092–1107.

Taylor, M., Bhagwagar, Z., Cowen, P. J., & Sharp, T. (2003). GABA and mood disorders. *Psychological Medicine, 33,* 387–393.

Taylor, S. E. (1991). The asymmetrical effects of positive and negative event: The mobilization–minimization hypothesis. *Psychological Bulletin, 110,* 67–85.

Thayer, R. E. (2001). *Calm energy: How people regulate mood with food and exercise.* London: Oxford University Press.

Thorndike, E. L. (1898). Animal intelligence: An experimental study of the associative process in animals. *Psychological Monographs, 2,* 1–109.

Wegener, D. T., & Petty, R. E. (1994). Mood management across affective states: The hedonic contingency hypothesis. *Journal of Personality and Social Psychology, 66,* 1034–1048.

Wegner, D. M., Erber, R., & Zanakos, S. (1993). Ironic processes in the mental control of mood and mood-related thought. *Journal of Personality and Social Psychology, 65,* 903–912.

Wilson, T. D., Centerbar, D. B., Kermer, D. A., & Gilbert, D. T. (2005). The pleasure of uncertainty: Prolonging positive moods in ways people do not anticipate. *Journal of Personality and Social Psychology, 88,* 5–21.

Part IV

Affect and Social Behavior

15

Affective Influences on Interpersonal Behavior: Towards Understanding the Role of Affect in Everyday Interactions

JOSEPH P. FORGAS

W hat is the role of affect in the way people perceive, respond to, and interact with each other? Are happy or sad persons better at creating a positive impression, making a successful request, or producing effective persuasive arguments? Does a happy mood predispose us to be more cooperative and optimistic in a negotiation? Most people are intuitively aware that their feelings do seem to have a profound influence on their thoughts, judgments, and behaviors. Philosophers and writers have also long been fascinated by the complex influence of affect on interpersonal relations. Few things make us more happy, or upset us more than the way others react to our interpersonal strategies. It is rather surprising then that the influence of affect on interpersonal behaviors received surprisingly little empirical attention in the past. This chapter will survey recent evidence suggesting that affective states indeed play a significant role in the way people plan and execute many everyday interpersonal strategies. Further, it will be argued that these effects can be largely understood in terms of the kind of information processing strategies people adopt when thinking about and planning their social interaction strategies. A comprehensive theory linking these processes, the Affect Infusion Model (AIM), will also be described (Forgas, 1995a, 2002).

HISTORY AND BACKGROUND

The study of interpersonal behavior has traditionally been one of the core areas of social psychology. However, when we consider the rich literature on impression management, verbal and nonverbal communication, social influence strategies or relationship formation, only a few studies have explicitly looked at the role of affect in these phenomena until quite recently. It was not until the early 1980s that psychologists such as Zajonc (1980, 2000) first argued that affective reactions often constitute the primary dimension of interpersonal behavior, and function as an independent and often dominant force in determining people's social strategies and responses. According to this view, affect is not just one of the three tradition-al faculties of the human mind—and the most neglected one at that—but one of the primary forces driving most interpersonal behaviors. Affective reactions large-ly determine how people perceive and cognitively represent everyday social episodes (Forgas, 1979, 1982), and how they categorize many kinds of social stim-uli (Niedenthal & Halberstadt, 2000).

This review will suggest that affect influences social behavior through its effects on the *content* and the *process* of cognition. Social living is only possible because humans possess an elaborate cognitive capacity to perceive and evaluate others, infer their intentions, and respond with sophisticated and highly adapt-able interpersonal strategies (Heider, 1958). Indeed, it has been suggested that the evolution of the immense computational capacity of the human brain was largely driven by the demands to coordinate ever-more complex and intricate interpersonal processes in increasingly sophisticated and adaptable human groups (Dunbar, 2004). The very recent and dramatic transformation of social life from the simple, face-to-face primary groups that characterized most of human history to contemporary, anonymous mass societies in the past few hun-dred years imposes ever greater challenges on individuals. As most of our social interactions now involve strangers and superficially known others, the cognitive demands of successful interpersonal behavior have also increased exponentially (Goffman, 1972; Heider, 1958). A number of theories as well as numerous empirical studies suggest that as cognitive strategies that drive behavior become more complex and elaborate, the influence of affective states also increases (Forgas, 1995a, 2000, 2001, 2002).

Many early social theorists saw affect as a subversive influence on effective interpersonal behavior (Machiavelli, 1961). Freud's psychoanalytic speculations also emphasized the dangerous and invasive character of affective impulses. However, this simplistic view has been challenged in recent years, as a conse-quence of important advances in neuroanatomy, psychophysiology, and social cognition, showing that affect is often a useful and even necessary component of adequate social responses (Adolphs & Damasio, 2001; Damasio, 1994; Ito & Cacioppo, 2001). The last few decades in particular produced much empirical research demonstrating the important functional role of affect in many social behaviors.

When thinking about affect, we need to distinguish between two qualitative-ly different kinds of affective phenomena: emotions and moods. Moods, unlike emotions, are relatively low-intensity, diffuse, and long-lasting affective states that are often subconscious and have no salient cause. Unlike more intense emotions, moods often escape our conscious attention. Paradoxically, their effects on social thinking and behavior tend to be potentially more insidious, enduring, and con-sistent, and may impact on both individual and group behaviors (Kelly & Spoor, this volume). Much research on the behavioral consequences of affect has focused on moods. In contrast, emotions are more intense, less durable, and are usually conscious with a great deal of cognitive content. Because emotions are replete with specific knowledge pertaining to their origin, cause, and consequences, the behavioral consequences of emotions tend to be less consistent and highly situation and context specific.

In this review we will consider two fundamental kinds of affective influences on interpersonal behavior: (1) theories and empirical studies that demonstrate that affective states influence the *content and valence* of social thinking and behavior, and (2) theories and studies that demonstrate that affect also influences the *process* that people adopt when responding to social situations.

AFFECT CONGRUENCE AND AFFECT INFUSION: FEELING GOOD, THINKING GOOD, AND ACTING GOOD

Perhaps the most universal influence of affect is that it colors our thoughts and responses in an affect-congruent manner. When we feel good, we tend to see the world through rose-colored glasses. When depressed, everything appears bleak and gloomy. Several early studies demonstrated affect-congruent influences on social behavior, although the mechanisms responsible for these effects were poorly understood. For example, Razran (1940) reported that affect had a marked mood-congruent effect on how people responded to attempts at persuasion. People who were made to feel bad by an aversive smell also made more negative judgments about unrelated issues than those who felt good after receiving a free lunch. Such spontaneous, and often unconscious, "affect congruence" appears to be a very common and reliable everyday phenomenon. Why exactly do these effects occur?

Psychoanalytic theories suggested that affective impulses may invade and color unrelated thoughts unless sufficient "pressure" is exerted to control them. Within such a framework, Feshbach and Singer (1957) found that attempts to suppress fear increased the tendency to see "another person as fearful and anxious" suggesting that "suppression of fear facilitates the tendency to project fear onto another social object" (p. 286). Alternative, conditioning theories maintained that such dynamic assumptions are not necessary, as affect may spontaneously attach itself to unrelated responses simply due to temporal and spatial associations. For example, people who feel bad because of the excessive heat and humidity in a room will respond more negatively to a person they just met in such a situation due to a conditioned association between their affect and the target person (Clore & Byrne, 1974). However, these effects are not universal, and neither psychoanalytic theories nor theories based on "blind" conditioning principles can explain the apparent situation- and context-sensitivity of affect infusion.

Two complementary psychological mechanisms responsible for such affect-congruent reactions were identified in recent affect-cognition theories. Affect may influence the *content and valence* of social behaviors through influencing *memory* processes (the affect priming theory; see also the chapter by Eich and Macaulay, this volume), and due to the mistaken inferential use of affect as information (the affect-as-information model).

According to the *affect priming theory*, affect should influence social behaviors through selectively priming and facilitating the use of affect-congruent constructs (Bower, 1981; Bower & Forgas, 2001). This model assumes that representations about the social world are linked to affective states within an associative network of memory. Experiencing an affective state thus automatically primes related constructs and memories, facilitating their use in constructive interpersonal tasks. Such affective priming of interpersonal behaviors is most likely in complex and demanding social situations that call for open, constructive processing that promotes the use of affectively primed information (Eich & Macauley, 2000; Fiedler, 2000; Forgas, 1995a, 2002; Sedikides, 1995). Recent neuroanatomical evidence provides strong convergent "evidence for the inseparable relation between emotion and other aspects of cognition. Our everyday experience also clearly shows that affect influences essentially all other aspects of cognitive functioning, including memory, attention, and decision making" (Adolphs & Damasio, 2001, p. 44).

As actors need to rely on past experiences and memory-based information to make sense of complex social events, the more complex or unusual a situation, the more likely that we will have to extensively search our memories to make sense of it, and the greater the likelihood that affect will influence the kind of ideas we access and the interpretations we make. Thus, affect infusion increases when an open, constructive thinking style is adopted to deal with difficult, unusual situations, as only this kind of thinking promotes the incidental use of affectively primed information (Forgas, 1995a, 2002). Thus, paradoxically, people are much more influenced by their temporary mood when responding to difficult, intractable personal problems in their romantic relationship, but mood effects are weaker when easier issues are considered (Forgas, 1994). Recent integrative theories such as the AIM (Forgas, 1995a) and accumulating evidence supporting it suggest that the nature and extent of affective influences on social behavior largely depend on the kind of information processing strategy people employ.

An alternative theory of affect congruence, the *affect-as-information* account (Schwarz & Clore, 1988), posits that people may sometimes directly use their affective state as information about a social situation. Rather than computing a response on the basis of the actual features of a situation, individuals may "ask themselves: 'How do I feel about it?'/and/in doing so, they may mistake feelings due to a pre-existing state as a reaction to the target" (Schwarz, 1990, p. 529). Thus, affective states may come to influence social behaviors because of an inferential error, as people misread their affective state and misattribute it to an unrelated person or situation. In empirical terms, this account is almost indistinguishable from the kind of conditioning theory advocated by Clore and Byrne (1974), except that affect and behavior are now linked as a result of an inferential mistake, rather than blind temporal and spatial associations. By definition, such a heuristic strategy is most likely when a person lacks sufficient interest, motivation, or resources to produce a more elaborate social response. For example, good or bad mood may facilitate affect-congruent responses in situations where more elaborate processing is unnecessary or impossible, such as responding to a telephone survey, or in an anonymous street survey where time and personal involvement are limited (Forgas & Moylan, 1987). Thus, in simple and poorly processed situations the "how do I feel about it?" heuristic can sometimes produce an affect-congruent response, but in more elaborately considered situations the memory-based affect priming process is more likely to be important.

There is good evidence for basic affect congruence in cognition. People in a happy mood remember more positive memories from their childhood, recall more happy events from the previous week, and remember better the words they have learnt when in a matching mood state (Bower, 1981; Eich & Macaulay, 2000; see also Eich & Macaulay, this volume). It is for this reason that people in a positive mood predominantly think about and remember happy, joyful experiences and tend to act in an optimistic, confident, and assertive manner. Negative mood in contrast triggers a stream of negative thoughts and ideas, leading to more cautious, pessimistic behavioral strategies.

Affect can also influence many other interpersonal tasks that require the use of memory-based information. For example, when people are asked to make sense of social scenes such as two people having an animated conversation, happy persons construct more cheerful, positive explanations (they are telling a joke), and those in a sad mood see a negative event (they are arguing; Bower, 1981). Ultimately, affect can also impact on interpersonal judgments about real people. In one study, we asked happy or sad participants to observe and rate their own and their partner's behaviors in a real videotaped social encounter (Forgas, Bower, & Krantz, 1984). Happy people "saw" far more positive, skilled, and fewer negative, unskilled behaviors both in themselves and in their partners than did sad subjects. These effects occur because affect directly influences the kinds of memories and interpretations that come to mind as observers try to make sense of complex and inherently ambiguous social behaviors. In other words, the same smile that is seen as warm and friendly by a person in a good mood can easily be judged as condescending or awkward by somebody in a bad mood.

These kinds of mood effects also influence how we interpret our own social behaviors and our successes and failures in real-life tasks such as passing an exam (Forgas, Bower, & Moylan, 1990). Part of the reason for these effects is that people tend to pay selective attention to affect-consistent rather than -inconsistent information (Forgas & Bower, 1987). Thus, affect appears to influence what we notice, what we learn, what we remember, and ultimately the kinds of judgments and decisions we make. However, this kind of spontaneous affect infusion is rather a fragile process, and can be easily reversed once people become aware of their mood states (Berkowitz, Jaffee, Jo, & Troccoli, 2000).

More Demanding Social Situations may Magnify Affective Influences

As noted earlier, affect infusion often seems significantly greater when people need to engage in more extensive and elaborate thinking in response to more demanding situations, as such a processing style increases the opportunity and the need to use mood-congruent information. For example, affect had a much greater mood-congruent effect on reactions to unusual, badly matched couples who required more elaborate interpretation, rather than typical, well-matched couples who were easier to interpret (Forgas, 1993, 1995b). The same kind of results are also obtained when people think about themselves: affect has a greater influence when interpreting less familiar, peripheral aspects of the self, but these effects are reduced when central, familiar features are judged (Sedikides, 1995).

Real-life interpersonal strategies show the same kind of context-specific affective bias. When happy or sad people were asked about their reactions to more or less serious conflicts in their intimate relationships, mood-congruent effects were consistently greater when more extensive thinking was required to deal with more serious rather than simple, routine conflicts (Forgas, 1994). Paradoxically, the more intimately we are acquainted with a person or an issue, the richer and more extensive the number of positive and negative memories we can call upon, and the more likely that affect may have a strong selective influence on what comes to mind and the kind of responses we formulate. This may be the reason why there are often extreme affective-induced fluctuations in the way people behave in their familiar personal relationship at different times, despite having very detailed and extensive knowledge about these situations.

As social interaction necessarily involves many rapid and largely subconscious cognitive decisions about alternative actions, we may expect that people in a positive mood should behave in a more confident, friendly, skilled, and constructive way than do those in a negative mood. This basic prediction was confirmed when we asked female undergraduates to interact with a confederate immediately after they were made to feel good or bad as a result of watching a mood-induction film (Forgas & Gunawardena, 2000). Independent raters blind to the mood manipulation found that happy students communicated more and did so more effectively, used more engaging nonverbal signals, were more talkative, and disclosed more about themselves. They were seen as acting in a more poised, skilled, and rewarding manner. Sad participants in contrast were judged as being less friendly, confident, and relaxed than were happy participants. It seems then that affect will infuse not only people's thoughts and judgments, but also their real-life social interactions. People are not usually aware of these effects. When questioned, students in this study did not realize that their behavior was in any way influenced by their moods. However, it seems that conscious effort and awareness can be quite effective in correcting for these mood effects (Berkowitz et al., 2000).

Affective Influences on Interpersonal Communication Strategies

Several studies now also show that affect has a significant influence on the way people communicate in social situations. Requesting—asking a person to do something for us—is almost always a difficult and complex interpersonal task (Gibbs, 1985). People must phrase their request with great care so as to maximize the likelihood of compliance (by being more direct), without risking giving offence (by not being *too* direct). Requesting thus involves inherent ambiguity and conflict and typically requires some degree of constructive, substantive processing.

Several experiments found that happy persons indeed interpret request situations in a more confident, optimistic way, and use more direct, impolite requests, while sad persons use more cautious, polite request forms. Further, these mood effects on requesting are much stronger when the request situation was demanding and difficult, and so required more extensive thinking (Forgas, 1998b, 1999a). Again, these effects were also found to occur in real-life interpersonal tasks. In one study, the actual requests used by students who were instructed to get a file from a neighboring office after receiving a mood induction were analyzed (Forgas, 1999b, Exp. 2). Even in this "real" situation, negative mood produced more polite, cautious, and hedging requests than did positive mood. In order to assess the processing styles responsible for these effects, participants' recall memory for the exact words used was also assessed. Recall accuracy—indicating more elaborate and detailed processing—was positively and significantly related to the degree of mood congruence in requests. This finding supports the theoretical prediction that affect infusion should be greater when more elaborate, substantive processing is used. The implications of such studies clearly extend to many real-life situations. The particular strategies used in an interpersonal task—and their success—will partly depend on the current mood state: when happy, people seem to construct the situation in a more confident and optimistic manner, and tend to prefer more direct behavioral approaches. When feeling down, more cautious and polite forms are used.

The Role of Affect in Responding to Social Situations

Ultimately affect may also influence how people respond to real-life interpersonal approaches, such as receiving an unexpected request (Forgas, 1998b). Responding to such approaches requires a rapid behavioral reaction based on the constructive cognitive processing of the situation that may be highly mood sensitive. In one unobtrusive study, affect was induced in unsuspecting library users by leaving mood-induction folders containing pretested pictures (or text) on unoccupied library desks. Arriving students were surreptitiously observed to ensure that they fully exposed themselves to the mood induction (almost everybody did). Soon afterwards, they were approached by another student (in fact, a confederate) who made an unexpected polite or impolite request for several sheets of paper needed to complete an essay. There was a clear mood-congruent pattern in responses: negative mood resulted in a more critical, negative response to the request and the requester and less compliance than did positive mood. These mood effects were greater when the request was impolite rather than polite, as impolite, unconventional requests are likely to require more elaborate and substantive processing. This explanation was confirmed by better recall memory for these impolite messages later on. Routine, polite requests in turn were processed less substantively, were less influenced by mood, and were also remembered less well later on.

Affect and Self-Disclosure Another important interpersonal communication task found to be highly affect sensitive is *self-disclosure*. It is through communicating increasingly personal and intimate information about ourselves that personal relationships are developed and a sense of self and identity is creat-ed. It turns out that being in a good or a bad mood significantly influences the extent to which individuals feel comfortable about disclosing personal information about themselves. We found that people who were induced to feel good were more willing to disclose more intimate information and did so sooner than did persons experiencing temporary negative affect, and this effect was even stronger when the partner reciprocated with matching levels of disclosure (Forgas, Laham, & Vargas, 2005).

In a way, it seems that by selectively priming positive thoughts, positive affect creates a sense of confidence and well-being that leads people to interpret their situation in an optimistic way, and allows them to act in a more open and confi-dent manner. Some researchers, like Yaacov Trope (see also this volume), sug-gested that positive affect can be considered a *psychological resource*. In their experiments, Trope and his colleagues (Trope, Ferguson, & Raghunanthan, 2001) found that people experiencing positive mood were more willing to seek out and cope with negative and threatening information about themselves, as long as they believed the threatening information to be potentially useful. Another example of the interpersonal benefits of good mood is in the area of negotiation and bargaining.

Affect and Negotiation: Affect Infusion into Bargaining Behaviors

Bargaining and negotiation by definition involve a degree of unpredictability and require careful planning and preparation. Several studies found that happy per-sons are more likely to make concessions (Baron, 1990), are more likely to be cooperative (Baron, Fortin, Frei, Hauver, & Shack, 1990), are less likely to be con-frontational (Carnevale & Isen, 1986), and tend to set themselves higher and more ambitious negotiating goals, expect to succeed more, and make plans and use strategies that are more optimistic, cooperative, and integrative than do peo-ple in a neutral or negative mood (Forgas, 1998a; Thomson, 2005).

In one illustrative series of experiments we investigated mood effects on zero-sum interpersonal and intergroup negotiations. After a positive or negative mood induction, participants engaged in an informal, interpersonal, and a formal, inter-group negotiating task. Those in a positive mood formulated more optimistic, cooperative, and integrative action plans, actually behaved less competitively, were more willing to use integrative strategies such as making deals, and as a result proved to be more successful at this task. We may understand these effects in terms of positive affect selectively priming more positive thoughts and ideas that lead to more optimistic expectations and the adoption of more cooperative and integrative bargaining strategies. These effects are largely automatic and sub-conscious, and few people realize that they occur at all. We also found that the degree of affect infusion was moderated by individual differences between negotiants. High scorers on measures such as machiavellism and need for approval were less influenced by mood than were low scorers on these measures. It seems that indi-vidual differences that predict the motivated processing of social information—such as self-esteem, social anxiety, and the like—tend to significantly moderate affective influences on social cognition and behavior (Ciarrochi & Forgas, 1999, 2000; Rusting, 1998, 2001). Overall, these results show that affect has a significant influence not only on people's constructive interpretation of social situations, but even on carefully planned strategic interpersonal behaviors.

Rather than looking at positive and negative mood, in a series of experiments van Kleef (van Kleef, 2004; van Kleef, de Dreu, & Manstead, 2004) investigated the role of distinct emotions *in a partner*, such as anger and happiness on negotiator strategies, using a computer-mediated negotiation task where the simulated "partner" displayed different emotions. Results showed that negotiators facing an angry opponent placed lower demands and made larger concessions, but those facing a happy opponent made smaller concessions. In a way, displaying motivated information processing, negotiators used the opponent's emotional state as information to guide their own bargaining strategies, conceding more to an angry than to a happy opponent. Anger was interpreted as signaling low tolerance, and happiness as signaling high tolerance. Negotiators also displayed emotional contagion, responding to the opponent's affective state with a matching emotion.

Affective Influences on Helping and Altruism

Although there has been extensive past research on the influence of affective states on helping and altruism (e.g., Salovey & Rosenhan, 1989), a detailed review of this rich literature is clearly beyond the scope of the present article. Generally, research found that positive affect consistently promotes altruism and helping; however, negative affect can also promote helping in some cases. Considerable uncertainty remains about the psychological mechanisms mediating these effects, and past explanations emphasized either cognitive or motivational principles (Salovey & Rosenhan, 1989). The evidence reviewed here suggests that different information processing strategies are likely to play an important role in moderating affective influences on helping behavior, a hypothesis that is readily amenable to future empirical testing.

The Role of Affect in Linking Attitudes to Behavior

Positive and negative affect seems to play an important role in how people deal with cognitive dissonance, and whether they will be motivated or not to maintain consistency between their behaviors and attitudes (Harmon-Jones, 2001; Petty, DeSteno, & Rucker, 2001). Leon Festinger proposed many years ago that the experience of negative affect accompanying cognitive dissonance can be a potent mechanism to produce attitude change (Cooper & Fazio, 1984; Harmon-Jones, 2001). Cognitive dissonance produces negative affect because discrepancy among cognitions undermines our clear and certain knowledge about the world, and thus our ability to engage in effective action (Harmon-Jones, 2001). Several studies suggest that positive affect reduces and negative affect increases dissonance reduction even if the source of affect is unrelated (Rhodewalt & Comer, 1979). And conversely, once consonance is restored, affective state also tends to improve (Harmon-Jones, 2001). It also appears that high self-esteem people seem generally better able to handle negative affective states (Harmon-Jones, 2001). It is interesting that qualitatively different dissonance experiences seem to trigger qualitatively different affective reactions. Belief disconfirmation is more likely to produce anxiety, whereas postdecisional dissonance is more likely to induce regret consistent with self-discrepancy theory that specifically predicts that different kinds of self-discrepancies evoke qualitatively distinct affective reactions (Higgins, 1989, 2001). Broadly speaking, it seems that positive affect enables individuals to tolerate dissonance without resorting to attitude or behavior change. Negative affect on the other hand tends to increase the aversive experience of dissonance and may hasten efforts to restore consonance. However, much work remains to be done in discovering the precise cognitive mechanisms responsible for moderating these effects.

Positive Affect as a Resource in Interpersonal Behavior

Affect also has an additional important influence on social behavior: positive mood may serve as a resource that allows people to overcome defensiveness and deal more effectively with potentially threatening situations (Trope et al., 2001). Dealing with threatening situations involves a powerful motivational conflict, and requires a trade-off between the immediate emotional cost and long-term gain. Trope and Neter (1994) found that people in a positive mood were more likely to voluntarily expose themselves to threatening information from others. In other words, positive mood functioned as a resource. This mood-as-a-resource hypothesis suggests that positive affect enables people to manage relevant but threatening social situations. The theory also suggests that those in a good mood may be better able to behave in a rational and effective way in otherwise difficult situations, such as in bargaining encounters (Forgas, 1998a). These effects may have important applied consequences. For example, people in positive mood responded more positively to threatening information about health risks, as the next section will also suggest.

Affect and Health-Related Behaviors

Positive or negative affective states may also influence health-related behaviors, and may ultimately also influence physical well-being (Salovey, Detweiler, Steward, & Bedell, 2001; see also Huppert, this volume). Numerous studies found a clear correlation between good moods and positive health outcomes (Salovey & Birnbaum, 1989). Several studies suggest that positive affect can influence health-related behaviors. Affect can influence beliefs about one's ability to manage one's health, and is an important predictor of actual health behaviors such as engaging in safe sex, smoking cessation, and adopting a healthy diet (Salovey, Rothman, & Rodin, 1998). Although the effects of affect on health-related behaviors appear robust and reliable, the psychological mechanisms responsible for these effects are not yet fully understood. Perhaps positive mood primes more confident and optimistic beliefs as was also found in other domains reviewed here, or alternatively positive affective states may directly influence the immune system and susceptibility to disease. Individual difference variables such as optimism, affect intensity, anxiety, hope, and affect regulation skills appear to moderate many of these effects (Salovey et al., 2001). It appears then that affect can have a highly important influence on behaviors related to health and illness. However, these effects are again subject to complex mediating influences that are receiving growing attention (Salovey et al., 2001).

Affect and Organizational Behavior

Although past research on organizational behavior was dominated by behaviorist and cognitive perspectives (Ilgen & Klein, 1989), affect is increasingly recognized as an essential component of the organizational experience (Baron, 1993; Forgas & George, 2001; George, 1990; George & Jones, 1996, 1997). Even mild affective states can have a significant mood-congruent influence on many organizational behaviors such as personnel selection (Baron, 1987), appraisal (Sinclair, 1988), consumer decisions (Ciarrochi & Forgas, 2000), and bargaining behaviors (Forgas, 1998a). Affective states also seem to play a critical role in work motivation and performance (Baron, 1993; George, 1989). These findings also suggest that affective influences on organizational behavior are also likely to be significantly moderated by different information processing strategies (Forgas & George, 2001).

So far we have focused on affect infusion, that is, the affect-congruent influence of feelings on the content of thinking and behavior. It is now time to turn to the other major consequence of affect on everyday behavior: affective influences on the process of thinking.

THE PROCESSING EFFECTS OF AFFECT ON SOCIAL BEHAVIOR

It turns out that affect may not only influence the content of cognition but may also impact on the *process* of cognition, that is, *how* people produce a response (Clark & Isen, 1982; Fiedler & Forgas, 1988). Different processing strategies promoted by different affective states can have a direct influence on the ensuing interpersonal behaviors. It was initially thought that good mood simply produces a more lazy, relaxed, and superficial thinking style, as feeling good "informs" us that the situation is safe and no particular effort is required. Bad mood in turn may function as a warning signal to be more careful and attentive. However, positive affect can also produce distinct processing advantages. People in a positive mood often adopt more creative, open, constructive, and inclusive thinking styles, and show greater cognitive and behavioral flexibility (Bless, 2000; Fiedler, 2000). It now appears that feeling good produces a thinking style that gives greater rein to our internal thoughts, dispositions, and ideas. In this mode of thinking individuals tend to pay less attention to external information, and tend to assimilate external details into their pre-existing knowledge about the world. Negative affect in contrast produces a more externally focused thinking style where accommodation to the demands of the external world takes precedence over internal ideas (Bless, 2000; Fiedler, 2001).

These differences in thinking style are consistent with evolutionary ideas that suggest that affect signals appropriate ways of responding to different situations. Positive affect tells us that the environment is benign and that we can rely on our existing knowledge in responding. Negative affect is more like an alarm signal, alerting us that the environment is potentially dangerous and that we need to pay close attention to external information. We now know that feeling good or feeling bad does make us deal very differently with the same social situation, as the studies below show.

Feeling Bad—but Thinking and Acting Effectively?

It is often assumed in everyday life that being in a good mood is not only more pleasant but also has universally desirable consequences. Organizational psychologists often assume that happy employers work better, are more flexible and creative, and create more customer satisfaction (Forgas & George, 2001). Despite the many obvious benefits of positive affect, the kind of careful, vigilant, and systematic attention to stimulus details typically recruited by negative moods can also be of considerable benefit in certain situations. For example, when responding to persuasive messages those in a negative mood tend to scrutinize the message more carefully and respond more in terms of message quality than do happy persons (Petty et al., 2001). People in a happy mood also tend to rely more on their pre-existing stereotypes when forming impressions about outgroup members (although other negative affective states, such as anger, can also increase the use of stereotypes; Bodenhausen, Mussweiler, Gabriel, & Moreno, 2001). Some clinical research also suggests that those feeling depressed are actually more realistic in how they see the world and themselves, and it is "normal" people who tend to distort reality in a positive direction.

Affective Influences on the Quality of Persuasive Messages: When Sad is Better?

Mild everyday mood states may thus influence how well we think and how well we do in demanding interpersonal situations, such as when we are trying to persuade others. In a recent series of experiments, we asked participants to try to produce effective persuasive arguments either for or against propositions such as (a) student fees should be increased, and (b) nuclear testing in the Pacific. When we asked subjects to do this immediately after a mood induction (Forgas et al., 2005), those in a negative mood consistently came up with higher quality persuasive arguments than did happy persons. The same effects were also obtained in a second study, when happy or sad people were asked to persuade a friend for or against Australia becoming a republic, and for or against a right-wing populist party. In a further experiment, individuals produced their persuasive arguments in interacting with a "partner" through a computer keyboard as if exchanging emails. Half the participants were promised a significant reward (movie passes) if they were successful. Those in a negative mood again produced and used higher quality arguments. However, the provision of a reward reduced the size of mood effects by imposing a strong motivational influence on how the task was approached.

Of course, the "real" efficacy of such persuasive arguments depends on how effective they are at producing real attitude change in people exposed to them. We tested this by assessing the relevant attitudes of students at the beginning of the year, and 2 months later exposing them to persuasive arguments on various topics written by persons who were either happy or sad at the time. We found that irrespective of the topic argued, those exposed to arguments written by sad persuaders showed greater actual attitude change than did persons reading the arguments by happy persuaders. These results suggest that mild negative moods promote a more careful, externally oriented processing style that is more attuned to the requirements of a given situation. However, a strong motivation to be effective can override these mood effects. The implications of such findings is that if a demanding interpersonal task is performed without any thought or awareness of affect, mood is likely to influence thinking style and the quality of the response. However, becoming aware that these effects occur and being motivated to overcome them is likely to be a highly effective control strategy.

Affective Influences on Intergroup Behaviors

It has long been assumed that affect plays an important role in how people behave towards members of outgroups (for reviews, see Bodenhausen et al., 2001). Based on psychoanalytic ideas and the frustration-aggression hypothesis, it was assumed that negative affect might contribute to intergroup aggression and discrimination. Conditioning processes may also play a role in explaining how regularly encountering and associating certain groups in aversive situations can elicit negative emotions such as anger and resentment, just as evaluative reactions to individuals can be influenced by conditioning (Clore & Byrne, 1974). In turn, associating encounters with outgroup members with positive feelings may produce more positive responses, according to the "contact hypothesis" (Allport, 1954).

Affect also influences intergroup behavior by influencing processing strategies. Thus, positive affect may promote more inclusive cognitive categorizations thus reducing negative intergroup behaviors (Bodenhausen et al., 2001). However, whether this effect is beneficial depends on whether the categories used are positive or negative, and whether they are used to discriminate between or unify outgroups and ingroups. According to some recent studies, when group membership is of low relevance, positive mood may facilitate the use of simple ingroup versus outgroup categories, and so increase negative responses to outgroups (Forgas & Fiedler, 1996). The experience of anxiety may also amplify reliance on stereotypes, increasing the tendency to respond to outgroups in discriminatory ways.

Recent experiments also found that trait anxiety can moderate the influence of negative affect on intergroup behavior (Ciarrochi & Forgas, 1999). Low trait anxious whites in the US reacted more negatively to a threatening Black outgroup when experiencing aversive mood. However, high trait anxious individuals responded in exactly the opposite manner, and produced more positive reactions. It seems that negative affect when combined with high trait anxiety triggered a more controlled, motivated response strategy leading to the reversal of socially undesirable intergroup responses.

Different negative affective states also have different processing consequences and so influence intergroup reactions. For example, sadness reduces but anger and anxiety may increase reliance on stereotypes (Bodenhausen et al., 2001). The process of "stereotyping" itself may involve at least four distinct cognitive operations that may be influenced by affect: the identification of the applicable category, activation of its contents, applying stereotyped features to the target, and correcting for inappropriate stereotyping.

For example, since positive moods often facilitate top-down, schematic processing (Bless, 2000; Fiedler, 2000), happy persons are more likely to rely on stereotype information (Bodenhausen et al., 2001; Forgas & Fiedler, 1996, Exp. 1). However, negative states other than sadness, such as anger or anxiety, may actually promote stereotyping according to evidence from several experiments (e.g., Bodenhausen et al., 2001). Once a category is activated, affect may also influence the amount of stereotyped information people *access*. If processing resources are limited fewer stereotyped details may be retrieved. In the simplest instance, once activated, stereotypic ideas can be directly used to produce responses. For example, we found that positive mood increased reliance on simple group stereotypes when making reward allocation decisions, but only when group membership was of low relevance (Forgas & Fiedler, 1996). At other times, stereotyped knowledge provides an initial influence on judgments that are likely to be supplemented and modified by other information (Bodenhausen et al., 2001). When group membership was made more personally relevant, it was people experiencing negative affect who behaved in a more discriminatory way towards outgroup members (Forgas & Fiedler, 1996, Exp. 2).

Ultimately, a motivated tendency to *correct* discriminatory reactions may also influence intergroup reactions, as people correct or recompute what appears to be an undesirable judgment. Negative affect may facilitate a cautious, defensive interpersonal style (Forgas, 1999a, 1999b), and persons feeling sad, guilty, or anxious seem to be more likely to engage in stereotype correction (Devine, 1989). Thus, negative affect sometimes functions as a warning signal, indicating the need for a motivated reassessment of potentially undesirable responses. This alerting effect of negative mood is particularly strong for individuals high on trait anxiety (Ciarrochi & Forgas, 1999). Thus, affect plays a complex role in intergroup behaviors, potentially influencing every stage of the stereotyping process. Contextual and situational factors again play a critical role in mediating these effects (Forgas, 1995a, 2002).

Negative Affect and Remembering Social Events

Another area where mild negative mood was shown to have significant beneficial effects is memory for social events. Remembering witnessed events accurately is not only important in everyday social behavior, but eyewitness accounts are also accorded special evidential status in the legal system. In several recent experiments, we evaluated mood effects on eyewitness accuracy (Forgas et al., 2005) by first allowing people to witness complex real-life social events. Some time later, good or bad mood was induced before they received questions that either included or did not include "planted", misleading information about the episodes. Those who were in a negative mood when exposed to misleading information were more accurate in remembering the episode and did not incorporate "false" details into their memory. Positive mood reduced accuracy, and increased the tendency to confuse misleading details with the original event. In other words, the more careful and externally oriented thinking style produced by mild negative moods can produce significant cognitive benefits and improve the accuracy of social memories. Reactions to many everyday interpersonal situations can be influenced by these effects, including important organizational decisions. For example, in a series of recent studies Stephanie Moylan (2000) showed that negative mood also tends to decrease the incidence of a variety of errors and distortions in performance assessment decisions. Although there has been much emphasis on the positive behavioral consequences of good moods, appreciating the potential benefits of mild negative mood states in certain problem-solving tasks can be equally important.

TOWARDS A THEORETICAL SYNTHESIS: THE AFFECT INFUSION MODEL (AIM)

Affect thus has a complex influence on both the content and the process of social cognition and the resulting interpersonal behaviors (Forgas, 2000, 2001). A comprehensive theory of these effects should specify the circumstances that promote or inhibit affect congruence, and should also define the processing conditions that lead to affect priming, or affect-as-information processes. The AIM (Forgas, 1995a, 2002) accomplished this by predicting that affect infusion should only occur in circumstances that promote an open, constructive processing style (Fiedler, 1991; Forgas, 1992b, 1995b). Constructive processing may be defined as those cognitive tasks that involve the active elaboration and transformation of the available stimulus information, require the activation and use of previous knowledge structures, and result in the creation of new knowledge from the combination of stored information and new stimulus details. As the AIM has been adequately described elsewhere, only a brief overview will be included here (Forgas, 1992a, 1995a, 2002).

The AIM identifies four alternative processing strategies people may use when responding to a social situation: *direct access*, *motivated*, *heuristic*, and *substantive* processing. These four strategies differ in terms of two basic characteristics: the degree of cognitive *effort* exerted in seeking a solution, and the degree of *openness* of the information search strategy (actively seeking and using new information to construct a response, or relying on existing knowledge). The combination of these two processing dimensions, quantity (effort) and quality (openness), produces four distinct processing styles: *substantive processing* (high effort/open), *motivated processing* (high effort/closed), *heuristic processing* (low effort/open, constructive), and *direct access processing* (low effort/closed). Affect infusion is most likely when a constructive strategy is used, such as substantive or heuristic processing, as these strategies are most likely to require the creation of a novel response. In contrast, affect infusion is unlikely when a task calls for highly directed and predetermined motivated or direct access processing (see also Fiedler, 2001, this volume).

The *direct access strategy* involves the direct retrieval of a pre-existing response, and is most likely when the task is highly familiar, and when no strong cognitive, affective, situational, or motivational cues call for more elaborate processing. As no constructive processing is required, affect infusion should not occur. *Motivated processing* involves highly selective and targeted thinking dominated by a particular motivational objective that also precludes open information search, and should be impervious to affect infusion (Clark & Isen, 1982). Motivated processing may also produce a reversal of mood-congruence effects (Berkowitz et al., 2000; Forgas, 1991; Forgas & Fiedler, 1996).

In contrast, both *heuristic* and *substantive* processing require constructive thinking and thus may facilitate affect infusion. *Heuristic processing* is most likely when the capacity or motivation to think more elaborately is impaired, and there are no "direct access" responses to fall back on. Heuristic processing can produce affect infusion when people rely on the "how do I feel about it" heuristics (Clore, Gasper, & Garvin, 2001; Schwarz & Clore, 1988). In most realistic situations people will need to engage in *substantive processing*, retrieving and combining memory-based knowledge with situational information. The AIM makes the interesting and counterintuitive prediction that affect infusion (and behavioral mood congruence) should be greater when more extensive processing is required to deal with more complex, demanding social tasks (Fiedler & Stroehm, 1986; Forgas, 1992b, 1993, 1995b, 1998a, 1998b, 1998c).

The AIM also specifies how features of the *task*, the *person*, and the *situation* influence processing choices, and recognizes that affect itself can influence processing preferences (for details, see Forgas, 1995a). The two key predictions of the AIM when applied to social behavior are that (a) affect congruence should be directly dependent on the degree of open, constructive processing required, and (b) negative moods may improve and positive mood impair the effectiveness of interpersonal strategies that call for the detailed and sensitive processing of situational information (such as the production of high-quality persuasive arguments). These implications have now been tested and confirmed in a number of experiments, as we have seen above.

SUMMARY AND CONCLUSIONS

This review suggested that even mild everyday moods can have a significant effect on how people behave in everyday social situations. The experiments reviewed show that feeling good or feeling bad has a marked effect on both the content and valence of interpersonal behaviors and the kind of information processing strategies that people employ. Affect can influence responses to outgroup members, the quality and originality of the persuasive messages, organizational and - health-related behaviors, the directness of requests, and the cooperativeness of bargaining strategies. Different information processing strategies play a key role in explaining these effects, as suggested by the AIM (Forgas, 1995a, 2002). In general, more extensive, substantive processing recruited by more difficult interpersonal tasks enhanced mood congruity effects (Forgas, 1992b, 1994, 1995b).

In contrast, affect infusion is absent when a task could be performed using a simple direct access strategy or a highly motivated strategy. In these conditions, there is less opportunity for affectively primed thoughts to influence the outcome (Fiedler, 1991; Forgas, 1995a). Several experiments also showed that affect infusion into social behaviors reliably occurs in many real-life situations. Even dealing with relationship conflicts can be subject to significant mood-congruent bias (Forgas, 1994). A full understanding of how affect influences interpersonal behaviors requires careful attention to the cognitive processes underlying these effects. Clearly a great deal more research is needed before we can fully understand the multiple influences that affect has on strategic interpersonal behaviors. Hopefully this review will help to stimulate further interest in this fascinating and rapidly developing area of inquiry.

ACKNOWLEDGMENTS

This work was supported by an Australian Professorial Fellowship from the Australian Research Council, and the Research Prize by the Alexander von Humboldt Foundation to Joseph P. Forgas. The contribution of Carrie Wyland, Liz Dunn, Simon Laham, Rebekah East, and Norman Chan to this project is gratefully acknowledged.

REFERENCES

Adolphs, R., & Damasio, A. (2001). The interaction of affect and cognition: A neurobiological perspective. In J. P. Forgas (Ed.), *The handbook of affect and social cognition* (pp. 27–49). Mahwah, NJ: Lawrence Erlbaum Associates, Inc.

Allport, G. W. (1954). *The nature of prejudice*. Reading, MA: Addison-Wesley.

Baron, R. A. (1987). Interviewers' moods and reactions to job applicants: The influence of affective states on applied social judgments. *Journal of Applied Social Psychology, 16*, 16–28.

Baron, R. A. (1990). Environmentally induced positive affect: Its impact on self-efficacy, task performance, negotiation and conflict. *Journal of Applied Social Psychology, 20*, 368–384.

Baron, R. A. (1993). Affect and organizational behavior: When and why feeling good (or bad) matters. In J. K. Murnighan (Ed.), *Social psychology in organizations: Advances in theory and research* (pp. 63–88). Englewood Cliffs, NJ: Prentice-Hall.

Baron, R. A., Fortin, S. P., Frei, R. L., Hauver, L. A., & Shack, M. L. (1990). Reducing organizational conflict: The role of socially induced positive affect. *International Journal of Conflict Management, 1*, 133–152.

Berkowitz, L., Jaffee, S., Jo, E., & Troccoli, B. T. (2000). On the correction of feeling-induced judgmental biases. In J. P. Forgas (Ed.), *Feeling and thinking: The role of affect in social cognition* (pp. 131–152). New York: Cambridge University Press.

Bless, H. (2000). The interplay of affect and cognition: The mediating role of general knowledge structures. In J. P. Forgas (Ed.), *Feeling and thinking: The role of affect in social cognition* (pp. 201–222). New York: Cambridge University Press.

Bodenhausen, G. V., Mussweiler, T. Gabriel, S., & Moreno, K. N. (2001). Affective influences on stereotyping and intergroup relations. In J. P. Forgas (Ed.), *The handbook of affect and social cognition* (pp. 319–343). Mahwah, NJ: Lawrence Erlbaum Associates, Inc.

Bower, G. H. (1981). Mood and memory. *American Psychologist, 36,* 129–148.

Bower, G. H., & Forgas, J. P. (2001). Mood and social memory. In J. P. Forgas (Ed.), *The handbook of affect and social cognition.* Mahwah, NJ: Lawrence Erlbaum Associates, Inc.

Carnevale, P. J., & Isen, A. M. (1986). The influence of positive affect and visual access on the discovery of integrative solutions in bilateral negotiations. *Organizational Behavior and Human Decision Processes, 83,* 235–259.

Ciarrochi, J. V., & Forgas, J. P. (1999). On being tense yet tolerant: The paradoxical effects of trait anxiety and aversive mood on intergroup judgments. *Group Dynamics: Theory, Research and Practice, 3,* 227–238.

Ciarrochi, J. V., & Forgas, J. P. (2000). The pleasure of possessions: Affect and consumer judgments. *European Journal of Social Psychology, 30,* 631–649.

Clark, M. S., & Isen, A. M. (1982). Towards understanding the relationship between feeling states and social behavior. In A. H. Hastorf & A. M. Isen (Eds.), *Cognitive social psychology* (pp. 73–108). New York: Elsevier-North Holland.

Clore, G. L., & Byrne, D. (1974). The reinforcement affect model of attraction. In T. L. Huston (Ed.), *Foundations of interpersonal attraction* (pp. 143–170). New York, NY: Academic Press.

Clore, G. L., Gasper, K., & Garvin, E. (2001). Affect as information. In J. P. Forgas (Ed.), *The handbook of affect and social cognition.* Mahwah, NJ: Lawrence Erlbaum Associates, Inc.

Cooper, J., & Fazio, R. H. (1984). A new look at dissonance theory. In L. Berkowitz (Ed.), *Advances in experimental social psychology* (Vol. 17, pp. 229–266). San Diego, CA: Academic Press.

Damasio, A. R. (1994). *Descartes' error.* New York: Grosste/Putnam.

Devine, P. G. (1989). Stereotypes and prejudice: Their automatic and controlled components. *Journal of Personality and Social Psychology, 56,* 5–18.

Dunbar, R. I. M. (2004). Social cognitiuon as a constraint on social interaction. *Journal of Cultural and Evolutionary Psychology, 2,* 181–194.

Eich, E., & Macaulay, D. (2000). Fundamental factors in mood-dependent memory. In J. P. Forgas (Ed.), *Feeling and thinking: The role of affect in social cognition* (pp. 109–130). New York: Cambridge University Press.

Feshbach, S., & Singer, R. D. (1957). The effects of fear arousal and suppression of fear upon social perception. *Journal of Abnormal and Social Psychology, 55,* 283–288.

Fiedler, K. (1991). On the task, the measures and the mood in research on affect and social cognition. In J. P. Forgas (Ed.), *Emotion and social judgments* (pp. 83–104). Oxford: Pergamon.

Fiedler, K. (2000). Towards an integrative account of affect and cognition phenomena using the BIAS computer algorithm. In J. P. Forgas (Ed.), *Feeling and thinking: The role of affect in social cognition.* New York: Cambridge University Press.

Fiedler, K. (2001). Affective influences on social information processing. In J. P. Forgas (Ed.), *The handbook of affect and social cognition* (pp. 163–185). Mahwah, NJ: Lawrence Erlbaum Associates, Inc.

Fiedler, K., & Forgas, J. P. (Eds.). (1988). *Affect, cognition, and social behavior: New evidence and integrative attempts* (pp. 44–62). Toronto: Hogrefe.

Fiedler, K., & Stroehm, W. (1986). What kind of mood influences what kind of memory: The role of arousal and information structure. *Memory and Cognition, 14,* 181–188.

Forgas, J. P. (1979). *Social episodes: The study of interaction routines*. London: Academic Press.

Forgas, J. P. (1982). Episode cognition: Internal representations of interaction routines. In L. Berkowitz (Ed.), *Advances in experimental social psychology* (Vol. 15, pp. 59–101). New York: Academic Press.

Forgas, J. P. (1991). Mood effects on partner choice: Role of affect in social decisions. *Journal of Personality and Social Psychology, 61*, 708–720.

Forgas, J. P. (1992a). Affect in social judgments and decisions: A multi-process model. In M. Zanna (Ed.), *Advances in experimental social psychology* (Vol. 25, pp. 227–275). New York: Academic Press.

Forgas, J. P. (1992b). On bad mood and peculiar people: Affect and person typicality in impression formation. *Journal of Personality and Social Psychology, 62*, 863–875.

Forgas, J. P. (1993). On making sense of odd couples: Mood effects on the perception of mismatched relationships. *Personality and Social Psychology Bulletin, 19*, 59–71.

Forgas, J. P. (1994). Sad and guilty? Affective influences on the explanation of conflict episodes. *Journal of Personality and Social Psychology, 66*, 56–68.

Forgas, J. P. (1995a). Mood and judgment: The affect infusion model (AIM). *Psychological Bulletin, 117(1)*, 39–66.

Forgas, J. P. (1995b). Strange couples: Mood effects on judgments and memory about prototypical and atypical targets. *Personality and Social Psychology Bulletin, 21*, 747–765.

Forgas, J. P. (1998a). On feeling good and getting your way: Mood effects on negotiation strategies and outcomes. *Journal of Personality and Social Psychology, 74*, 565–577.

Forgas, J. P. (1998b). Asking nicely? Mood effects on responding to more or less polite requests. *Personality and Social Psychology Bulletin, 24*, 173–185.

Forgas, J. P. (1998c). Happy and mistaken? Mood effects on the fundamental attribution error. *Journal of Personality and Social Psychology, 75*, 318–331.

Forgas, J. P. (1999a). On feeling good and being rude: Affective influences on language use and request formulations. *Journal of Personality and Social Psychology, 76*, 928–939.

Forgas, J. P. (1999b). Feeling and speaking: Mood effects on verbal communication strategies. *Personality and Social Psychology Bulletin, 25*, 850–863.

Forgas, J. P. (Ed.). (2000). *Feeling and thinking: The role of affect in social cognition*. New York: Cambridge University Press.

Forgas, J. P. (Ed.). (2001). *The handbook of affect and social cognition*. Mahwah, NJ: Lawrence Erlbaum Associates, Inc.

Forgas, J. P. (2002). Feeling and doing: Affective influences on interpersonal behavior. *Psychological Inquiry, 13*, 1–28.

Forgas, J. P., & Bower, G. H. (1987). Mood effects on person perception judgements. *Journal of Personality and Social Psychology, 53*, 53–60.

Forgas, J. P., Bower, G. H., & Krantz, S. (1984). The influence of mood on perceptions of social interactions. *Journal of Experimental Social Psychology, 20*, 497–513.

Forgas, J. P., Bower, G. H., & Moylan, S. J. (1990). Praise or Blame? Affective influences on attributions for achievement. *Journal of Personality and Social Psychology, 59*, 809–818.

Forgas, J. P., & Fiedler, K. (1996). Us and them: Mood effects on intergroup discrimination. *Journal of Personality and Social Psychology, 70*, 36–52.

Forgas, J. P., & George, J. M. (2001). Affective influences on judgments and behavior in organizations: An information processing perspective. *Organizational Behavior and Human Decision Processes, 86*, 3–34.

Forgas, J. P., & Gunawardena, A. (2000). *Affective influences on spontaneous interpersonal behaviors*. Unpublished manuscript, University of New South Wales, Sydney, Australia.

Forgas, J. P., & Moylan, S. J. (1987). After the movies: The effects of transient mood states on social judgments. *Personality and Social Psychology Bulletin, 13*, 478–489.

Forgas, J. P., Laham, S., & Vargas, P. (2005). Mood effects on eyewitness memory: Affective influences on susceptibility to misinformation. *Journal of Experimental Social Psychology, 41*, 574–588.

George, J. M. (1989). Mood and absence. *Journal of Applied Psychology, 74*, 317–324.

George, J. M. (1990). Personality, affect, and behavior in groups. *Journal of Applied Psychology, 75*, 107–116.

George, J. M., & Jones, G. R. (1996). The experience of work and turnover intentions: Interactive effects of value attainment, job satisfaction, and positive mood. *Journal of Applied Psychology, 81*, 318–325.

George, J. M., & Jones, G. R. (1997). Experiencing work: Values, attitudes, and moods. *Human Relations, 50*, 393–416.

Gibbs, R. (1985). Situational conventions and requests. In J. P. Forgas (Ed.), *Language and social situations* (pp. 97–113). New York: Springer.

Goffman, E. (1972). *Frame analysis*. London, UK: Penguin.

Harmon-Jones, E. (2001). The role of affect in cognitive dissonance processes. In J. P. Forgas (Ed.), *The handbook of affect and social cognition*. Mahwah, NJ: Lawrence Erlbaum Associates, Inc.

Heider, F. (1958). *The psychology of interpersonal relations*. New York: Wiley.

Higgins, E. T. (1989). Self-discrepancy theory: What patterns of self-beliefs cause people to suffer? In L. Berkowitz (Ed.), *Advances in Experimental Social Psychology, 22*, 93–136.

Higgins, E. T. (2001). Promotion and prevention experiences: Relating emotions to non-emotional motivational states. In J. P. Forgas (Ed.), *The handbook of affect and social cognition*. Mahwah, NJ: Lawrence Erlbaum Associates, Inc.

Ilgen, D. R., & Klein, H. J. (1989). Organizational behavior. *Annual Review of Psychology, 40*, 327–351.

Ito, T., & Cacioppo, J. (2001). Affect and attitudes: A social neuroscience approach. In J. P. Forgas (Ed.), *The handbook of affect and social cognition*. Mahwah, NJ: Lawrence Erlbaum Associates, Inc.

Machiavelli, N. (1961). *The prince*. London, UK: Penguin.

Moylan, S. J. (2000). *Affective influences on organisational decisions*. Unpublished PhD thesis, University of New South Wales, Sydney.

Niedenthal, P., & Halberstadt, J. (2000). Grounding categories in emotional response. In J. P. Forgas (Ed.), *Feeling and thinking: The role of affect in social cognition* (pp. 357–386). New York: Cambridge University Press.

Petty, R. E., DeSteno, D., & Rucker, D. (2001). The role of affect in attitude change. In J. P. Forgas (Ed.), *The handbook of affect and social cognition*. Mahwah, NJ: Lawrence Erlbaum Associates, Inc.

Razran, G. H. S. (1940). Conditioned response changes in rating and appraising sociopolitical slogans. *Psychological Bulletin, 37*, 481–497.

Rhodewalt, F., & Comer, R. (1979). Induced-compliance attitude change: Once more with feeling. *Journal of Experimental Social Psychology, 15*, 35–47.

Rusting, C. (2001). Personality as a mediator of affective influences on social cognition. In J. P. Forgas (Ed.), *The handbook of affect and social cognition*. Mahwah, NJ: Lawrence Erlbaum Associates, Inc.

Rusting, C. L. (1998). Personality, mood, and cognitive processing of emotional information: Three conceptual frameworks. *Psychological Bulletin, 124(2),* 165–196.

Salovey, P., & Birnbaum, D. (1989). Influence of mood on health-relevant cognitions. *Journal of Personality and Social Psychology, 57,* 539–551.

Salovey, P., Detweiler, J. B., Steward, W. T., & Bedell, B. T. (2001). Affect and health-relevant cognition. In J. Forgas (Ed.), *Handbook of Affect and Social Cognition* (pp. 344–370). Mahwah, NJ: Lawrence Erlbaum Associates, Inc.

Salovey, P., & Rosenhan, D. L. (1989). Mood states and prosocial behavior. In H. L. Wagner & A. S. R. Manstead (Eds.), *Handbook of psychophysiology: Emotion and social behavior* (pp. 371–391). Chichester, England: Wiley.

Salovey, P., Rothman, A. J., & Rodin, J. (1998). Health behavior. In D. T. Gilbert, S. T. Fiske, & G. Lindzey (Eds.), *The handbook of social psychology* (4th ed., Vol. 2, pp. 633–683). New York: McGraw-Hill.

Schwarz, N. (1990). Feelings as information: Informational and motivational functions of affective states. In E. T. Higgins & R. Sorrentino (Eds.), *Handbook of motivation and cognition: Foundations of social behaviour* (Vol. 2, pp. 527–561). New York: Guilford Press.

Schwarz, N., & Clore, G. L. (1988). How do I feel about it? The informative function of affective states. In K. Fiedler & J. P. Forgas (Eds.), *Affect, cognition, and social behavior* (pp. 44–62). Toronto: Hogrefe.

Sedikides, C. (1995). Central and peripheral self-conceptions are differentially influenced by mood: Tests of the differential sensitivity hypothesis. *Journal of Personality and Social Psychology, 69(4),* 759–777.

Sinclair, R. C. (1988). Mood, categorization breadth, and performance appraisal: The effects of order of information acquisition and affective state on halo, accuracy, information retrieval, and evaluations. *Organizational Behavior and Human Decision Processes, 42,* 22–46.

Thomson, L. (2005). *The mind and the heart of the negotiator.* New Jersey: Prentice-Hall.

Trope, Y., Ferguson, M., & Raghunanthan, R. (2001). Mood as a resource in processing self-relevant information. In J. P. Forgas (Ed.), *The handbook of affect and social cognition* (pp. 256–274). Mahwah, NJ: Lawrence Erlbaum Associates, Inc.

Trope, Y., & Neter, E. (1994). Reconciling competing motives in self-evaluation: The role of self-control in feedback seeking. *Journal of Personality and Social Psychology, 66,* 646–657.

Van Kleef, G. A. (2004). *Emotion in social conflict: The interpersonal effects of emotions in negotiations.* Amsterdam, Holland: Kurt Lewin Institute.

Van Kleef, G. A., de Dreu, C. K. W., & Manstead, A. S. R. (2004). The interpersonal effects of anger and happiness in negotiation. *Journal of Personality and Social Psychology, 86,* 57–76.

Zajonc, R. B. (1980). Feeling and thinking: Preferences need no inferences. *American Psychologist, 35,* 151–175.

Zajonc, R. B. (2000). Feeling and thinking: Closing the debate over the independence of affect. In J. P. Forgas (Ed.), *Feeling and thinking: The role of affect in social cognition* (pp. 31–58). New York: Cambridge University Press.

16

Emotional Intelligence and Interpersonal Behavior: A Theory and Review of the Literature

JOSEPH CIARROCHI and JOHN T. BLACKLEDGE

O ne thing is striking about human beings: In the absence of any observable threat or external privation, we behave badly toward each other, perhaps more so than any other animal behaves toward its own kind. We murder in the name of love, religion, and honor. Up to 38% of people in a workplace reported experiencing bullying (McAvoy & Murtagh, 2003), and 50% of people have betrayed someone in their current social network (Jones & Burdette, 1994). Employee theft is pervasive and causes one in three business failures. Forty-three percent of people who steal do so out of vindictiveness or the desire to get even (Furnham & Taylor, 2004). Wherever you find more than one human gathered together for any period of time, you might observe many forms of aversive interpersonal behavior, including verbal abuse, name calling, back stabbing, rudeness, ridicule, teasing, ostracism, emotional withholding, and bullying. Why do humans have such difficulty getting along?

Emotion is often seen as one of the causes of interpersonal problems. Anger often gets the blame for destructive social behavior, and anxiety gets the blame for avoidant social behavior. The main focus of the chapter is on why some people respond ineffectively to emotions, acting in a way that is aversive and inconsistent with their own social goals. That is, why do humans so often behave in a way that is emotionally unintelligent?

DEFINITIONS

Our chapter focuses on processes that are presumed to promote emotionally intelligent behavior (EIB) and indirectly reduce suffering. It is critical to distinguish between emotional intelligence (EI) and EIB. EI refers to people's ability to process emotions and deal effectively with them. EI refers to people's *potential*. In contrast, "emotionally intelligent behavior" refers to how effectively people actually behave in the presence of emotions and emotionally charged thoughts.

Simply put, emotionally unintelligent behavior occurs when emotions impede effective action, and EIB occurs when emotions do not impede effective action or when emotions facilitate effective action. EI (as an ability) is one set of processes hypothesized to promote EIB. There are other potential processes, many of which will be discussed in this chapter.

Perhaps a few examples of EIB will clarify our definition. If you are anxious, does that feeling stop you from socializing (we assume that this would be inconsistent with your goal of meeting new people)? If you are very angry at your friend, do you hit him (assuming your goal is to maintain friendly relations)? If you feel sad, does this stop you from caring for a loved one (assuming you value such "care")? These are three examples of emotionally unintelligent behavior. The processes that we specify in this chapter are hypothesized to help people act more intelligently and more effectively pursue their personal values and goals when they feel anxious, angry, or sad.

In our model, EIB is presumed to reduce unnecessary suffering. Thus, reduced suffering is essentially an aftereffect of people moving toward what they value (or engaging in EIB). For example, if people feel sad but continue to maintain their social relationships, they may be less likely to experience depression because their abilities to consistently engage in personally meaningful and vital activities would be expected to minimize depression over the long term. Similarly, if someone experiences anxiety about meeting a new person and still makes the effort to meet the person, they will be less likely to experience excess anxiety and regret. In contrast, if they avoid meeting new people when they feel anxious, then they may ironically experience more anxiety about meeting new people (see the section on Effective emotional orientation).

Our review focuses on processes that are presumed to both promote EIB and be modifiable by an intervention. By talking about these processes, we do not make any assumptions about whether the processes refer to either a "potential" or a "tendency." The ultimate purpose of everything done within our EI approach is about intervening to help people lead better, more vital lives. Thus, we are not interested in EI-relevant measures in themselves, but rather how these measures facilitate effective interventions.

WHY ARE PEOPLE SO EMOTIONALLY UNINTELLIGENT WHEN INTERACTING WITH OTHER PEOPLE?

The theory we will now describe is taken from two interrelated sources: relational frame theory (RFT) (Hayes, Barnes-Holmes, & Roche, 2001) and acceptance and commitment therapy (ACT) (Hayes, Strosahl, & Wilson, 1999). ACT has been tested in the field and RFT has been tested in the lab under highly controlled conditions, and both have found substantial empirical support during the last two decades (Hayes, Masuda, Bissett, Luoma, & Guerrero, 2004). RFT and ACT suggest two core factors that lead to low EI and low interpersonal effectiveness.

Factor 1: Believing Unhelpful Evaluations and Rules

Research has shown that words can carry the stimulus functions of the events or experiences they designate even when these words have not been associated with classical or direct operant conditioning (Hayes et al., 2001). For example, the word "shock" will carry with it some of the aversive functions of shock itself, even if the word has not been directly paired with an actual shock. A large body of empirical RFT studies have demonstrated that many of the ways we think about (or "frame") our experiences are derived indirectly from past experiences, that these derivations often occur along the arbitrary dimensions (e.g., dimensions such as relative worth or importance) with no objective formal or physical referents to verify them, and that many such derivations are made even when they do not correspond well to the actual contingencies we experience (Hayes et al., 2001). This phenomenon so far appears to be unique to language-able humans and to cause a unique set of pervasive problems (Hayes et al., 2001).

What does all this mean for the social world? First, it means that verbalizing about painful social interactions can itself be painful (as when we ruminate about a past social conflict). Second, verbal process can transform the way we behave socially, even in the absence of contact with social contingencies. For example, if you are told a stranger is "toxic," you might avoid that person, without ever having had bad experiences with him. Third, when we frame (i.e., verbally link) a particular social experience with a negative evaluation, the stimulus functions of that experience are transformed and become correspondingly more negative or aversive than they actually are from the perspective of a nonverbal organism (or, more precisely, than they actually would be from a direct contingency perspective). For example, if a man frames marital relationship problems as "hopeless" and his actions within the marriage as "unforgivable" and proves that he is "worthless," this is most likely to result in ineffective action and enhanced unpleasantness.

RFT makes a distinction between "having" a thought and "believing" it. By "believe," we mean that certain verbal contents have a controlling role in behavior. For example, we can have the evaluation "I am unlovable" and this evaluation may prevent us from engaging in social behavior (in which case we say the evaluation was believed). In contrast, we could have the same evaluation and act in a way that makes it likely that we will meet a lover (e.g., attend a social function). Importantly, RFT posits that whether or not symbols are believed depends on context. For example, in a context where evaluations are mindfully observed, they may be experienced as fleeting sounds, rather than as "truth" that must guide behavior. In this instance, words like "I am unlovable" may have no impact on behavior.

Factor 2: Avoiding Private Experience

The previous sections establish that verbal reports can take on many of the stimulus functions of actual experience. This makes it possible for us to evaluate the verbal reports as "bad" and to try to avoid them, just as we would avoid something aversive in the external environment. Words also allow us to create labels for private experiences. For example, we label various sensations and thoughts as "anxiety." We can then evaluate anxiety as "bad" and seek to avoid it. Finally, language allows us to create various senses of self. We develop a sense of "I" and this "I" can be evaluated as inadequate, worthless, special, and powerless. If the "I" becomes too aversive, we may seek to escape it through alcohol, gambling, or work.

Unfortunately, experiential avoidance does not appear to work in the long run. Research has shown that when subjects are asked to suppress a thought, they later show an increase in this suppressed thought as compared with those not given suppression instructions (Wenzlaff & Wegner, 2000). Indeed, the suppression strategy may actually stimulate the suppressed mood in a kind of self-amplifying loop (Feldner, Zvolensky, Eifert, & Spira, 2003). Thought suppression has been found to be associated with heightened pain experience (Sullivan, Rouse, Bishop, & Johnston, 1997), anxiety (Koster, Rassin, Crombez, & Naring, 2003), poorer ratings of quality of sleep and longer estimates of sleep-onset latency when thoughts are suppressed during the presleep period (Harvey, 2003), and increases in the reinforcing effect of alcohol when urges to drink were suppressed by heavy drinkers (Palfai, Monti, Colby, & Rohsenow, 1997). Similar results have been found in the coping literature. Avoidant coping strategies predict negative outcomes for substance abuse, depression, and effects of child sexual abuse (for review, see Hayes et al., 1999).

Bringing It All Together: Believing, Avoiding, and Behaving Aversively

Figure 16.1 summarizes essential aspects of our theory. Believing, avoiding, and emotional awareness are all hypothesized to be interconnected. Believing unhelpful rules and evaluations is expected, in many contexts, to be linked to increased avoidance and reduced emotional awareness. For example, if you have the evaluation "I am unlovable" and fully believe it, such an evaluation is likely to be quite averse. It may prompt you to avoid situations that evoke the evaluation (Figure 16.1: B → C) (Herbert & Cardaciotto, in press). The evaluation may also come to so dominate your world that you become insensitive to environmental contingencies and less aware of others' emotions and behaviors that might be inconsistent with the evaluation (B → A). For example, when couples are angry with each other and evaluating each other negatively, they tend to be less aware of emotions that are inconsistent with their partner being "bad." For example, they may fail to notice when their partner is displaying signs of affection (Flury & Ickes, 2006). The low awareness of affection may in turn make it more likely to believe the partner is "bad" (A → B).

Figure 16.1 also suggests that avoidance behavior may reinforce believing (C → B). For example, if you believe "I am too anxious to be around others" and avoid others, you may be reinforced by the momentary avoidance of social anxiety. The rule itself that led to the avoidance of anxiety thus becomes reinforced and "more" believed. Consistent with this view, there is evidence that the tendency to engage in experiential avoidance is associated with believing unhelpful rules and self-evaluations (Ciarrochi, Robb, & Godsell, 2005; Ciarrochi, Scott, Deane, & Heaven, 2003b). There is also evidence that believing unhelpful negative self-evaluations is

	Context	
Factors that may often elicit problematic verbal rules & evaluations	**Factors that foster defusion (the disbelieving of rules and evaluations)**	**Factors that increase experiential acceptance** Mindfulness exercises
Being close to another human being, learning how another has performed (better or worse than you); being in the presence of a powerful or successful other Being denied power, verbal abuse, name calling, rudeness, ridicule, teasing, criticism, accusation, blame, ostracism, threats, withholding, devaluing, bullying	Mindfulness exercises Use of metaphors to see and experience private events in a new way Repetition and altering the sound or speed of verbal formulations Manipulations that undermine confidence in reason giving	Increasing awareness of link between behavior and social contingencies Encouraging person to experiment with willingness, acceptance, and exposure Values clarification; identifying when avoidance leads away from values
	(B) Believing unhelpful rules , evaluations, and other symbolic stimuli **Evaluations** about feelings, life, the self, and other people **Rules** about the self, about controlling emotions, about how emotions "make" us act , and about how people and life "should" not make us upset	
(A) Moment to moment awareness of own and others' emotions and behaviors Identifying own and other feelings Empathic accuracy Accurate identification of how own social behavior affects others	−	**(C) Behavior serving to avoid unpleasant thoughts and feelings** <u>Observable behaviors</u> Blaming, bullying, teasing, criticizing, arguing, social avoidance, ostracism, drug and alcohol abuse <u>Private behaviors</u> Social comparison, private denigrating, anger, rumination

FIGURE 16.1   The role of context in believing, being aware, and defensive social behavior.

associated with lower and more inaccurate awareness of moment-to-moment emotions and behavior. For example, socially anxious people have a bias to believe negative social evaluations and tend to underestimate their own social skills and overestimate people's negative appraisals (Ciarrochi, Eaton, Funder, & Riggio, 2005; Rapee & Lim, 1992).

Finally, there is strong evidence that high avoidance is associated with low awareness (A → C; C → A) (Ciarrochi et al., 2005; Taylor, 2000). Individual difference measures of awareness and avoidance tend to be negatively correlated (Ciarrochi et al., 2005). In addition, people who are low in awareness tend to engage in behaviors that appear to be in the service of avoiding emotions (e.g., alcohol abuse) (Taylor, 2000). One explanation for the link between avoidance and awareness is that emotionally unaware people cannot fully work through and assimilate difficult emotional events. Consequently, they may turn to ineffective avoidance strategies to manage their emotions.

A REVIEW OF THE INDIVIDUAL DIFFERENCE LITERATURE AND ITS LINK TO EMOTIONALLY INTELLIGENT BEHAVIOR

We will now describe EI-relevant dimensions that are derived from the model. Then, we review a number of individual difference measures that appear to tap into the dimensions and discuss their relationship to interpersonal behavior. Two important points should be kept in mind while reading our discussion of EI-relevant measures. First, with few exceptions, these measures were not specifically designed to measure the EI-relevant dimension. Thus, they imperfectly measure the proposed dimension. Second, our discussion is not to be taken as an attempt to re-label old measures as "EI." Rather, it focuses on these older measures and the decades of research associated with them in order to get a better understanding of the processes that lead to EIB.

Dimension 1: Effective Emotional Orientation

Effective emotional orientation (EEO) involves willingness to have private experiences (e.g., anxiety), when doing so fosters effective action (Figure 16.2). It also involves accepting the inevitability of unpleasant affect and negative self-evaluation, and recognizing that these private experiences do not have to stop us from pursuing a valued direction (Hayes et al., 1999). People low in EEO chronically attempt to escape or get rid of their unpleasant private experiences.

Thought Suppression The *White Bear Suppression Inventory* (Wegner & Zanakos, 1994) assesses the tendency to avoid unpleasant thoughts. Research indicates that this form of avoidance can be ineffective. It tends to be associated with anxiety, depression, poor relationship quality, and low levels of social support (Ciarrochi, 2005; Ciarrochi et al., 2005). Richards and Gross (2000) provide evidence that emotional suppression impairs incidental memory for information presented

EI-relevant process	Individual Difference
1. Effective emotional orientation	Mindfulness
Willingness to have emotionally charged private experiences (thoughts, images, emotions) when doing so fosters effective action	Thought suppression
	Avoidant coping
Accepting the inevitably of a certain amount of unpleasant affect and negative self-evaluation	Blaming
Understand that private experiences do not have to stop one from pursuing a valued direction (and therefore one doesn't have to get rid of them)	Ineffective parenting style
	Reassurance seeking
2. Using emotion and emotional knowledge as information to inform effective action	Mindfulness
	Identifying emotions
	Level of emotional
Identifying emotions in self and others	awareness
Understanding the appraisals that activate different	
emotions	Empathic accuracy
Understanding how emotions progress over time	
Being aware of other people's emotions in the moment	Ability-based EI measures
3. Defusing from unhelpful rules, evaluations, and other symbolic experience	Mindfulness
	Dysfunctional attitudes
Looking *at* emotionally charged thoughts, rather than *through* them. Seeing them for what they are: fleeting thoughts that come and go; not what they seem to be: 'realities', facts, dangers that must be avoided	Dire need for power
	Dire need for approval
	Beliefs about the need for
Seeing that emotionally charged thoughts about life are not equivalent to life	rigid structure
Being able to be mindful of moment to moment experience (either internal or external)	
4. Defusing from unhelpful self-concepts	Mindfulness
Looking *at* self-evaluations, rather than through them	Self-esteem/acceptance
	Narcissism
Escaping the perceived need to defend self-esteem	Self-esteem stability
	Social comparison tendency
Recognizing that emotionally charged evaluations of the self do not have to stop us from pursing our goals	Prejudice
5. Effective action orientation	Effective action orientation
Ability to take action that is consistent with social goals and values, in the context of: impulses, fears, lack of	Impulsiveness
confidence, uncertainty, exhaustion, fatigue, physical pain, intense emotion	Ego control
	Personal strivings
Awareness of own values and their relative importance	
	Character, mettle, courage
Ability to sustain committed action in the face of inconsistent feedback, frustration, and failure	

FIGURE 16.2   Processes that are hypothesized to promote emotionally intelligent behavior.

while suppression is taking place, suggesting that suppression may impair the processing of social information (see Figure 16.1, B → A link). At the same time, suppression may increase the impact of the to-be-avoided social information. Wegner and Gold (1995) showed that suppressing thoughts about past relationships showed a rebound in thoughts for a no longer desired relationship. Lane and Wegner (1995) showed that attempts to keep and suppress a secret thought lead to increased intrusions of that thought.

Acceptance and Action Questionnaire The acceptance and action questionnaire (AAQ) (Bond & Bunce,2003; Hayes et al., 2003) measures the willingness to experience thoughts, feelings, and physiological sensations without having to control them or let them determine one's actions. In a longitudinal paradigm, Bond and Bunce (2003) found that the AAQ predicted mental health and an objective measure of workplace performance . In another study, participants high in emotional avoidance (high on the AAQ) showed more anxiety in response to CO_2 (biological challenge), particularly when instructed to suppress their emotions (Feldner et al., 2003). Finally, research has shown that low acceptance is associated with lower relationship satisfaction, few numbers of social supports, and less satisfaction with social support (Ciarrochi, 2005).

Excessive Reassurance Seeking Excessive reassurance seeking (ERS) has been defined as the stable tendency to persistently seek assurances from others that one is lovable and worthy (Joiner, Metalsky, Katz, & Beach, 1999). Cross-sectional research has shown a clear link between ERS and depression (Joiner, Alfano, & Metalsky, 1992; Joiner & Metalsky, 1995). Importantly, longitudinal research has shown that ERS predicts future depression (Joiner & Schmidt, 1998; Potthoff, Holahan, & Joiner, 1995). In addition to potentially causing depression, ERS also appears to have adverse social consequences. Several studies have found that people high in ERS tend to be evaluated negatively by others and socially rejected (Joiner & Metalsky, 1995; Katz & Beach, 1997).

Blaming Behavior Blaming behavior may often be used to avoid anxiety, loneliness, and hurt (Cordova, Jacobson, & Christensen, 1998). For example, if people blame their partner for a marital breakdown, they may be able to defend against such self-evaluations as "I am not good enough to be in a relationship" and "I am unlovable." Research has examined the impact of an acceptance-based couple's therapy on in-session expressions of blame (Cordova et al., 1998). The acceptance therapy led couples to engage in more nonblaming descriptions of problems and fewer expressions of "hard" emotions such as anger (compared to a therapy that did not emphasize acceptance). In general, success in behavioral marital therapy seems to be improved by working on acceptance of genuine incompatibilities and idiosyncronicities of marital partners (Christensen, Atkins, Berns, Wheeler, Baucom, & Simpson, 2004; Jacobson, 1992; Koener, Jacobson, & Christensen, 1994).

Acquiescent/Coercive Parenting Styles If child noncompliance is observed, there are at least two common and ineffective parental responses: acquiescence to the child's demands or dramatic and emotional escalation of demands on the child. Research suggests that both of these styles lead to behavioral problems (Murrell, Coyne, & Wilson, 2005; Patterson, 1982) .Why do parents stick to such styles if they do not work? Murrell et al. (2005) suggest that part of what reinforces poor parenting style is that it helps parents to modify, in the short term, unpleasant self-evaluations and feelings. For example, if a child misbehaves, the parent may have aversive thoughts such as "I am a bad parent/person/failure."

Thus, the aversiveness of the misbehavior is due not just to the misbehavior itself but also to the parents' aversive evaluations about themselves and the child. An ineffective parenting style might be a quick way to get the child to comply in the short term and make these unpleasant evaluations "stop." Unfortunately, such strategies do not seem to work in the long run, as the child's behavior gets worse (Murrell et al., 2005).

Dimension 2: Using Emotion as Information

The second dimension of EI involves the ability to use emotions and emotional knowledge as information to inform effective action (see Figure 16.2). There are a number of aspects to this dimension, but we will focus on one, namely, skill at identifying emotions. This ability is crucial to using emotion as information because emotions often provide us with important information about our desires and about the social world. For example, anxiety can result from the appraisal that someone might do something undesirable in the future. Anger results from the appraisal that someone has acted unfairly and this has resulted in something undesirable (Ortony, Clore, & Collins, 1988). The emotionally unaware person is hypothesized to not be able to use emotional signals as a guide to effective social action. For example, they may not know that they are angry and about to "explode" or that they are experiencing anxiety and avoiding an important social interaction.

Alexithymia   Alexithymia is a condition that involves difficulty identifying and describing emotions, minimizing emotional experience, and focusing attention externally rather than internally (Taylor, 2001). The Toronto Alexithymia Scale (TAS-20) is one of the most commonly used measures of alexithymia and has been shown to be related to a number of important life outcomes. For example, the alexithymia subscales—difficulty identifying and describing emotions—are related to a variety of negative indices of well-being (e.g., depression) (Ciarrochi et al., 2003b). Alexithymics are also at significantly higher risk than the general population for developing psychological disorders, including anxiety disorders (Parker, Taylor, Bagby, & Acklin, 1993; Zeitlin & McNally, 1993), eating disorders (Jimerson, Wolfe, Franko, Covino, & Sifneos, 1994), and substance abuse disorders (Taylor, 2001). Medical conditions that have been linked with alexithymia include hypertension (Salminen & Saarijarvi, 1999; Todarello, Taylor, Parker, & Fanelli, 1995), gastrointestinal and bowel problems (Porcelli, Leoci, Guerra, Taylor, & Bagby, 1996), and chronic pain (Cox, Kuch, Parker, Shulman, & Evans, 1994). Additionally, alexithymia has also been linked with early mortality (Kauhanen, Kaplan, Cohen, Julkunen, & Salonen, 1996).

Given that alexithymics suffer from more emotional disorders, physical problems, and alcohol abuse, we would expect this variable to have a dramatic effect on their social world. Two studies suggest this might be the case. In a large-scale study of men, Kauhanen, Kaplan, Julkunen, Wilson, and Salonen (1993) found that alexithymics were more likely to be unmarried and to have low levels of social contacts and acquaintances. Similarly, Ciarrochi (2005) found that the difficulty identifying subscale of the TAS-20 was related to low relationship satisfaction and low quantity and quality of social support.

Level of Emotional Awareness Scale   The Level of Emotional Awareness Scale (LEAS) is a performance test rather than a self-report measure (Lane, Kivley, Du Bois, Shamasundara, & Schwarz, 1995). People low in emotional awareness tend not to use specific emotion terms (sadness, anger) to describe their emotional experience. Instead, they focus on cognitions (I'd feel confused), bodily sensations (I'd feel tired), and undifferentiated emotional states (I'd feel bad). Research has shown people high in emotional awareness are less likely to allow moods to bias their judgments in mood-congruent directions (Ciarrochi, Caputi, & Mayer, 2003a). Other research suggests that emotionally aware adults have a higher number of social supports (Ciarrochi et al., 2003a). More recently, Bajgar found that emotionally aware boys are less likely to be involved in anger outbursts and fights and emotionally aware girls are more likely to be popular with their peers (Bajgar & Deane, 2004).

Emotional Perception and Understanding in Young People   This research typically involves behavioral assessment strategies, since young people presumably are not be able to accurately use self-reports. Barth and Bastiani (1997) presented young children (aged 4–5) with facial expressions of classmates (who were told to produce one of five different emotions) and had them identify the emotion being expressed. Teachers and peers rated each student in terms of social competence and popularity, respectively. The research found that a bias to see anger in faces was linked to negative dependency (e.g., asking for help when not really needed) and peer acceptance (Barth & Bastiani, 1997). Other related research suggests that children with greater understanding or awareness of emotions have been identified by their parents as having better social skills (Philippot & Feldman, 1990) and are rated as more likable and popular with their peers (Cassidy, Parke, Butkovsky, & Braungart, 1992; Denham, McKinley, Couchoud, & Holt, 1990). In observational studies, children with greater understanding of emotion display less anger and greater prosocial behavior with a peer (Garner & Estep, 2001) and lower conflict and higher cooperative pretend play with a friend (Dunn & Cutting, 1999).

Ability-Based Measures of Emotional Intelligence   Much of our discussion has focused on self-report measures, because these map most clearly to our model (Figure 16.2). However, important research has been undertaken using an ability measure of EI, the Mayer–Salovey–Caruso Emotional Intelligence Test (Mayer, Salovey, & Caruso, 2002). This measure has been shown to be reliable, distinctive from personality and IQ tests, and to be related to a number of important social outcomes (Ciarrochi, Chan, & Caputi, 2000; Mayer, Caruso, & Salovey, 1999). It correlates with empathy and the quality of interpersonal relationships (Ciarrochi et al., 2000), interpersonal skill of managers (Mayer, Salovey, & Caruso, 2004; Rosete & Ciarrochi, 2005), deviant behavior such as drug abuse and bullying (Mayer et al., 2004; Trinidad & Johnson, 2002), satisfaction with social relationships (Lopes, Salovey, & Straus, 2003), and quality of social interactions (Lopes, Brackett, Nezlek, Schutz, Sellin, & Salovey, 2004).

Dimensions 3 and 4: Defusing from Unhelpful Rules, Evaluations, and Other Symbolic Stimuli

From an ACT/RFT perspective, the problem with unhelpful verbal formulations is not that they occur, but rather that one believes them when they occur. Thus, ACT interventions typically target the believability of thoughts, rather than the form or frequency of such thoughts (see Figure 16.1 for "believability" manipulations).

This brings us to the third and fourth dimension of EI, both of which involve undermining the power of unhelpful verbal formulations. We will use the term "fused" to mean that a particular verbal formulation (e.g., "I am unlovable") has a controlling role in behavior (e.g., stopping one from socializing). "Fusing" and "believing" are used in a roughly synonymous fashion. Figure 16.2 lists the key components of this skill (Dimensions 3 and 4). Defusion involves manipulations that undermine the harmful stimulus functions of particular verbal stimuli. Such manipulations are expected to eventually lead to stable individual differences in the ability to defuse from unhelpful verbal contents. We focus on the individual difference measures that are likely to be impacted by defusion manipulations.

Mindfulness   Mindfulness of private experience is an example of a practice that can promote defusion (see Figure 16.1 for other examples of defusion manipulations). It also involves elements of acceptance and awareness of emotional states, so it cuts across many of the EI-relevant dimensions. Mindfulness involves a non-judgmental noticing of sensations, thoughts, and memories (private events) as they occur from moment to moment. This practice is hypothesized to help people experience private events as an unfolding, changing process of living, rather than as a fixed part of the self (Hayes, 2002). For example, people can view their moods as equivalent to their "self" (I am depressed), or they can experience the mood, and the evaluation of the mood, as it is (e.g., I am labeling these unpleasant sensations as "depression." I am having the evaluation that "I am depressed."). Such context shifts help people to see their private experience for what it is—streams of thought, fleeting sensations (defusion)—rather than what it says it is—fixed, facts, dangers that must be avoided (Hayes et al., 1999; Kabat-Zinn, 1990).

The Mindfulness Attention Awareness Scale   The Mindfulness Attention Awareness Scale (MAAS) measures people's tendency to be mindful of moment-to-moment experience. This scale has been shown to relate to various aspects of well-being and to how effectively people deal with stressful life events (Brown & Ryan, 2003). Intervention techniques that are likely to increase mindfulness have been shown to reduce stress and other negative mood states (Alexander, Swanson, Rainforth, & Carlisle, 1993; Speca, Carlson, Goodey, & Angen, 2000; Teasdale, Segal, & Williams, 1995). The improvements in mood appear to be associated with better peer relationships (Alexander et al., 1993).

Fusing with Unhelpful Rules and Evaluations   The Dysfunctional Attitudes Scale (DAS) (Weissman, 2000) is commonly used in clinical practice and measures the extent people believe, or fuse with, certain unhelpful thoughts. It can be divided into two dimensions (Blatt, Quinlan, Pilkonis, & Shea, 1995; Brown, Hammen, Craske, & Wickens, 1995). The first dimension is about the "dire need" for power and success, and includes beliefs that relate to perfectionism (being perfectly achieving), performance evaluation, not seeming weak, and a need for admiration and control. The second dimension relates to acceptance, and includes feeling a "dire need" for social acceptance, love, and approval. The DAS (and similar scales) has been shown to relate to well-being, discriminate between clinical and nonclinical groups, and predict changes in well-being in a longitudinal design (Blatt et al., 1995; Brown et al., 1995). The dire need for power and success has been shown to be related to poor personal relationships and lower quality social support in normal populations (Ciarrochi, 2005).

Another group of measures reflects unhelpful beliefs about uncertainty (e.g., "that uncertainty is awful or intolerable"). These include measures of intolerance of uncertainty (Dugas, Gagnon, Ladouceur, & Freeston, 1998), rigidity (Neuberg & Newson, 1993), and ambiguity (Frenkel-Brunswik, 1949). These measures have been shown to relate to depression and anxiety in both clinical and normal populations (Dugas et al., 1998; Freeston, Rheaume, Letarte, Dugas, & Ladouceur, 1994). More research is needed to investigate the role of uncertainty beliefs in social behavior.

Other measures reflect fusion with unhelpful self-concepts (Figure 16.2, Dimension 4). Low self-esteem seems to involve at least two parts: negative evaluations of the entire self (I am worthless) and fusion with these evaluations. In other words, one could have a negative self-evaluation yet not believe (fuse with) it. It appears to be reasonably well-established that low self-esteem is associated with higher levels of negative affect (Blascovich & Tomaka, 1991), lower social competence, poorer relationships, and reduced social support (Ciarrochi, 2005; Frankel & Myatt, 1996; Kim & Cicchetti, 2004).

What is somewhat more surprising is that some aspects of high self-esteem have been associated with poor well-being and social behavior, at least in some circumstances (Kernis, Grannemann, & Barclay, 1989; Rhodewalt, 2001). For example, the Narcissist Personality Inventory (NPI) assesses a person's sense of grandiosity, self-importance, and specialness (Raskin & Terry, 1988). Narcissists scan the social context for evidence that supports their elevated sense of self and tend to construct high self-esteem in the absence of objective evidence. Their self-esteem is fragile, and they are prone to respond to threatening feedback with shame, humiliation, anger, and interpersonal aggression (Rhodewalt & Eddings, 2002).

A related line of research has examined individual differences in the stability of self-esteem. Stability can be measured by administering a standard self-esteem inventory at multiple times, and then using the variance between different measurements to predict outcomes (Kernis et al., 1989). People who have unstable high self-esteem have been shown to experience more anger and hostility, perhaps because they feel the "need" to defend their self-worth (Kernis et al., 1989). Other research shows that unstable self-esteem is associated with goal-related affect characterized by greater tenseness and less interest (Kernis, Paradise, Whitaker, Wheatman, & Goldman, 2000).

Social Comparison From an RFT perspective, social comparison involves putting one's self-concept in a "frame" of comparison with another (I am better than you; I am worse than you). The reason comparison frames are sometimes problematic is not because they occur: social comparison is expected to occur in just about any language-able human. Rather, it is because the social comparisons are believed. Research suggests that unhappy people are more likely than happy people to engage in and believe social comparison processes. They feel worse when someone performs better than them (Lyubomirsky & Ross, 1997), and feel better when others perform worse, even if they also performed poorly. In contrast, happy people's mood appears to be more dependent on actual performance, rather than on how others performed.

Prejudice The topic of prejudice is much too large to discuss in detail here, but we note some key features of this domain that fit well with the present model. Prejudice involves framing oneself in an equivalence relationship with a group (e.g., *I* = white) and in nonequivalence or opposition to outgroups (e.g., "I am not black. I am the opposite of a conservative."). Thus, benefits to one's group come to be equivalent to benefits to oneself. Similarly, one can engage in social comparison processes, where one's group is viewed as better or worse than other groups.

Prejudice can be understood in terms of the model presented in Figure 16.1. Essentially, unhelpful attitudes about one's group and outgroups fall under "Believing unhelpful rules and evaluations (B)." Such attitudes are associated with inaccuracies or biases in moment-to-moment awareness of other people's behaviors (Figure 16.1; B ←→ A) (Fisk, 2004). The attitudes and self-concepts are also associated with avoidance behavior (Figure 16.1; B ←→ C). For example, people high in Right-Wing Authoritarianism engage in prejudiced behavior to defend against (or avoid) perceived threats to ingroup values in a "dangerous" world (Adorno, Frenkel-Brunswick, Levinson, & Sanford, 1950; Altemeyer, 1988). People high in Social Dominance Orientation engage in prejudiced behavior to defend against perceived threats to ingroup status in a "competitive" world (Fisk, 2004; Pratto, Sidanius, Stallworth, & Malle, 1994). Similarly, terror management theory posits that people engage in prejudice behavior to defend against thoughts of death (Pyszczynski, Greenberg, & Solomon, 1999). Such defending is presumed to increase self-esteem and give people the illusion that, through their group, they will live beyond their lifetime. Importantly, much of this defending is targeting unpleasant thoughts (e.g., self-esteem, insecurity) and feelings (terror, anxiety), rather than actual threats in the material world.

EFFECTIVE ACTION ORIENTATION

Effective action orientation involves the ability to take value-congruent action in the context of strong emotions and self-doubts. It also involves the ability to sustain this action even in the face of inconsistent feedback, frustration, and failure (see Figure 16.2). Some more colloquial terms for this dimension might be "character," "courage," or "mettle."

One of the major causes of ineffective action orientation, from an RFT perspective, is that people often believe unhelpful rules or "reasons" about their emotions and other private experiences. For example, they often believe that "confidence is needed to do something important," that anxiety "stops" them from taking action, and that anger "makes" them act aggressively.

The *Action-State Orientation Scale* measures people's ability to move from a desired goal state to some future goal state (action orientation) versus their tendency to engage in persistent, ruminative thoughts, which reduces the resources available for goal striving (Diefendorff, Hall, Lord, & Strean, 2000). Strong action orientation is associated with lower levels of anxiety, depression, and rigidity, higher levels of positive attitudes, and positive job-related behavior (Diefendorff et al., 2000; Heckhausen & Strang, 1988; Kuhl & Beckmann, 1994).

The *Self-Control Scale* is another measure of action orientation (Tangney, Baumeister, & Boone, 2004). Self-control involves the ability to "...interrupt undesired behavioral tendencies and refrain from acting on them" (Tangney et al., 2004) (p. 274). Research has demonstrated the validity of this scale and shown that high self-control is related to higher grade point average, lower levels of anxiety and depression, less alcohol abuse, and better relationships (Tangney et al., 2004).

Self-control can be measured using behavioral tasks, as well as the self-report. Specifically, a substantial amount of developmental research has looked at children's ability to delay gratification in particular situations (Mischel, Shoda, & Peake, 1988; Shoda, Mischel, & Peake, 1990; Wulfert, Block, Ana, Rodriguez, & Colsman, 2002). For example, one study offered adolescents $7 immediate payment or $10 one week later (Wulfert et al., 2002). Compared to students who delayed gratification, those who chose the immediate fee showed more self-regulatory failures, such as greater use of drugs and greater academic underperformance. In another study, preschool children were offered the choice of one marshmallow immediately versus two at a later time. This task predicted performance 10 years later. Specifically, it was found that the children who delayed gratification were more academically and socially competent and more able to deal well with frustration and stress (Mischel et al., 1988).

CONCLUSIONS

One of the most important goals in psychology is to reduce suffering and improve people's ability to get along with each other. One way to do this is to investigate why some people are particulary resilient and socially effective. If we can identify what skills these effective people have, then presumably we can teach the skills to others. Researchers have identified dozens of individual differences that are potentially important (Figure 16.2). Indeed, it seems like new individual difference measures are created every day.

The individual difference research has undoubtably been important. However, looking at the field as a whole, the different areas of research do not present a coherent picture. Researchers investigating one type of individual difference (e.g., alexithymia) rarely refer to research in other domains (e.g., dysfunctional attitudes, impulsivity). The field consists of a wide variety of seemingly unrelated measures.

This chapter attempted to bring all these measures together under a common theoretical (RFT) and intervention (ACT) framework. We sought to show how the measures can be understood in terms of three interrelated processes, namely, fusing, avoiding, and being aware. We briefly described the sorts of interventions that could seek to influence these three processes [see Figure 16.1, top and Hayes et al. (1999) for a book length treatment]. If the model presented in this chapter is accurate, then interventions that target prejudice, social anxiety, and marital problems can utilize similar kinds of technologies and be understood in terms of similar psychological processes.

One thing is strikingly different about our model compared to every other EI model (Ciarrochi, Forgas, & Mayer, 2001). We do not assume that EI consists of the ability to manage emotions or other private experiences. Indeed, we have argued that attempts at emotional management are often part of the problem, rather than the solution. We acknowledge that attempts to control emotions are sometimes effective. We just do not view control as *essential* to EIB. However, our EI model does suggest that letting go of first-order change strategies (direct attempts to modify private experiences) will result in second-order benefits. That is, when people are willing to accept the pain that occurs as a normal part of life, they will be less likely to suffer. And, they will be less likely to make others suffer.

REFERENCES

Adorno, T. W., Frenkel-Brunswick, E., Levinson, D. J., & Sanford, R. N. (1950). *The authoritarian personality.* New York: Harper.

Alexander, C. N., Swanson, G. C., Rainforth, M. V., & Carlisle, T. W. (1993). Effects of the transcendental meditation program on stress reduction, health, and employee development: A prospective study in two occupational settings. *Stress and Coping: An International Journal, 6,* 245–262.

Altemeyer, B. (1988). *Enemies of freedom: Understanding right-wing authoritariansim.* San Fransisco, CA: Jossey-Bass.

Bajgar, J., & Deane, F. P. (2004). *Does emotional awareness help in the popularity stakes?* Unpublished manuscript.

Barth, J. M., & Bastiani, A. (1997). A longitudinal study of emotion recognition and pre-school children's social behavior. *Merrill-Palmer Quarterly, 43(1),* 107–128.

Blascovich, J., & Tomaka, J. (1991). Measures of self-esteem. In J. P. Robinson, P. R. Shaver, & L. S. Wrightsman (Eds.), *Measures of personality and social psychological attitudes* (Vol. 1, pp. 115–160). New York: Academic Press.

Blatt, S. J., Quinlan, D. M., Pilkonis, P. A., & Shea, M. (1995). Impact of perfectionism and need for approval on the brief treatment of depression: The National Institute of Mental Health Treatment of Depression Collaborative Research Program revisited. *Journal of Consulting and Clinical Psychology, 63(1),* 125–132.

Bond, F. W., & Bunce, D. (2003). The role of acceptance and job control in mental health, job satisfaction, and work performance. *Journal of Applied Psychology, 88(6),* 1057–1067.

Brown, G. P., Hammen, C. L., Craske, M. G., & Wickens, T. D. (1995). Dimensions of dysfunctional attitudes as vulnerabilities to depressive symptoms. *Journal of Abnormal Psychology, 104(3)*, 431–435.

Brown, K. W., & Ryan, R. M. (2003). The benefits of being present: Mindfulness and its role in psychological well-being. *Journal of Personality & Social Psychology, 84(4)*, 822–848.

Cassidy, J., Parke, R. D., Butkovsky, L., & Braungart, J. M. (1992). Family-peer connections: The roles of emotional expressiveness within the family and children's understanding of emotions. *Child Development, 63(3)*, 603–618.

Christensen, A., Atkins, D. C., Berns, S., Wheeler, J., Baucom, D. H., & Simpson, L. E. (2004). Traditional versus integrative behavioral couple therapy for significantly and chronically distressed married couples. *Journal of Consulting and Clinical Psychology, 72(2)*, 176–191.

Ciarrochi, J. (2005). *Avoidance and dysfunctional beliefs as predictors of relationship satisfaction and quatity and quanity of social support.* Unpublished manuscript.

Ciarrochi, J., Caputi, P., & Mayer, J. D. (2003a). The distinctiveness and utility of a measure of trait emotional awareness. *Personality and Individual Differences, 34(8)*, 1477–1490.

Ciarrochi, J. V., Chan, A. Y. C., & Caputi, P. (2000). A critical evaluation of the emotional intelligence construct. *Personality and Individual Differences, 28(3)*, 539–561.

Ciarrochi, J., Eaton, L. G., Funder, D. C., & Riggio, R. (2005). *Behavioral assessment of social competence.* Unpublished manuscript, Wollongong.

Ciarrochi, J., Forgas, J. P., & Mayer, J. D. (Eds.). (2001). *Emotional intelligence in everyday life: A scientific inquiry.* Philadelphia, PA: Psychology Press/Taylor & Francis.

Ciarrochi, J., Robb, H., & Godsell, C. (2005). Letting a little nonverbal air into the room: Insights from acceptance and commitment therapy. Part 1: Philosophical and theoretical underpinnings. *Journal of Rational-Emotive and Cognitive-Behavior Therapy, 23(2)*, 79–106.

Ciarrochi, J., Scott, G., Deane, F. P., & Heaven, P. C. L. (2003b). Relations between social and emotional competence and mental health: A construct validation study. *Personality and Individual Differences, 35*, 1947–1963.

Cordova, J. V., Jacobson, N. S., & Christensen, A. (1998). Acceptance versus change interventions in behavioral couple therapy: Impact on couples' in-session communication. *Journal of Marital and Family Therapy, 24(4)*, 437–455.

Cox, B. J., Kuch, K., Parker, J. D., Shulman, I. D., & Evans, R. J. (1994). Alexithymia in somatoform disorder patients with chronic pain. *Journal of Psychosomatic Research, 38(6)*, 523–527.

Denham, S. A., McKinley, M., Couchoud, E. A., & Holt, R. (1990). Emotional and behavioral predictors of preschool peer ratings. *Child Development, 61(4)*, 1145–1152.

Diefendorff, J. M., Hall, R. J., Lord, R. G., & Strean, M. L. (2000). Action-state orientation: Construct validity of a revised measure and its relationship to work-related variables. *Journal of Applied Psychology, 85(2)*, 250–263.

Dugas, M. J., Gagnon, F., Ladouceur, R., & Freeston, M. H. (1998). Generalized anxiety disorder: A preliminary test of a conceptual model. *Behaviour Research and Therapy, 36(2)*, 215–226.

Dunn, J., & Cutting, A. L. (1999). Understanding others, and individual differences in friendship interactions in young children. *Social Development, 8(2)*, 201–219.

Feldner, M., Zvolensky, M., Eifert, G., & Spira, A. (2003). Emotional avoidance: An experimental test of individual differences and response suppression using biological challenge. *Behaviour Research and Therapy, 41(4)*, 403–411.

Fisk, S. (2004). *Social beings: A core motives approach to social psychology.* New York: Wiley.

Flury, J., & Ickes, W. (2006). Emotional intelligence and empathic accuracy. In J. Ciarrochi, J. Forgas, & J. Mayer (Eds.), *Emotional intelligence in everyday life: A scientific inquiry* (2nd ed.). Philadelphia, PA: Psychology Press/Taylor & Francis.

Frankel, F., & Myatt, R. (1996). Self-esteem, social competence and psychopathology in boys without friends. *Personality and Individual Differences, 20(3),* 401–407.

Freeston, M. H., Rheaume, J., Letarte, H., Dugas, M. J., & Ladouceur, R. (1994). Why do people worry? *Personality and Individual Differences, 17(6),* 791–802.

Frenkel-Brunswik, E. (1949). Intolerance of ambiguity as an emotional and perceptual personality variable. *Journal of Personality, 18,* 108–143.

Furnham, A., & Taylor, J. (2004). *The dark side of behaviour at work: Understanding and avoiding employees leaving, thieving, and deceiving.* New York: Palgrave Macmillan.

Garner, P. W., & Estep, K. M. (2001). Emotional competence, emotion socialization, and young children's peer-related social competence. *Early Education and Development, 12(1),* 29–48.

Harvey, A. G. (2003). The attempted suppression of presleep cognitive activity in insomnia. *Cognitive Therapy and Research, 27(6),* 593–602.

Hayes, S. C. (2002). Buddhism and acceptance and commitment therapy. *Cognitive and Behavioral Practice, 9(1),* 58–66.

Hayes, S. C., Barnes-Holmes, D., & Roche, B. (Eds.). (2001). *Relational frame theory: A post-Skinnerian account of human language and cognition.* New York: Kluwer Academic/Plenum Publishers.

Hayes, S., Masuda, A., Bissett, R., Luoma, J., & Guerrero, L. F. (2004). DBT, FAP, and ACT: How empirically oriented are the new behavior therapy technologies? *Behavior Therapy, 35,* 35–54.

Hayes, S. C., Strosahl, K. D., & Wilson, K. G. (1999). *Acceptance and commitment therapy: An experiential approach to behavior change* (Vol. 16). New York, NY: The Guilford Press.

Hayes, S. C., Strosahl, K. D., Wilson, K. G., Bissett, R. T., Pistorello, J., Polusny, M., Dykstra, T. A., & Batten, S. V. (2003). *The acceptance and action questionnaire (AAQ) as a measure of experiential avoidance.* Unpublished manuscript.

Heckhausen, H., & Strang, H. (1988). Efficiency under record performance demands: Exertion control—an individual difference variable? *Journal of Personality and Social Psychology, 55(3),* 489–498.

Herbert, J. D., & Cardaciotto, L. (in press). A mindfulness-based perspective on social anxiety disorder. In S. Orsillo & L. Roemer (Eds.), *Acceptance and mindfulness based approaches to anxiety: Conceptualization and treatment.* New York: Kluwer/Plenum.

Jacobson, N. S. (1992). Behavioral couple therapy: A new beginning. *Behavior Therapy, 23(4),* 493–506.

Jimerson, D. C., Wolfe, B. E., Franko, D. L., Covino, N. A., & Sifneos, P. E. (1994). Alexithymia ratings in bulimia nervosa: Clinical correlates. *Psychosomatic Medicine, 56(2),* 90–93.

Joiner, T. E., Alfano, M. S., & Metalsky, G. I. (1992). When depression breeds contempt: Reassurance seeking, self-esteem, and rejection of depressed college students by their roommates. *Journal of Abnormal Psychology, 101(1),* 165–173.

Joiner, T. E. Jr., Metalsky, G. I., Katz, J., & Beach, S. R. H. (1999). Depression and excessive reassurance-seeking. *Psychological Inquiry, 10(4),* 269–278.

Joiner, T. E. Jr., & Schmidt, N. B. (1998). Excessive reassurance-seeking predicts depressive but not anxious reactions to acute stress. *Journal of Abnormal Psychology*, *107(3)*, 533–537.

Joiner, T. E., & Metalsky, G. I. (1995). A prospective test of an integrative interpersonal theory of depression: A naturalistic study of college roommates. *Journal of Personality and Social Psychology*, *69(4)*, 778–788.

Jones, W. H., & Burdette, M. P. (1994). Betrayal in relationships. In A. L. Weber & J. H. Harvey (Eds.), *Perspectives on close relationships* (pp. 243–262). Needham Heights, MA: Allyn & Bacon.

Kabat-Zinn, J. (1990). *Full catastrophe living: Using the wisdom of your body and mind to face stress, pain, and illness.* New York: Dell Publishing.

Katz, J., & Beach, S. R. H. (1997). Romance in the crossfire: When do women's depressive symptoms predict partner relationship dissatisfaction? *Journal of Social and Clinical Psychology*, *16(3)*, 243–258.

Kauhanen, J., Kaplan, G. A., Cohen, R. D., Julkunen, J., & Salonen, J. T. (1996). Alexithymia and risk of death in middle-aged men. *Journal of Psychosomatic Research*, *41(6)*, 541–549.

Kauhanen, J., Kaplan, G. A., Julkunen, J., Wilson, T. W., & Salonen, J. T. (1993). Social factors in alexithymia. *Comprehensive Psychiatry*, *34(5)*, 330–335.

Kernis, M. H., Grannemann, B. D., & Barclay, L. C. (1989). Stability and level of self-esteem as predictors of anger arousal and hostility. *Journal of Personality and Social Psychology*, *56(6)*, 1013–1022.

Kernis, M. H., Paradise, A. W., Whitaker, D. J., Wheatman, S. R., & Goldman, B. N. (2000). Master of one's psychological domain? Not likely if one's self-esteem is unstable. *Personality and Social Psychology Bulletin*, *26(10)*, 1297–1305.

Kim, J., & Cicchetti, D. (2004). A longitudinal study of child maltreatment, mother-child relationship quality and maladjustment: The role of self-esteem and social competence. *Journal of Abnormal Child Psychology*, *32(4)*, 341–354.

Koener, K., Jacobson, N., & Christensen, A. J. (1994). Emotional acceptance in integrative behavioral couple therapy. In S. Hayes, N. Jacobson, V. Folette, & M. Dougher (Eds.), *Acceptance and change. Content and context in psychotherapy* (pp. 109–118). Reno, NV: Context Press.

Koster, E. H. W., Rassin, E., Crombez, G., & Naring, G. W. B. (2003). The paradoxical effects of suppressing anxious thoughts during imminent threat. *Behaviour Research and Therapy*, *41(9)*, 1113–1120.

Kuhl, J., & Beckmann, J. (1994). *Volition and personality: Action versus state orientation.* Gottingen: Hogrefe & Huber Publishers.

Lane, J. D., & Wegner, D. M. (1995). The cognitive consequences of secrecy. *Journal of Personality and Social Psychology*, *69(2)*, 237–253.

Lane, R. D., Kivley, L. S., Du Bois, M. A., Shamasundara, P., & Schwarz, G. E. (1995). Levels of emotional awareness and the degree of right hemispheric dominance in the perception of facial emotion. *Neuropsychologia*, *33(5)*, 525–538.

Lopes, P. N., Brackett, M. A., Nezlek, J. B., Schutz, A., Sellin, I., & Salovey, P. (2004). Emotional intelligence and social interaction. *Personality and Social Psychology Bulletin*, *30(8)*, 1018–1034.

Lopes, P. N., Salovey, P., & Straus, R. (2003). Emotional intelligence, personality, and the perceived quality of social relationships. *Personality and Individual Differences*, *35(3)*, 641–658.

Lyubomirsky, S., & Ross, L. (1997). Hedonic consequences of social comparison: A contrast of happy and unhappy people. *Journal of Personality and Social Psychology*, *73(6)*, 1141–1157.

Mayer, J. D., Salovey, P., & Caruso, D. (2004). Emotional intelligence: Theory, findings, and implications. *Psychological Inquiry, 15(3)*, 197–215.

Mayer, J. D., Caruso, D. R., & Salovey, P. (1999). Emotional intelligence meets traditional standards for an intelligence. *Intelligence, 27(4)*, 267–298.

Mayer, J. D., Salovey, P., & Caruso, D. R. (2002). *Mayer-Salovey-Caruso emotional intelligence test (MSCEIT) user's manual.* Toronto, Canada: MHS Publishers.

McAvoy, B. R., & Murtagh, J. (2003). Workplace bullying: The silent epidemic. *BMJ: British Medical Journal, 326(7393)*, 776–777.

Mischel, W., Shoda, Y., & Peake, P. K. (1988). The nature of adolescent competencies predicted by preschool delay of gratification. *Journal of Personality and Social Psychology, 54(4)*, 687–696.

Murrell, A. R., Coyne, L. W., & Wilson, K. G. (2005). ACT with children, adolescents, and their parents. In S. C. Hayes & K. D. Strosahl (Eds.), *A practical guide to acceptance and commitment therapy* (pp. 249–273). New York: Springer Science.

Neuberg, S. L., & Newson, J. T. (1993). Personal need for structure: Individual differences in the desire for simpler structure. *Journal of Personality and Social Psychology, 65(1)*, 113–131.

Ortony, A., Clore, G., & Collins, A. (1988). *The cognitive structure of emotion.* New York: Cambridge University Press.

Palfai, T. P., Monti, P. M., Colby, S. M., & Rohsenow, D. J. (1997). Effects of suppressing the urge to drink on the accessibility of alcohol outcome expectancies. *Behaviour Research and Therapy, 35(1)*, 59–65.

Parker, J. D., Taylor, G. J., Bagby, R., & Acklin, M. W. (1993). Alexithymia in panic disorder and simple phobia: A comparative study. *American Journal of Psychiatry, 150(7)*, 1105–1107.

Patterson, G. R. (1982). *Coercive family process.* Eugene, OR: Castalia.

Philippot, P., & Feldman, R. S. (1990). Age and social competence in preschoolers' decoding of facial expression. *British Journal of Social Psychology, 29(1)*, 43–54.

Porcelli, P., Leoci, C., Guerra, V., Taylor, G. J., & Bagby, R. (1996). A longitudinal study of alexithymia and psychological distress in inflammatory bowel disease. *Journal of Psychosomatic Research, 41(6)*, 569–573.

Potthoff, J. G., Holahan, C. J., & Joiner, T. E. (1995). Reassurance seeking, stress generation, and depressive symptoms: An integrative model. *Journal of Personality and Social Psychology, 68(4)*, 664–670.

Pratto, F., Sidanius, J., Stallworth, L. M., & Malle, B. F. (1994). Social dominance orientation: A personality variable predicting social and political attitudes. *Journal of Personality and Social Psychology, 67(4)*, 741–763.

Pyszczynski, T., Greenberg, J., & Solomon, S. (1999). A dual-process model of defense against conscious and unconscious death-related thoughts: An extension of terror management theory. *Psychological Review, 106(4)*, 835–845.

Rapee, R. M., & Lim, L. (1992). Discrepancy between self- and observer ratings of performance in social phobics. *Journal of Abnormal Psychology, 101(4)*, 728–731.

Raskin, R., & Terry, H. (1988). A principal-components analysis of the Narcissistic Personality Inventory and further evidence of its construct validity. *Journal of Personality and Social Psychology, 54(5)*, 890–902.

Rhodewalt, F. (2001). The social mind of the narcissist: Cognitive and motivational aspects of interpersonal self-construction. In J. P. Forgas & K. D. Williams (Eds.), *The social mind: Cognitive and motivational aspects of interpersonal behavior* (pp. 117–198). Cambridge: Cambridge University Press.

Rhodewalt, F., & Eddings, S. K. (2002). Narcissus reflects: Memory distortion in response to ego-relevant feedback among high- and low-narcissistic men. *Journal of Research in Personality, 36(2)*, 97–116.

Richards, J. M., & Gross, J. J. (2000). Emotion regulation and memory: The cognitive costs of keeping one's cool. *Journal of Personality and Social Psychology, 79(3)*, 410–424.

Rosete, D., & Ciarrochi, J. (2005). *The role of emotional intelligence in managerial effectiveness.* Unpublished manuscript, Wollongong.

Salminen, J., & Saarijarvi, S. (1999). Alexithymia: a facet of essential hypertension. *Hypertension, 33*, 1057–1061.

Shoda, Y., Mischel, W., & Peake, P. K. (1990). Predicting adolescent cognitive and self-regulatory competencies from preschool delay of gratification: Identifying diagnostic conditions. *Developmental Psychology, 26(6)*, 978–986.

Speca, M., Carlson, L. E., Goodey, E., & Angen, M. (2000). A randomized, wait-list controlled clinical trial: The effect of a mindfulness meditation-based stress reduction program on mood and symptoms of stress in cancer outpatients. *Psychosomatic Medicine, 62(5)*, 613–622.

Sullivan, M. J. L., Rouse, D., Bishop, S., & Johnston, S. (1997). Thought suppression, catastrophizing, and pain. *Cognitive Therapy and Research, 21(5)*, 555–568.

Tangney, J. P., Baumeister, R. F., & Boone, A. L. (2004). High self-control predicts good adjustment, less pathology, better grades, and interpersonal success. *Journal of Personality, 72(2)*, 271–322.

Taylor, G. J. (2000). Recent developments in alexithymia theory and research. *Canadian Journal of Psychiatry, 45(2)*, 134–142.

Taylor, G. J. (2001). Low emotional intelligence and mental illness. In J. Ciarrochi & J. P. Forgas (Eds.), *Emotional intelligence in everyday life: A scientific inquiry* (pp. 67–81). Philadelphia, PA: Psychology Press/Taylor & Francis.

Teasdale, J. D., Segal, Z., & Williams, J. M. G. (1995). How does cognitive therapy prevent depressive relapse and why should attentional control (mindfulness) training help? *Behaviour Research and Therapy, 33(1)*, 25–39.

Todarello, O., Taylor, G. J., Parker, J. D., & Fanelli, M. (1995). Alexithymia in essential hypertensive and psychiatric outpatients: A comparative study. *Journal of Psychosomatic Research, 39(8)*, 987–994.

Trinidad, D. R., & Johnson, C. A. (2002). The association between emotional intelligence and early adolescent tobacco and alcohol use. *Personality and Individual Differences, 32*, 95–105.

Wegner, D. M., & Gold, D. B. (1995). Fanning old flames: Emotional and cognitive effects of suppressing thoughts of a past relationship. *Journal of Personality and Social Psychology, 68(5)*, 782–792.

Wegner, D. M., & Zanakos, S. (1994). Chronic thought suppression. *Journal of Personality, 62(4)*, 615–640.

Weissman, A. (2000). Dysfunctional Attitude Scale (DAS). In K. Corcoran & J. Fischer (Eds.), *Measures for clinical practice: A sourcebook* (Vol. 2, pp. 187–190). New York: Free Press.

Wenzlaff, R. M., & Wegner, D. M. (2000). Thought suppression. *Annual Review of Psychology, 51*, 59–91.

Wulfert, E., Block, J. A., Ana, E. S., Rodriguez, M. L., & Colsman, M. (2002). Delay of gratification: Impulsive choices and problem behaviors in early and late adolescence. *Journal of Personality, 70(4)*, 533–552.

Zeitlin, S. B., & McNally, R. J. (1993). Alexithymia and anxiety sensitivity in panic disorder and obsessive-compulsive disorder. *American Journal of Psychiatry, 150(4)*, 658–660.

17

Affective Influence in Groups

JANICE R. KELLY and JENNIFER R. SPOOR

G roup researchers have long acknowledged the importance of a group's emotional life to its performance, development, and health. Until recently, however, relatively little research has directly examined the role of affect in group performance. During this same time, individual-level researchers investigating social phenomena have acknowledged that moods and emotions have profound influences on many areas of cognitive functioning. For example, mood has been found to affect judgments, persuasion, and person perception, and it appears to do so through influencing the processes of memory, attention, and type of information processing (see, for example, Forgas, 1992, 2002; see also Clore & Storbeck, this volume; Bless & Fiedler, this volume; and Forgas, this volume). Recent group-level models suggest that group affect might also have similarly important influences on group performance through its impact on information and emotion sharing processes of groups (Kelly, 2001; Kelly & Barsade, 2001).

This chapter reviews the current literature on affective influences in small, interacting, task-oriented groups. We have broadly organized the chapter around an input-process-outcome model with group performance as a primary focus (see Figure 17.1). Using our model as a framework, we examine various types of affective experiences as potential inputs affecting group process. We argue that, just as individuals experience a variety of affective states, so might groups. We provide initial evidence for these group-level affective experiences and also examine various theoretical and empirical issues concerning the definitions of group-level affect, and the measurement and manipulation of these states. We next examine affective influences involved in group process. Specifically, we discuss research and theory regarding how affective states are shared among group members, how groups engage in affect regulation in order to maintain or change an existing affective state, how affect impacts the sharing of information, and how affect exerts an influence on other aspects of group process, such as coordination of group member efforts and leadership. Finally, we review the existing literature on group outcomes, focusing in particular on affective and performance outcomes. Throughout our discussion, we also highlight several unresolved issues for future research and theory development.

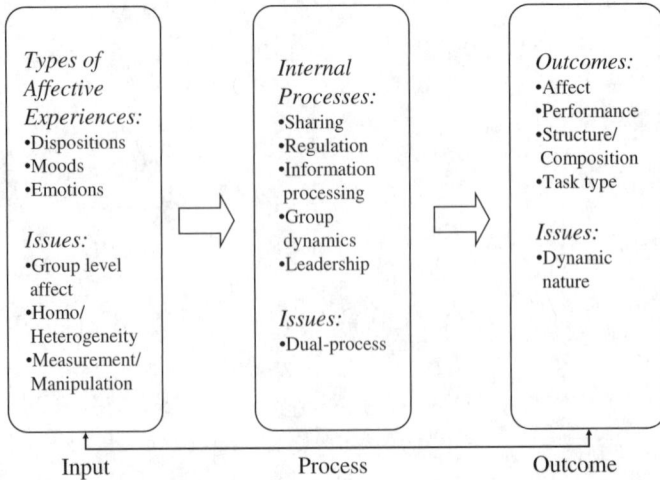

FIGURE 17.1   Affective influences in groups.

TYPES OF AFFECTIVE EXPERIENCES

Although affective factors have been central to many theories of group life, there has as yet been no agreed on definition, nor agreed on measure, of group mood or emotion. Researchers have defined a variety of types of emotional experiences that may occur primarily in group settings. For example, "group cohesiveness" refers to the affective ties that bind a group together, or to a sense of solidarity that may develop over the course of group interaction (Hogg, 1992). "Emotion contagion" refers to the spread of affect from one group member to another (Hatfield, Cacioppo, & Rapson, 1994). The "mob mind" also suggests a type of group-level affective experience (McDougall, 1923). However, none of these emotional concepts have explicitly been identified as a group-level mood or emotion. We suggest that just as individuals experience a variety of affective states, groups can also be characterized by a variety of affective experiences that may serve as input factors affecting group performance. We briefly define three such experiences at the group level—dispositional group affect, group moods, and group emotions—and then discuss unresolved issues for future research.

Individual and Group Affective Dispositions

At the individual level, dispositional affect is defined as a person's characteristic level of affect (Lazarus, 1991). Similarly, George (1990, 1996) suggested that some groups may be characterized by a dispositional level of affect. She suggests that "group affective tone" can be used to describe the group's characteristic level of positive or negative affect. More specifically, group affective tone is defined as a homogeneous or internally consistent level of dispositional affect that develops in some groups. Although not all groups develop a group affective tone, George

(1996) argues that several processes, such as selection, common history, and socialization, facilitate and encourage its development.

Individual and Group Moods

At the individual level, moods are generally defined as low intensity, diffuse feeling states that, as opposed to more intense emotions, are generally not directed toward specific targets (Forgas, 1992; Isen, 1984; see also Clore & Storbeck, this volume). Individual-level researchers have been particularly interested in mood states since, given their lack of target specificity, they have the potential to affect many kinds of judgments and evaluations. We suggest that groups also experience similar kinds of low intensity affective states. For example, Barsade (2002) and Totterdell, Kellet, Teuchmann, and Briner (1988) traced the migration of mood states across individuals in a group through the process of emotional contagion. In addition, Bartel and Saavedra (2000) provide evidence that both members of a group and outside observers are able to accurately judge group mood.

Individual and Group Emotions

Emotions can be distinguished from both dispositional affect and moods in that they tend to have a readily apparent source, tend to be relatively short in duration, and are more focused and intense (Frijda, 1994). Emotions are more likely to change beliefs (Schwarz, Bless, & Bohner, 1991; see also Bless & Fiedler, this volume), disrupt activity (Lazarus, 1991; see also Smith, David, & Kirby, this volume), and motivate specific actions and behaviors (see Baumeister, Vohs, & Tice, this volume; Smith, David, & Kirby, this volume; and Forgas, this volume). While these features may have interesting implications for group processes and outcomes, almost no empirical research has examined the effects of intense emotions on group processes, which may reflect the difficulty in measuring such brief affective states. However, a recent study by Duffy and Shaw (2000) found that group envy resulted in reduced group performance as a consequence of social loafing, less cohesiveness, and diminished group potency.

Unresolved Issues

Group-Level Affect Although a number of researchers have described and investigated group affect, there seems to be little agreement as to what exactly a group-level mood or emotion is. Is group mood simply a summary of the variety of individual-level moods present in the group, or is it something more than the sum of these parts? George (1996), for example, posits that group affective tone only exists when it is shared across group members (e.g., with high intragroup agreement in individual-level dispositional affect). Are similar conditions (shared levels) necessary to define group moods and group emotions as well? And importantly, are there group-level affective constructs that predict unique outcomes apart from individual-level predictions (see, for example, Grawitch, Munz, & Kramer, 2003a)?

Homogeneity and Heterogeneity of Group Affect   Integrally related to the issue of group-level affect are issues of homogeneity and heterogeneity of group member mood. Can affectively heterogeneous groups still be considered to have a group mood? And as above, are unique effects predicted by homogeneous versus heterogeneous group moods and emotions? There seems to be some agreement that a variety of forces tend to push group members toward similar affective states. Kelly and Barsade (2001) and Barsade and Gibson (1998) have recently suggested that a variety of both "top-down" and "bottom-up" processes may create a group-level mood or emotion. Norms for emotion displays may also encourage the expression of particular affective experiences and inhibit the expression of others, thus pushing members toward expressing common affect (Rafaeli & Sutton, 1989). In addition, group members may enter the situation with individual-level affective experiences that combine with or influence other members' feelings. In fact, Kelly and Barsade (2001) define group emotion as the result of these two forces working together.

Measurement and Manipulation of Group Affect   Methods for assessing group mood have also been recently developed. As discussed above, George (1990, 1996) argues that high levels of intermember consistency are necessary for group affective tone to exist. If such consistency exists, then individual-level reports of affect may be combined into a group average that reflects the group's affective tone. If intermember consistency does not exist, then an affective tone does not exist for that particular group.

Alternatively, Bartel and Saavedra (2000) have shown evidence that group mood can be reliably recognized by those outside of the group and can be measured through observation. They argue that mood convergence among group members occurs through the synchronization of behavioral mood information. Their "Guide to Work Group Mood" therefore consists of a set of behavioral indicators of the eight mood categories of the mood circumplex. They reported significant correlations between self-report and observer ratings of mood, validating their group mood assessment instrument, as well as significant within-group agreement in mood, demonstrating the affective homogeneity that constitutes a group mood.

Although there is growing consensus on how to measure pre-existing moods, experimental manipulations of group mood are relatively sparse. Most researchers have relied on traditional, and individual-level, methods of inducing mood (e.g., Forgas, 1992; Grawitch, Munz, Elliot, & Mathis, 2003b; Grawitch et al., 2003a; Hertel, Neuhof, Theuer, & Kerr, 2000), such as exposing participants to films, music, or memories with sad or uplifting content. Although these manipulations generally produce relatively large changes in individuals' reported mood, they are potentially problematic in that they are inherently individualistic. Kelly (2003) proposed a group-level manipulation in which group members discussed neutral or uplifting topics before engaging in the primary task. These manipulations produced smaller but reliable differences in participants' perceptions of the group's affective state.

Other potential group-level manipulations of affect could be developed. Groups could be asked to engage in fun or boring tasks, while groups with a history might be asked to discuss recent or negative events that have affected the group as a whole. However, group discussion manipulations of negative mood may be complicated by the fact that group interaction often leads to increases in positive mood (Hinsz, Park, & Sjomeling, 2004). Laboratory manipulations of emotions may also be somewhat difficult, but might include providing the group with a success or failure experience, or introducing some kind of intergroup conflict.

INTERNAL GROUP PROCESSES

As described above, there are a variety of affective states that may serve as input to the group interaction process. Group interaction process refers to the exchange of information—cognitive, affective, and behavioral—that occurs as groups interact face-to-face. We next discuss emotional exchange/sharing, affect regulation, information exchange, and other aspects of group dynamics that may be impacted by or involve affective inputs.

Sharing of Affect among Group Members

As described above, processes exist that appear to homogenize moods and emotions within groups of interacting members through the transference of emotional states. These processes include both implicit and explicit processes of affect sharing (Kelly & Barsade, 2001). The nonconscious process that has received the most empirical attention is emotional contagion, which refers to the spread of an individual's affective state to nearby individuals. Although stereotypes of emotional contagion revolve around the spread of powerful emotional experiences (e.g., panic or the "mob mind"), the spread of less intense emotions in the form of "primitive emotional contagion" is far more common (Hatfield et al., 1994). Primitive emotional contagion is defined as "the tendency to automatically mimic and synchronize facial expressions, vocalizations, postures, and movements with those of another person and, consequently, to converge emotionally" (Hatfield, Cacioppo, & Rapson, 1992, pp. 153–154).

Several processes may facilitate emotional contagion. For example, several empirical studies suggest that we mimic others' emotionally expressive behavior. Mimicry may be either direct and conscious (Bavelas, Black, Lemery, & Mullett, 1987) or relatively nonconscious and automatic (Bernieri, Reznick, & Rosenthal, 1988; Cappella, 1981). Other primarily nonconscious processes also serve to support the contagion process and the development of shared affect within the group (Kelly & Barsade, 2001). Specifically, interaction synchrony, or behavioral entrainment, is thought to underlie emotional contagion (Condon & Ogston, 1966; Hatfield et al., 1994; Kelly, 1988; McGrath & Kelly, 1986). According to the social entrainment model (McGrath & Kelly, 1986), when individuals interact, their temporal patterns of behavior often become synchronized or mutually entrained. Synchronization of expressive behavior may also serve to reinforce mimicry responses, thus reinforcing emotional contagion.

Affect Regulation in Groups

Emotional contagion is a relatively automatic and nonconscious process, but more explicit mechanisms of affect regulation may also exist. For example, groups may be motivated to maintain particular levels of affect within the group. Several theorists have proposed that emotions correspond to status within a group. For example, Houser and Lovaglia's (2002; Lovaglia & Houser, 1996) theory of status-emotional compatibility suggests that group members expect high status group members to experience positive emotions and low status group members to experience negative emotions. Similarly, Kemper (2000) has proposed links between emotional responses and changes in one's relative status within a group. He suggests that increases in one's own relative status should be associated with happiness, while decreases in one's relative status should be associated with anger or depression (depending on the reasons for the status change). From these perspectives, status differences within a group may be one factor that promotes heterogeneous levels of affect among groups (see also George, 2002).

Spoor and Kelly (2004) have suggested that groups may also engage in explicit affect regulation strategies when specific group outcomes are desired (see Erber & Markunas, this volume, for a similar argument at the individual level). Drawing on an evolutionary perspective, they suggest that positive affective states within groups promote cooperation while negative affective states may promote collective action in response to negative aspects of the environment. Thus, they suggest that explicit affect regulation strategies may communicate larger group goals among the group members. In contrast to affect regulation to maintain status differences, this type of affect regulation stresses the importance of homogeneous levels of affect within groups.

In their research on naïve theories of group mood, Kelly and Spoor (in press) recently suggested an additional impetus for explicit affect regulation. They argue that just as individuals possess naïve theories regarding other social phenomena, individuals may also possess naïve theories regarding how mood affects group interaction. Their research suggests that there is some consensus regarding the content of naïve theories and that these theories may subsequently bias perceptions of a group interaction. They further speculate that group members' naïve theories may motivate group members to engage in affect regulation when their theory suggests that the current affective state is potentially harmful for the group.

Affect and Information Processing in Groups

Drawing heavily on individual-level information processing theories, an emerging perspective within small groups research is to conceptualize groups as information processors (Hinsz, Tindale, & Vollrath, 1997). Kelly (2001) has argued that group moods may shape group information processing in a parallel manner as at the individual level. She proposes that group information processing may "look" like individual information processing except that at the group level information processing occurs "out loud" and can be indexed via patterns of information exchange. Thus, happy individuals often prefer relatively heuristic, top-down processing, while sad individuals often prefer relatively systematic, bottom-up processing (Forgas, 1992, 1995; Schwarz, Bless, & Bohner, 1991; see also Clore & Storbeck, this volume; Bless & Fiedler, this volume; and Forgas, this volume). In groups, heuristic processing may be reflected in the use of simple decision rules (e.g., majority wins) and short discussion time, whereas systematic processing may be reflected in longer total discussion time and fewer topic changes (indicating more elaboration).

Preliminary evidence for the influence of mood on group information processing is provided by Forgas (1990), who induced positive, negative, or neutral moods in individual participants. Participants were then asked to make evaluative ratings of nine person categories, either individually or as a group. Consistent with previous research, individual judgments were biased in a mood-consistent manner. However, group discussions tended to accentuate the bias of positive moods but attenuate the bias of negative moods. Presumably, group members in negative moods engaged in more controlled information processing, and thus were less influenced by their mood. We believe that Kelly's (2001) group information processing approach has tremendous potential for understanding mood effects in groups.

Other Aspects of Group Dynamics

Coordination and Cooperation Affective inputs may affect not only what information is exchanged, but also how that information is exchanged. For example, high levels of interpersonal and task cohesion may also have an impact on the group's ability to coordinate efforts and to contribute equally to a task, which may subsequently affect group performance (Zaccaro & McCoy, 1988). Similarly, positive affect among group members may also affect the group's ability to coordinate information exchange and to appropriately utilize group resources.

Mood states may also affect motivation to persist on a task. For example, Martin, Ward, Achee, and Wyer (1993) suggest that bad moods signal that goals have not been satisfied, and thus lead to continued behavior toward that goal, whereas positive moods signal that goals have been satisfied, and thus lead to the discontinuation of behavior directed toward that goal. Research by Sanna, Parks, and Chang (2003) supports this mood effect for members working on social dilemma tasks.

Leadership Leaders play a crucial role in shaping group process, and one facet of effective leadership is the ability to manage group emotions. For example, the transformational leadership style is widely considered to be one of the most effective forms of leadership, and several theorists have suggested that transformational leaders are adept at using emotions to motivate and communicate their vision to subordinates (Ashkanasy & Tse, 2000; Bass & Avolio, 1994).

Leadership research has also addressed the direct impact of leaders' moods on group performance. In a study of work teams in a customer service context,

George (1995) found that the leaders' positive mood during the last week predicted supervisors' perceptions of the groups' performance, even after controlling for the groups' affective tone. However, group positive affective tone was unrelated to the leaders' positive affect, which George attributed to the relatively hierarchical structure of the work teams. She speculated that groups in which leaders and group members worked together closely to complete tasks would show a stronger relationship between the group's affective tone and the leader's mood.

Other research is concerned with how a leader's emotional reactions to group outcomes shape group interaction. For example, Pescolido (2002) suggests that one role of emergent leaders is to serve as "emotion managers". Pescolido suggests that emergent leaders may help to manage the group's responses to uncertain situations (e.g., receiving ambiguous feedback) by modeling an emotional response. An interesting aspect of this approach is that any group member may serve as a manager of group emotions at various times throughout the group's history.

Unresolved Issues of Affect and Group Process

A Dual-Process Approach   One potential avenue for research is to explore the extent to which affective influences in groups are relatively conscious and deliberate or nonconscious and automatic. Research on affective processes at the individual level suggests multiprocess approaches (Forgas, 2002). With regards to affect sharing, there is clear evidence for nonconscious processes (e.g., emotional contagion), but as discussed in the section on affect sharing, the evidence for conscious processes is sparse (but see Kelly & Barsade, 2001, for such potential conscious processes).

An alternative dual process perspective would involve a two-stage sequence of affective influences. Groups may experience different affective states in a relatively automatic way. If the group does not explicitly recognize the affective state, it may infuse the group's interaction and information processing. However, when groups recognize the affective influences, they may then engage in explicit strategies to correct or suppress the mood. Mood suppression and correction are potentially resource intensive (Baumeister, Bratslavsky, Muraven, & Tice, 1998; Richards & Gross, 2000). Thus, correcting for mood effects may have negative consequences in terms of group performance. Preliminary support for these processes at the group level is suggested by Spoor and Kelly's (2003) recent research on mood regulation in groups. In this study, positive or negative group moods were manipulated via a group discussion manipulation. Group members were also given norm information suggesting that a particular mood state was most beneficial for group performance. When the norm differed from the manipulated mood, the groups performed more poorly on a subsequent decision-making task. Presumably, when the norm was inconsistent with their current mood state, groups attempted to regulate the mood, resulting in decreased attention to the primary task and reduced performance.

AFFECT INFLUENCES ON GROUP PERFORMANCE AND OTHER OUTCOMES

Affective Outcomes

Although we have focused on affect as either an input factor or a factor directly affecting group interaction processes, affective states may also be an outcome of interaction. Consequently, these affective states may be reinforced in the group, to serve as a new input factor. Cohesion is one of the most widely studied group affective states (Kelly & Barsade, 2001). Although too broad a literature to discuss here, recent reviews (e.g., Mullen & Copper, 1994) suggest that the cohesiveness construct comprises interpersonal attraction, task commitment, and group pride, and is both an antecedent and a consequence of group interaction (Levine & Moreland, 1990). Thoits (1996) suggests that intentionally manipulating extreme emotions might, at least temporarily, aid therapy groups in developing group solidarity and cohesion. Consequently, therapy groups might be more successful in dealing with their problems. This research suggests that affect may serve as both an input and an output factor for group interaction.

Although behavioral entrainment and interaction synchrony underlie emotional contagion, these processes may directly lead to increases in positive affect through creating a more efficient interaction (see also, Spoor & Kelly, 2004). Several studies examining group and dyadic interaction demonstrate that both processes are linked to outcomes related to affect in groups, including group rapport (Tickle-Degnan & Rosenthal, 1987) and liking for the interaction partner (Kelly, 1987). In a similar fashion, research demonstrates that nonconscious mimicry of one's interaction partner smoothes the interaction, resulting in greater rapport, liking, and positive affect (Lakin, Jefferis, Cheng, & Chartrand, 2003).

Performance Outcomes

A large body of literature suggests that different affective experiences can have important influences on group performance. For example, cohesion is often implicated in successful performance of various types of groups (Mullen & Copper, 1994). More generally, a positive emotional character or "internal group harmony" has been cited as the most important component in determining the quality of group outcomes (Hackman, 1991). However, only a handful of investigators have examined the effects of group mood on performance.

In a study of sales teams, George (1990) found that group affective tone predicted a number of important outcomes related to performance. Positive group affective tone was negatively related to absenteeism, while negative group affective tone was negatively related to customer-directed prosocial behavior. Given the nature of these teams, this study provides evidence that affect in groups may have important consequences for group performance.

A few studies have also examined the effect of mood states on cooperative choices among small group members. For example, Hertel and Fiedler (1994) induced positive and negative moods in members playing four-person Prisoner's Dilemma Games. They found that positive mood states did not directly increase cooperative choices, but rather increased the variability of responses. More recently, Hertel et al. (2000) examined the effects of positive and negative moods in the context of a chicken dilemma game. In this study, individuals in positive moods tended to rely on heuristics, and so were more likely to imitate their partners' behavior. Negative moods induced more systematic processing of information and led to more rational decision-making outcomes, such that individuals defected when others' cooperation was high, but cooperated when others' cooperation fell below a critical level.

Recent experiments by Grawitch and his colleagues (Grawitch et al., 2003a, 2003b) demonstrate that group members' mood states may impact creative performance. For example, Grawitch et al. (2003a) induced positive, neutral, and negative moods before groups completed a creative problem-solving task. They found that positive mood groups outperformed both neutral and negative mood groups in terms of both overall creativity and efficiency. Outside observers also rated the negative mood groups as having a more negative affective tone, more negative reactions to the task, and a stronger relationship-orientation (and less task orientation) than the other groups.

In another study, Grawitch et al. (2003b) found that, compared to neutral mood groups, positive mood groups generated more original and important ideas on a brainstorming task. Interestingly, they also found that positive mood groups reported less overall satisfaction when they had more autonomy in choosing the topics to brainstorm. They suggested that neutral mood groups may have capitalized on their autonomy to engage in mood management, thus using the task to improve their mood. Positive mood groups may have been primarily interested in maintaining their positive mood state. Thus, in the low autonomy conditions, the extra effort of defining the task may have decreased the group members' positive mood states.

These studies demonstrate that mood can have important implications for performance in a group context. However, each of these studies operates from different theoretical perspectives concerning the potential effects of affect on group behavior, each explores vastly different types of groups and group tasks, and each defines group affect in a different manner.

Task Type as Moderator

One clear avenue for future research is to examine how the nature of the group's performance task interacts with affective influences. It seems fairly straightforward, both from individual-level research and the available group research, that the actual impact of affective states on group performance will vary depending on the type of task. The concept of process-performance fit (Hutson-Comeaux & Kelly, 1996; Wood, 1987) suggests that changes in interaction process do not have uniformly positive or negative effects on group performance, but rather performance effects depend on the fit between interaction process and requirements for successful performance on any particular task. For example, Grawitch's research (e.g., Grawitch et al., 2003a, 2003b) demonstrates that tasks involving creative thinking may be facilitated by positive mood states in groups, which may facilitate broader and divergent thinking (Fredrickson, 2001). At the same time, both information processing models and mood management models suggest that positive moods may sometimes hinder decision-making groups from fully elaborating and discussing alternatives, especially if such activities would attenuate the group's positive mood.

We might also expect different process-performance fits for intellective or judgmental tasks (Laughlin, 1980). For both types of tasks, the process-performance fit likely depends on a variety of factors. As discussed above, positive moods may increase the group's reliance on heuristics or simple decision rules, which may be helpful on judgmental tasks if it facilitates the group's ability to make their decision quickly. On the other hand, these same heuristics may be harmful if group members hesitate to voice dissenting opinions (e.g., to avoid conflict). Negative moods may allow group members to discuss dissenting opinions, but the negative affective state may lead to a spiraling of negative interaction and group conflict (see also the discussion in the next section on the dynamic nature of affective influences).

Unresolved Issues

The Dynamic Nature of Group Affect   Future research examining the role of affect in groups will also have to consider the potentially dynamic and cyclical nature of these effects. Because of their limited duration, studies of ad hoc lab groups generally only focus on one aspect of the input-process-output relationship. While these studies provide insight into causal relationships, they may not be able to capture the ways in which affect is reinforced within a group that interacts over an extended period of time. Positive or negative affect within a group may influence the types of tasks the group seeks out, the risks the group is willing to take, and the way that the group responds to performance feedback, which may subsequently reinforce the initial mood state. Similarly, the group performance itself may influence the affective state. Certainly a "job well done" reinforces positive affect, while poor performance may increase negative affect. The resultant positive affective state may lead to diminished performance on future tasks if processing decreases, or improved efforts designed to maintain the positive affect. Similarly, negative affect may lead to improved performance if the group becomes more vigilant and engages in more systematic processing, and the group may also be able to draw on the experience to increase cohesiveness and task commitment. On the other hand, negative affect may be debilitating for a group, perhaps resulting in increased conflict and a reduction of effort (if there is hopelessness).

CONCLUSIONS

Kelly and Barsade (2001) recently commented that affect is alive and well and living in groups. Researchers have long acknowledged that many aspects of affective phenomena have interpersonal antecedents and consequences

(Wallbott & Scherer, 1986), and that emotional expression has an important impact on social interaction (see all chapters in this volume). However, an empirical examination of affective influence in groups is a relatively recent area of inquiry. There are many potential avenues for future research, only some of which we have outlined here.

ACKNOWLEDGMENT

This work was supported by a National Science Foundation Grant (#BCS-0132258) to the first author.

REFERENCES

Ashkanasy, N. M., & Tse, B. (2000). Transformational leadership as management of emotion: A conceptual review. In N. M. Ashkanasy, C. Hartel, & W. Zerbe (Eds.), *Emotions in the workplace: Developments in the study of the managed heart* (pp. 221–235). Westport, CT: Quorum Books.

Barsade, S. G. (2002). The ripple effect: Emotional contagion and its influence on group behavior. *Administrative Science Quarterly, 47*, 644–675.

Barsade, S. G., & Gibson, D. E. (1998). Group emotion: A view from top and bottom. In D. H. Gruenfeld, B. Mannix, & M. Neale (Eds.), *Research on managing groups and teams* (pp. 81–102). Stamford, CT: JAI Press.

Bartel, C., & Saavedra, R. (2000). The collective construction of work group moods. *Administrative Science Quarterly, 45*, 802–836.

Bass, B. M., & Avolio, B. J. (1994). *Improving organizational effectiveness through transformational leadership*. Thousand Oaks, CA: Sage.

Baumeister, R. F., Bratslavsky, E., Muraven, M., & Tice, D. M. (1998). Ego depletion: Is the self a limited resource? *Journal of Personality and Social Psychology, 74*, 1252–1265.

Bavelas, J. B., Black, A., Lemery, C. R., & Mullett, J. (1987). Motor mimicry as primitive empathy. In N. Eisenberg & J. Strayer (Eds.), *Empathy and its development. Cambridge studies in social and emotional development* (pp. 317–338). New York: Cambridge University Press.

Bernieri, F. J., Reznick, J. S., & Rosenthal, R. (1988). Synchrony, pseudosynchrony, and dissynchrony: Measuring the entrainment process in mother–infant dyads. *Journal of Personality and Social Psychology, 54*, 243–253.

Cappella, J. N. (1981). Mutual influence in expressive behavior: Adult–adult and infant–adult dyadic interaction. *Psychological Bulletin, 89*, 101–132.

Condon, W. S., & Ogston, W. D. (1966). Sound film analysis of normal and pathological behavior patterns. *Journal of Nervous and Mental Diseases, 143*, 338–347.

Duffy, M. K., & Shaw, J. D. (2000). The Salieri syndrome: Consequences of envy in groups. *Small Group Research, 31*, 3–23.

Forgas, J. P. (1990). Affective influences on individual and group judgments. *European Journal of Social Psychology, 20*, 441–453.

Forgas, J. P. (1992). Affect in social judgments and decisions: A multiprocess model. In M. Zanna (Ed.), *Advances in experimental social psychology* (Vol. 25, pp. 227–275). New York: Academic Press.

Forgas, J. P. (1995). Mood and judgment: The Affect Infusion Model (AIM). *Psychological Bulletin, 117*, 39–66.

Forgas, J. P. (2002). Feeling and doing: Affective influences on interpersonal behavior. *Psychological Inquiry, 13*, 1–28.

Fredrickson, B. L. (2001). The role of positive emotions in positive psychology: The broaden-and-build theory of positive emotions. *American Psychologist, 56*, 218–226.

Frijda, N. H. (1994). Varieties of affect: Emotions and episodes, moods, and sentiments. In P. Ekman & R. J. Davidson (Eds.), *The nature of emotion: Fundamental questions*. Oxford, UK: Oxford University Press.

George, J. M. (1990). Personality, affect, and behavior in groups. *Journal of Applied Psychology, 75*, 107–116.

George, J. M. (1995). Leader positive mood and group performance: The case of customer service. *Journal of Applied Social Psychology, 25*, 778–794.

George, J. M. (1996). Group affective tone. In M. A. West (Ed.), *Handbook of work group psychology* (pp. 77–93). Chicester, UK: Wiley.

George, J. M. (2002). Affect regulation in groups and teams. In R. G. Lord, R. J. Klimoski, & R. Kanfer (Eds.), *Emotions in the workplace: Understanding the structure and role of emotions in organizational behavior* (pp. 183–217). San Francisco: Jossey-Bass.

Grawitch, M. J., Munz, D. C., & Kramer, T. J. (2003a). Effects of member mood states on creative performance in temporary workgroups. *Group Dynamics: Theory, Research and Practice, 7*, 41–54.

Grawitch, M. J., Munz, D. C., Elliot, E. K., & Mathis, A. (2003b). Promoting creativity in temporary problem-solving groups: The effects of positive mood and autonomy in problem definition on idea-generating performance. *Group Dynamics: Theory, Research and Practice, 7*, 200–213.

Hackman, J. R. (1991). Group influences on individuals in organizations. In M. D. Dunnette & L. M. Hough (Eds.), *Handbook of industrial and organizational psychology* (Vol. 3., pp. 199–267). Palo Alto, CA: Consulting Psychologists Press.

Hatfield, E., Cacioppo, J., & Rapson, R. L. (1992). Emotional contagion. In M. S. Clark (Ed.), *Emotion and social behavior* (pp. 151–177). Newbury Park, CA: Sage.

Hatfield, E., Cacioppo, J., & Rapson, R. L. (1994). *Emotional contagion*. New York: Cambridge University Press.

Hertel, G, & Fiedler, K. (1994). Affective and cognitive influences in a social dilemma game. *European Journal of Social Psychology, 24*, 131–145.

Hertel, G., Neuhof, J., Theuer, T., & Kerr, N. L. (2000). Mood effects on cooperation in small groups: Does positive mood simply lead to more cooperation? *Cognition and Emotion, 14*, 441–472.

Hinsz, V. B., Park, E. S., & Sjomeling, M. (2004, May). *Group interaction sustains positive mood and diminishes negative mood*. Paper presented at the meeting of the Midwestern Psychological Association, Chicago, IL.

Hinsz, V. B., Tindale, R. S., & Vollrath, D. A. (1997). The emerging conceptualization of groups as information processors. *Psychological Bulletin, 121*, 43–64.

Hogg, M. A. (1992). *The social psychology of group cohesiveness: From attraction to social identity*. New York: Harvester Wheatsheaf.

Houser, J. A., & Lovaglia, M. J. (2002). Status, emotion, and the development of solidarity in stratified task groups. In S. R. Thye & E. J. Lawler (Eds.), *Group cohesion, trust, and solidarity: Advances in group processes* (Vol. 19, pp. 109–137). Amsterdam: Elsevier.

Hutson-Comeaux, S. L, & Kelly, J. R. (1996). Sex differences in interaction style and group task performance: The process-performance relationship. *Journal of Social Behavior and Personality*, *11*, 255–275.

Isen, A. M. (1984). Toward understanding the role of affect in cognition. In J. R. S. Wyer & T. Srull (Eds.), *Handbook of social cognition* (pp. 170–236). Hillsdale, NJ: Lawrence Erlbaum Associates, Inc.

Kelly, J. R. (1987). *Mood and interaction*. Unpublished doctoral dissertation, University of Illinois, Urbana-Champaign, IL.

Kelly, J. R. (1988). Entrainment in group interaction and task performance. In J. E. McGrath (Ed.), *The social psychology of time: New perspectives* (pp. 89–110). Thousand Oaks, CA: Sage.

Kelly, J. R. (2001). Mood and emotion in groups. In M. A. Hogg & R. S. Tindale (Eds.), *The Blackwell handbook of social psychology* (Vol. 3, pp. 164–181). Oxford, UK: Blackwell.

Kelly, J. R. (2003, May). *Group mood and group decision making*. Invited talk presented at the meeting of the Midwestern Psychological Association, Chicago, IL.

Kelly, J. R., & Barsade, S. G. (2001). Mood and emotions in small groups and work teams. *Organizational Behavior and Human Decision Processes*, *86*, 99–130.

Kelly, J. R., & Spoor, J. R. (in press). Naïve theories of the effects of mood in groups: A preliminary investigation. *Group Processes and Intergroup Relations*. Manuscript submitted for publication.

Kemper, T. D. (2000). Social models in the explanation of emotions. In M. Lewis & J. M. Haviland-Jones (Eds.), *Handbook of emotions* (Vol. 2, pp. 45–58). New York: Guilford Press.

Lakin, J. L., Jefferis, V. E., Cheng, C. M., & Chartrand, T. L. (2003). The chameleon effect as social glue: Evidence for the evolutionary significance of nonconscious mimicry. *Journal of Nonverbal Behavior*, *27*, 145–162.

Laughlin, P. R. (1980). Social combination process of cooperative, problem-solving groups at verbal intellective tasks. In M. Fishbein (Ed.), *Progress in social psychology* (Vol. 1, pp. 127–155). Hillsdale, NJ: Lawrence Erlbaum Associates, Inc.

Lazarus, R. S. (1991). *Emotion and adaptation*. New York: Oxford University Press.

Levine, J. M., & Moreland, R. L. (1990). Progress in small group research. *Annual Review of Psychology*, *41*, 585–634.

Lovaglia, M. J., & Houser, J. A. (1996). Emotional reactions and status in groups. *American Sociological Review*, *61*, 867–883.

Martin, L. L., Ward, W., Achee, J. W., & Wyer, R. S. (1993). Mood as input: People have to interpret the motivational implications of their moods. *Journal of Personality and Social Psychology*, *64*, 317–326.

McDougall, W. (1923). *Outline of psychology*. New York: Scribner.

McGrath, J. E., & Kelly, J. R. (1986). *Time and human interaction: Toward a social psychology of time*. New York: Guilford Press.

Mullen, B., & Copper, C. (1994). The relation between group cohesiveness and performance: An integration. *Psychological Bulletin*, *115*, 210–227.

Pescolido, A. T. (2002). Emergent leaders as managers of group emotion. *The Leadership Quarterly*, *13*, 583–599.

Rafaeli, A., & Sutton, R. I. (1989). The expression of emotion in organizational life. In L. L. Cummings & B. M. Staw (Eds.), *Research in organizational behavior* (pp. 1–42). Greenwich, CT: JAI Press.

Richards, J. M., & Gross, J. J. (2000). Emotion regulation and memory: The cognitive costs of keeping one's cool. *Journal of Personality and Social Psychology*, *79*, 410–424.

Sanna, L. J., Parks, C. D., & Chang, E. C. (2003). Mixed-motive conflict in social dilemmas: Mood as input to competitive and cooperative goals. *Group Dynamics: Theory, Research, and Practice, 7*, 26–40.

Schwarz, N., Bless, H., & Bohner, G. (1991). Mood and persuasion: Affective states influence the processing of persuasive communications. In M. P. Zanna (Ed.), *Advances in experimental social psychology* (Vol. 24, pp. 161–199). San Diego, CA: Academic Press.

Spoor, J. R., & Kelly, J. R. (2003, February). *Situational norms and group mood: Implications for task performance.* Paper presented at the meeting of the Society for Personality and Social Psychology, Los Angeles, CA.

Spoor, J. R., & Kelly, J. R. (2004). The evolutionary significance of affect in groups: Communication and group bonding. *Group Processes and Intergroup Relations, 7*, 398–416.

Thoits, P. A. (1996). Managing the emotions of others. *Symbolic Interaction, 19*, 85–109.

Tickle-Degnan, L., & Rosenthal, R. (1987). Group rapport and nonverbal behavior. *Review of Personality and Social Psychology, 9*, 113–136.

Totterdell, P., Kellet, S., Teuchmann, K., & Briner, R. B. (1988). Evidence of mood linkage in work groups. *Journal of Personality and Social Psychology, 74*, 1504–1515.

Wallbott, H. G., & Scherer, K. R. (1986). The antecedents of emotional experiences. In K. R. Scherer, H. G. Wallbott, & A. B. Summerfield (Eds.), *Experiencing emotion: A cross-cultural study* (pp. 69–97). Cambridge, UK: Cambridge University Press.

Wood, W. (1987). Meta-analytic review of sex differences in group performance. *Psychological Bulletin, 102*, 53–71.

Zaccaro, S. J., & McCoy, M. C. (1988). The effects of task and interpersonal cohesiveness on performance of a disjunctive group task. *Journal of Applied Social Psychology, 18*, 837–851.

18

Affect and the Regulation of Interdependence in Personal Relationships

JOHN G. HOLMES and DANU B. ANTHONY

*I*n recent years, models of affect and emotion have increasingly emphasized the functional role that affect plays in helping people adapt to their environments. Theories of affect in close relationships have made similar assumptions, depicting relational affect as a guidance system that regulates people's interdependence with a significant other. In this chapter, we will first review the most prominent theories of affect and emotion, with an eye to pointing out their common themes regarding the regulation of risk in relationships. This will be followed by a discussion of recent work on the "dependence-regulation model" (Murray & Holmes, 2000). This model suggests that a particular set of emotions are functionally related in a regulatory system that modulates risk-taking behavior in close relationships. Specifically, feelings such as anxiety and social pain (hurt feelings), which signal perceived risk, are theorized to elicit feelings of social distance and anger—affect that controls the degree of relational interdependence a person is willing to risk.

THE EMOTIONS-IN-RELATIONSHIPS MODEL

The most prominent theory in the field has been Berscheid's (1983/2002) emotions-in-relationships model (ERM). Berscheid adapted Mandler's (1975) discrepancy detection theory to the relational context. Mandler argued that detecting *change* in our environments is critical to survival. The discrepancy between the world as currently perceived and the world as we have known it in the past serves to signal that new ways of behaving are necessary to protect ourselves or to enhance our welfare. Unexpected disruption of routines or goal pursuits results in autonomic nervous system (ANS) arousal that has priority status in consciousness. Unexplained arousal results in scanning of a situation to locate its cause (e.g., Schachter, 1964) so that relevant adjustments may be made. These ideas are similar to Gray and McNaughton's (2000) notion of a "comparator" monitoring system, which they link primarily to a behavioral inhibition system (BIS).

Berscheid sees violated expectancies as the basis for both negative and positive emotions, linking them to the BIS and BAS (the behavioral activation system), respectively. She argues that the infrastructure of a close relationship serves to produce conditions conducive to people experiencing their most intense emotions. Individuals in close relationships are very dependent on each other for the attainment of many important plans and goals, so that violated expectancies have potent consequences for the individual's welfare. Further, individuals in close relationships hold clearer and more numerous expectations for each other than do individuals in more superficial relationships, resulting in increased opportunities for expectancy violation.

Berscheid's ERM predicts that negative emotion will result when a partner unexpectedly interferes with the attainment of an important personal or couple goal. Berscheid notes that goals and plans have a hierarchical structure, and that the disruption of even everyday behavioral routines can result in upset if they are nested in a series of higher-order plans. Thus, the negative affective reaction spurred by the disruption of a goal sequence serves as a signal warning individuals to make behavioral adjustments to protect their interests and reduce their exposure to interpersonal risk. Consequently, couples whose concrete goals and preferences do not correspond well experience more upset, anger, and conflict, even if they have no explicit awareness of their lack of goal complementarity (Holmes & Dal Cin, 2005).

On the other hand, Berscheid notes that people will often have no awareness of the extent to which their routines and goal pursuits are "meshed" with those of a partner. This enmeshment of goals within a couple can create a situation in which individuals rarely experience goal disruptions, resulting in low levels of emotion. In such a situation, individuals may not realize the extent of their dependence on their partner (a "stagnant relationship"). Sometimes it is only an intense negative reaction to separation or relationship dissolution that leads a person to understand the degree to which he or she depended on the other for the attainment of significant goals.

According to the ERM, positive emotion will result when the consequences of a violated expectation are perceived to enhance an individual's welfare, as when a partner facilitates the achievement of an important goal. Holmes and Dal Cin (2005) found that couples whose goals are largely compatible experience a sense of "well-being" when goals are facilitated unexpectedly. Of course, the ultimate emotion, passionate love, will be facilitated by a variety of factors, among them an unexpectedly quick realization that "someone so wonderful actually cares for me."

Berscheid and Walster (1974), inspired by Schachter (1964), proposed a two-component theory of love. They suggested that passionate love develops when an individual is very aroused physically and contextual cues suggest that "passion" is the appropriate label for that arousal. Interestingly, they suggest that a variety of emotional experiences associated with physiological arousal (e.g., anxiety, frustration, rejection, sexual excitement) are instrumental in producing and enhancing passionate feelings through misattribution processes. This literature is too extensive to review in detail here (see Berscheid & Regan, 2005). Instead, we want to focus on the functional aspects of love and its relation to the general attachment system.

THE ATTACHMENT SYSTEM AND EMOTIONS

Shaver, Hazan and their colleagues conceptualize passionate love as a biological process that has been designed by evolution to facilitate attachment between two adult sexual partners (Hazan & Diamond, 2000; Hazan & Shaver, 1987). They have noted that key features of infant–caregiver attachment are remarkably similar to those of adult romantic love, including idealization, absorption, and physical proximity seeking. However, two key differences are the more reciprocal, equal-power, caregiving that occurs between adults and the fact that sexual desire is normally part of the experience. The authors suggest that prototypical adult romantic love involves the integration of three independent, biologically based behavioral systems: attachment, caregiving, and sexuality. Sternberg (1986) had earlier made a similar point, suggesting that "love" involves a weighted contribution of three components that can be viewed as a triangle: intimacy, commitment, and passion.

In recent years considerable progress has been made in studying the possible biological bases of passionate or romantic love and the psychological and biochemical differences between it and its neighbor, companionate love (i.e., an attachment bond without passion). For instance, passionate love is associated with elevated levels of androgens such as testosterone, as well as high levels of the neurotransmitters dopamine and norepinephrine (and low levels of serotonin) (Fisher, 1998). Meyers and Berscheid (1997) found that people have a relatively clear prototype of passionate love that includes strong sexual desire, exclusivity and obsession with the partner. Indeed, serotonin levels of those feeling passionately in love were not different from those diagnosed with obsessive–compulsive disorder, while both differed from controls (Marazitti, Akiskal, Rossi, & Cassano, 1999).

Meyers and Berscheid also report that people code themselves as being "in love" in the passionate stage, compared to simply experiencing feelings of "love" in companionate relationships. Similarly, Shaver, Morgan, and Wu (1996) suggest that the statement "I love you" could refer to the type of love experienced in attachment, caregiving, or sexual attraction relationships. They conclude that passionate love, being "in love," actually involves a mix of all three of these behavioral/emotional systems. Companionate love, on the other hand, is seen as an attachment bond characterized by feelings of affection and tenderness, as well as an emotional dependence on the other for feelings of security and happiness (Shaver et al., 1996). Recent research indeed suggests that attachment is associated with a different set of biological processes than passionate love, including elevated levels of neuropeptides, oxytocin, and vasopressin. The working assumption of this research is that the attachment emotion system evolved to motivate individuals to engage in positive social behaviors and to sustain their affiliative connections long enough to complete species-specific parental duties (Fisher, 1998).

In their seminal paper, Shaver et al. (1996) marshal arguments for considering love as a basic emotion. In accord with Izard's (1991) views, they note that at first blush love appears to be complex, to be more than a single emotion. Izard notes that "the one we love can make us very angry. Some people think that their greatest frustrations and their most intense anger are elicited by people they love. …the intense involvement between two people who love each other makes possible the arousal of strong emotions of various kinds" (p. 394). Shaver et al. concur with Lazarus (1991) that this definition of love refers to "a social relationship rather than an emotional process or state, a relationship that could involve the emotion of love at some times and not others, as well anger, guilt, and jealousy" (p. 274).

Shaver et al. argue that it is only the momentary feelings of "surge love" that meets the criteria that emotion theorists such as Izard have used to determine the "basic emotions." Thus they believe it is important to distinguish, as Lazarus does, between this state-like, momentary reaction that comes and goes, and the "dispositional" kind of love that instead describes the quality of an ongoing relationship, which the authors term "relational love" (p. 81). The latter is a bond that develops between romantic partners and, as Izard suggests in the quote above, it can be associated with a variety of emotions, not just "surge love." This is because, in the ordinary course of its operation, the attachment behavioral *system* generates a variety of emotions.

The attachment system, according to Shaver et al. (1996), was "co-opted" into the adult romantic realm from an infant attachment system, which was designed to maintain optimal proximity to a caregiver. According to Bowlby (1979, p. 69), the attachment system consists of a number of different functional processes that facilitate achievement of this overall goal. First, it is a monitoring system for whether the attachment figure is sufficiently available and responsive [similar to the Leary & Baumeister (2000) notion of a "sociometer," which monitors social inclusion]. If this monitoring results in a negative or uncertain conclusion about caregiver availability, *anxiety results*. If the anxiety cannot be reduced by efforts to re-establish proximity and closeness, the situation is likely to arouse *anger*. On the other hand, if monitoring typically results in reassurance of the strength of the bond, "the unchallenged maintenance of the bond is experienced as a source of *security*." Interestingly, Bowlby also suggests that "the renewal of a bond is experienced as *joy*."

Shaver et al. (1996) suggest another possible cascade of emotions that can result from the attachment system. In their view, if anxiety about caregiver responsiveness is resolved by the appraisal that, at a particular moment, a significant other is available, responsive and caring, a momentary surge of love will result. It is this form of "surge love" that they consider to be a basic, universal emotion. These ideas are quite consistent with Berscheid's ERM, considering that love surges are hypothesized to depend on positive partner behavior that resolves uncertainty about possible responsiveness and caring.

This theoretical model developed by Shaver et al. (1996) is quite impressive in its ability to distinguish longer-term, more "dispositional" feelings (as they label them) from momentary, state emotions, and to link negative emotions such as anxiety and anger to the complex issue of "love." However, there have been almost no efforts by attachment theorists to test the "state" model empirically (for a review of the influence of mood and emotional states on social cognition, see Forgas, this volume). Further, the "relational love" aspect of the model has largely been explored by focusing on the personality side of the "disposition" notion. That is, investigators have found that individuals with a secure *personality* "style" report stronger feelings of love and security, whereas those with insecure styles report either more anxiety or reduced closeness to partner.

These results are of course important, but they do not directly capture the notion of "relational love" or security that Bowlby proposed, where the focus would be on the quality of feelings of attachment and security in a *specific* relationship, and how those feelings would relate to momentary emotions. These are the issues central to a related theoretical perspective, the dependence-regulation model proposed by Murray and Holmes (2000).

THE DEPENDENCE-REGULATION MODEL

Our earlier research had shown that intimates in close relationships typically have positive illusions about their partner, seeing them even more positively than their partners see themselves. This work resulted in the serendipitous observation that people with low self-esteem (LSE) were far less likely to see their partner in such generous, idealistic ways than people with high self-esteem (HSE) (Murray, Holmes, & Griffin, 1996). In fact, we noticed that there was extensive evidence in the literature that LSE was associated with less satisfying close relationships, though the exact mechanisms responsible for the link remained a mystery. We speculated that part of the answer might have to do with LSE people (needlessly) doubting their partner's positive regard and love.

To explore this idea, we asked both members of dating and married couples to describe how they saw themselves on a set of interpersonally oriented qualities, then how they saw their partner, and finally how they believed their partner saw them (our measure of perceived regard) (Murray, Holmes, & Griffin, 2000). Acting like naïve realists (and self-verification theorists), people with LSE incorrectly assumed that their partner saw them in the same relatively negative light as they saw themselves. Ironically, this effect emerged even though LSE people reported wanting their partner to see them much more positively than they saw themselves (and even though their partner actually did see them as positively as they had hoped). Perhaps most crucially, dating and married intimates who believed that they were less well regarded by their partner in turn found less to value in the partner. Insecurities about a partner's regard thus appeared to constrain the idealization process, leading people to maintain a cautious distance in their relationships by defensively seeing their partner in a less generous light.

This pattern of results was reminiscent of Holmes and Rempel's (1989) speculation about how people might resolve the serious, but common, problem of how to cope with feelings of insecurity about a partner's regard and affections. The solution suggested was that people would actively regulate (inter)dependence—only letting themselves risk feeling attached and committed to their partner to the extent that they felt confident of their partners' reciprocated affections. Integrating these ideas, Murray et al. (2000) proposed a *dependence-regulation model*. This model suggests that, in the face of risk, people regulate their dependence (and thus their vulnerability) in a relationship by self-protectively "pulling away" from the partner, reducing feelings of love and closeness, devaluing the partner, and disengaging from the relationship.

Dependence-Regulation Dynamics across Time

Murray et al. (2000) found longitudinal support for the model, with people's (often unwarranted) initial doubts about their partner's regard predicting less generosity in their view of the partner (as well as more conflict and doubt and less love) as dating relationships progressed. They also found that when intimates felt less positively regarded initially, their overall self-esteem became more negative over time. This seemed important evidence for the sociometer model of self-esteem (Leary & Baumeister, 2000), as it clearly links perceptions of acceptance from a close other with changes in self-esteem over time.

These observed changes over time represent an analysis of the dynamics of close relationships that remains at a general level, and can be characterized as focusing broadly on "relational love" (Shaver et al., 1996). At this broad level, the logic of the dependence-regulation model is a good fit with the attachment system conceptualization discussed earlier. Both models can be interpreted in terms of parallel cognitive and affective processes, with the emotions presumably providing the motivational impetus for adaptive action (see Figure 18.1). The perceived regard construct is a cognitive summary of people's estimation of how much they are valued and loved by a *particular* partner in a close relationship, and can thus be considered a relationship-specific sociometer. It is tied logically and empirically to one's expectations of responsiveness from one's partner, expectations which many writers deem central to evolutionary arguments about evolved psychological mechanisms for regulating relationship behavior (see Reis, Clark, & Holmes, 2004).

The affect construct tied to appraisals of perceived regard is probably best described as simply "feelings of security or insecurity." In our research we have

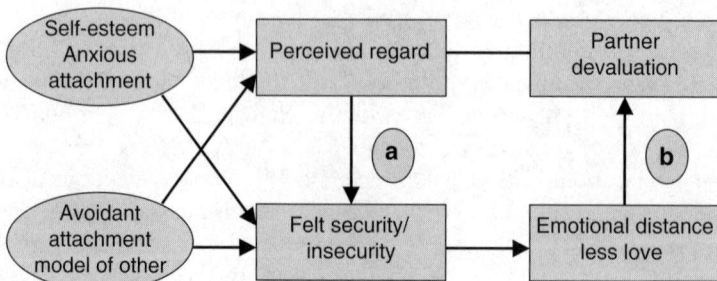

FIGURE 18.1. Dependence-regulation system.

found that feelings of insecurity reflect a combination of the reality of the partner's actual lowered commitment and caring, as well as biased construals based on chronic personality traits. Specifically, high attachment anxiety or LSE (as previously described) result in more felt insecurity, as do high levels of attachment avoidance. The feelings of "unease" associated with felt insecurity are experienced as anxiety by people with a negative "model of self" (LSE or high attachment anxiety) and as vulnerability or discomfort with closeness by people with a negative "model of other" attachment avoidance.

The dependence-regulation model assumes that felt insecurity is a warning sign that triggers defensive regulatory responses. The emotional reactions elicited by felt insecurity would be reduced feelings of closeness and love. Figure 18.1 indicates how this decrease in emotional closeness might spur changes in cognition to bring thoughts into line with affect. The result of this is self-protective devaluation of the partner and relationship, which serves the function of minimizing dependence and the potential magnitude of the loss expected by insecure people. If the feeling of insecurity is sufficiently strong and the person feels "devalued," the reaction to the associated "hurt feelings" is also likely to be one of anger (which we will discuss below).

A Situational Analysis of Felt Security

Our goal in more recent research is to demonstrate that dependence-regulation dynamics not only describe long-term adjustments in relationships, but also predict cognitive and affective reactions to everyday events (the momentary affective states described by Shaver et al., 1996). That is, we believe that risk regulation is an ongoing microprocess, one that can be quite revealing of the inter-relations among various affective states in relationships. Similar approaches to studying affect through self-regulation processes are described in chapters by Baumeister et al., Erber and Markunas, and Haselton and Ketelaar in this volume.

Consider the flow diagram in Figure 18.2. Imagine that a man named Harry finds himself in a situation of interdependence with his wife Sally and one day he notices that she is in a bad mood and is acting in a distant way (a potentially threatening event). Many people might feel a bit rejected, at least momentarily. However, under what circumstances might this fleeting feeling be taken as a sign that one's partner's affections are waning? We predicted that people with *chronic* concerns about their partner's regard would be quick to perceive behavior like Sally's as rejection, and then to "make mountains out of molehills" by generalizing from it to a larger meaning about their partner's feelings. The associated affective reaction to such perceived rejection would be acute "social pain" or hurt feelings, a topic we return to later.

On the other side of the coin, confident expectations that the partner values the self might inoculate people against all but the most obvious signs of a partner's rejection in everyday social interactions. The result would be a discounting of the meaning of potentially offending behaviors, such as Sally's moodiness. Indeed, our past work suggested that people are strongly motivated to feel secure in their most significant relationships (e.g., Murray, Holmes, MacDonald, & Ellsworth, 1998).

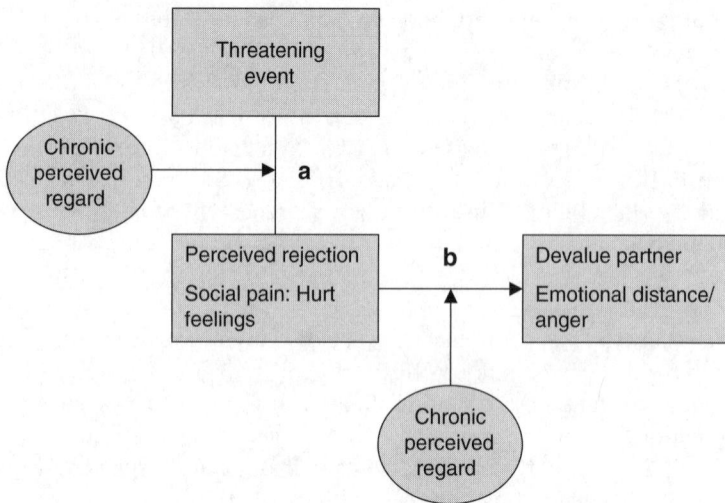

FIGURE 18.2   A situational analysis of felt security regulation.

Given this, we expected to find that people who feel chronically valued by their partner would actively compensate for potential concerns by recruiting thoughts to help
them embellish their partner's love. Thus, the "appraisal-sensitivity" link between a
threatening event and temporarily lowered perceived regard, or hurt feelings (path
a in Figure 18.1), is moderated by a person's chronic state of perceived regard.

In a similar way, we also expected that chronic perceived regard would moderate the capacity to stay connected and attached to a partner in situations that pro-
voke feelings of hurt and rejection (path b). Intimates with low chronic perceived
regard may be most likely to react to the acute pain of rejection with anger, or by
taking the defensive step of distancing from their partner, the source of the hurt.
After all, devaluing one's partner, reducing feelings of closeness, and lashing out
behaviorally all serve self-protective motivations by reducing investment in the
relationship. In contrast, people with high chronic perceived regard are predicted
to use their firm sense of felt security as a resource, allowing them to take the risk
of taking constructive steps to enhance or promote the value of the relationship.

Research is quite consistent with this model. For instance, Murray and her
colleagues have demonstrated such patterns of responses in the real-life behavior
of married couples, as measured through daily diaries (Murray, Bellavia, Rose, &
Griffin, 2003). People who felt chronically less valued by their spouses (often LSE
individuals) felt more hurt and rejected on days when their partner reported a bad
mood, inconsiderate behavior, or a conflict (see Figure 18.3). Such hurt feelings
then led to more self-reported anger and emotional distance the next day, accompanied by behavior that was hostile and controlling, according to their partner.
This bad behavior was understandably annoying to partner. Thus, the result of this
dependence-regulation sequence may have been a self-fulfilling prophecy, in that
the bad behavior at its end may have provoked real rejection, which was only
feared to exist in the beginning. In stark contrast, people with chronically high

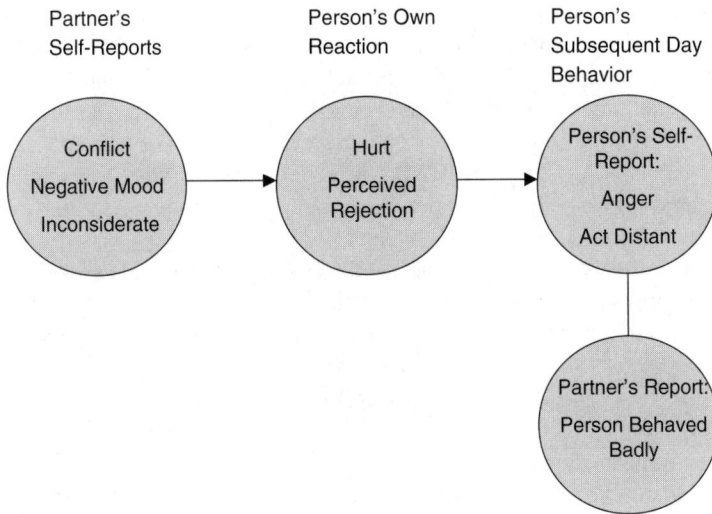

Partner's Self-Reports	Person's Own Reaction	Person's Subsequent Day Behavior
Conflict / Negative Mood / Inconsiderate	Hurt / Perceived Rejection	Person's Self-Report: Anger / Act Distant

Partner's Report: Person Behaved Badly

FIGURE 18.3   Low perceived regard people's reactions.

perceived regard actually felt *more* accepted by their spouse the day after a threatening event, and also reacted to difficulties by drawing closer to the partner. Such constructive reactions to potential insecurity would clearly serve as a consolidating force in the relationship.

Conceptual replications of these dynamics are evident in both experimental studies and field research. People who are likely to doubt their partner's acceptance, by virtue of low global self-esteem, chronic attachment-related anxiety, or chronic rejection sensitivity, react to feeling rejected in ways that reduce and minimize dependence. Specifically, people with LSE respond to experimentally induced anxieties about their partner's possible rejection by depending less on their partner for comfort (Murray et al., 1998) and by evaluating their partner's qualities more negatively (Murray et al., 1998; Murray, Rose, Bellavia, Holmes, & Kusche, 2002). The need to downplay the value and importance of the partner (the source of the hurt) is sufficiently powerful in that derogation effects emerge on the very qualities that typically reveal people's positive illusions about their partner (Murray et al., 1996). These devaluing processes also emerge whether these acute rejection anxieties are completely imagined in response to a newly discovered fault in the self (Murray et al., 1998) or arise in response to the partner's behavior (Murray et al., 2002).

For example, Murray et al. (2002) explored people's reactions to potential evidence that their partner had concerns about their relationship. An example of "evidence" presented was a biased inventory that informed participants that a partner's occasional irritation and impatience were signs of "unspoken complaints." In all of the studies, LSE people read too much into "problems," seeing them as a sign of a partner's waning affections; they then reacted to this risk by derogating the partner and reducing closeness. HSE people were less sensitive to potential signs of rejection. Moreover, they reacted to "problems" by actually *increasing* their ratings of their partner's acceptance and their own feelings of closeness, compared to controls. Clearly, people with a chronic high positive regard are motivated to protect both their sense of felt security and their positive image of the relationship (Murray, Holmes, & Collins, 2005).

Evidence from other laboratories is also consistent with these ideas. For instance, more anxiously attached women displayed greater anger towards their partner in a situation in which their partner may not have been as responsive as they hoped (Rholes, Simpson, & Orina, 1999). After discussing a serious problem in their relationship, more anxiously attached men and women reported greater anger and hostility (as compared to anxious people discussing a minor problem, or secure people discussing either problem), and they also downplayed their feelings of closeness and commitment (Simpson, Rholes, & Phillips, 1996). To the extent that expression of anger is a means of trying to control the partner's behavior, such sentiment reduces dependence.

Additionally, in a situation in which participants accurately inferred their partner's positive thoughts about available and attractive opposite-sex others, intimates high on attachment-related anxiety reactively reported feeling less close to the offending partner (Simpson, Ickes, & Grich, 1999). Women chronically high on rejection sensitivity also responded to a *potential* partner's disinterest by evaluating that person more negatively (Ayduk, Downey, Testa, Yen, & Shoda, 1999). In day-to-day interactions with a romantic partner, rejection-sensitive women were also more likely to initiate conflicts on days after they felt rejected by their partner, and simply priming rejection-related words activated hostility-related thoughts (Ayduk et al., 1999).

Interestingly, a major school of clinical intervention, emotion-focused marital therapy (Greenberg & Johnson, 1988; see Johnson & Talitman, 1997 for an outcome study), follows a logic that closely corresponds to the dependence-regulation model. The therapy is based on attachment theory and assumes that "secondary, *reactive* emotional responses" (italics ours) are often the result of primary goals being thwarted. Thus, for instance, anger is often a presenting problem in therapy, but one that should not become its focus. It should be bypassed in order to focus on the underlying primary emotional process that caused the anger to begin with: feeling hurt, rejected, or vulnerable. The authors argue that if these underlying feelings are dealt with effectively, new interaction cycles that facilitate the growth of trust and safety can result. Essentially, it was a lack of feelings of trust and safety that was the basic problem causing conflict and lack of closeness in the first place. Indeed, in an empirically based study of therapy outcomes, the amount of trust developed at follow-up predicted intimacy and satisfaction.

THE THREAT-DEFENSE SYSTEM AND THE SOCIAL PAIN HYPOTHESIS

Recently, Geoff MacDonald, who worked on the original dependence-regulation model (Murray et al., 1998), has written a review suggesting that social exclusion or relational devaluation is experienced as painful because reactions to rejection are mediated, quite literally, by aspects of the physical pain system (MacDonald & Leary, 2005). Basically, the authors suggest that in evolutionary development the physical pain system was "co-opted" to aid social animals in responding to threats to exclusion. Essentially, we developed learning mechanisms aimed at associating cues from a monitor of social distance (a sociometer) with response mechanisms that triggered relevant social approach/avoidance tendencies. Learning such associations serves the critical biological imperative of a "need to belong" (Baumeister & Leary, 1995), a motivation that is viewed as critical for survival in our primitive past.

Because of the strong relation between pain and threat-defense response mechanisms (Gray & McNaughton, 2000; Panksepp, 1998), pain affect would provide a pathway by which exclusion cues could trigger quick defensive reactions aimed at improving one's level of social inclusion. Panksepp's ideas about the "panic" neural system in young animals seem close to Bowlby's (1982) attachment system concepts, with separation linked to distress vocalizations and response options designed to restore proximity to the parent. The benefit of having a social pain system that is overlaid onto the physical one is that social exclusionary cues would be experienced as *painful*, resulting in physiological changes that promote timely and urgent action, such as aroused ANS and analgesia (Gray & McNaughton, 2000). Given that social exclusion would have been almost as dangerous to our ancestors as physical injury, an equally urgent warning and reaction system would have been highly beneficial.

Recent laboratory studies by Twenge, Baumeister, and colleagues support the hypothesis that analgesia and action-preparedness are the body's reactions to social pain. For instance, in one set of studies, the authors inform participants that they likely face a life of being alone, a significant threat to social inclusion. People in this situation tend to act in a less cognitively complex, intelligent way (Baumeister, Twenge, & Nuss, 2002), engage in self-defeating, "dumb" behaviors (Twenge, Catanese, & Baumeister, 2002), and react as if they are experiencing an inner "numbness" (Twenge, Catanese, & Baumeister, 2003). That is, they surprisingly seem to be in a "deconstructed" state where they experience few emotions. Such a state seems to ward off potentially intense negative affect and defend against an awareness of the self's deficiencies that may have led to the rejection. Thus, it appears that overt anger may not mediate the aggressive responses that very typically accompany the experience of exclusion (e.g., Twenge, Baumeister, Tice, & Stucke, 2001).

MacDonald and Leary also conclude from their review that felt devaluation often leads to aggression, noting that "aggression seems like an odd response....unlikely to increase others' acceptance" (p. 41). Aggression is a more understandable response, however, if rejection is a primal threat leading to social pain that triggers a panic reaction. Defensive aggression would often be a relatively automatic response that is functional in physical threat contexts, but less functional in social threat contexts. Further, exclusion may prime an automatic defense that may be difficult to override and control, given the limited cognitive resources available for reappraisal (Baumeister et al., 2002).

Despite the evidence that aggression and assertiveness is the dominant response to exclusion, the panic and pain systems are generally seen as triggering preparedness for all of the fight/flight/freezing threat response options. The "flight" response in humans seems more similar to withdrawal and avoidance, of the sort described in the dependence-regulation model, and it is seen as more likely when an "escape route" is available. "Freezing" seems most akin to depressive affect and helplessness when no escape is possible. The critical question for researchers, then, is to specify the relational conditions that will determine the form that the threat response will take in close relationships where the person is generally dependent on the relationship and does not want to imperil it at a conscious level.

Specifically, research by Twenge, Baumeister, and colleagues has typically used a rather dramatic manipulation of exclusion, one that has broad negative implications for the self. In contrast, in our dependence-regulation research we are normally trying to understand reactions to potential relational devaluation or lack of responsiveness. In such circumstances of milder "social pain," the analgesic, numbing effects might be much weaker (see Williams, Case, & Govan, 2003) and, as we indicated earlier, anger may be the first response to feeling hurt in an ongoing relationship.

The dependence-regulation model generally emphasizes "flight" reactions such as emotional distancing and cognitive devaluing of the relationship as a broad response to feeling hurt. Individuals who are dispositionally prone to avoidance may be especially likely to adopt such reactions (Murray et al., 2005). Nonetheless, the evidence reviewed above suggested that hostile, bad behavior was commonly combined with such distancing responses, despite its potentially self-defeating nature. This was particularly true for individuals with LSE or high attachment anxiety. (This reaction seems in contrast to attachment theorists' claims that highly anxious individuals' natural reaction is to try to increase proximity in the face of threat.) Admittedly, some of this bad behavior may function as a "protest," to signal one's hurt to the partner (see Simpson et al., 1996; Williams et al., 2003), or it might reflect a desire for control in the absence of trust (Holmes & Rempel, 1989). But our hunch is that some of the hostility expressed by people who fear rejection by their partner is a relatively primitive response spurred by social pain, a hypothesis that is supported by our earlier review of people's self-reports of anger and implicit emotional reactions.

CONCLUSION

Theories of emotion in close relationships hinge on the notion that people's emotions play a functional role in regulating their interdependence with significant others. There is strong evidence that anxiety reflects people's insecure expectations about how a partner will care for them and respond to their needs. The warning systems of such individuals will show increased appraisal sensitivity for identifying potential threats. There is growing evidence that perception of a threat to acceptance results in hurt feelings that resemble "social pain." Such experiences of felt insecurity or social pain trigger defensive reactions, motivating individuals to regulate their dependence on the person who inflicted the pain. While there is considerable evidence of such regulation, the form it will take in terms of flight or fight responses is not yet clear. Finally, the role of anger as a mediator of fight responses is ambiguous at this point and the issue may hinge on the seriousness of the signs of social rejection. Anger may result in the context of the subtle or ambiguous exclusion cues common to ongoing close relationships, whereas emotional numbness may occur in contexts where one faces full relational exclusion.

REFERENCES

Ayduk, O., Downey, G., Testa, A., Yen, Y., & Shoda, Y. (1999). Does rejection elicit hostility in rejection sensitive women? *Social Cognition*, *17*, 245–271.

Baumeister, R. F., & Leary, M. R. (1995). The need to belong: Desire for interpersonal attachments as a fundamental human motivation. *Psychological Bulletin*, *117*, 497–529.

Baumeister, R. F., Twenge, J. M., & Nuss, C. K. (2002). Effects of social exclusion on cognitive processes: Anticipated aloneness reduces intelligent thought. *Journal of Personality and Social Psychology*, *83*, 817–827.

Berscheid, E. (1983/2002). Emotion. In H. H. Kelley, E. Berscheid, A. Christensen, J. Harvey, T. Huston, G. Levinger, E. McClintock, L. Peplau, & D. Peterson, (Eds.), *Close relationships* (pp. 110–168). Clinton Corners, NY: Percheron Press.

Berscheid, E., & Regan, P. (2005). *The psychology of interpersonal relations*. Upper Sadle River, NJ: Prentice-Hall.

Berscheid, E., & Walster, E. (1974). A little bit about love. In T. Huston (Ed.), *Foundations of interpersonal attraction* (pp. 355–381). New York: Academic Press.

Bowlby, J. (1979). *The making and breaking of affectional bonds*. London: Tavistok.

Bowlby, J. (1982). *Attachment and loss (Vol. 1: Attachment)*. London: Hogarth Press.

Fisher, H. (1998). Lust, attraction and attachment in mammalian reproduction. *Human Nature*, *9*, 23–52.

Gray, J. A., & McNaughton, N. (2000). *The neuropsychology of anxiety*. New York: Oxford University Press.

Greenberg, L., & Johnson, S. (1988). *Emotionally focused therapy for couples*. New York: Guilford.

Hazan, C., & Diamond, L. M. (2000). The place of attachment in human mating. *Review of General Psychology*, *4*, 186–204.

Hazan, C., & Shaver, P. (1987). Romantic love conceptualized as an attachment process. *Journal of Personality and Social Psychology*, *52*, 511–524.

Holmes, J. G., & Dal Cin, S. (2005). *Goal compatibility in couples and the relation to psychological processes*. Unpublished manuscript, University of Waterloo.

Holmes, J. G., & Rempel, J. K. (1989). Trust in close relationships. In C. Hendrick (Ed.), *Review of personality and social psychology: Close relationships* (Vol. 10, pp. 187–219). Newbury Park: Sage.

Izard, C. E. (1991). *The psychology of emotions*. New York: Plenum.

Johnson, S., & Talitman, E. (1997). Predictors of success in emotionally focused marital therapy. *Journal of Marital and Family Therapy*, *23*, 135–152.

Lazarus, R. S. (1991). *Emotion and adaptation*. New York: Oxford University Press.

Leary, M. R., & Baumeister, R. F. (2000). The nature and function of self-esteem: Sociometer theory. In M. P. Zanna (Ed.), *Advances in experimental social psychology* (Vol. 32, pp. 2–51). San Diego, CA: Academic Press.

MacDonald, G., & Leary, M. R. (2005). Why does social exclusion hurt? The relationship between social and physical pain. *Psychological Bulletin, 13(2),* 202–223.

Mandler, G. (1975). *Mind and emotion.* New York: Wiley.

Marazitti, D., Akiskal, H., Rossi, A., & Cassano, G. (1999). Alteration of the platelet serotonin transporter in romantic love. *Psychological Medicine, 239,* 741–745.

Meyers, S., & Berscheid, E. (1997). The language of love: What a difference a preposition makes. *Personality and Social Psychology Bulletin, 23,* 347–362.

Murray, S. L., Bellavia, G., Rose, P., & Griffin, D. (2003). Once hurt, twice hurtful: How perceived regard regulates daily marital interaction. *Journal of Personality and Social Psychology, 84,* 126–147.

Murray, S. L., & Holmes, J. G. (2000). Seeing the self through a partner's eyes: Why self-doubts turn into relationship insecurities. In A. Tesser, R. B. Felson, & J. M. Suls (Eds.), *Psychological perspectives on self and identity* (pp. 173–198). Washington: APA Press.

Murray, S. L., Holmes, J. G., & Collins, N. (2005). *The relational signature of felt security.* Unpublished manuscript.

Murray, S. L., Holmes, J. G., & Griffin, D. (1996). The benefits of positive illusions: Idealization and the construction of satisfaction in close relationships. *Journal of Personality and Social Psychology, 70,* 79–98.

Murray, S. L., Holmes, J. G., & Griffin, D. W. (2000). Self-esteem and the quest for felt security: How perceived regard regulates attachment processes. *Journal of Personality and Social Psychology, 78,* 478–498.

Murray, S. L., Holmes, J. G., MacDonald, G., & Ellsworth, P. (1998). Through the looking glass darkly? When self-doubts turn into relationship insecurities. *Journal of Personality and Social Psychology, 75,* 1459–1480.

Murray, S. L., Rose, P., Bellavia, G., Holmes, J., & Kusche, A. (2002). When rejection stings: How self-esteem constrains relationship-enhancement processes. *Journal of Personality and Social Psychology, 83,* 556–573.

Panksepp, J. (1998). *Affective neuroscience: The foundation of human and animal emotions.* London: Oxford University Press.

Reis, H., Clark, M., & Holmes, J. G. (2004). Perceived partner responsiveness as an organizing construct in the study of intimacy and closeness. In D. J. Mashek & A. Aron (Eds.), *Handbook of intimacy and closeness* (pp. 201–225). Mahwah, NJ: Lawrence Erlbaum Associates, Inc.

Rholes, W. S., Simpson, J. A., & Orina, M. M. (1999). Attachment and anger in an anxiety-provoking situation. *Journal of Personality and Social Psychology, 76,* 940–957.

Schachter, S. (1964). The interaction of cognitive and physiological determinants of emotional state. In L. Berkowitz (Ed.), *Advances in experimental social psychology* (Vol. 1, pp. 49–80). New York: Academic Press.

Shaver, P. R., Morgan, H., & Wu, S. (1996). Is love a "basic" emotion? *Personal Relationships, 3,* 81–96.

Simpson, J. A., Ickes, W., & Grich, J. (1999). When accuracy hurts: Reactions of anxious ambivalent dating partner to a relationship-threatening situation. *Journal of Personality and Social Psychology, 76,* 754–769.

Simpson, J. A., Rholes, W. S., & Phillips, D. (1996). Conflict in close relationships: An attachment perspective. *Journal of Personality and Social Psychology, 71,* 899–914.

Sternberg, R. J. (1986). A triangular theory of love. *Psychological Review*, 93, 119–135.

Twenge, J. M., Baumeister, R. F., Tice, D. M., & Stucke, T. S. (2001). If you can't join them, beat them: Effects of social exclusion on aggressive behavior. *Journal of Personality and Social Psychology*, 81, 1058–1069.

Twenge, J. M., Catanese, K. R., & Baumeister, R. F. (2002). Social exclusion causes self-defeating behavior. *Journal of Personality and Social Psychology*, 83, 606–615.

Twenge, J. M., Catanese, K., & Baumeister, R. F. (2003). Social exclusion and the deconstructed state: Time perception, meaninglessness, lethargy, lack of emotion, and self-awareness. *Journal of Personality and Social Psychology*, 85, 409–423.

Williams, K., Case, T., & Govan, C. (2003). Impact of ostracism on social judgments and decisions: Explicit and implicit processes. In J. Forgas, K. Williams, & W. Von Hipple (Eds.), *Responding to the social world: Implicit and explicit processes in social judgments and decisions*. New York: Psychology Press.

Index

A